THE
DAMIENS AFFAIR
AND THE UNRAVELING OF THE *ANCIEN RÉGIME*
1750-1770

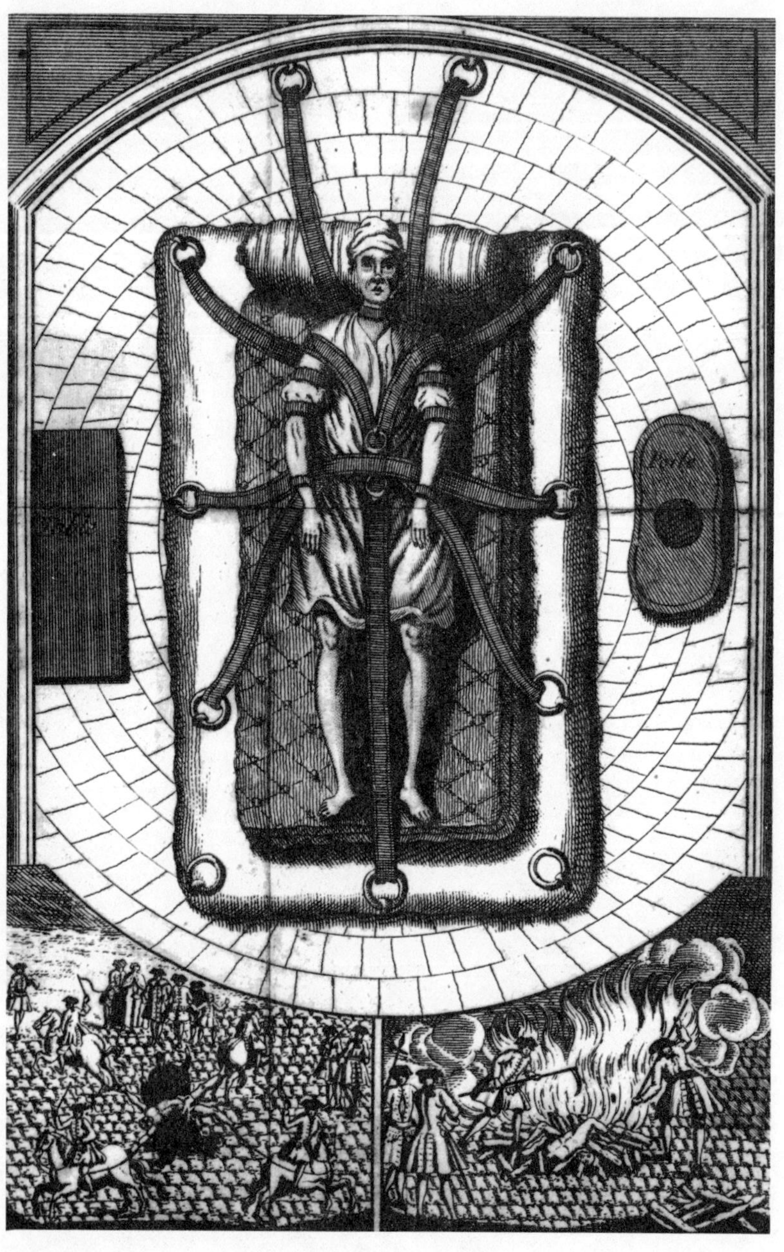

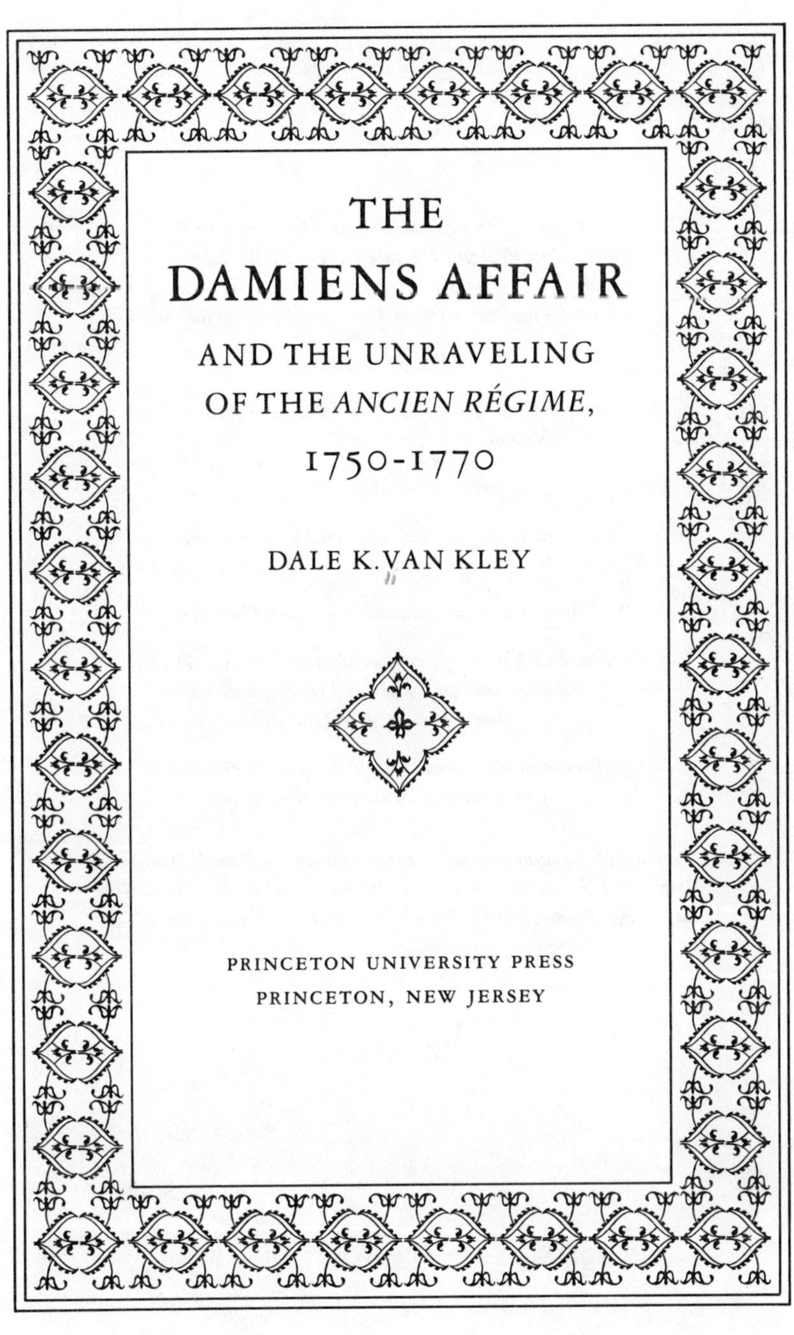

THE DAMIENS AFFAIR

AND THE UNRAVELING OF THE *ANCIEN RÉGIME*, 1750-1770

DALE K. VAN KLEY

PRINCETON UNIVERSITY PRESS
PRINCETON, NEW JERSEY

Published by Princeton University Press, 41 William Street, Princeton, New Jersey 08540
In the United Kingdom: Princeton University Press, Guildford, Surrey

Library of Congress Cataloging in Publication Data will be found on the last printed page of this book

ISBN 0-691-05402-9

Publication of this book has been aided by a grant from the Harold W. McGraw Fund of Princeton University Press

This book has been composed in Linotron Garamond

Clothbound editions of Princeton University Press books are printed on acid-free paper, and binding materials are chosen for strength and durability.

Printed in the United States of America by Princeton University Press, Princeton, New Jersey

Frontispiece: Damiens strapped to his mattress in the Tour de Montgomery.
Inset left: Damiens being dismembered by four horses in the place de Grève.
Inset right: Damiens' dismembered body being burned in the place de Grève.

To my parents, John and Stella,
for Christmas, 1983

Contents

Preface and Acknowledgments

IT HAS LONG BEEN my conviction that the mixed religious, ecclesiastical, and political disputes related to the papal bull *Unigenitus* in eighteenth-century France should occupy a central place in the ongoing discussions concerning the breakdown of the Old Regime and the ideological origins of the French Revolution. The present book represents another in a succession of attempts to trace the contours of that place. This task, difficult enough for the "century of lights," is not made the easier by the tendency of most "secular" historians to relegate ecclesiastical or "church" history to a wholly separate and irrelevant category of endeavor and of most ecclesiastical historians to rest content with their ghettolike existence as long as their dogmatic slumbers are not unduly disturbed. Hence the title's scrupulous avoidance of anything that might smack of religious or ecclesiastical history. It is a book first and foremost about eighteenth-century France and only secondarily about the French Catholic church. Of those predisposed against such a view who have nonetheless taken the bother to read this preface, I beg whatever indulgence they can muster and at least the patience to hear me out.

But why Damiens? Why remain entrenched in the century's middle decades rather than storm the 1770s and 1780s to demonstrate, say, the continuity between Jansenist-Gallican modes of political discourse and those more immediately preceding the French Revolution. A hundred times in the beginning stages of the present project I was tempted to abandon Damiens to his fate and attempt—or more modestly begin to attempt—something on the model of Bernard Bailyn's book on the ideological origins of the American Revolution. But aside from the facts that such a project is far vaster than the one for which I had been originally funded and is probably beyond my abilities in any event, I was for better or worse convinced by Steven Kaplan of Cornell University that it would be wiser for the time to stay with a project possessed of a social dimension and capable of showing that the arguments of parlementary lawyers and Jansenist clerics resonated beyond the cabinets of the Palais de justice and the sacristies of the Saint-Etienne-du-Mont parish. Hence Damiens. Yet it remains a book partly about the ideological origins of the French Revolution, although viewed from a certain distance; moreover, it goes without saying that I eagerly await the results of the revisionist efforts undertaken by Professors Keith Michael Baker and Robert Darnton, hoping perhaps presumptuously that the last two decades of the Old Regime's existence will look somewhat altered to them in the light of the immediately preceding decades of *Unigenitus*-dominated controversies.

Like many others before me, I long labored on my chosen subject under the illusion that I labored alone as well as in obscurity. It was not, indeed, until I had finished my research in France and had returned to this country that Professor Pierre Rétat of the University of Lyons reached me with the news that he was working with several others on a cooperative study of the Damiens affair and kindly invited me to contribute a chapter or an introduction. With the Atlantic between us all efforts at effective collaboration proved futile. But owing principally to Professor Rétat's thoughtfulness in forwarding his *équipe*'s chapters as they were written, we managed to steer quite clear of each other, they concentrating on the reactions of the press and I on the event's political and ideological context. I have consequently been able to rely on their authority in precisely those areas where my own research was thin, and my only regret is that I was unable to do as much for them. Besides this obvious difference in focus, the chief features that distinguish their approach from mine are a tendency to take somewhat less seriously than I do the mixed Jansenist and parlementary content of Damiens' self-confessed motivation and a perhaps *Annales*-inspired squeamishness at the spectre of narrative history maintained in the very act of heralding the "return of the event."

Among historians and specialists in this country I am most

deeply indebted to Daniel Carroll Joynes of the University of Chicago. When we met five or six years ago at the Bibliothèque de Port-Royal, I was able to introduce him to the Le Paige collection and help him identify some unsigned letters, but since then he has more than repaid these initial favors with painstaking readings of the manuscript for this book, the generous use of his own notes and microfilms, and his unfailing encouragement and enthusiasm. When it appears, his own work on eighteenth-century Jansenist constitutional thought will complete some of the argument tentatively advanced here and carry the story into the critical Maupeou period. A special word of thanks must also go to Professor Robert Palmer whose *Catholics and Unbelievers in Eighteenth-Century France* first aroused my interest in this subject and whose kind interest and encouragement have accompanied me throughout the present study. The manuscript for this study profited as well from the critiques of Princeton University Press' two still anonymous readers, and if I did not adopt all of their suggestions, it was not because I thought them devoid of merit. Professors Keith Baker, David Bien, John LaGrand, Robert Palmer, Alexander Sedgwick, and Timothy Tackett, as well as my colleagues David Diephouse and Edwin J. Van Kley, have all read parts of the manuscript, which has benefited in more ways than I can possibly recall by their wise counsels. The mercifully surgical attentions of Princeton University Press' Tam Curry amputated the manuscript's many remaining redundancies and curtailed its several spavined metaphors. Finally, the Calvin College History Department Colloquium should be commended for its exemplary patience in hearing parts of the manuscript read to it at reportedly breakneck speed.

In Europe Professor François Furet gave the manuscript an eleventh-hour reading and encouraged me to address myself more directly to the question of the desacralization of the monarchy. As usual m. André Gazier welcomed me cordially at the Bibliothèque de Port-Royal and permitted me to hunt and gather at will in the Le Paige collection's still largely uncharted vastness. To Professors Jacques LeBrun of the *Etudes*, Bruno Neveu of the *Ecole pratique des Hautes Etudes*, and Robert

Shackleton, then of the Bodleian Library, I owe innumerable bits of archival and bibliographical advice and the pleasure of their spirited conversation. And to mlle Hélène Walbaum, a veritable woman for all seasons, I owe the mundane but indispensable discovery of a central and affordable apartment for my family and me in Paris. This stay and the research I did then was made possible by a John Simon Guggenheim Fellowship supplemented by a Calvin College sabbatical leave of absence for the academic year 1976-1977. A postdoctoral fellowship from the University of Wisconsin's Institute for Research in the Humanities, also supplemented by a Calvin College leave of absence for the academic year 1979-1980, enabled me to find the time to compose the manuscript, a task made infinitely more pleasurable than it would otherwise have been by the institute's relaxed ambiance and high-spirited luncheon conversations. Modest but strategic stipends from the now unfortunately defunct Calvin Foundation made our stays in both Paris and Madison more comfortable than they would otherwise have been.

My wife's and three children's patience at being repeatedly dislodged and transported into foreign environments in the train of an historian in quest of an unespecially holy grail is not the least among the factors in this book's completion. My wife Sandra also read parts of the manuscript and made valuable stylistic observations. My colleagues and neighbors George and Lucie Marsden and Richard and Phyllis Mouw, whose undiluted Calvinism renders them infinitely better adapted than I am to this time and place, deserve credit for tolerating a Calvinist hopelessly backslidden into Jansenist despair. Last but not least, Sondra Ostenson, Wanda Schultz, Amy Plantinga, and Sonja Jager typed most of the manuscript; to them, my thanks for their patience in the face of a notoriously hieroglyphic hand.

Dale K. Van Kley
Calvin College
January 1983

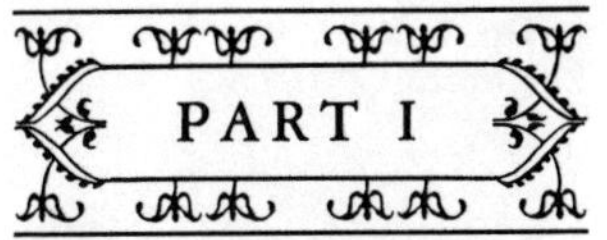

PART I

The Damiens Affair

Introduction

THE RIGOROUS COLD that came in with the French New Year in 1757 affected soldier, courtier, and sovereign alike. On the morning of January 5 in La Vilette, near Paris, one Jean-François Le Clerc, a veteran gunner on his way back from Linchaus to Douai on roundabout business for the king, took refuge in a cabaret where he warmed himself with a *demi-septier* of wine after removing a handkerchief that he had secured around his face "to protect himself from the cold." Cold comfort indeed, this stop, because had he only kept his handkerchief over his mouth or not entered the cabaret in the first place, he would not have grumbled indiscreetly about the king in the presence of others, calling him a "bugger" (*bougre*) who made a soldier travel "120 leagues malapropos" and predicting that if he persisted in imitating his most unfortunate ancestors "something similar could happen to him before long."[1]

The same cold had driven the maligned king in question, Louis XV, from the drafty, unheatable apartments of the château of Versailles to the relative warmth of the Trianon palace. On the evening of the same day, however, after a dinner in celebration of the Epiphany, the king briefly returned with part of the court to the larger château to visit his favorite daughter, madame Victoire, detained there with a cold. Finding her health improved, he ordered his carriage to await him at 5:30 at the foot of the staircase leading from the new guardroom on the northeast side of the court. There, at 5:45 precisely, he began his descent, accompanied by the dauphin, the duc d'Ayen, the duc de Duras, the marquis de Montmirail, and the king's first and second equerry, and surrounded by his personal bodyguard.[2] The duc de Richelieu lingered behind this group, for the moment preferring the shelter of the guardroom door to the ceremonial wait in the wind-swept courtyard below. Night had already fallen, and the glare of the guardsmen's torches might have obscured the marshal's view in any event. But it was rather his big muff, in which he had "hidden his visage to protect himself from the cold," that prevented him from witnessing a singular occurrence.[3] As the king was about to descend the last step of the staircase, a tall somebody cloaked in a greyish-brown riding coat with a hat still conspicuously on his head broke through the protective row of guards, violently pushed aside an officer of the One Hundred Swiss, and seizing the king's shoulder with one hand, plunged a knife blade into his majesty's right side with the other.[4]

A moment of confusion followed. The unknown somebody retreated to a position near the waiting coach, where according to one witness he "kept his eyes fixed on the king, and resembled a drunken madman."[5] Despite the claim of Pierre-Charles Selim, one of the king's foot valets, to have arrested him on the spot, the would-be assassin somehow found the leisure to wipe the blood from the blade and conceal the knife in one of his pockets. The king abandoned the supporting arm of Henri-Camille de Beringhen, his first equerry, lurched forward a few steps, and cried, "someone has touched me," or "I have just been punched." After feeling his side and finding his hand stained with blood, the king announced that he had been wounded and pointed to his assailant, who had his hat still on his head, saying, "it is that man over there who has hurt me. Arrest him and do him no harm." He then ascended the staircase unassisted.[6]

By the time the king reached his bedroom, pandemonium reigned in his stead. Clean clothes, bedsheets, and domestic help were all lacking because the king had not been expected to stay there that night. Those in attendance therefore unceremoniously undressed his majesty and stretched him out on the bare mattress. In the absence of the king's first surgeon, Germain de La Martinière, who was of course at Trianon, the dauphin's first surgeon Prudent Hevin bled the king, but he lacked the courage to explore the wound, which was more than sufficiently bleeding the king on its own. And in place of the king's Jesuit confessor, Père Desmarets, who was absent in faraway Paris, one of his almoners hurriedly fetched the last sacraments and exhorted the king until the abbé Soldini, almoner of the Great Common, arrived and began a general confession, for the king was by now convinced that his end was near and his salvation at stake. He designated the dauphin as lieutenant general, announced to all and sundry that the realm would be better governed under his heir, and apologized to the queen and his daughters for the scandal of his private life.[7]

The scene was in every respect so deplorable that the queen, less than cheerfully greeted by her husband with the words, "I am assassinated, madame, I am assassinated," is supposed to have fainted upon seeing it. Yet the same coach that carried the queen from Trianon also brought the king's first surgeon, La Martinière, who was finally able to examine the wound more closely. The assassin's knife, he found, had entered the king's right side between the fourth and fifth ribs, making an incision only three inches deep and avoiding all vital organs. At least two circumstances had collaborated to produce this result. First, the unsuccessful assassin had elected to use the shorter blade or penknife, instead of the larger blade that the knife also contained. Second, this blade had first to penetrate the four or more layers of heavy clothing—overcoat, coat, vest, and several foldings of shirt—in which his majesty had tried to stay warm that day.[8] In this instance, for once, the cold had done some good.

In any case, La Martinière was of the opinion that if the king had only been "a simple particular," he could have been up in his dressing gown the very next day; Hevin would not have forbidden him to tend to business; and the king's physician François Quesnay, doing them one better, did not think that the wound would have prevented another from attending a ball. On the eighth of January the last reports on the king's health appeared on the door of the Paris Hôtel de Ville.[9] We have it on the dubious but colorful testimony of madame de Campan that shortly after the assassination the marquis de Landsmath, an unreconstructed soldier and commandant of the king's venery, brusquely entered the king's apartment where he found the prostrate prince surrounded by his tearful daughters and the dauphine. "Get these mourners out of here," he barked, and when at the king's nod they had gone, he seized a chamber pot, presented it to his majesty and commanded him to "piss, cough, and spit" in that order. Having observed the successful performance of these functions, he announced to the king that his wound was "nothing" and predicted that in a few days they would "hunt down a stag."[10]

More than a few days passed, however, before the king did much of anything. At first the possibility that the knife blade had conveyed poison seemed to justify continued anxiety, and the king spent a rather sleepless first night in the company of Père Desmarets, who had returned from Paris to hear the king confess a second time. But when both the examination of the knife blade and the interrogation of the assassin effectively dispelled this fear, a siege of moroseness took hold and kept the king mainly abed and out of communication with his sometime mistress and now indispensable friend, the marquise de Pompadour. Toward those with permission to see him he "cast a chagrined glance which appeared to say, 'Look at your king whom a wretch tried to assassinate and who is the most unhappy person in his kingdom' "; and when after he healed someone expressed satisfaction over his recovery, he responded, "Yes, the body is doing well, but this (pointing to his head) is doing very badly, and this is impossible to heal."[11]

What it all seemed to presage to seasoned observers of the court was the imminent "conversion" of the king, the dismissal of the marquise de Pompadour, and a reorientation of domestic policy, if not of foreign policy, in the direction of the "devout" or Jesuitical party at court. Apologies to the queen, repeated confessions to a Jesuit, a new confidence in the dauphin, who was reputedly the head of the court's "devout" opposition—these were all signs announcing "a great change at the court" deemed imminent by the marquis d'Argenson as late as January 15.[12] Yet about that very time the king paid a brief visit to the marquise de Pompadour, and it was not to send her away. By January 19 the duc de Luynes could note that the king had "resumed the same train of life, and madame de Pompadour also," and by the twenty-third the king had finally hunted a deer, presumably with Landsmath. By the end of the year it was clear to both Luynes and the cardinal de Bernis that the marquise de Pompadour was more powerfully entrenched at court than ever. Life at court had clearly resumed its erstwhile rhythms.[13]

The same was soon true of the realm. When news of the king's accident became widely known in Paris on the morning of January 6, the consternation, according to lawyer Edmond Barbier, was "general, and there were very few people who did not break out in tears." Only the "great cold," he said, prevented all of Paris from simultaneously gathering in the streets and in the churches, where prayers of forty hours were said at the behest of the archbishop of Paris. The duc de Luynes also reported a "prodigious affluence" of people attending the *neuvaine* in the church of Sainte-Geneviève, and he thought the "affection and disquietude of the people" to be just as marked as in 1744, when the king had fallen dangerously ill while on campaign at Metz.[14] Nonetheless, the marquis d'Argenson, who did not share Barbier's and Luynes' approval of the king's recent domestic policy, thought that this "grief" was largely restricted to the *bons bourgeois* while the *bas peuple* remained "mute" because of the king's late actions against the magistrature and in favor of the bishops. Perhaps, as d'Argenson suggested, it was because the king distrusted the Parisians' affections, or simply because of his strained relations with the archbishop of Paris at that time—in exile at Conflans—that no solemn mass or *Te Deum* was celebrated in Paris in response to the king's recovery until March 6, and then only as a purely ecclesiastical ceremony.[15] But the theatres at least reopened on the ninth of January, and the rest of the realm soon resounded with masses and *Te Deum*s followed by more profane rejoicings such as banquets and balls that went on through the night. Even the Protestants in Languedoc and the Jews in Alsace gave thanks.[16]

The assassination attempt occurred in the midst of a full-scale political crisis. On December 13, 1756, the king had personally come to Paris and in an unpopular bed of justice (*lit de justice*) forced his parlement of Paris to "register" an edict and two declarations, all directly or indirectly related to the ecclesiastical and religious disputes dividing the parlement from the episcopacy since 1750. In protest against this forced registration all of the councillors in the parlement's lower judicial chambers, the *enquêtes* and *requêtes*, tendered their resignations, followed by more than half of the councillors in the senior chamber, or *Grand' chambre*, leaving only about twenty-five magistrates to go through the motions of administering justice. And since neither the lawyers nor the attorneys were willing to work for the rump Grand' chambre, its motions remained mimelike indeed. At roughly the same time the king's most recent fiscal declaration, that of July 7, 1756, prolonging the first twentieth tax, or *vingtième*, and creating a second, had encountered strenuous resistance from provincial parlements at Rouen, Bordeaux, Besançon, but especially Rennes, where the parlement's opposition was reinforced by that of the estates of Brittany simultaneously meeting in the same city.[17]

The attempted assassination created an eerily calm eye in the midst of this hurricane. News of the attack no sooner reached Paris than the "striking" councillors from the parlement's chambers of enquêtes and requêtes began gathering at the hôtel of the president Pierre Alexis Dubois, where they decided to assemble the whole parlement in the Palais de justice at 5:00 o'clock Thursday morning to await the royal response to their collective offer to take back their resignations and give "marks" of their fidelity—on condition, it is true, that the king at least orally suspend the execution of the most offensive of the declarations that provoked these resignations. And when the news reached Rennes on the evening of January 7, the provincial estates postponed all further discussion of the vingtième and sent three of their delegates to Versailles to inquire concerning the king's health, thereby falsely creating the impression that they had consented to the vingtième. But the bright day of reality soon dissipated these misty nocturnal reconciliations. The dauphin refused to shoulder the responsibility for answering the enquêtes's offer to take back their resignations except to refer the matter to the king, who decided that only the Grand' chambre—in effect, its remaining twenty-five members—should conduct the trial of the unsuccessful assassin. By the thirteenth of January this rump Grand' chambre was again remonstrating to the king concerning the edict and declarations and still requesting the reunification of all the parlement's chambers. The reconciliation between Rennes and its wounded king ended abruptly on January 11 when two magistrates of the parlement of Brittany were arrested by royal *lettres de cachet* for having encouraged the estates' continued resistance to the vingtième. And though the estates finally consented to this tax on January 16, the aggrieved parlement still had to be reckoned with.[18] Decidedly, politics were returning to normal, in the sense at least that "normal" had come to be experienced since 1750.

But if court, realm, and political relations between them were soon returning to their well-worn ruts, things would never be quite the same for the king's unfortunate assailant. After first seizing him, the king's foot valet Pierre Selim succeeded in setting him down on a stone bench and getting his hat respectfully off his head before being joined by any number of the king's guards, who dragged him off less ceremoniously to the new guardroom. There he was searched, stripped, confusedly questioned, and then "informally" tortured by the application of red-hot pincers to his ankles on the order of the keeper of the seals, Machault d'Arnouville, who hoped in this manner to get a prompt avowal of the man's accomplices,[19] for the man's warnings to the guards that they "take care of the dauphin" plus his avowal that his accomplices were "very far away" had stimulated his torturers' already ingrained prejudice that he could not have acted alone.[20] In any case, the lieutenant general of the royal court's *prévôté* soon arrived, put a stop to Machault's informal "question," and had the prisoner conducted to the criminal chamber where shortly later he

> found the said particular of tall stature, bearing light chestnut hair, clothed in a grey English drugget, a beggardly velvet coat, a red silk shag culotte, and a unicolored hat . . . , to the interrogation of whom we have proceeded, such as it follows, after having taken from him the oath to tell us the truth, and having advised

> him that he will be judged by Sovereign Judgment, so that he has no appeal to expect:
>
> 1. Asked his name, surname, age, quality, profession, residence and birthplace,
>
> Said he was François Damiens, forty years old, a native of Culoy five leagues from Arras, and refused to say his quality and profession and residence. . . .[21]

The next day the king's attorney duly lodged a judicial accusation (*plainte*) enabling the lieutenant to hear testimony and retroactively making the first interrogation an official or "judicial" one. However "informal" a physical assault upon the king, the law would henceforth make it as formal as possible. The gears of judicial machinery were now engaged; even here a kind of normality had reasserted itself.

What happened on January 5, 1757, arguably made hardly a dent on the course of events to follow. Unlike, say, François Ravaillac's assassination of Henry IV in 1610, Damiens' less than mortal attack in 1757 did not produce one of the "thirty days which made France."[22] The diplomatic revolution that realigned France with her traditional enemy, the Austrian Habsburgs, against her erstwhile ally Brandenburg Prussia, was two-thirds complete by the time Damiens assaulted the king; it was brought to formal conclusion later the same year with the signing of the Second Treaty of Versailles.[23] Conceivably, the assassination attempt might have altered the course of the Seven Years War, because the simultaneous disgrace of the secretaries of war and the navy, which was undoubtedly related to the Damiens affair, surely unsettled the conduct of the war by breaking the continuity of the administration and augmenting even further the dubious influence of the marquise de Pompadour.[24] Be that as it very speculatively may, this disastrous war was, however, well under way by the beginning of 1757 and would have probably continued as long as it did, Damiens or no. The political crisis then afflicting France, dividing the clergy from the parlements and resulting in the cessation of justice in a large part of the realm, would very probably have ended the way it did and perhaps even when it did, at the time of the parlement's scheduled *vacances* in September 1757.[25] And though the Damiens affair figured as evidence against the Jesuits during the controversy surrounding their order a few years later, the affair at best facilitated the suppression of that order but might also have retarded it, depending on the perspective chosen.[26] The affair's unquestionable effects on censorship and political justice in France were probably more sensational than lasting.

To a much larger extent, however, than many spectacularly successful and influential political assassinations in history, this one revealed much about the polity in which it occurred. Episodes in the assassin's biography as well as his announced motivation unmistakably pointed to the mixed political, ecclesiastical, and religious disputes that had reached the boiling point shortly before Damiens' attempted assassination. The identity of the contending parties to these controversies was highlighted by Damiens' trial itself—his informal one before public opinion as well as his judicial one by the leftover Grand' chambre—as parlementary magistrates and their Jansenist allies laid conspiratorial blame for the attempted assassination upon the Jesuit order, the ultramontanist episcopacy, and their lay allies at Versailles, while these latter groups more defensively blamed the Jansenist-infiltrated parlements and their incendiary antiroyal rhetoric. And the outcome of what had been the principal issue in these contentions, the refusal of sacraments controversy, became apparent immediately after Damiens' trial as the recovered king disregarded his magistrates' resignations and tacitly acknowledged their right to control the public administration of the sacraments. This contest, however, is not fully intelligible without reference to the underlying conflict of ideas about the nature of the state, the church, and the relations between them, a conflict pitting Gallican-Jansenist constitutionalism against ultramontanist absolutism and attaining sharper articulation in the context of the Damiens affair. The fact, moreover, that someone as socially undistinguished as Damiens was motivated in his act by some of these ideas showed that they were not limited to elites, a fact that became clearer in the context of the many other humbly born subjects arrested for *mauvais discours* (seditious things said) in the wake of the Damiens affair and interrogated in consequence. Finally, both elite and popular forms of political opposition—and the interplay between them—as revealed in the Damiens affair anticipate important dimensions of the French Revolution; they therefore shed light on some obscure and neglected ideological origins of this renowned and much studied upheaval.

All these dimensions and more were contained in the event, although the event itself was hardly the cause of them. Like a catalyst, it hastened the crystallization of certain ideological and political patterns and configurations that had long been in the process of formation. But above all, it revealed them. Like a bolt of lightning in a stormy night, the event suddenly and brilliantly illuminated the political, intellectual, and even some features of the social landscape in France.

Damiens

The Domestic Servant

BY MID-JANUARY the combined efforts of the magistracy and the police had filled in the missing spaces that remained after the assassin's first four or five interrogations. His full name was Robert-François Damiens, although he had usually called himself François; he came from the village of Tieulloy in Artois, although its inhabitants indeed pronounced it Culoy or Cueilloloy; and he was in fact forty-two years old, although it was still most common in the eighteenth century not to know one's precise age.[1] It is probably not evidence of deviousness on his part that Damiens gave his age as forty, thirty-six or thirty-seven, and thirty-nine in his first three interrogations respectively.[2] At the time of his arrest he was an unemployed domestic servant with no fixed address, having only recently returned to Paris after a six-month visit to his native province of Artois. Before that, however, he had served a wide variety of masters, mainly but not exclusively in Paris and many although by no means all from the parlementary magistracy. From the last of his masters, an international merchant named Jean Michel, he had stolen a sum of 240 louis, for which his arrest had been ordered the previous July, and which explains, in part, his trip to Artois. Of his immediate family, his wife, seventeen-year-old daughter, and younger brother, who was also a domestic servant, lived in Paris; an aged father, an older brother, and a widowed younger sister still lived in Artois.[3]

Stated in bare outline, the would-be assassin's biography seemed unremarkable even to his judges and contemporaries—so unremarkable, in fact, as to be incommensurate with the enormity of his act, a cause unequal to its effect. The judges' first instinct was therefore to regard Damiens as only the most visible part of a much larger cause, the passive, venal agent of a dark and far-flung conspiracy. From the beginning of his trial to its very bitter end, their greatest efforts were accordingly devoted to persuading him to reveal his accomplices, the true and hidden authors of his crime. Only when this quest proved utterly fruitless were they driven to conclude that he had acted alone. But they tried at least to invest his madness with gigantic proportions. If he was not a religious fanatic, a throwback to the Ravaillacs and Jacques Cléments of the age of religious warfare, he was then a political fanatic who got heated up about matters that did not concern him. Most of all, however, he was a "monster," a "scoundrel" of unprecedented perversity, an aberration of nature for which no nation, no province, could ultimately be held responsible.[4]

Yet even in much greater detail, the banality of Damiens' biography remains recalcitrant to these constructions and rather resembles the careers of any number of others who left their native provinces to seek their fortunes in Paris and tragically failed to find them. His family was poor, his father having early sunk from the status of independent *fermier* to that of simple day laborer who could ill afford the ten children his wife bore him before her death around 1729. It was undoubtedly this death rather than the fourteen- or fifteen-year-old boy's "incorrigibility"—consisting, apparently, in his mediocre performance with a plow—that prompted his father to send Robert-François to be raised by his maternal great uncle Jacques-Louis Guillemant, a well-to-do grain merchant and cabaret owner in nearby Béthune.[5] In any case, no hard evidence exists to substantiate the "official" conclusion that he was recalcitrant from "his tenderest youth." When asked about Robert-François' behavior as a boy, the most reliable witness on the subject, his father, answered on one occasion that he had behaved "very well" and on another that he had been "a little libertine," judgments that may well cancel each other out but fall short of substantiating the nickname "Robert the devil" that the prince de Cröy, governor of the province of Artois, claimed to have encountered in his investigations there.[6]

Damiens himself testified that he remained with Guillemant for about four years and only left because his uncle "wanted to make him study and he had no taste for that"; indeed, he remained only technically literate for the rest of his life. Apparently Guillemant also tried to apprentice Damiens to a local locksmith with no better success, and at some personal cost. Damiens then left his uncle, and after a two-year stint as apprentice wig maker or cook in Artois left the province as well. Retrospectively alleging youthful "levity" and a "desire to see the country," he attached himself to a captain of the Swiss regiment as a domestic servant in 1733 and accompanied his new master on campaigns, among them the siege of Philipsburg in 1734.[7]

Although domesticity thereafter remained his sole profession, a tendency to change masters frequently and to irritate some of them with "impertinences" and "vivacities" continued as evidence, perhaps, of a certain instability and independence. Arriving in Paris with "the fever" after the siege of Phillipsburg, he left the service of Captain Dubas and obtained a position as common valet in the Jesuit college of Louis-le-Grand on the rue Saint-Jacques, where a distant relative, one Jean-François Neveu, also served as maître d'hôtel. Here he remained from around 1736 to 1739 or 1740, serving both in the refectory and as a lackey for some of the students. But this deceptively long stay was interrupted midway by an eleven-month-long dismissal for reasons that are obscure—Damiens said his employers wanted to take him off wine for something he had done or said—and finally terminated altogether, according to Neveu, because of "impertinences he said against the Jesuits." During his temporary loss of Jesuitical sufficient grace, Damiens briefly served a certain Calobeau on the rue Vivienne, and before its definitive loss, he married Elizabeth Molerienne, a domestic servant of Irish origin who lived in the nearby cloister of Saint-Etienne-des-Grès (now, approximately, the rue Cujas). He nonetheless remained on friendly terms with some of the Jesuit professors at Louis-le-Grand;

Père de Launay, in particular, continued to act as a sort of protector, recommending him for a position as late as 1753.[8]

It was in fact Damiens' marriage, not his impertinences, that caused his final dismissal from Louis-le-Grand, because most domestic servants were supposed to be bachelors so that they could stay in the houses they served.[9] This is undoubtedly the reason why Damiens thereafter presented himself as single, called himself by the common nickname "Flammand," and according to his daughter always made a "mystery," even to his family, of the masters he served.[10] He was simply afraid they might come to see him, giving away his quality as husband and father. Asked during the trial which masters Damiens had served, his wife could remember only a few. And of these, the comte de Maridor admitted that he discovered only after hiring Damiens that he had a family and that his name was not simply "Flammand"; Bèze de Lys, whom Damiens served personally for a considerable time, never apparently knew him by any other name.[11] Such an arrangement could hardly have been beneficial for a marriage. And indeed his wife complained that Damiens had "always lived badly with her, being often out of work," that he was "often drunk and chased women" including a "mistress called Manou." When he gave her money, he often "threw it at her as if she were a dog."[12]

Being an occasional wine-imbibing, petticoat-chasing wife-beater does not of course make Damiens unique; the volume of complaints to this effect in the records of the Parisian commissioners of police stands as evidence that such problems were at least as legion in the eighteenth century as they are today. Of Damiens' case in particular, it is well to recall that his wife's remarks were neither unsolicited by her interrogators' questions nor made under circumstances when it was particularly easy to remember anything pleasant about him. Despite his recent theft, however, both she and their daughter seemed genuinely happy to see him when he returned from Arras to spend the 1757 New Year with them in Paris; and Damiens, for his part, was not wholly devoid of concern for their welfare. The majority of his unquestionable lies under oath were uttered "in fear that [they] would be harmed, having no knowledge of the crime he committed": he denied having any family at all until January 18, and it was not until near the end of his trial that he explicitly admitted to having seen his wife, daughter, and younger brother in Paris shortly before attacking the king. When in February he first learned that his entire family had been arrested and imprisoned, he was first "furious" but then "wept," bitterly protesting their innocence.[13]

Resuming Damiens' traces around 1740, these undeniably form a more irregular impression after his marriage and final departure from the Jesuits. According to Damiens' testimony in the interrogation of January 18, he proceeded successively to serve the comte de Bouville, officer in the gendarmerie, on the rue du Temple for twenty-six months, ending in his dismissal "not knowing the reason"; Monsieur Boulenger (probably Bellenger d'Essenlis), councillor in the parlement, on the rue du Paradis, for "around twenty-six or twenty-seven months"; Louis-Anne Séguier, councillor in the parlement, rue Saint-Antoine, for "around nine months"; Dumetz de Ferrière, maître d'hôtel, "for less than a year"; the comte de Raymond "for around fifteen months," including a trip to Bavaria and Ingolstadt but not to Angoulême where Damiens refused to follow him; Bèze de Lys, councillor in the parlement, on the rue des Maçons, for "two years in two different times," the first ending with his master's imprisonment in the fortress of Pierre-en-Cise, the second terminated "for vivacities"; Dupré de La Grange-Bleneau, councillor in the parlement, for seven months; madame la maréchale de Montmorency, on the rue Jacob, for "seven months," including a "journey to Chaton with her"; the comte de Maridor for two years, whose employ he left because "he got bored in the country of Maine"; Mahé de La Bourdonnaye, gouvernor of Pondicherry, on the rue d'Enfer, "until his death which could not have been more than a year or so"; madame de Verneil Saint-Rheuse, on the rue Grange-Batelière, who dismissed him after "around six months" because "she cast horoscopes, and having repeatedly studied his hand, predicted that he would be broken on the wheel"; a certain Le Paige, ecuyer of the dauphine, who dismissed him "after six weeks or so" because he "did not find him strong enough to suit his fancy"; and finally Jean Michel, a merchant in St. Petersburg, whose Parisian quarters on the rue des Bourdonnois Damiens fled after only two days, having stolen 240 louis from his master's portfolio.[14]

This run-down contains serious lapses and errors of memory, however, which were uncorrected by any investigations at the time. Assuming this succession to have begun around 1740 after Damiens' definitive dismissal by the Jesuits, simple addition yields a total of at most thirteen and a half years, which gets us up to 1753, but hardly to July 1756 when Damiens finally left Paris for Artois. This time unaccounted for further expands with the knowledge that Damiens exaggerated the time he served with many if not all these masters. The periods that elapsed between his various "conditions" undoubtedly account for a fraction of these extra years, since his wife complained that he was often "out of work."[15] But his wife also remembered his having served the councillor Louis Barré of the parlement's second chamber of enquêtes, whom Damiens mentioned in none of his interrogations; and in one of his interrogations Damiens rather vividly recalled serving Le Corgne de Launay, a theology professor at the Sorbonne, even though he did not think to include him in the list recited on January 18.[16] What is more, the order in which Damiens listed his masters on this date is almost certainly mistaken. Even if we can believe that Damiens followed the comte de Raymond to Bavaria and Ingolstadt while maintaining a wife and by that time a child in Paris (and not, as the parlement's secretary, Alexandre-André Le Breton, reconstructed it, before he was ever married or even settled in Paris in the first place), there remains the fact that, in his very first interrogation at Versailles, Damiens recalled a significantly different if very fragmentary order: the comte de Maridor, *then* Bèze de Lys, then La Bourdonnaye, and finally Saint-Rheuse.[17] This is surely the correct order in view of the facts that Maridor, who had the decency to talk to Damiens and make a juridical deposition, recalled that "Flammand" had served him seven years earlier, around 1750, and that the period of Damiens' service to Bèze de Lys coincided with the height of the refusal of sacraments controversy between the parlement and the archbishop of Paris, from about 1752 to 1754. The dates of his service to Mahé de La Bourdonnaye as given by his widow in deposition—October 1753 to sometime in January 1754—further enable us to situate this service *between* the periods of longer service to Bèze de Lys, who was exiled from Paris and imprisoned in Pierre-en-Cise beginning in May 1753 and took Damiens back for awhile after the recall of the parlement in September 1754.[18] These corrections are important, because they place Damiens' career as a rather "good" domestic servant before his demonstrably unsettling experience as Bèze de Lys' personal lackey in the early 1750s.

The fact that Damiens could be a reasonably good domestic servant is amply testified to by numbers of his former masters, at least before his service to Bèze de Lys. The comte de Maridor hired him upon the favorable testimony of the maréchale de Montmorency, who said that "aside from wine and a certain lightheadedness" he was a good servant, "faithful, pious, and perfectly obedient." The comte de Maridor himself claimed to have dismissed Damiens because of a "domestics' quarrel" having nothing to do with boredom in the province of Maine, and after eleven months, not two years as Damiens claimed. He also observed that Damiens "was quarrelsome in wine," with a character "difficult to define, being unstable, except that he liked to put order (*mettre la police*) everywhere and threaten all those who did him any injustice or whatever he imagined to be such." Yet this did not prevent Maridor from acknowledging in the same deposition that "he always appeared to be faithful and possessed of piety, that he approached the sacraments from time to time, heard mass nearly every day, served well and was intelligent."[19] La Bourdonnaye's widow, Charlotte-Elizabeth Combaut d'Auteuil, likewise testified that Damiens' service had been "très exact." Damiens had come to them on the recommendation of the père de Launay, the principal of Louis-le-Grand, and left only because he aspired to the position of maître d'hôtel rather than that of *laquais-frotteur* eventually offered him after La Bourdonnaye's death. Damiens returned these compliments in the course of the judicial confrontations with these witnesses. Maridor, he said, had been a "good master who had always given him good counsel and inspired him with the principles of religion"; and had he always remained in the service of La Bourdonnaye, "he would never have committed his crime. . . ."[20]

It remains nonetheless true that such favorable testimonies struggle upstream against the unfavorable impression created by Damiens' cascadelike succession of positions in the course of fifteen or twenty years. In the eighteenth century the domestic servant was still accounted part of the household, and the good domestic servant therefore faithfully served a single master just as the faithful son did not abandon his father. Damiens' younger brother Louis had exemplified this ideal, serving the councillor Charles-Louis Aubin for fifteen years. The only reason Damiens could give for not having done likewise was "that he could not get along with them [his masters], or otherwise they dismissed him."[21] Yet this negative impression is somewhat mitigated by at least two considerations. First, it is demonstrably untrue, as quasi-official truth on his subject came to have it, that he had served more than sixty masters.[22] From fifteen to twenty lies more modestly in the vicinity of reality. Second, the trend among domestics nationally after mid-century was in Damiens' direction, that is of greater mobility, increasingly giving the lie to the legal fiction that domestics were part of the households they served.[23] Besides Damiens himself, nine other domestic servants including his wife, younger brother, and sister-in-law got caught in the web of his affair, and of the eight who were questioned about their previous masters, the most stable changed masters on an average of every five years or so, another did so every four, three did so at the rate of every three years give or take a half, and two in less than two. Of these latter, the twenty-two-year-old Quentin Ferard, called "Condé," from Lorraine would have served about as many masters as Damiens had by a comparable age if he continued at his youthful pace; and the forty-seven-year-old Noel Roi, called "Roi," from Franche-Comté had served an impressive total of seventeen including his present one, a notary at the Châtelet.[24] Asked why he changed masters so frequently, he did little better than Damiens: "Said that it was because of some discontents and irritations [*fatigues*] he experienced in the said houses."[25] The model domestic servant Louis Damiens was probably the exception, hardly the rule.

The more or less unexceptional character of Damiens' career as a domestic servant holds equally well for his vivacities and impertinances. What precisely these might have amounted to is not first of all made clear by the testimony except that they usually had to do with wine; they seem in any case to have been related to only two or three of his dismissals, from the Jesuits in the 1730s, from Bèze de Lys in the 1750s, and from Sainte-Rheuse in 1755 or 1756. The latter complained that *after* she had dismissed him because of bad service and a "sinister physiognomy," the "said Flammand" committed the "insolence" of throwing some stones at the window of her *cabinet de toilette* while she was there and at the windows of her coach when he thought she was in it.[26] But even assuming all this to be true—Damiens vigorously denied these allegations and there is some reason to believe him—what does it amount to in a city where it was not uncommon to see a "domestic without a condition" in the pillory on some public square with a sign in front of and behind him reading, "A Lackey Insolent Toward His Master," or in worse ways punished for the same offense.[27] Just to restrict our views to admittedly random soundings in the year 1757 alone, consider the Paris *guet*'s rounds of September 16 through 18, which included the arrest of Jacques Lyonnais, a domestic servant, for having struck his master, the sieur de La Marguerit, sometime captain of the cavalry; of a domestic servant named Germain Petit for having "insulted madame de Montigny, his mistress, in her own residence"; and of Jacques Marconer, domestic servant, at the request of the chevalier de Jorris, captain of the regiment of Honderville, "whom he insulted."[28] Or if domestics named "Flammand" be preferred, consider the plight of one Jean-Jacques Chaponel, a lawyer in the parlement of Paris residing on the rue Neuve in the parish of Saint-Eustache, whose "perfidious" domestic "named Flammand" disappeared on April 4 with his lent wardrobe, after being fired for "bad manners and impertinences"; or one François Perie, a horse-master living in the rue des Orties Buttes in the parish of Saint-Roch, who was on March 14 and for no discernible reason "atrociously vilified" and nearly stabbed by a "furious particular" named Denis Ornauld, commonly known as "Flammand," his former domestic now "without condition."[29]

A certain glimpse of Damiens' variety of impertinances and vivacities are furnished, however, by the trial and interrogations themselves. Just minutes after his arrest he told the keeper of the seals, Machault d'Arnouville, that he was a "wretch" for having "betrayed his company," a clear and even knowledgeable reference to Machault's role in preparing the lit de justice of December 13, 1756, and he assured the marquis de Sourches, grand provost of France, that he knew him well, having once served his son-in-law the comte de Bouville.[30] Interrogated on the *sellette* on March 26 before the rump Grand' chambre and the princes and peers of the realm, he not only "remained untroubled by the sight of such an august assembly" but "recognized and named numbers of his judges, . . . even permitting himself a few pleasantries."[31] He told the duc de Noailles, for example, that he looked chilly sitting there in his white stockings and suggested he move nearer the fire; and he assured his chief interrogator, Denis-Louis Pasquier, that though he spoke "like an angel" and surely deserved on that account to be chancellor, it remained as true as the fact that he stood before the crucifix that there existed no conspiracy. Pressed by Pasquier on precisely how he had spent his last three hours in Paris before coming to Versailles, Damiens responded that he had passed them in the company of a "grosse dondon" endowed with a "very fine figure" who deserved to be more widely known than she was.[32]

If these are representative of Damiens' vivacities, one might better call them familiarities. They proceeded quite naturally from the mouth of a person who, however humble his social status and origin, had seen the high and mighty at close and even intimate quarters and had finished by losing the requisite distance and respect. For all the trial's talk about Damiens' low social condition or estate, this could not have been inferred from the profession of domesticity alone. As an occupation domesticity was not, strictly speaking, congruous with any particular social status or situation; it ran the gamut of the social hierarchy from the king's noble pages to the lowliest scrubwoman serving the meanest bourgeois. The equivalent of no social place, it naturally encouraged a tendency not to know one's place, and this was particularly true of servants of illustrious houses who wore their master's livery and carried the noble sword.[33]

In the last analysis, the most remarkable feature about the list of Damiens' former masters is not so much its length as its exalted quality and distinction. From an authentically ancient military noble family such as La Bourdonnaye to an illustrious parlementary name such as Séguier, from the Jesuits on the rue Saint-Jacques or the fanatically "jesuitical" Le Corgne de Launay at the Sorbonne to the parlementary firebrand Bèze de Lys on the rue des Maçons, from another old noble family such as Montmorency to parvenu court nobility such as Sainte-Rheuse and her lover, the marquis de Marigny alias Abel Poisson, the list spans the top of the social and political spectrum of the expiring Old Regime and reads like *le tout Paris* of the eighteenth century. If Damiens was indeed the nobody portrayed by his judges and the press, he was at least a nobody not unknown by some pretty important somebodies, which partly accounts for the strangely reticent, embarrassed quality of his trial and surrounding investigations. Asked somewhat innocently by the criminal lieutenant Le Clerc Du Brillet how he knew "so many persons at court and in the magistracy," he impertinently asked in turn whether, "having for so long resided in Paris, he was not in a position to know many people?"[34] Epitomizing, perhaps, both his irreverence and his refusal to be nobody was his reply to the question of whether he knew that it was the "usage to remove one's hat when the king passed by, and why he had his on his head in the presence of his majesty while the latter passed by to climb into his coach on the fifth of the present month": he said that "the good Lord evidently permitted that in order that he be recognized."[35]

Quite unexceptional, then, in his less than perfect marriage, his many masters, and his infamous insolences, Damiens does not even escape banality by stealing 240 louis from the last of his masters, the merchant Jean Michel, on July 6, 1756. It is worth insisting at the outset, however, that this was in all likelihood Damiens' only theft, despite the more or less official "truth" that he had previously stolen from any number of his masters.[36] It is true that Pierre-François Desvaux, tutor of La Bourdonnaye's children, half accused Damiens of stealing fifty louis that were found missing from the secretary at the time Damiens was serving Desvaux particularly, but aside from Damiens' vehement denial, this accusation is perhaps best viewed in the perspective of the sentence of perpetual galley labor that Desvaux himself incurred twenty-six years later for having "diverted and dissipated" for his personal use 552,377 livres of the La Bourdonnaye fortune.[37] Not another scrap of evidence exists suggesting domestic theft prior to service with Jean Michel.

In any case, domestic theft was a common enough crime, certainly more common than the two or three death penalties dispensed by the Châtelet in Paris each year would suggest. Because eighteenth-century law regarded domestic theft as a kind of parricide or father-assault and therefore punishable by death, most victimized masters probably contented themselves with full or partial restitution of the stolen sum and simple dismissal of the offending servant rather than exacting the law's full pound of flesh and attracting a sort of adverse publicity. The Parisian police evidently connived at such informal settlements, since they received many more complaints concerning such thefts than ever assumed the form of judicial proceedings.[38] In Damiens' case the victimized master lost no time in declaring the theft to the local commissioner of police (Jean-Pierre Laumonier, July 7, 1:00 P.M.) but nine full days were allowed to elapse between this declaration and the order for Damiens' arrest. Meanwhile, both Michel and the police located Damiens' wife and daughter, who were given clearly to understand that "out of consideration for the family the said Damiens would not be arrested provided that they could find him and have him return the sum he had stolen."[39] Even after Damiens surfaced in Saint-Omer and his arrest was decreed, the family continued zealously to occupy itself with the restitution of the stolen sum, presumably on the assumption that the worst could yet be avoided. It is true, however, that by that date Damiens' brother Louis in Paris warned the family in Artois that Michel was "no longer the master" of Damiens' fate which was now rather in the hands of "the whole constabulary of France" and that the best that could be hoped for Damiens was that "he never be caught and that there never by any further question of him."[40]

But the potentially elusive quality of the domestic thief perhaps also accounts for the disproportion between complaints and judicial proceedings. Would Damiens ever have been caught had he not returned to stab the king? Especially vulnerable, it seems, were masters in precisely Michel's situation, who hurriedly hired a lackey on the strength of a recommendation or two without otherwise inquiring very closely into his previous career, social connections, or even name. Take the example of the baron de Traverse, who on March 27, 1757, the day before Damiens suffered his horrible execution, came to complain to Commissioner Louis-Charles Roland about a certain "Baptiste" whom he had hired as a pantry servant (*garçon d'office et de cuisine*) on November 18 of the previous year. Since he had needed a servant in a hurry, he had contented himself with Baptiste's certificates and assurances that he was single, although he found it strange that Baptiste slept elsewhere seven nights a week; he also accepted Baptiste's not very convincing explanation that he had a dangerously sick cousin to care for. Time passed, and the baron bought a commode for keeping his money. He always took the precaution of taking the key with him on periodic trips to Versailles, but he had given various other keys to Baptiste for safekeeping at the time of his hire. One day, upon returning from Versailles, Traverse found ten louis missing but no evidence that the drawer had been forced. On the next trip to Versailles, he took all the money with him, and when he returned sooner than expected, he found one of the keys he had given to Baptiste jammed in the lock of the commode. By now suspicious, he alerted another, more trustworthy domestic servant named La Vie who eventually observed Baptiste more or less in the act. Baptiste then promptly disappeared.[41]

It turned out, of course, that Baptiste was not single and that his name was not simply Baptiste, but rather Jean-Baptiste Sumo, or Humo; he lived with his wife above a butcher's shop on the rue du Four Saint-Germain near the Croix Rouge. The so-called Baptiste eventually reappeared, and the baron had him promptly arrested, but in other respects his name could have been Damiens or Flammand. Damiens was only a bit cleverer, having not gotten the key to the commode stuck in the lock of the armoire (as in the baron's case, a single key opened more than it was supposed to) and having somehow not disturbed the ribbons on either side of the otherwise quite open portfolio that contained the money.[42] And unlike Baptiste, Flammand fled not only his master in the rue des Bourdonnois but also Paris, only stopping briefly at Saint-Etienne-des-Grès to see a wife and daughter whose existence Michel did not yet suspect.[43]

Damiens' next moves were sickeningly predictable, however—and in fact were accurately predicted. Since at least 1754 the Damiens family had been parties to a lawsuit involving the inheritance of a maternal uncle in Béthune, a son, no doubt, of the Jacques-Louis Guillemant who had cared for the adolescent Damiens from 1729 to 1733. Upon the recommendation, probably, of the Damiens brothers in Paris who both served magistrates at the time, the case was appealed the same year from the superior council of Artois to the parlement of Paris, where it was still pending on the report of the councillor Jean-Nicolas de La Guillaumie as late as March 1756. Evidently despairing of ever obtaining a judgment by a court perpetually preoccupied with political and ecclesiastical affaires du temps, however, the parties finally decided to settle out of court.[44] This settlement might very well have taken Damiens back to his native province in any case; as it was, he had been making noises for some time about wanting to return to "his country." Things were hardly improving for him in Paris. On the contrary, his last two or three conditions were unmistakable comedowns from what he had known before; at forty-two years old he was nowhere in sight of his self-defined goal of becoming maître d'hôtel in a distinguished house. With sadistic but pinpoint accuracy the police inspector Courtaillon warned the provost of the constabulary in Saint-Omer on July 14, 1756, that "this clown" could be expected to surface in that town quite soon, "if not to establish himself there, at least to look dazzling for a couple of days."[45]

By that time Damiens was indeed in Saint-Omer and behaving in every respect the way Courtaillon had foreseen. Arriving in Arras on the morning of July 7 by way of mail coach from Paris, Damiens promptly rented a horse and traveled to nearby Hermanville, then to Manin where he negotiated with three Guillemant aunts and their husbands, all parties to the suit over the Guillemant inheritance. Unable to accommodate, Damiens returned to Arras on the eighth in order to issue a request against two of these parties with an attorney named Sohier. Having at the same returned his rented horse, Damiens took the mail coach the following day to the town of Béthune for an equally unproductive visit with a madame Marchand, a stepdaughter of the deceased Guillemant uncle, then went on to spend the night in a cabaret in Aire near both Saint-Omer and Arques where his father, older brother, sister-in-law, and younger sister all resided.[46]

At 7:00 o'clock on the morning of the tenth Damiens made his triumphal entry into Saint-Omer. Not finding his brother at home, he was directed by his sister-in-law to the merchant for whom her husband worked as a journeyman wool carder. There Damiens introduced himself after his twenty-five-year absence, then carried his brother reluctantly off to a nearby cabaret where, according to the older and more sober Antoine-Joseph, Damiens began "to spend money as if it were hay." He gave his sister-in-law a gold louis and an écus of six livres; he bought his brother nearly three hundred livres worth of wool "so that he could work for his own account instead of being the poor, day-laboring wool carder that he was." "Your fortune is made," he benevolently exulted, while announcing his own intention of entering the wool business and fraternally sharing the profits. Finding his brother's quarters too humble for his taste, he chose instead to stay with his younger widowed sister, Catherine, to whom he gave fifty-four livres to add to her furnishings. But he saw to it that his brother augmented his own as well: a hundred écus for his brother "so that he could dress himself more properly"; a dress, mattress, and pillow for his fifteen-year-old niece; six table knives and some faience dishes for the household. While making the latter purchases on Sunday after mass, Robert-François "allowed himself every sort of *gasconnade*," and when his brother wondered aloud what purpose faience served "for poor wretches like us," Damiens shot him a "very evil sidelong glance."[47]

After the same mass on Sunday, July 11, the local boy turned Parisian dandy clearly gave his family to understand that he possessed "no religion." According to his brother's friend, the shoemaker Pierre-François Le Clerc, Damiens "fretted impatiently" in church, murmuring against his brother who wanted to stay until vespers. Instead, he stalked out with his father and retired to the first cabaret they encountered in Arques where, eventually being joined by his brother and Le Clerc, he "made fun of his brother for being so religious" and of his young niece "for going to church so often." At his sister's he slept late and consumed a lot of wine and beer.[48]

Damiens' family was of course not a little curious about where all the money came from, not altogether convinced that it represented uniquely the product of his savings in Paris over the years.[49] Then, on July 13, came the fateful letter from younger brother Louis in Paris, informing the family of Robert-François' theft of 240 louis from his last master's portfolio. Confronted with this evidence by his brother and sister the next day, Damiens "entered into a furor so violent that they feared for their lives and reputation as a family." Damiens said he had not stolen that much, that "plenty of merchants had stolen larger sums," that he would return to Paris at the first opportunity to "break Michel's neck." He then went to an apothecary, bought fifteen sous worth of arsenic, and by his own admission swallowed it with a glass of water in an apparent attempt to end his life. During the ensuing illness he displayed "every sort of folly and anxiety: he cried occasionally, said he did not fear death so much as the dishonor of his family."[50] Urged after his recovery to help restitute the sum and confess to a priest, he refused to do either and instead declaimed against priests, maintaining that they could not be trusted because they revealed confessions. When his sister presented him with holy water, he "taxed her with bigotry"; when his brother proposed the counsels of the curé Fenes of the parish of Sainte-Marguerite, he accused this "*{foutu}* curé" of being "another of your *dévôts*" or a Jansenist "with whom he wished to have no commerce," depending on whether the testimony of his brother or the shoemaker is to be preferred.[51]

From this point onward Damiens' behavior became indeed that of a man at the end of his tether, although it is well in evaluating it to consider that such was objectively his situation in life. It is not altogether surprising to find a man in a desperate situation behaving desperately. On July 16 the Châtelet officially ordered his arrest; by the twenty-third or twenty-fourth, the constabulary was actually looking for him in Saint-Omer. His arrest at this point would almost certainly have entailed a sentence of death on the gibbet in Paris. He was a man condemned and dishonored, his dreams in smoke. At best he could merely survive.

With the curé and chanter of Sainte-Marguerite, Damiens' brother Antoine-Joseph concocted the expedient of having Damiens admitted—or committed—to a house of the order of the Good Sons in Saint-Venant, an order that had been founded for more or less such purposes during the previous century, where it was hoped that the good brothers would both facilitate the sinner's conversion and force him to relinquish the money.[52] Damiens appears at least momentarily to have consented to the plan, but only on the condition that he first be allowed to glimpse the sea. So on the twenty-third his brother and sister accompanied him to Dunkerque and Fort Mardik, where they stayed with his sister's relatives. There Damiens appeared "sad and distant from time to time," left a snuffbox behind, and bought a new riding coat—the same one he later wore when attacking the king. Having in the meantime ascertained that the constabulary had invested the Damiens' houses in Saint-Omer, the two brothers circumvented this town on their way to Saint-Venant, only to find, when they arrived there toward the end of July, that the superior of the house of Good Sons would not accept Damiens without a lettre de cachet or the authorization of a judge or intendant.[53] As this was out of the question, no other recourse remained, it seemed, than to seek the security of the Austrian border, which they crossed by paying off the border constabulary on July 27 or 28.[54]

For a brief moment the brothers remained together in a cabaret in Ypres where they presented a most remarkable contrast: the one a citified dandy with his frizzled hair and somewhat pretentious get-up consisting of a red culotte and vest and cinnamon-colored volant topped by a new brownish riding coat and gold-bordered hat; the other the very embodiment of provincial misery, with his pale, emaciated face, straight dull black hair, and cover of bluish, indistinguishable rags. Yet both were in their early to middle forties and were visibly brothers by virtue of their bean-pole stature—five feet, four or five thumbs—and their long aquiline noses. They parted the next day, not forever but very nearly so, Antoine-Joseph returning to Saint-Omer and Damiens remaining in Ypres.[55]

For the next five months Damiens frittered away his life in Flemish and Artesian cabarets and auberges, morningless nights in strange beds and aimless walks in unfamiliar places:

Ypres, Jacques Vantolle's cabaret (three or four days): Damiens "went into the village on only a single occasion." Otherwise, "he remained alone in his room and very often in bed. When he took walks, it was always in the orchards behind the house and never in the streets. When he encountered strangers, he always looked upset. He always talked to himself in his room and seemed very agitated."[56]

Zutnoland, Pierre-Roland Peel's cabaret (about eight days): "He took solitary walks around the house, and very often remained in his bed." One time after Damiens had had himself bled, his host found him abed "bathing in his blood, with the bandage no longer on his arm." Asked "why he let his blood flow freely without calling for help," he answered that "apparently this happened while he was sleeping." When the host's wife replaced the bandage, Damiens' blood "spurted out like a jet, so agitated was his interior." The host suspected that Damiens had either "lost his mind or done something evil, observing him always alone and upset."[57]

Poperingue, Jacobus Messelin's cabaret (until the end of August): "He was very sober and always spoke to himself; even with other people he always moved his lips as if he were speaking." During Damiens' stay here "he had no commerce with anyone at all; he sometimes took walks in the streets of the village, but more often remained in bed. Sometimes he walked six or seven times around the church near the prévôté, always with a preoccupied air."[58]

Poperingue, Petronille Hameau's mercery shop (about two weeks): "He always had a worried look and seemed very upset"; his hostess had no doubt that Damiens had committed some crime. He complained much about being unable to sleep, for which he bought some drugs which she judged to be poppy heads. During his entire stay here "he hardly ever went out and had no relations with anyone." He left on September 10 after being informed that the village magistrate wanted to see him.[59]

Fies in Artois, cousin François-Joseph Tailly's farm (until the end of October): The "said Damiens never went to see anyone in the area except occasionally to François Decroix's cabaret in Fies to drink and play cards with whomever he might meet there." The cousin "noticed that Damiens was closed within himself and often talked alone, sometimes remaining abed for two or three days" on the pretense of sickness. On one occasion he had himself bled.[60]

Fies, cousin Jean-Baptiste Lejosne's farm (a couple of days in October): Damiens "was always dreamy and talking to himself . . ."; he had "no relation with anyone" and "remained abed the greater part of the time." Reproached for his "uneasy and somber mood, Damiens explained that he had killed someone in Paris." He left a good hunting knife behind.[61]

Autreville, cousin Jean-Clément-Dominique Damiens' farm (a single night in early November): Damiens rose at 11:00 A.M. and during dinner had an "uneasy air, approaching madness, talking to himself. . . ." The cousin "heard Damiens mutter some things between his teeth without being able to make them out or even imagine what he was saying except for the intention of sleeping the next night at Lefevre's in Hermanville."[62]

Villiers-Chatel, Antoine-Luc Beaucourt's house (two weeks): Damiens "did not speak coherently, and had a distant and interior air."[63]

Arras, Marc-Antoine Réant's cabaret (perhaps a week): Réant "was afraid of him and tried to get rid of him."[64]

Arras, François Saget's auberge (most of December): Damiens had "a distracted look and often talked alone, and when anyone asked him what was wrong, he would answer: 'Oh, I have a head full of ideas.' " Otherwise, "he spoke to no one, went to the estaminet once in a while where he drank seriously without getting drunk." While staying here, he had himself bled again, even demanded that the surgeon "make a bigger cut so that the bad blood could get out." The surgeon also gave him some opium grains for the sake of sleep, and when these had no effect, some poppy tea. Here Damiens left two old pairs of pants, a brown vest, a shirt, and a collar.[65]

Arras, the Ecu de France where the coaches departed for Paris (December 25-28): He "rose late, was taciturn, and never went out except to go to the tavern to drink a shot without talking." On Monday, second day of Christmas, "he dressed so late he missed mass."[66]

Yet even amidst these appearances of total disintegration, a few fragments of method can be discerned. Damiens never lost sight of the inheritance affair that a familial procuration obtained before the discovery of his theft empowered him to conclude. While staying for a while in November with his cousin Pierre-Guislain Lefevre, for example, Damiens went to nearby Hermanville to obtain a copy of his grandfather's death certificate and to Avesne-le-Compte to find the marriage contracts of his two maternal aunts in Manin. On December 3 and 6, moreover, he concluded transactions in Arras with these two aunts and the madame Marchand of Béthune, which netted him sums further divided among the family by means of a quittance signed with his father on December 22. In all of these transactions he signed as "Robert-François Damiens, Bourgeois of Paris, there residing," giving evidence of social aspirations tenuously resisting the catastrophic assault of his recent experiences.[67]

At the same time, Damiens clung tenaciously to what remained of the money stolen from Jean Michel. He went so far as to return to his father's house in Arques for a brief visit in September in order to recover fourteen louis he had left with his sister, threatening to "dishonor his family by having himself hung in the public square of Saint-Omer if they were not returned to him." These he obtained, mainly through the peace-keeping efforts of his father, but he was less successful in recovering the three hundred livres that he had given his brother to purchase wool. Antoine-Joseph had already resold this wool along with the other household presents Damiens had foisted upon him, all with a view toward restituting the stolen sum.[68]

Yet such fragmentary evidence of purpose can no more obscure the eccentricities of Damiens' behavior during this period than the general desperateness of his situation can totally account for them. His desire to see the sea, his apparent attempt on his life, repeated purges of his own "bad blood," and above all, his incessant talking to himself all suggest the theme of eighteenth-century folly or unreason. This theme is reinforced by the fact that testimony relating to it is not restricted to the period in question but spans Damiens' entire career as domestic servant in Paris. Two witnesses who knew Damiens as early as the late 1730s while working at Louis-le-Grand remembered him as someone with a "taciturn character," often "talking alone" or appearing "to talk inwardly," from whom "everyone fled" and from whom "no one could extract a word."[69] As late as 1755 or 1756 Louis-Claude Perier, first commissioner of the king's buildings, who recognized Damiens as madame de Verneil Sainte-Rheuse's valet, recalled meeting him "numbers of times in the streets, gesticulating, talking to himself and even so audibly that one might have almost overheard what he was saying"; Sainte-Rheuse herself complained that Damiens' "reasonings were without coherence," that "when she wished to send him on errands he excused himself on the pretext of vapors with which he pretended to be attacked," and that he talked to himself.[70]

But the most striking testimony concerns the very troubled period in Artois and Flanders in the late summer and autumn of 1756. A certain Nicolas Playoust, a stocking merchant and artisan who for two weeks shared room and bed with Damiens at Petronille Hameau's in Poperingue, reported that Damiens "hardly ever slept" and instead "talked to himself the whole night long without his having been able to distinguish a single word." On one occasion, when Playoust had obligingly accompanied Damiens to the town of Rochebrune, Damiens barricaded the door of the room they rented but remained "very agitated" in spite of this precaution; then at one o'clock in the morning he took refuge in the cabaret's cellar from which he was retrieved only with force.[71] François-Joseph Bourbier, a blacksmith who spent an afternoon and evening with Damiens in a cabaret in Nedonchel near Fies, vividly recalled Damiens' anxiety while awaiting his cousin Lejosne who was retrieving a valise Damiens had left in Poperingue, as well as the giddy "gaiety" occasioned by the cousin's arrival with the suitcase toward evening. Damiens immediately ordered a bottle of wine and five or six pieces of lamb to be put on the grill and paid the whole bill himself.[72]

Given the quasi-official verdict that Damiens acted as a solitary *fou*, it is somewhat surprising that more was not made of these symptoms, especially in view of the fact that eighteenth-century "psychology" was not incapable of making a certain sense of them. The concept of melancholia, for example, could not only have made sense of Damiens' much commented upon "taciturnity," "inwardness," and habit of talking to himself but, joined as it already was to that of "mania," could have accounted for the crazy oscillation from depression to giddiness observed by Bourbier in the cabaret.[73] The doctors Foubert and Boyer, appointed by the parlement to preserve

Damiens intact for the spectacle of the execution, likewise reported on February 26 that "since the last interrogation . . . he has fallen into a kind of discouragement and melancholy whose persistence alone is remarkable, its being rather common for him to pass alternatively from one of these states to another."[74] Again Damiens' frequent complaints of "incommodities" and even "vapors" lend themselves well to the century's concept of "hypochondria," just as the already associated concept of "hysteria" might have shed light on his equally noted "agitations." As if confusedly conscious of "folly" himself, Damiens exposed himself to water, traveled from place to place, had himself repeatedly bled to release his "bad blood"—all remedies suggested by eighteenth-century doctors for "insanity or unreason."[75]

With the possible exception of the prince de Cröy who thought Damiens "atrabilious," contemporaries did not really exploit this body of suggestible evidence.[76] The remarkable testimonies of Playoust and Bourbier were included in the trial only to mollify the prince de Conti's insistence that the court extend its investigations directly into Artois and proved uninteresting even to him because they failed to suggest the conspiracy he thought existed there. The same was roughly true of the token former masters and fellow domestics heard in deposition. Included at Conti's behest, they said very little that anybody wanted to hear at the time. Numbers of opportunities simply to find out something about Damiens were cavalierly passed up, such as that presented by François Boussin, master of German flute, who on January 15 came to Police Commissioner Miché de Rochebrune to say that he had known Damiens, his family, and something about his relationship to the La Bourdonnaye family.[77] No further questions were asked, no follow-up undertaken.

The only facet of Damiens' "folly" that seemed to interest his interrogators related to his obsession, confided to his brother, sisters, and Playoust, with a horoscope cast or "sinister predictions" made by Verneil Sainte-Rheuse and her chambermaid, to the effect that he would do something awful and be broken on the wheel and which he regarded as having been fulfilled by his theft of July 6.[78] But his judges' somewhat obscure fascination with this subject probably has much more to do with their tireless quest for a motivation at once simple, temporally precise, and in a sense exterior to Damiens, and which possessed the additional advantage of not leading in the direction of the parlement of Paris but rather toward Versailles—Sainte-Rheuse was madame de Pompadour's brother's mistress—as well as toward a Verneil, a name associated with Ravaillac's assassination of Henry IV.[79]

Damiens' Religion

SUCH EXAMPLES of erratic and (to us) psychotic behavior did not greatly interest Damiens' judges, however. What rather preempted their attention—and what they indeed regarded as a species of "folly"—was Damiens' profession of political, patriotic, and in a sense altruistic motives in attacking the king. In fact, Damiens consistently maintained in his interrogations that his intention had not really been to kill the king, and he persuasively argued that had he wanted to do so he would have used the longer blade of his knife and taken advantage of the ample time to deliver two or three blows instead of just one. What he had rather attempted to do, he said, was "to touch the king" and by this means "prompt him to restore all things to order and tranquility in his States"—in effect, to convey disinterested political advice.[80] To his aristocratic judges, such words coming from a "vile" domestic servant socially incapable of such high political motivation represented an "insolent excuse" masking the more sordid prospect of material gain, held out, no doubt, by the true aristocratic conspirators behind the scenes. A man of Damiens' humble social station could only have been motivated by considerations of narrow self-interest, which in the absence of personal contact and therefore quarrel with the king must have been provided by some outside agent. But to the extent his judges were eventually persuaded by his sincerity on this point, they regarded it as the height of "nonsense," the very essence of his "detestable folly."[81]

Yet his judges did not despair of finding elements of self-interest in even this unlikely domain. One clue they briefly pursued was suggested by an unlaundered and extrajudicial deposition by the comte de Maridor, who said that the police had arrested Damiens' daughter at the time of the great "children's kidnapping" riot in Paris in 1750 and that Damiens had written an insolent letter to the lieutenant of police Nicolas-René Berryer threatening him with harm if he did not release her. He had never seen the original letter, Maridor said, but only a copy that Damiens had shown him.[82] That this riot particularly affected Damiens seemed partially corroborated by an off-handed comment he made to his cousin Lejosne in Fies that "there was once a riot in Paris." Asked by his interrogators on January 29 to what purpose he made this remark, Damiens responded that such riots had always occurred. Asked in turn if he had not referred "to the only one that occurred on the subject of the children, he said he had that one in mind like the others." Asked finally whether this one had "affected him particularly," he said it had not.[83]

This line of inquiry hence reached the dead end it deserved. Even for us it would be in a sense both satisfying and appropriate to be able to root Damiens' political radicalization in something so specific and personal as the great riot or rather series of riots that swept through Paris in the spring of 1750 in response to the rumor that the police were arresting children to ship to the colonies, and which so frightened Louis XV that he thereafter ceased traversing Paris on his trips from Compiègne to Versailles. But Damiens' claim that his then eleven-year-old daughter was among those arrested by the police is surely another of his gasconades, as is the story about the letter to the lieutenant of police. The police, or rather disguised and subaltern agents of the police, indeed arrested children in 1750—not, to be sure, to send to the colonies, but in response to complaints of their playing games that involved money and throwing stones at the newly erected street-lamps in Paris. But they arrested neither girls of any sort in this connection nor any children of either sex on the left bank of Paris where Damiens lived. The solitary reference to girls being arrested in the voluminous trial occasioned by this affair is so visibly a product of an eleven-year-old imagination as not to warrant adult consideration.[84] It is not even clear, finally, that Damiens was himself in Paris at the time; he was more probably at the Maridor château of Saint-Ouen in Maine.[85]

That Damiens indiscreetly talked about this riot at the time, however, and that he made it his personal affair to the extent of telling others that his daughter had been arrested and claiming to have threatened the lieutenant of police suggests that the event had indeed greatly excited him. Yet this much should not have so surprised his judges, even in the absence of any solid evidence of personal interest. Domestic servants were easily the most conspicuous group to have actually participated in all of the 1750 Parisian riots and, lest this be attributed solely to their inherent visibility—they wore their masters' livery—they also constituted the largest single category of those arrested in connection with this affair. If Damiens himself had not actually participated in or directly observed one of these riots—the nearest one occurred in the rue de l'Hirondelle near the pont Saint-Michel, still a long walk from either Saint-Etienne-des-Grès or Maridor's Parisian residence on the rue du Vieux Colombier near Saint-Sulpice—he could have undoubtedly talked to comrades who had.[86]

But while his judges strained to hear such nearly inaudible clues, Damiens himself loudly and forthrightly proclaimed that "religion" had been his motive in attacking the king.[87] Initially this avowal enabled Damiens' judges to cast him in the altogether traditional and familiar mold of religious fanatic, a throwback to the confessionally motivated assassins of the late sixteenth and early seventeenth centuries. Indeed, they never wholly abandoned the attempt to understand him in this way—far from it, as we shall observe. Yet at least two obstacles stood in the way of such an interpretation. First, there was the accumulating evidence of Damiens' *irreligion*, such as his affected impiety at Saint-Omer and his distrust of priests and confessions. "We were wrong in thinking that the criminal was religious; he has no [religion] at all," wrote the prince de Cröy from Saint-Omer to the marquis de Sourches, grand provost of France, on January 19.[88] And second, there was Damiens' seemingly eccentric definition of religion. Reminded that the "principles"of "holy religion" condemned the "horrible action" he had just committed, he responded that he understood by religion that "three-fourths of the people are perishing." Asked what "idea" he had of religion, he answered that his idea was that "one ought not to refuse the sacraments to people who live holy lives and who pray to God in church every day from morning till night." In this and other interrogations he typically coupled these themes: the "misery" of the people and the refusal of sacraments.[89] Little wonder, then, that his interrogators accused him of using religion as a "mask" or that the attorney general thought that he understood religion "rather poorly."[90]

But did he? If the attorney general or the parlementary interrogators had sincerely wished to know what Damiens meant by "religion," they had only to attend to what they themselves meant by it every time they informed the king that his "religion" had been "surprised"—that is, his sense of justice and goodness had been abused or taken advantage of. That this is basically what Damiens meant by it, too, is attested to by his equally loud proclamation that his intention in attacking the king had been "to render [his majesty] more disposed to hear [his parlement's] remonstrances, to dispense justice, and cease heeding the pernicious advice of his ministers."[91] The words echoed many a parlementary remonstrance, many a "representation" by the first president to the king.

To an extent, this is even true of one of the subthemes of Damiens' religion, namely the misery of the people. It is not likely, to be sure, that Damiens either saw or heard the parlement of Paris' warnings against the "inexpressible sequence of injustices" and "extreme misery" likely to ensue from the king's fiscal declarations of July 7, 1756, which most notably prolonged the first vingtième created in 1749 and imposed yet a second for the duration of the war then beginning.[92] These representations and "articles for remonstrances" are dated August 5 and 13 respectively, more than a month, that is, after Damiens had left Paris for Artois, whose provincial estates were murmuring against the same fiscal measures. But as a domestic in the service of either the comte de Maridor or Bèze de Lys, he might have remembered the parlement's remonstrances of June 7, 1750, which forthrightly informed his majesty that the "excessive dearness (*cherté*) of the most vital provisions, . . . the poor reduced to the impossibility of surviving," and "the diminution of all subjects by an excess of misery" were the "inevitable results" of his "multiple impositions." Or if his memory were still stronger, Damiens might have also recalled, while serving the magistrates Bellenger d'Essenlis or Séguier in 1741, the parlement's eloquent supplications of that year in behalf of his majesty's subjects afflicted by a "calamity shared by all conditions" and "exhausted by the dearth that hardly leaves them enough to subsist on."[93] When, while looking for the reassuring element of sordid self-interest in Damiens' pronouncements on the subject, his parlementary interrogators objected that he had served "in houses where he could not have perceived the misery of the people" and that "the epoque [of this misery] is too distant," Damiens could very well have responded that at least he had heard about this misery, because the houses in question were more or less their own. As it was, they could not accept Damiens' insolent appropriation of what they considered their exclusive right to altruism. "What is good for only oneself," he responded, "is good for nothing."[94]

The "epoque," for that matter, was not far removed either. Damiens need not have either read or heard parlementary remonstrances or recalled epoques as distant as 1750 or—what his judges undoubtedly had in mind—1741; he had only to keep his ear to the ground in 1756. The subsistence crisis of 1756-1757, it is true, does not register very spectacularly on a graph of French grain prices for the eighteenth century; certainly it did not rival those of 1709-1710, 1725-1726, 1740-1741, 1768-1772, or 1788-1789. But it was at least comparable to those of 1748-1749 or 1751-1752, and it grew more acute in proportion as one traveled west and north in France, to Normandy, Hainault, Flanders, and Artois—precisely where Damiens spent the six months preceding his return to Paris at the end of December 1756. In fact, the crisis of 1756-1757 was largely restricted to areas bordering the English Channel, which were affected by heavy rains during the harvest of 1756.[95] In England, where the price of wheat reached its highest point in the century since the catastrophic winter of 1709-1710, "many insurrections" broke out "on account of the scarcity of corn and the high prices of provisions, in response to which the parliament was finally persuaded to forbid the further exportation of wheat and shut down the distilleries."[96] Across the channel the prince de Cröy found the area around the port of Calais afflicted by a "general dearth" and "menaced by revolt" when he arrived there on May 29, 1757, and he promptly "warned the court" and took "necessary measures."[97] In Normandy the Parisian magistrate Jean-Baptiste Saget, in exile in that province, reported to his friend Lefebvre de Saint-Hilaire on April 21 that a *setier* of wheat, which ordinarily sold for fifteen livres, was then selling for the astronomical price of forty-two, and he challenged his correspondent to "conceive of the misery that results in the public." To find a scapegoat for this public, the parlement of Rouen had fined a poor curé five hundred livres for having hidden "a rather considerable stock of wheat under some straw."[98]

Both the misery and the new royal taxes gave rise to a good deal of talk, and one did not need to stray very far from Damiens' path to hear it. One letter written by a "simple," "small," and not altogether literate "personage" near Amiens and received by the attorney general during the Damiens affair implored the king to "deliver and relieve his people" from the "famine" and "sufferings" that had reduced them to "the last misery" and effectively rendered them "unable," he added, "to give any deniers to his majesty." Unlike this subject, however, who attributed the "great dearth" to the recent suppression of the Feast of the Apostles in his diocese, another anonymous and still more illiterate correspondent of the attorney general's, this one from Lyons, placed causal responsibility squarely on the shoulders of "the Fifteenth by name" who ran the risk of getting "purged" as a "tyrant" like Henry III or Henry IV if he did not soon restore the parlement to its "first function," "withdraw the terrible vingtième," and enable his people to have "some bread to eat."[99] But to move a bit closer to Damiens, he was apparently not the only Parisian domestic undeterred by his masters' ease from talking about misery and high prices, because two out of three letters discovered on the persons of domestics arrested in connection with the Damiens affair and retained by the attorney general made mention of popular misery and the high price of bread, apropos of both Paris and Amiens.[100] And to move still closer, m. Bataille, the attorney general's substitute in Arras, with whom Damiens had indirectly inquired while there in October concerning the order for his arrest, never tired of complaining in letters to his superior in Paris of the "infinitely high prices," "shortage of wheat," and "extreme misery encountered in the province." Charged with the expiatory task of destroying the house in which Damiens was born, he thought it "not at all exorbitant," given present conditions, to give the carpenter twelve livres a day for his labor and charitably suggested that the house's debris be auctioned off and the accruing profits distributed to the parish poor "who were running the risk of starving to death."[101] Damiens himself would hardly have objected.

If concern over misery, taxes, and the high price of grain was common in 1756-1757, so also was Damiens' identification of the merchants as responsible agents. Indeed, even his choice of a merchant as the ideal master to steal from was typical, as was his opinion that he was almost entitled to do so because "plenty of merchants had stolen other sums."[102] In a closely related affair the arrested leader of a Santerre-based robber band, hard pressed to divert his judges' attention from his own activities, seized the occasion of both the Damiens affair and the high price of grain to report a supposed conspiracy against the king's life. Significantly, he pointed his finger at two wealthy merchants in the area, Claude Lefort of Hargest and François Dangest of Vauvillier, whom he also accused of buying grain in order to sell it abroad—in effect, of speculating on the people's misery.[103] Damiens, too, apparently thought of himself as a species of Louis Mandrin, for on at least two occasions while in Artois he was reproached by relatives for giving money to the poor.[104]

Yet no more than in the remonstrances of the parlement of Paris was popular misery the most prominent motif in Damiens' religion. What overshadowed new taxes and high prices in Damiens' account of his motivation was the archbishop of Paris' refusal of sacraments to "good people who were worthy of receiving them" and the king's refusal to heed the remonstrances of the parlement of Paris. "If the king had only lopped off the heads of three or four bishops," he blurted immediately after his capture, "this would not have happened"—meaning by "bishops" those who thought as did the archbishop of Paris.[105] Queried repeatedly by his interrogators concerning the "veritable epoque" or precise "moment" of his resolution to attack the king, Damiens consistently responded that it was "since the time of the affairs of the archbishop and the parlement"—that is, "three or four years ago," the "time of the first refusals [of sacraments] by the archbishop." Even under torture, Damiens persisted in saying that it was "the archbishop by all his evil ways," specifically his "refusal of sacraments," who had motivated this crime, which he could nonetheless have resisted had the king only listened to his parlement's remonstrances on the subject. He was not being inconsistent, then, in also maintaining that he had resolved upon his plan only after seeing "what little heed the king paid to the representations of his parlement."[106] "If he had attempted to kill the king," Damiens told his guards in prison, "it was because his majesty had not listened to the remonstrances of his parlement." His attack on the king, in effect, was an exceptionally strong, nonverbal sort of remonstrance on behalf of the parlement of Paris.[107]

Unlike popular misery and the high price of bread, the subject of the refusal of sacraments calls for a preliminary word of explanation. Ever since the arrival of the papal bull *Unigenitus* (1713) in France, which condemned 101 "Jansenist" and Gallican propositions from a book by the oratorian Pasquier Quesnel, a tendency was discernible among some French bishops to construe continued opposition to this bull as heresy and to punish ecclesiastics who appealed it to an ecumenical council with deprivation of the sacraments of the Eucharist and extreme unction. But this tendency never assumed the form of a systematic campaign until around 1750 when a group of zealous "constitutionary" bishops led by Christophe de Beaumont, the young and newly elevated archbishop of Paris, began systematically refusing these sacraments to anyone who would not produce a *billet de confession*, a written attestation that one had been confessed by an "orthodox" priest, that is, one who had accepted the bull *Unigenitus*. Although these measures affected primarily ecclesiastics and aimed to uproot a kind of Jansenist church within the French Catholic church, they frequently grazed laymen as well, for instance, the Châtelet councillor sieur Coffin, who was refused the sacraments in 1750. This in itself might have prompted the parlement of Paris to intervene on behalf of the archbishop's victims, but the parlement was also legally persuaded that the episcopacy was overstepping its constitutional bounds, violating both the letter of its canons by adding confessional requirements unauthorized by the rituals and even the spirit of the bull *Unigenitus* by wrongly transforming it into a "rule of faith," something that precisely distinguished dogma from error. At first timidly, then with steadily mounting audacity, the parlement therefore waded into the quarrel, in specific cases ordering priests in at least a roundabout fashion to administer the sacraments. Caught visibly off guard by the dimensions the quarrel rapidly assumed, the king vacillated, maneuvered, but generally sided with the bishops and their "spiritual jurisdiction," which was under attack, he thought, by his secular courts' actions and remonstrances. The controversy reached its zenith in 1753—Damiens' "three or four years ago"—when the parlement tried to indict the archbishop of Paris and the king finally exiled the parlement after the latter refused to suspend legal proceedings against sacrament-refusing priests. But it was still raging in 1757 and was closely related to the resignation of most of the magistrates of the parlement of Paris on December 13-14, 1756.[108]

That a lowly domestic servant should have found these high

jurisdictional and theological quarrels so gripping may seem surprising to us, and it certainly embarrassed and mystified his interrogators who "objected that what occurred regarding the archbishop could never have determined a man of his sort to commit his crime." Damiens responded that "he had nothing else to say, except that if [the archbishop] had not refused the sacraments, none of this would have happened." Thoroughly unconvinced, his interrogators again probed for the potentially explanatory element of self-interest: "Asked whether he himself had ever sustained a refusal of sacraments, or one of his relatives or friends, he answered no, that he did not even present himself." When they asked him in turn what idea he had of religion, they were struck by the boomerang of their own rhetoric: he "responded that he had the idea that one ought not refuse the sacraments to people who live well, and who pray to God every day from morning till night," a near quotation from the parlement's remonstrances of April 15, 1752.[109]

What should rather surprise us, however, is that his judges should have seemed surprised at all by these responses. Damiens, after all, had served as the councillor Bèze de Lys' personal lackey during the height of the refusal of sacraments controversy around 1752-1754; in that capacity he had worn de Lys' livery and accompanied his master to and from parlementary sessions at the Palais de justice, where he had sometimes waited long hours for these sessions to end. It was here, he said, in the "rooms of the Palais waiting for the end of the [parlement's] deliberations," that he had first "formed his execrable design." It was the discourses of "lawyers, councillors, and ecclesiastics" who "said very loudly in the rooms of the Palais" that "the king risked much by not preventing the evil conduct of the archbishop of Paris" that had "heated up his head."[110] Or was it perhaps on the rue des Maçons, where both Bèze de Lys and the Jansenist councillor Rolland de Challerange lived, that the idea first occurred to Damiens? Under torture, he said that it was here, while "returning from the Palais," that a certain Dominique Gautier, intendant of the marquis Louis-Joseph Le Maistre de Ferrières, yet another Jansenist and parlementary family, had suggested that if only someone could "touch" or "hit" the king, the parlement could punish the archbishop of Paris and prevent further refusals of sacraments.[111]

Damiens was not the only domestic servant to have become "heated up" on his master's side of this controversy. In an unedited, extrajudicial deposition a certain Marguerite Lafaye, another of Bèze de Lys' former domestics, reported that "Flammand" was in the habit of assembling the parlementary *lacquetaille* around the gaming table in the Palais de justice and conducting mock trials of the archbishop of Paris, assigning the role of first president, attorney general, *greffier*, and hangman by throws of the dice. Damiens might have taken the lead in this macabre entertainment, but he evidently found plenty of willing participants.[112] More remarkable, perhaps, is the testimony of the archbishop's principal lackey, delivered over wine on May 5, 1752, to a police informant, that one of his comrades who was imprudent enough to go to the Palais de justice on private business wearing the archepiscopal livery had found himself insulted and nearly assaulted as a spy by the parlementary lackeys. The archbishop, he said, had since taken to sending his domestics on errands without livery.[113] Moreover, if Damiens' judges had looked with different spectacles on the letters they seized between Robert-François' brothers, Louis and Antoine-Joseph, they might have attached significance to the fact that Louis, also the servant of a parlementary magistrate, never failed to mention the latest developments in the refusal of sacraments controversy and devoted one entire letter to the subject, presented with a parlementary bias. To the police and judges in search of evidence for a conspiracy, however, all this was anodyne "domestic gossip."[114]

Popular interest in and excitement over the controversy was not limited to domestics serving one or the other of the principal contestants. The memoirs of both the lawyer Edmond Barbier and the marquis d'Argenson fairly bristle with references to popular demonstrations and even small-scale riots in Paris in favor of the parlement and against the archbishop on the occasion of the refusal of sacraments to appellants of the bull *Unigenitus*. But if these be suspect as excessively "literary" sources, what is one to make of a duel fought between two procurator's clercs in 1752 over differing opinions about the archbishop's refusal of sacraments to appellants of *Unigenitus* and reported to the police commissioner by a wounded participant; or the "more than twenty women and several *colporteurs*, posted and bought by Jansenist money" who in April of the same year publicly taunted the archbishop with a hostile parlementary *arrêt* while he led a canonization procession through the streets adjacent to the cathedral; or the riot that nearly ensued on August 6, 1754, and was only prevented by the hasty arrival of the Paris guard after an inebriated bourgeois of Paris began yelling in a cabaret in the rue de la Harpe on behalf of "religion," which was persecuted, in his opinion, by the parlement of Paris, notwithstanding the latter's exile at that time.[115]

Of particular relevance to Damiens are the reports of a police observer following the funerals, in 1752, of Louis "the pious," duc d'Orléans, who died reputedly a Jansenist, and the abbé Le Merre, an appellant priest who died having been refused the last sacraments by Bouëttin, curé of Saint-Etienne-du-Mont. Commenting on the latter event, the police observer underscored the violent language of the "populace," which threatened to "stone" (*assommer à coup de pierres*) the offending curé as a "wretch" (*malheureux*) should he "dare to show himself"—he had fled after the parlement ordered his arrest—and enthusiastically offered to "serve as his hangman" (*chacun étoit prêt de lui servir de bourreau*) should the parlement legally condemn him. "Many persons" thought that the parlement had been too lenient in its treatment of the curé, that it should even have tried the archbishop of Paris, who issued the orders the curé had obeyed: "In acting this way, more than five hundred thousand citizens would have accompanied the parlement to Versailles and supported its representations to the king, who was ignorant of the vexations with which they [the priests] make his most faithful subjects suffer."[116]

It is not difficult to recognize here the essentially popular source of the surgical language and reactions of a Damiens, who thought the whole problem consisted in the "too kind" king's unwillingness to lop off three or four mitered heads, who arranged mock trials of the archbishop with his fellow parlementary lackeys, and who, according to Marguerite Lafaye, another domestic at Bèze de Lys', was forever bragging that "if only the first president would give him a free hand (*main levée*) to go arrest (*enlever chez lui*) that archbishop in order to try him," he would "acquit himself well of the commission."[117] That this was banal and popular language should hardly be surprising, since the "crowd" at Le Merre's funeral was gathered around the church of Sainte-Geneviève, just a stone's throw, as it were, from Damiens' home at Saint-Etienne-des-Grès, and Damiens might very well have been a member of it. As Damiens himself tirelessly insisted, "all the world" or "the public generally" talked in this manner against the prelate and his priests, both "in the streets and the cafés" of Paris and in the towns of Flanders and Artois, "Frenchmen and foreigners alike."[118]

Likewise further enlightened by reference to talk from "below" are Damiens' religious and sacramental conceptions. For Damiens, who thought religion consisted in not refusing the sacraments to "people who live well"—as for this crowd, which thought that Le Merre had been "unjustly refused the sacraments, because he had lived well"—religion was an essentially moral or ethical affair. The doctrinal dimension of the refusal of sacraments controversy quite escaped them. In the duc d'Orléans' funeral crowd, on the other hand, we again encounter Damiens' coupled themes of hunger or "misery" and the refusal of sacraments—bread in either case, it might be observed, of which the king could not deprive his subjects without evident injustice. The police observer reported that the populace believed that this saintly prince, who had once been refused the sacraments, had been "taken away" by God so that he would no longer have to witness the "horrors that the government tolerated, both in the church and among the people, who have no bread. . . ." The marquis d'Argenson, as usual quite sensitive to popular echoes, in effect acknowledged the same linkage when he observed in the wake of Damiens' coup that "tempers are too agitated by religion and misery."[119]

What, if anything, makes Damiens stand out from among this anti-episcopal crowd is only the degree of his personal and psychic involvement in these controversies. From the time he worked for "Bèze de Lys and some other councillors of the parlement," his wife complained, he declaimed about the parlement "like a hair brain," speaking "badly of priests" and adding that "if he were in charge, he would know how to give the parlement its due, that it would not be treated as it was. . . ." Fellow domestic Julien Le Guerinays remarked similarly that every time he met him, Damiens wanted to talk about the bull *Unigenitus* and billets de confession. Even as lacquais frotteur to the La Bourdonnaye family in 1753, that is, after his first period of service to Bèze de Lys, Damiens acquired a household reputation as "the first newsmonger (*nouvelliste*) of the quarter," going "almost every day to the terrace of the Luxembourg to ask for news, or to read it." Damiens "always seemed informed about when the parlement's assemblies began and ended," and when asked how he knew this, "he responded only that he knew very well."[120]

So intense was the anticlericalism Damiens acquired through the agency of this controversy that he ceased altogether to frequent the sacraments and extended his hostility toward priests to all without distinction. His wife reported that he thought priests generally, not only some, "ruined the realm"; Marguerite Lafaye remembered that on one occasion, when she pointed out to him a crucifix in the passage of Sainte-Geneviève near Saint-Etienne-du-Mont, "he responded as an atheist who does not believe anything"; and we have noted the impiety with which he scandalized his family in Saint-Omer, going so far as to condemn even Jansenist priests.[121] In response to questions about these matters, he was brutally specific: "Asked how long ago he had gone to confession and approached the sacraments, he said that he went three or four years ago, but that the archbishop gave such wonderful examples that he has not gone there since." Or again, "asked what made him lose his sentiments of piety, he said that it was the trouble he observed among the priests." Damiens' religion did not survive his respect for its ministers.[122] A good thirty years before the Revolution, in the absence of any discernibly "enlightened" influence and by means of the sole agency, apparently, of the refusal of sacraments controversy, Damiens was already "de-christianized," almost a sans culotte—except for the culotte; Damiens not only wore one but retained an envious respect for the aristocracy.[123]

Damiens' case nonetheless brings to mind the marquis d'Argenson's well-known comments about the dramatic decline in the number of communicants in the Paris parishes of Saint-Côme, Saint-Eustache, and Saint-Sulpice in 1753, at the height of the refusal of sacraments controversy. "One should not attribute the decline of religion in France to English philosophy," he judged, "which has only made a hundred or so converts in Paris, but to the hatred conceived against priests which runs to excess these days."[124] The relationship between this decline and the current affaires du temps was further underscored by the attorney general's retired father, also named Guillaume-François Joly de Fleury, who in 1752 warned the archbishop of Rouen that "the bulk of the people who still possess some religion are revolting against their bishops in connection with the refusal of sacraments and billets de confession."[125] In the absence of Parisian Old Regime parish records, which unfortunately perished in the destruction of 1830, no quantitative corroboration based on confessions at *Pâcques* is possible for these judgments. But police records seem to bear out the more qualitative emphasis upon "hatred" and revolt, which went so far, according to d'Argenson, that priests "hardly dare show themselves in the streets without being hooted."[126] To restrict ourselves again to the temporal vicinity of the Damiens affair, let us commiserate with Père Gervais, the prior of a Carmelite house in Charenton, who was stabbed on the evening of January 10, 1757, by one of two "workers" on the rue des Prouvaires as he was returning to the Paris Carmelite residence on the rue de Vaugirard; or the abbé de La Grive, *porte-Dieu* of the parish of Sainte-Marguerite, who having carried the sacraments to one of the parish sick on the morning of February 8, 1757, found himself "insulted" on his way home by a certain Jacques Reynard, journeyman carpenter; or the sieur Mathieu Flint, finally, another porte-Dieu at Sainte-Marguerite, who was stabbed and hit on March 7, 1758, by two individuals on the rue Verte, one of whom had lured him there with a request for the last sacraments in behalf of a supposedly dying woman who lived on that street.[127] Evidence such as this suggests that Damiens was not altogether unique and that the refusal of sacraments and other *Unigenitus*-related controversies might have played a more important role in the development known as dechristianization than they are generally credited with doing.

In any event, these ecclesiastical affaires du temps continued to interest Damiens sporadically even after his theft and its subsequent discovery in Artois permanently darkened his life. Jean-François Neveu, probably one of the first people Damiens saw upon arriving in Arras, remembered that Damiens "appeared very predisposed against the ecclesiastics in the current controversies, and very attached to the parlement"; and to his cousin Pierre-Guislain Lefebvre, in Hermanville, Damiens "speechified in a manner to show that he was very attached to the parlement, very little to the ecclesiastics." On July 11 in Saint-Omer he told his brother and the shoemaker Pierre-François Le Clerc about some recent cases of the refusal of sacraments, adding "that if the king knew his business, he would hang several ecclesiastics in order to impose upon the rest." To Antoine-Luc Beaucourt, finally, in early November, Damiens "spoke vaguely in disjointed phrases, but he appeared . . . to favor not the ecclesiastics, but the parlement."[128]

Then came the news of the mass resignations of the parlement of Paris on December 13-14, provoked in part by a royal declaration that took the episcopacy's side in the refusal of sacraments controversy.[129] For Damiens, who first heard the news from the attorneys Sohier and Dufour in Arras, this event acted as a catalyst that once and for all combined in his mind the never too distinct elements of his private, personal crisis and that of the realm. Never perfectly parallel, the lines of the two finally intersected here, with fatal consequences for both. "Everything is lost," he mumbled in the presence of

Nicolas Breuvart, grain measurer in Arras, "look at the realm knocked down; and as for me, I am ruined for good; look at the lousy affair on my back." And in the presence of Martin-Philippe Neveu, speaking "all alone" around December 23: "Look at my poor wife ruined, my poor little wife is f[outu]."[130]

About the same time, even earlier in fact than the news of the king's lit de justice of December 13, another, more ominously discernible theme began to make itself heard above Damiens' otherwise indistinct and subterranean mumblings. "If I return to France, yes, I will return there," he said to Nicolas Playoust while in Poperingue, "and if I die, the greatest on earth will die also, and you will hear of me." To François-Joseph Bourbier, a bit later in Fies, Damiens said, or rather muttered, that he intended to join a good regiment or "go talk to the king," and he told Nicolas Breuvart that he absolutely had to return to Paris where "he would be spoken of."[131] What the news of December 13 did, evidently, was to crystallize these amorphous regicidal urgings into a fixed resolution by holding out, to Damiens, a forward escape from his purely personal dilemma.[132] He could wipe out the guilt of a petty parricide—the theft from his master—with the penance of a grandiose one—an attack on his king—in a sacrament that demanded no untrustworthy priests as intermediaries and that the archbishop could not refuse. He would then "die like Jesus Christ amidst pain and torments" and "render a great service to the state" by contributing to the "cares and efforts of the parlement, which is maintaining religion and the state."[133]

For Damiens, the time had now come for action, which seemed purposeful for the first time since July:

Arras, Tuesday, December 28: Using the name "Breval," he boarded the Paris-bound mail coach in which he was joined by a tonsured cleric, a Dominican monk, and a sergeant of the regiment of Poitou. During the journey, he mostly slept or pretended to sleep, but while awake he looked around with distracted eyes and displayed "a great curiosity for political news," forcing the passengers to listen to a public reading of the *Gazette de France* in the town of Roye. Discussing the troubles between the parlement and the clergy, he told the young cleric that "if several bishops had not been left so tranquil, the peace could have been maintained."[134]

Paris, Friday, December 31, 2:00 P.M.: The coach arrived in Paris at the *barrière* Saint-Martin, where Damiens, fearing the sergeant intended to conscript him, took a fiacre with the cleric to the rue de Poitiers in the Marais. From there he made his way to a cabaret on the rue Beaubourg and sent a Savoyard errand boy to tell his brother that someone wanted to see him there. Resplendent in his red vest and new riding coat, he brushed aside his brother's reproaches and informed the astonished Louis that he had returned to Paris "because of the affairs of the parlement, that he was angry that these were not yet terminated—discourses that he delivered with a great deal of passion." When Louis refused to recommend an auberge to him on the grounds that his theft was everywhere known, Damiens responded angrily that he should have gone directly to Versailles. When Louis at least told him where his wife and daughter then lived, Damiens then embraced his brother and took his leave, telling him that they had probably seen each other for the last time.[135]

Around 5:00 or 5:30 P.M. Damiens arrived at the house of madame Ripandelly on the rue du cimetière Saint-Nicolas-des-Champs, where his wife now worked as cook. Finding that his wife was out on errands at les Halles, he was invited by the chambermaid to wait for her in the kitchen. When his wife arrived around 6:00 P.M., she embraced him and upon his assurances that he did not intend to stay long and would soon be on his way back to Artois, she allowed him to spend the night in her room on the third floor.[136]

Paris, New Year's Day, January 1: Damiens "very politely" received the New Year's compliments of the domestic Charles Hurillon when the latter encountered him in his wife's room, still in bed at 11:00 A.M. Damiens' eighteen-year-old daughter, Marie-Elizabeth, was also there, having come from Saint-Etienne-des-Grès where she still lived. Damiens might have gone out briefly that day on the pretense of reserving a coach for Arras, perhaps actually to attend mass. At some point during this stay at Ripandelly's, he secretly placed what remained of the stolen money in a sack on the manteau of the kitchen fireplace, evidently hoping that his wife would eventually find it there.[137]

Paris, Sunday, January 2: Damiens, as usual still in bed, received a visit by his daughter and the family's seamstress friend, the widow Wattebled, who lived on the place de l'Estrapade. Damiens seemed happy to see Wattebled, listened patiently to her reproaches, and apparently tried to assure both that he had not returned to Paris to have himself hung and dishonor the family, that he intended to return to Arras shortly and join a regiment. Later that evening Damiens and his wife accompanied Wattebled and Marie-Elizabeth as far as a cabaret near Saint-Merry on the rue Saint-Martin, where they remained for a time over beer.[138]

Paris, Monday, January 3, 7:00 P.M.: After spending another day in his wife's room, Damiens left the Ripandelly house in the company of his wife and daughter, then took his leave of them on the rue Saint-Martin near the rue aux Ours around 8:00 P.M. In parting, Damiens told his wife and daughter that he would probably return to Artois, there to engage himself with a captain who would take him to the colonies. But he may well have also mumbled something to his daughter about going to Versailles "to talk to the king and put the present affairs in order."[139]

Damiens went to the rue de l'Université, faubourg Saint-Germain, where he entered a cabaret owned by a former fellow domestic at the college of Louis-le-Grand. Unable to find him, Damiens ate, supped, and fell asleep. He left after being awakened by the innkeeper's apprentice around 10:45 P.M.[140] He then boarded a coach from Paris to Versailles at 11:00 P.M., arriving at his destination around 2:30 A.M. Unable to find an open auberge, he took refuge at the bureau of the court's carriages, where an attendant permitted him to sleep on the straw mattresses.[141]

Versailles, Tuesday, January 4, 7:00 A.M.: Damiens took a room under the name "Lefevre," *marchand-négociant*, in an auberge owned by Antoine Fortier on the rue Satory. After eating some bread and drinking a half bottle of wine, he slept until mid-afternoon.[142] He then left the auberge around 3:00 P.M. and wandered across the château courtyard, visiting merchants' quarters and conversing with chairmen and other domestics. Later he warmed himself in a cabaret on the rue des Récollets, where he ate some more bread and drank some more wine.[143] Damiens returned to his auberge at 11:00 P.M. and asked Fortier for some chicken. When Fortier offered some lamb instead, Damiens "flew into a rage, assumed a very imperious tone, and said, swearing: 'This f[outu] Versailles, one can never finish any business; now it's the king who has left for Trianon until Saturday!' " He ate some salad and lamb and went to bed.[144]

Versailles, Wednesday, January 5, 8:00 A.M.: Damiens rose and asked the innkeeper's wife to send for a surgeon so that he could have himself bled. It was so cold that the woman thought he was jesting and responded that he could not have chosen a better time. Damiens was later to claim that if he had only been bled, he would not have done what he shortly did.[145] Damiens left the auberge about 10:00 A.M., giving the keys to the garçon. Sometime later he returned to the château courtyard where a guard thought he remembered him walking and pacing aimlessly. Around 4:00 or 5:00 P.M. Damiens encountered someone who asked him, "Well?" to which he responded, "Well, I am waiting." Or was the exchange the reverse of what the guard remembered, as Damiens later maintained?[146]

The king arrived at the château from Trianon at 5:30 P.M. to see his sick daughter. Damiens insinuated himself into the immediate vicinity of the staircase where the king was shortly expected, by "conversing with the king's postillons and guards though he did not know them."[147] At 5:45 P.M. the king began his descent of the staircase. The Artesian "marchand-négociant," waiting in the obscurity of the staircase's base, was soon to discover that he could finish his business in Versailles after all.

Damiens' Masters as Judges

Les Affaires du Temps

DAMIENS WAS NOT tried by the parlement of Paris or even by its whole Grand' chambre, for these institutions had temporarily ceased to exist in the wake of the king's lit de justice and the mass resignations that followed. Refusing to reconstitute the parlement in response to the "striking" magistrates' collective offer to take back their resignations, the king instead confided Damiens' trial to the Grand' chambre's remaining ten "loyal" presidents and approximately fifteen councillors, to which he added a number of retired or honorary councillors and the princes and peers of the realm.[1] For this reason alone Damiens' trial took place in a charged political atmosphere, his case unintelligible except in the glare of the larger affair pitting the realm's magistracy against the episcopacy supported by the king.

Moreover, the same issues involving the bull *Unigenitus* and the refusal of sacraments that divided these two parties entered massively, as we have noted, into Damiens' announced motivation; the same lit de justice and mass resignations that politicized his trial had also prompted his return from Arras to Paris and Versailles. The relationship between Damiens' affair and the wider "affaires du temps" was hence not only extrinsic and circumstantial, but intrinsic and essential as well, so that a preliminary glance at these *affaires* becomes the more imperative. And among the royal measures forcibly registered at the December 13 lit de justice that provoked the magistrates' mass resignations was precisely a declaration forbidding the parlement from ordering on its own "secular" authority that the sacraments be administered to opponents or appellants of the papal bull *Unigenitus*.[2]

Unigenitus was the last and most thorough in a series of papal acts condemning French Jansenism, a movement of Augustinian piety within the French and Flemish Catholic church accenting the indomitable influence of human sin or "concupiscence" in the absence of "charity" bestowed only by divine predestination through an all-powerful or "efficacious" grace.[3] Ascetic, austere, and most otherworldly (unlike Calvinism) when it took root in the 1640s and first flowered in the Sorbonne and the convent of Port-Royal near Paris, this movement had by the advent of *Unigenitus* become thoroughly mixed up with and virtually inseparable from two older elements in the repertory of French traditions, namely Gallicanism and the parlement's constitutionalism. Gallicanism, whose lineage dates immediately from the reign of Philip the Fair in the fourteenth century, laid claim to the French, or Gallican, church's complete independence from Roman canonical usages and the right to judge doctrine concurrently with Rome; while parlementary constitutionalism, with more recent origins in the sixteenth century, emphasized the parlement's essential place in the French "constitution" and important right, as presumed successor to the medieval court of peers and even the Merovingians' spring meetings with the *leuds*, or barons, to reject, modify, or freely consent to the royal edicts and declarations sent to it for registration by the king.[4] These traditions were in turn related in that the parlement especially prided itself on being a staunch defender of the Gallican "liberties," although as construed by the parlement's secular magistrates and legists, this properly ecclesiastical tradition meant not only the Gallican church's independence from Rome but also the church's dependence upon the state or king in all but the most spiritual matters. This latter emphasis was eventually expressed conversely as the king's accountability to God alone for his temporal administration in the first of the four Gallican liberties with which the general assembly of the Gallican church spelled out the tradition in 1682.

How these originally quite heterogeneous elements coalesced

is bound up with the circumstances of Jansenism's condemnation in France. The papacy was persuaded to condemn it in 1653 under the influence of the then-powerful Jesuit order, which espoused the very opposite theological tendencies and perceived in Jansenism the reincarnation of the heresies of Calvinism and Baianism. The French monarchy and much of the episcopacy with which the Jesuits were likewise influential vigorously seconded and to an extent anticipated the papacy's efforts, in part because they were concerned that Jansenist independence and accent on individual conscience might undermine the universe of hierarchy and subordination. Persecuted by monarchy, papacy, and episcopacy, Jansenism found a refuge within the lower reaches of the clergy and obtained a certain protection from the parlement of Paris, which feared that the papacy was using Jansenism as a pretext for undermining the Gallican tradition. Simultaneously the parlement gave unprecedented expression to its constitutional pretensions during the mid-seventeenth-century civil war known as the Fronde.[5]

This much already grouped Jansenism, Gallicanism, and parlementary constitutionalism in a common opposition to papacy, monarchy, and Jesuitism, but *Unigenitus* itself welded them into a coherent if not altogether internally consistent oppositional point of view. Solicited by the setting "sun king" and promulgated by Clement XI in 1713, this bull unwisely offended both Augustinian and Gallican sensibilities. The 101 propositions it chose for condemnation from Pasquier Quesnel's book, *Réflexions morales sur le Nouveau testament*, included not only unquestionably Jansenist theological tenets—efficacious grace's invincible power over the human will, for example, or the unworthiness of all works not proceeding from "charity"—but ethical judgments such as "an unjust excommunication should never prevent one from doing one's duty," thereby giving substance to the Gallican nightmare of a pope unsettling domestic tranquility in France by unjustly excommunicating her king.[6] Though the bull, predictably, provoked the hostility of the parlement of Paris and, less predictably, a sizeable proportion of the episcopacy, the monarchy had engaged its authority in the bull's behalf and persisted in attempting to enforce it as a law of both church and state. Under the ministry of André-Hercules, cardinal de Fleury, the monarchy gradually weeded out opponents of the bull from the episcopacy, expelled them wholesale from the Sorbonne, and tried in 1720 and again in 1730 to get the parlement of Paris to register it without reservations. But however successful these measures were in achieving their immediate goals, they succeeded in the longer run only in creating an even broader and more popular front of opposition, called the *parti janséniste*, sustained by an increasingly articulate and subversive point of view.[7]

The mentality in question combined the themes of Jansenism, Gallicanism, and parlementary constitutionalism, but the result somehow exceeded the sum of its constituent parts. In the name of doctrinal Augustinianism it denounced the neo-Pelagianism and accommodating morality, or Molinism, of the Jesuit order and called upon all good Catholics to uproot them. In the name of episcopal Gallicanism it denounced the "foreign" influences of the Jesuit order and the Jesuit-dominated papacy and called upon "patriots" and "all good Frenchmen" to eradicate them. In the name of parlementary Gallicanism it denounced the "spirit of domination" and "system of independence" of the Gallican bishops and their grand vicars and called upon the monarchy to subjugate them. And in the name of parlementary constitutionalism it denounced the "despotism" and "arbitrariness" of this same monarchy, or at least its ministers, and called upon all good "patriots" to oppose them. It opposed the "court of Rome" in the name of the Roman "Holy See," "ministerial despotism" in the name of the monarchy's best interests, and the Gallican bishops in the name of true or pristine Gallicanism.[8] But it was no less effective for being thus circular and so closely shadowing what it opposed. It focused hostility against what seemed to be a syndrome of oppression: as the marquis d'Argenson saw it, things "ecclesiastical, ultramontanist, and inquisitorial," or more specifically, "the episcopacy, the Jesuits and ambitious abbés," and royal ministers who governed the realm "arbitrarily and without remedy."[9]

Constituting the front lines of the political forces united by this mentality were Jansenist priests and members of religious orders who had appealed *Unigenitus* to an ecumenical council and who were vulnerable on that account to interdicts, the refusal of sacraments, and even imprisonment in the Bastille on orders by their ecclesiastical superiors. An example already encountered is the curé of Sainte-Marguerite at Saint-Omer, or in general, the "best priests" or the "priests of the party of the parlement" whom Damiens sometimes overheard talking in the "rooms of the Palais." Those who more properly belonged in the Palais de justice, namely, the hard-core parti janséniste of the parlement of Paris, made up the lay wing of the front lines. Examples among the magistrates are Rolland de Challerange, the abbé Chauvelin, Robert de Saint-Vincent, Lefebvre de Saint-Hilaire, Guillaume II Lambert, Clément de Feillet, and Henri de Revol; and among lawyers, the abbés Gabriel-Nicolas Maultrot, Claude Mey, Charlemagne Lalourcé, Jean-Baptiste Gerbier, and Louis-Adrien Le Paige.[10] But both clerical and lay contingents could put into the field much larger groups, the first from among the lower ranks of the clergy, the second from among all those in any way connected with the law, who without being in any theological sense Jansenists, nonetheless shared the front line's outrage over the episcopal and ministerial highhandedness represented by the bull *Unigenitus* and its enforcement in the land. In fact, in this loose sense much of the population of Paris could be accounted Jansenist, at least if we can believe such observers as Barbier and d'Argenson who never tired of saying that "all Paris is Jansenist."[11]

Opposing the parti janséniste was the less popular but more stellar *parti dévôt*, represented at the court by the queen, the dauphin, and the king's daughters; also by the duc de La Vauguyon, governor of the royal children; the comte d'Argenson, secretary of war; the bishop of Mirepoix, Jean-François Boyer, in charge of episcopal appointments (the *feuille des bénéfices*); and the chancellor Lamoignon de Blancmesnil. But it included as well the still influential Jesuit order, most of the episcopacy, and large parts of the clerical second order together with their numerous lay dependencies. After 1749 the parti dévôt was sometimes known as the "archbishop's party" because its standard bearer was by all accounts Christophe de Beaumont, newly elevated archbishop of Paris, whose zeal in behalf of *Unigenitus* only slightly exceeded that of such sacrament-refusing colleagues as Orléans de La Motte of Amiens, Montmorency de Laval of Orléans, Poncet de La Rivière of Troyes, Caritat de Condorcet of Auxerre, and Antoine de Brancas of Aix. Together these bishops—the five or six, perhaps, that Damiens would have liked to have seen beheaded—were known as "constitutionary" bishops, inasmuch as they favored the "constitution" *Unigenitus*, not parlementary constitutionalism.[12] On the contrary, because they looked generally to the monarchy for support, their conception of the monarchy tended to be more "despotic" or free of constitutional restraints than that of the parlement and its adherents. Similarly, in defending their own authority, indirectly under attack by way of the bull, they also defended the papal authority that promulgated this document and tended in consequence to become more propapal or ultramontanist, less Gallican, than their parlementary and Jansenist foes.[13]

When the refusal of sacraments controversy suddenly erupted around 1750, the stakes in the battle between these parties were already very high, much higher than the various issues considered individually might suggest. Confusedly under debate between them were questions of no less import than the authority within the church, whether vested in the pope, the ecclesiastical hierarchy, or the whole body of the faithful; than sovereignty within the state, whether concentrated in the king or ultimately diffused throughout the nation; than the proper relationship between these communities, whether of mutual or unequal dependence or whether they should be coterminate at all; than even the nature of the Christian religion, whether something internal and purely spiritual and whether external and physical as well.[14] These larger questions related the bewildering multiplicity of issues to each other and invested each with ideological force. Embedded in the debate over the administration of the Parisian Hôpital général in the early

1750s, for example, were not only the particular questions of Jansenism, administrative personnel, and budgetary irresponsibility but the more explosive issues of lay or clerical, parlementary or royal control over this important and powerful institution.[15]

The underlying modernity of this contest is easily lost sight of amidst the joustlike rhetorical trappings with which it was fought. Gallican and Jansenist pamphleteers were thoroughly convinced that they were reliving the religious wars of the sixteenth and early seventeenth centuries and that the Jesuit-dominated Catholic League of those wars was resurrecting before their very eyes. The archbishop of Paris, Christophe de Beaumont, to believe one pamphleteer writing in the context of the Damiens affair, was the "chief" of this new league, a pastoral instruction he published its "first signal of combat" or manifesto.[16] Or if such rhetoric be dismissed as insincere propaganda, listen to the Jansenist lawyer Louis-Adrien Le Paige as he tried privately to persuade his patron, the prince de Conti, on December 9, 1756, to resume relations with the king and head off if at all possible the imminent lit de justice: "We have here the same situation, the same audacity in the clergy, the same league on the part of the false zealots, the same instability and . . . weakness on the part of the prince." Just as Henry III was "sometimes for the clergy, sometimes for the parlement, and sometimes in between" but "was finally forced to declare himself the chief of the league that he abhorred," so it was to be feared that the vacillatory Louis XV in following a similarly uneven course would infallibly come to the same unfortunate end, namely, "to die at the hands of the league itself."[17]

The episcopacy also relived the sixteenth century, occasionally complaining of a "league"—of Protestant-like heretics, this one—"formed against the church and her ministers," a veritable "conjuration" like that of Amboise "concluded against the adorable body of Jesus Christ, in order to surrender it hand and foot to his most cruel enemies."[18] More often, however, they walked painfully in the footsteps of the church fathers of the fourth and fifth centuries, persecuted, as were they, by a combination of pagans, heretics, and well-meaning but misled emperors. Christophe de Beaumont adopted the persona of Saint Ambrose doing holy battle with the emperor Valentinian, while his friend and colleague Orléans de La Motte assumed the mantle of Athanasius persecuted by the emperor Constantius.[19] Rosset de Ceilcs of Tours trod the rock-strewn path of Saint Hilary of Poitiers in his trials with the same heretical emperors.[20] In still other moods many agreed that "even the centuries the least favorable to the church furnished no precedents" to the reign of Louis XV, that "religion was in greater danger than it had ever been," and that the direst of apocalyptic predictions were about to be realized.[21]

Damiens' self-declared motivation made it impossible in any case to quarantine his particular affair from this wider ideological and political contagion, despite a certain attempt by the official press to do so. But by refusing to accept the resigned magistrates' olive branch of January 6 and in choosing thereby to perpetuate the political crisis that began on December 13, the king linked the latter to the Damiens affair even more closely than it might otherwise have been, for to restrict the number of Damiens' judges to those who had not resigned on December 13 was to entrust his trial to a small handful of magistrates whose very claim to constitute the parlement was hotly disputed and whose integrity and independence from a Jesuit-tainted Versailles was open to question. The royal council's decision to add the princes and peers of the realm might have increased the number of Damiens' judges, but it did not fundamentally change the situation since their role was primarily passive, restricted to hearing the interrogations and other procedures performed by the four judges commissioned to this effect by what remained of the parlement's Grand' chambre.[22] Whether anybody wanted it to or not, therefore, Damiens' trial became a constituent and complicating factor in this larger political conflict, a pebble contributing its own considerable ripples to already troubled waters.

The trial's contamination by the wider political conflict extended even to the royal council's seemingly innocent decision to convoke the princes and peers of the realm, for the royal council had consistently opposed the parlement's "invitations" to the princes and peers as a body to join in its deliberations ever since it first attempted to do so in order to try the archbishop of Paris in December 1752. A constitutional controversy had ensued from this opposition, focusing on whether the parlement might invite the princes and peers to deliberate independently of royal consent; the controversy reached crisis proportions shortly before the Damiens affair in connection with the parlement's conflict with a rival Paris court called the *Grand conseil*. Beginning as a petty jurisdictional squabble over whether the Grand conseil possessed the exclusive right to try cases involving its own members, the conflict broadened and deepened when the king came to the conseil's defense and the parlement invited the princes and peers to discuss the threat that, in its opinion, this defense posed to the "fundamental" laws of the realm. The king then predictably forbade the princes and peers to respond to the parlement's invitation—eventually provoking a formal protest on their part—and the parlement just as predictably protested the king's prohibition.

This conflict, still unresolved at the beginning of 1757, was related to ecclesiastical conflicts of longer duration in that the parlement not unjustifiably suspected the king of grooming the Grand conseil as a docile replacement for the parlement of Paris where both ministry and episcopacy could "register" whatever declarations they pleased.[23] It was also related to the Damiens trial, because by subsequently inviting the princes and peers to try Damiens, the king was asserting the monarchy's exclusive right to convoke them while flattering their sense of independent importance, thereby sundering their emerging constitutional alliance with the parlement.

The royal council soon had reason to regret its decision to convoke the princes and peers, for it transformed into one of Damiens' judges the king's cousin Louis-François de Bourbon, prince de Conti. Conti had long functioned as the king's unofficial counselor in both foreign affairs and in the ecclesiastical controversies dividing the parlement from the clergy; in the latter capacity he had contributed importantly to ending the parlement's long exile from May 1753 to September 1754.

But in the course of the year 1756, Conti had in stages broken with the king, partly for reasons of foreign policy, partly because the king's domestic policy was then clearly taking the antiparlementary turn that ended in the lit de justice of December 13. By the time of Damiens' trial, therefore, no royal connection remained to restrain the prince's steady descent into the ranks of the parlementary opposition, which could exert gravitational force of its own by means of his legal council, consisting of the councillor Jean-François-Alexandre de Murard and the Jansenist lawyers Jean-Baptiste Gerbier, Pothouin, and Le Paige. Since around April 1756 Le Paige, the prince's personal archivist and *bailli* of his privileged residence at the temple of the Order of Malta, especially incarnated the parlement's parti janséniste and during the Damiens trial "stoked the fire" in the prince's "loins," in the chagrined expression of the court reporter Denis-Louis Pasquier.[24] Open hostility toward the rump Grand' chambre, disdain for its pretension to constitute in any sense the parlement, the darkest suspicions concerning the conduct of the trial, and a determination to use the trial itself to press the battle against the Jesuits and the episcopacy—all these dispositions of the parti janséniste thus acquired a willing and eloquent spokesman among the princely judges themselves.

Plots and Conspiracies

WILLINGNESS to allow the wider affaires du temps to impinge upon Damiens' trial was not restricted to the prince de Conti or the parti janséniste, however. All direct participants in or literate observers of the century's political conflicts—the whole political nation, in short—were willing enough to allow Damiens to play a role in these conflicts, but on their own peculiar terms. These terms rigorously denied Damiens' independent role in the attack on the king and stipulated that he be a more or less passive instrument in the service of one or the other of the contending parties in the unfolding political drama. He had to be the mere agent of a conspiracy, or at best a political domestic servant.

These terms were implicitly contained in a maxim that not even the intensest bombardment by contrary evidence seemed able to dislodge from the minds of Damiens' contemporaries. The maxim held that no person of humble social extraction such as Damiens could have independently conceived the idea of killing or hurting the king, because the necessary motivation would be lacking. In order to possess this motivation, one would have had to be personally offended by or otherwise in direct conflict with the king and therefore move in some exalted social circles. Since this was demonstrably not Damiens' situation, it was assumed there would have been one or more highly placed intermediaries who had received the requisite motivation in a "natural" way, that is, from their immediate environment; and they then would have communicated it "artificially" to someone of lower social rank by means of such extraneous motivations as the offer of money or the guarantee of salvation. Despite periodical high-class rabble-rousing and the satisfaction they visibly received from the support of the crowd, nearly all parlementary magistrates instinctively thought in these terms to the extent that they thought about the matter at all. Despite its inherent social snobbism, their assumption could be justified by up-to-date Enlightenment sensationalist psychology, which insisted upon the environmental origins of all men's ideas.

The conspiratorial theme was sounded at the very outset of Damiens' ordeal by Jean-Marie de La Brou de Vareilles, the ensign of the king's guards, who informed the "wretch," "[it is] not possible for you [diminutive] to have brought yourself to the abominable crime that you have just committed without accomplices."[25] The theme was further embellished by the Gallican and Jansenist press, which confirmed to its public midway through the trial, "if it is true, as we are assured, that [the assailant] was born and lived in a base condition, it is evident by virtue of that alone that he is only an emissary of secret enemies who communicated to him their furors," because "a man without a name or status in civil society could not have had any sort of personal discontent that armed him against his king. On the other hand," added this pamphleteer, "nothing stands in the way of his being venal or seduced."[26] The theme reached a kind of fugal climax toward the end of the trial when, in response to his interrogators' assurances that it was "not possible for a solitary person [of his sort, they meant to say] to conceive, retain, and execute the cruel design that he had unhappily consummated without being stimulated in that direction by views suggested to him," Damiens responded wonderfully that "what has never happened before has happened on this occasion" and that his interrogators had only to "see it before their very eyes."[27]

The fact that this elitist assumption was deeply entrenched in his contemporaries' minds and not simply invented for Damiens' benefit in order to justify the search for a conspiracy can be illustrated in other distantly related cases. In far off Château-Gontier, for example, an apprentice tanner and deserter from the regiment of Piedmont named François Bellier was denounced and arrested for having loudly proclaimed in two cabarets on different days that if he had been in Damiens' place, he would not have "missed his shot" but would have killed the "sacred bugger" (*sacré bougre*). Asked by the local criminal lieutenant if he knew or had ever seen the king, Bellier responded negatively. Then, rising to his point, this zealous provincial magistrate "protested to the accused that since he had neither seen the king nor knew him it could not happen that he had conceived his detestable projects by himself without these having been inspired or suggested to him by some other persons" and demanded that he declare his "accomplices."[28] Apparently no category existed in the magistrate's mind for someone simply blowing off steam at the king's expense. It remained for the journeyman hatter Jean Aveque to turn the tables on his socially superior interrogators by means of these assumptions in the spring of 1758. Denounced, arrested, and *embastillé* for having spoken too favorably of Cromwell, Ravaillac, and the parlement of Paris at the time of the latter's exile in 1753-1754, Aveque responded to Police Commissioner Miché de Rochebrune's questions about these remarks by denying that he had uttered them. Then he added that however believable they were coming from the mouth of a "highly placed (*en place*) individual who did not consider himself sufficiently rewarded," they were absurdly attributed to "the respondent whose low estate is not compatible with the said horrible discourses. . . ."[29] Whether this represents "internalization" or sheer cleverness on Aveque's part the sociologist can perhaps best untangle.

Damiens could not of course have taken Aveque's tack, because he was on trial not for what he reportedly said but what he indisputably did. Despite his eloquent and after January 7 consistent protestations that he had acted alone, Damiens himself lent credence to speculation that he had acted with the help of accomplices by some inconsiderate remarks that escaped him shortly after his arrest. He warned his guards, for example, that they should "take care of the dauphin" who "had better not appear" because "his life is not secure"; and in reply to the guards' questions about his accomplices, he asserted that they were "very far away" and exclaimed, "what a world of people implicated!"[30] In his first interrogation he told Le Clerc Du Brillet that "if he named all those who had taken part, everything would be finished," and in the second, that he would reveal his accomplices to the grand provost alone, and only after he had received the king's pardon. When questioned about these remarks later, Damiens consistently answered that his warnings regarding the dauphin were meant to divert his guards' torturous attentions, and as for the others, he did not remember uttering them, but if he had, they were "discourses in the air" emitted by his spinning head.[31] But the damage was done. Nearly everyone thereafter chose to regard his initial avowals as ingenuous truth, the subsequent denials as calculated subterfuge.

Most unshakably convinced of Damiens' representing a conspiratorial effort were members of the parti janséniste, who were also quite certain of the quarter from which the conspiracy arose. Most indefatigable in assembling all the bits and scratches of evidence to this effect were the prince de Conti's advisor Louis-Adrien Le Paige, "to whom all threads converged when one wanted to deal with the prince," and the Troyen lawyer Jean-Pierre Grosley, a Jansenist in at least a political sense if not in a rigorously theological one. Le Paige, who left behind him two volumes of manuscripts on the Damiens affair in an impeccable but minuscule hand, passed this ammunition on to the prince de Conti, who used it in the plenary judicial sessions that began on February 12. Grosley took the same sort of case before the public by means of anonymous pamphlets such as *Lettre d'un patriote, Réflexions sur l'attentat commis le 5 janvier contre la vie du roi*, and *Déclaration de guerre contre les auteurs du parricide*.[32] These, especially the first, were so violent in tone and so impugned the integrity of the judges trying Damiens that the rump Grand' chambre condemned them roundly in an arrêt of April 30, seizing the occasion to solicit and register a draconian royal declaration brandishing the death penalty against all writers and publishers of such productions.[33] But the similarity of content, even of style, between Le Paige's manuscript notes and Grosley's pamphlets, especially the *Lettre d'un patriote*, make it admissible to suspect that Le Paige had a hand in their composition as well.[34]

In any event, Le Paige, Grosley, and others experienced no difficulty in assembling a considerable body of evidence suggesting the existence of a conspiracy. Besides the evidence furnished by Damiens himself, they pointed to cases of several people who seemingly knew about the event before it actually happened: a thirteen-year-old pensionary in the community of Saint-Joseph in Paris, for example, who was said to have announced as early as the afternoon of the day of the assassination that the king had been assassinated or soon would be; a letter from the wife of a Paris-based, Prussian-born shoemaker to a curé in Hargest-en-Santerre, dated two days before the assassination, promising "very surprising news" for the following Thursday, January 6; yet another letter, this one also dated January 3, from a Parisian apprentice to a relative in Péronne, predicting that "terrible things" were soon to happen; and a "discourse," finally, heard in Arras or Compiègne, that before long something would happen at Versailles that would make a loud noise in the land. No less a person than the comte de Zaluski, grand referendary of Poland, had received a visit from someone the day before the assassination announcing an imminent conspiracy against the state and the French royal house and imploring him to alert the king.[35]

Evidence also abounded of a more cloak and daggerish sort. About two and a half weeks before the assassination someone named Dubreuil who lived in Versailles received an anonymous letter warning him to "flee" because "the blow has failed"; this Dubreuil, it was rumored, had either been arrested or otherwise made to disappear lest he say too much. The wife of a shoemaker living on the rue Mazarine reported that several days before the assassination she was visited by four men wearing swords who asked her what king she acknowledged, whether it was Louis XV; when she responded affirmatively, they threateningly told her that she would not do so for very long and then left. A soldier from the Gardes françaises named Simon de Morsy reported that someone had offered him three hundred louis for assassinating the king, and when he declined, was given a louis to keep silent. And what about the two fully bridled horses found tied to the gate of the château of Versailles and subsequently claimed by no one; or the two assassinated men found on the road from Versailles to Trianon on the very evening of the assassination; or the two men on horseback observed by a woman of Versailles only a moment after the assassination and who, as soon as one had informed the other that the "blow" had just "failed," sped off in the same direction?[36]

While gathering all these pieces of Damiens' puzzling conspiracy, Le Paige, Grosley, and magistrates such as Robert de Saint-Vincent began to suspect the existence of another, this one involving the principal members of the rump Grand' chambre and the lieutenant of police, Nicolas-René Berryer, possibly acting on secret orders from Versailles. The purpose of this second conspiracy was to cover up or suppress altogether the traces of the first, to stop proceedings short of uncovering the true authors of the assassination or at least to keep their identity a secret and make it look as if Damiens had acted on his own. What else could explain the "incredible negligence" of the judicial procedure, the unseemly haste to execute the would-be assassin, the Grand' chambre's precaution to assign as Damiens' interrogators, judges as corruptible or compliant as the presidents René-Charles Maupeou and Mathieu-François Molé and the councillors Denis-Louis Pasquier and Jean-Jacques Severt? Why such resistance from Pasquier and Maupeou in the plenary judicial sessions that began on February 12 to the prince de Conti's numerous and public-spirited suggestions: to conduct a judicial investigation in Artois, or at least to read the prince de Cröy's full report of his extrajudicial investigations in that province; to read the guards' journal of Damiens' remarks in prison; or to hear all his former masters and fellow domestics in formal, judicial deposition?[37]

Two suspicions gradually assumed substantial form. The first was that the royal ministry or perhaps the king himself had decided for reasons best known to themselves to consign Damiens' trial to superficiality. This was undoubtedly the reason why the king (or was it the dauphin?) decided not to end the political crisis by reassembling the whole parlement, for the assembled chambers, reasoned Grosley, would have had "too many eyes, too much light, too much activity for discovering all the branches of a conspiracy. . . ." It was also "impossible," reasoned Robert de Saint-Vincent, to "explain otherwise" the king's decision to exile sixteen of his most zealous resigned magistrates, including Saint-Vincent, from Paris on January 16. Even their unofficial activity, reasoned this Jansenist magistrate, constituted too great a threat to the charade being staged in the Palais de justice. It was even rumored that Police Lieutenant Berryer had shown the court's reporter Denis-Louis Pasquier a letter written in the hand of the king himself instructing Pasquier not to "touch the bishops" and in general to stop the investigations at whatever point Berryer specified.[38] This rumor lent substance to the second suspicion, namely, that there were really two trials underway, the one "public and for show" in the Palais de justice, the other an "occult" but quite serious one conducted by Berryer in the fortress of the Bastille. Innumerable people were seen being taken into the Bastille, many of them Jesuits.[39]

In regard to the double aspect of the proceedings and the desire to conclude them as rapidly as possible, these suspicions were not very wide of the mark. It is altogether true that those principally conducting the trial—the four commissioners with the attorney general, Guillaume-François Joly de Fleury, and his substitute, Jean-Pierre Pierron—wished to "hasten as much as we can" the conclusion of the trial, in the words of the attorney general himself.[40] It is also true that the police arrested considerable numbers of people in connection with the Damiens affair, whom either Miché de Rochebrune or Berryer himself interrogated at the Bastille and whose cases never surfaced at the public judicial proceedings but instead remained "extrajudicial," in the somewhat euphemistic terminology of the day. What can be said on behalf of these men is that their object was somewhat more innocent than that imagined by Gallican-Jansenist critics, consisting not so much in a desire to cover up a conspiracy as to avoid a public scandal, or what they called an *éclat*. Their view was that what was fit for public attention was the ritual avenging of the crime—the execution, the destruction of Damiens' natal house—but not the crime itself, which as something akin to sacrilege was better hidden from view.[41]

It was all the more deflating, then, when at the prince de Conti's insistence the attorney general rendered account of Berryer's discoveries in the plenary session of March 2. The "very surprising news" promised by the Prussian-born Parisian shoemaker Guillaume Kattman's wife, Marguerite Delapine, in her letter to the curé of Hargest turned out to be the imminent duel between the maréchal de Bellisle and the duc de Biron, the return of the parlement of Paris, and the exile of the archbishop of Paris. When by January 6 none of these events had materialized, this quite illiterate couple had their local *écrivain public* write a letter recounting the attempted assassination of the king.[42] The "something terrible" darkly alluded to in the January 3 letter from Fidelle-Amable Chauveau, a Parisian jeweler's shopkeeper, to his cousin in Péronne, turned out to be something quite terrible indeed: no less than a "revolution in the state resulting from the suppression of the parlement," which he expected the king to undertake any day. However enlightening on the subject of Damiens' "whole public generally," this "news" did not much interest judges in quest of a conspiracy.[43] The "discourse" heard in Arras or Compiègne, finally, although not discussed in the plenary session of March 2, was almost surely the disgruntled mutterings of the gunner Le Clerc in the cabaret of La Vilette with which this narrative began. Le Clerc's hearsay predictions concerning the king were without specificity: at the most, "something might happen to him before long" if he did not change his ways, such as a "revolt."[44]

The same banality generally held true for the cloaks and daggers, which under closer investigation turned out to be ordinary riding coats and mainly decorative swords. The shadowy Dubreuil was one of the king's comedians, and the mysterious message his cook received from a sword-bearing, riding-coat-wearing person informed him that "everything had been discovered," not that the "blow had failed." Dubreuil himself reported the matter to the police on January 9, and he no more knew what to make of it than the police were subsequently able to. The shoemaker's wife on the second floor of the rue Mazarine—Dubray, strangely close to Dubreuil—was accosted by the four sword-bearing particulars on January 15, not several days before the assassination; oddly enough, no other occupants of the building reported comparable visits or knew anything about hers.[45] The soldier from the Gardes françaises was twenty-two-year-old Félix Ricard, not his companion in thievery Simon de Morsy. Although on March 2 the court indeed ordered the arrest of the merchant Claude Lefort whom Ricard had accused of offering him money to kill the king, it was already abundantly clear from the interrogations that Ricard had sustained in Montdidier that his accusations amounted to nothing more than an attempt at once to settle a personal score and divert his judges' attention from his own nefarious activities.[46] The two bridled horses before the gate of the château of Versailles and the two men on horseback were never the object of any formal deposition and remained somewhere near the bottom of the judicial trashcan of hearsay and unsubstantiated rumor.

With time the remaining "evidence" similarly dissipated

like the morning mist. The prince de Conti was able himself to clarify the conspiratorial predictions made to the grand referendary of Poland the day before the assassination. He reported to the court on March 9 that, having arranged an informal "confrontation" between Count Zaluski and a certain eighty-five-year-old abbé named Michel Passerat de La Chapelle who had begun revealing his farfetched plots to the police in 1755, Zaluski had recognized the senile abbé as the one who had visited him on January 4. In any case, his rendition of a plot had nothing to do with Damiens, and moreover greatly embarrassed both the parlement and the royal ministry because its agents were the Habsburgs, since May 1756 allies of France.[47] On the other hand, the affair of Marguerite Descouflet, the thirteen-year-old pensionary who reported foreknowledge of the assassination, quite seriously occupied the court until March 17. Descouflet herself admitted as early as January 13 to Police Commissioner Rochebrune that, in order to appear "better informed about news" than her fellow pensionaries, she had pretended in conversations on January 6 to have known about the assassination the day it occurred. What prolonged the agony of this simple matter was that her good friend Marie Geoffroy kept insisting that Descouflet had told her on the afternoon of the fateful day itself that the king had been assassinated, or soon would be. It was not until March 17 that she confessed before the full court that she, too, had lied out of *étourderie*. By that time, unfortunately, both Geoffroy, Descouflet, and Descouflet's older sister Marie-Jeanne had made the tour of the prisons of the Conciergerie.[48]

Despite this eagerness to have done with Damiens' trial and their visible reluctance to pursue the evidence in certain compromising directions, it cannot be plausibly maintained that the much maligned magistrates directing the procedure were unconcerned with a conspiracy. The four interrogators in particular relentlessly pursued Damiens on this subject from one end of the trial to the other—at the expense, for the twentieth-century historian, of more interesting questions. January 25: "Questioned for the third or fourth time to declare the persons who participated in the conspiracy, and to tell their names, their places of residence, and the place where they assembled to form it; said he had already responded several times that there was no conspiracy, and that there is no reason to disturb anyone on that account because there is nothing to be found." The same interrogation, a couple of questions later: "Asked once again to declare the names of his accomplices, and the place where they could have been when he said that they were already far away; said there are no accomplices, and permits messieurs the commissioners the liberty to think what they please." March 17: "Represented to him that he flatters himself in vain with the thought of imposing upon Justice, that she has in her hand the authority necessary to constrain him to tell the truth, . . . and that he ought therefore freely and voluntarily to declare today who are his accomplices; said he had already answered any number of times, and now assures us again, that there are no accomplices, . . . that if any existed he would declare them, but that one could rummage the world around without finding any." March 18: "Asked the names of the persons with whom he supped [at Versailles], and whether among others he supped with the person to whom he spoke under the vault of the chapel at Versailles, and whether it was not in the said cabaret where they gave each other rendezvous; said he supped alone, that he already told us numbers of times that thanks to the good fortune of France there was neither a conspiracy nor any conspirators."[49] On through the plenary interrogation before the whole court (March 26), the interrogation under torture (March 28), and down to the execution and grave itself—or wind, in this case—Damiens' judges tirelessly posed the same questions and received the same spirited denials.

Despite all this negative evidence, two unanswered questions preoccupied the judges as well as the public at large and fueled continuing speculation about the existence of a conspiracy. The first had to do with Damiens' whereabouts in Paris on the evening of January 3 between approximately 8:00, when he took leave of his wife and daughter on the rue Saint-Martin, and 11:00, when he boarded the coach for Versailles. Was it then that he met with his fellow conspirators? Did they at that time settle upon the last details of their plot? And, if not, why was Damiens so evasive on the subject, maintaining successively that he had spent the time with some "girls" on the rue Gilles-Coeur, that he had supped in a cabaret in the rue Condé near the Comédie française, that he had languished on the floor above a butcher's shop in the same street after being "hooked" by a *fille de joie*, and on March 28 finally, under torture this time, that he had supped and fallen asleep in a cabaret in the rue de l'Université vis-à-vis the rue de Poitiers.[50] The unaccounted for three hours seemed all the more sinister in the light of a rumor that Damiens had been observed in the presence of two persons who, at the end of this term, accompanied him to the coach for Versailles and bade him "bon courage, bon succès."[51]

The second unanswered question concerned the two mysterious men, one rather tall with a brownish riding coat and a unicolored hat, the other somewhat shorter but with the same general attire and with his hair *en bourse*, whom one of the king's door sentinels observed in conversation beneath the vault of the château's chapel between 5:00 and 5:30 on the evening of January 5, not long before the attempted assassination. As the guard recalled it, the smaller man approached the other with the question, "Well (*Eh bien*)?" to which the taller man, whom the guard later recognized as Damiens, responded, "Well, I am waiting (*Eh bien, j'attends*)." The evidence strongly suggested that Damiens had assured a fellow conspirator that he was still waiting to kill the king only a short while before he attempted to do so, at 5:45 the same evening.[52] When interrogated concerning this encounter Damiens was in this instance very consistent. He admitted that the exchange in question took place but insisted throughout the trial and even under torture that the guard had confused the words and their speakers: that it was he, Damiens, who had asked, "Well?" and the other who responded, "Well, I am waiting." This mysterious other he further identified as a man he had met in a cabaret in Versailles who had obtained the permission of the duc de Chaulnes, then governor of Picardy, to show a certain "machine" he had invented to the comte de Noailles, the younger brother of the captain of the king's bodyguards. He was still waiting to do so when Damiens by chance encountered him on the château grounds and remembered to ask him about it.[53]

Happily, the first of these questions can now be definitively laid to rest though it has in a sense remained unanswered until now. Near the very end of the still extant manuscript trial record lie the depositions of a certain Jean-Baptiste Ternois, a wine merchant established in the rue de l'Université vis-à-vis the rue de Poitiers, and his twenty-three-year-old apprentice, Louis La Croix. Summoned, evidently, by the greffier Le Breton after Damiens' confession under torture, the two admitted on April 22 that Damiens who had known Ternois as a fellow domestic servant at Louis-le-Grand nineteen years earlier indeed appeared looking for Ternois at the latter's cabaret in the rue de l'Université around 9:00 or 9:30 the evening of January 3. Not finding him present, Damiens fell asleep over wine and dinner, then left after being awakened by La Croix around 10:45 P.M. without having seen Ternois, who insisted that he never left the cellar where he was busily drawing wine. Damiens, then, told the truth under torture.[54] The only reason Damiens lied about the matter was that he did not want to compromise an acquaintance; the only reason the truth never became public knowledge is that the attorney general never officially requested an additional *information*, or judicial injunction to hear testimony, which would have authorized or rendered "judicial" the further depositions of Ternois and La Croix. The result was that these depositions could not, juridically speaking, find a place in the trial record that was printed later that year.

The matter of Damiens' conversation with somebody outside the château of Versailles is indeed more mysterious, although its mystery consists partly in why it so mystified contemporaries. What is baffling, properly speaking, is why the judges found it so insuperably difficult to accept Damiens' simple explanation that he had conversed with a man he had recently met who was waiting for an opportunity to show a machine of his own contriving to the duc d'Ayen. The content of this explanation was hardly the product of Damiens' unaided imagination. Michel-Ferdinand d'Albert d'Ailly, duc de Chaulnes and governor of Picardy, was indeed an amateur scientist with a lively interest in machines, or inventions, of all sorts, who had sometimes used his influence to help inventors get their contrivances subventioned and adopted for use by the state, as in the case of Marc-René de Montalembert's new cannons in 1755.[55] What is more, there was indeed such a man in Versailles at the beginning of January 1757. He had demonstrated some sort of "automate" in Picardy to the duc de Chaulnes, who had given him permission to show it to the comte de Noailles at Versailles. In a letter dated February 3 the comte de Saint-Florentin, secretary of the king's household, ordered Police Lieutenant Berryer to arrest the man but at the same time urged that there was no good reason to suspect him and that he be released immediately after being interrogated.[56] If he spent any time in the Bastille at all, no trace of it exists in what remains of its archives.

The fact that *l'homme machine*, as we shall christen him, was treated with such consideration and was able so successfully to obscure his traces that he escapes positive identification even today points to one possible impediment to contemporaries' capacity to accept Damiens' explanation. *L'homme machine* was manifestly somebody who, if not of sizable social proportions himself, at least enjoyed specific connections with and the protection of considerable personages at court whose own reputations could not have remained untainted by that of a protégé guilty of conversing with an unemployed domestic servant less than an hour before the latter assaulted the king. Through the screen of contemporaries' discreet references the silhouettes of powerful protectors can be glimpsed who were motivated not by a desire to cover up a conspiracy but by the desire to save both themselves and somebody they knew from the mortal stigma of close proximity to the king's assailant and his act.[57] The hypothesis cannot be excluded that this man was the marquis de Montalembert himself, there to demonstrate another of his military "machines" to the comte de Noailles. In that case, Montalembert would have enjoyed the protection not only of the comte de Noailles and the duc de Chaulnes but very likely of Damiens himself. Both he and Damiens were simultaneously present at the seige of Phillipsburg during the War of the Polish Succession in 1734, and it is not impossible that Damiens recognized him—and then denied that he did, out of the same stubborn loyalty toward nearly everyone he had ever encountered that prompted him to deny the existence of his family and lie about his whereabouts in Paris on the evening of January 3.[58]

Be that as it may, a simpler consideration stood in the way of accepting Damiens' explanation. For *l'homme machine* was of tall stature not only socially, but physically as well—at least five feet five or six "thumbs." He did not therefore match the sentinel's description of someone *smaller* than Damiens—five feet at best.[59] But what if instead of mixing up only the roles of the two speakers in the exchange he overheard, as Damiens thought, the sentinel more plausibly mixed up the identity of the conversants themselves, thinking Damiens was the taller of the two when in fact the reverse was the case. At a certain distance and in the enveloping night Damiens would on this hypothesis have appeared comparatively short standing next to his taller conversant. Both were wearing brownish riding coats and unicolored hats; the sentinel moreover described the smaller man as wearing his hair in a taffeta pouch, or *en bourse*, and from thirty-five to forty years old, which was also approximately Damiens' age and the way he was wearing his hair at the time. The fact that the sentinel recalled having exchanged a few banal remarks with the taller of the two men before the conversation between them changes nothing, for though the sentinel thought he recognized the taller person when confronted with Damiens, Damiens did not recognize him.[60]

What lends some additional credence to this hypothesis is that yet another guard, this one on duty in the queen's guardroom in the late afternoon of January 5, observed a "rather tall" person wearing a brownish riding coat and a worn unicolored hat who entered the room around 3:30 P.M. and left around 4:00 P.M. Thinking in retrospect that he might have been the king's assailant, he was later confronted with Damiens but failed to recognize in him the person he had seen. Damiens, for his part, insisted that he had never entered that or any of the château's rooms.[61] But the guard's testimony nonetheless demonstrates the existence of another person wearing a riding coat and a unicolored hat who was perhaps as tall if not taller than Damiens and who was at large on the château premises on the afternoon and early evening of January 5. He might also have been *l'homme machine* with whom Damiens conversed.

What is certain is that the judges did not exercise their heads about this or any other hypothesis and signally failed either to pose the appropriate questions or arrange the obvious confrontations that would have cleared the matter up, to one degree or another.[62] Instead, they chose to entertain only the rather implausible hypothesis that Damiens cooked up the story of *l'homme machine*, which coincidentally corresponded with a certain reality, and that it was someone else with whom Damiens spoke, possibly a co-conspirator, who presumably fled after the event. The trial therefore ended with a contumacious order for the arrest of a *quidam*, or "somebody," who might ironically have been Damiens himself.[63] As it stood, the contumacy served only to provoke the arrest of any number of unfortunate vagabonds and mendicants in the months and years to follow.[64] If for every political assassination there must be a shadowy figure or a grassy knoll, then this was surely it. But what the incident demonstrates is not so much a reluctance to pursue a dark conspiracy, which as a hypothesis was both preferred and thoroughly investigated in this instance, as a reluctance to follow the evidence down even the most well-lit streets if it thereby risked compromising or merely embarrassing the wrong—or rather right—sorts of people. It was this sort of reluctance that gave the trial its distinctive character and condemned it in advance to sterile results.

Jansenists and Jesuits

THE EVASIVE character of the trial grew more pronounced in proportion to its ever more direct bearing upon the wider political and ideological conflicts of the day, the famous affaires du temps. This was the unintended consequence of the judges' assumptions, for if, as conventional wisdom dictated, Damiens had necessarily acted with the help of accomplices, the resultant conspiracy must have proceeded from one of the two corners of the political and ideological ring; the possibility that it might have come from a power hostile to France, such as England, was rather quickly discarded, necessitating an investigation in either of these other directions.[65] But if in spite of the reigning assumption Damiens was not the agent of a conspiracy in the narrowest, most venal sense, as the results of the investigations seemed increasingly to indicate, it then followed that he was a kind of religious fanatic, doctrinally motivated by one or the other of the contending politico-ecclesiastical parties and therefore the agent of at least a kind of second order conspiracy. This pushed the trial into the diffuse realm of doctrine, rhetoric, and opinion, therefore even more decisively into the regions of the affaires du temps.

The interrogators made a show, at least, of uncovering Damiens' Jansenist connections, however perilously close to home this was for them as magistrates in the parlement of Paris. Not, of course, that any of the interrogators were Jansenists in any rigorously theological or religious sense of the term—Jean-Jacques Severt was even a member of the Jesuits' lay congregation—but as magistrates they had protected full-fledged Jansenists and were caught up willy-nilly in a movement that associated elements of Jansenism, Gallicanism, and parlementary constitutionalism in a common front of opposition to royal and ecclesiastical authority. Any Jansenist connection ran the risk of reflecting back on them and on the institution they represented. But if a pure Jansenist element could be separated from its Gallican and parlementary alloys, and if Damiens could be shown to be simply a religious zealot, then the damage might be minimized, at least as far as the parlement of Paris was concerned.

The search for Damiens' Jansenist ties struck gold in the person of his brother Antoine-Joseph and his associations in Saint-Omer, for Antoine-Joseph turned out to be the catechumen of the Jansenist Fenes brothers, curé and chanter of the parish of Sainte-Marguerite in Saint-Omer, and frequently in attendance at their garden conventicles on the subject of Père Quesnel's propositions and the bull *Unigenitus*.[66] It was with stupefaction that Jacques-Charles-Alexandre Vanden Driesche, lieutenant of the constabulary in Saint-Omer, discovered 140 bound volumes of theological, catechetical, and devotional literature, mainly of Jansenist inspiration, in Antoine-Joseph's modest house at the time of the latter's arrest on January 10, 1757. Asked how a journeyman wool carder who was "hardly well to do (*peu aisée*)" and had not thirty livres worth of furniture in his house had managed to amass a library worth two hundred livres or more, Antoine-Joseph responded, in impeccably Jansenist fashion, that he had purchased the greater part "with his savings, much preferring study to going to the cabaret," although some of the books had been given to him by the late curé of Saint-Sépulchre and the present curé of Sainte-Marguerite.[67] It was one of these volumes entitled *Prières et instructions chrétiennes* by Père Quesnel that Antoine-Joseph gave his brother Robert-François the previous July or August, and that was discovered on Damiens' person on January 5. It was the same curé of Sainte-Marguerite who helped Antoine-Joseph try to restore the sum his brother stole and whose good confessional offices the unrepentant thief had spurned.[68]

That is where the connection stopped, however. When asked whether he had attended the Fenes brothers' conventicles, Robert-François could answer honestly that he knew nothing about them, for he was not a Jansenist in that sense.[69] He scorned, as we have noted, his brother's piety and detested his Jansenist priests. Although in other contexts he could speak in defense of the "best priests" who were refused the sacraments, it was the manifest injustice and ecclesiastical highhandedness represented by these refusals that moved him, certainly not the doctrinal issues involved. And although he could sound vaguely Jansenist when he said he hated the Jesuits' "way of thinking," his claim to doctrinal sophistication hardly sustained the one test he accidentally provoked. Asked on one occasion why he thought so badly of ecclesiastics, he responded that he did not think badly of them all but only of "Molinists and those who refuse the sacraments," who "apparently believe in two Gods although there is only one"—a reference, evidently, to the two-tiered system of natural and supernatural morality credited to the seventeenth-century Jesuit theologian Luis Molina and associated with the whole Jesuit order. Asked further whether he had read any book that contained this doctrine, he said he did not remember; asked whether he had read any book that refuted this doctrine, he did not remember that, either, but ventured that one had "no need of books in order to know it."[70] Decidedly, this was not Damiens' terrain.

All the less reason, therefore, to suppose Damiens had anything to do with the convulsionary sects that had arisen, in the 1730s, in response to the king's closing the cemetery of Saint-Médard where devotees of the deceased Jansenist deacon François de Paris had gathered to witness miraculous cures and experience convulsions.[71] On the basis of the devotional book by Quesnel found in his possession and his declamations against the priesthood some Jesuits bruited it about as early as January 8 that Damiens was a Jansenist of a convulsionary stripe. A former sectarian named Pierre-Paul Boucher de La Timonière, who had denounced a convulsionary plot against the king as early as 1750, was arrested and newly interrogated in the Bastille on January 31; and the attorney general at the urging of the duc de Noailles was still looking for an obscure convulsionary connection as late as March.[72] It would have been comforting to such as he, if Damiens *had* to have Jansenist connections, to locate them on the movement's lunatic fringe against which even the parlement of Paris had proceeded in the 1730s. But though Damiens might well have known the two laundresses of the rue Saint-Etienne-des-Grès who were devotees of the deacon's cult in the 1750s and could probably recognize madame Rolland de Challerange of the rue des Maçons who was a faithful at Saint-Médard while Damiens worked for Bèze de Lys, his connections with the movement were no more substantial than these.[73]

There was even less to uncover in the way of connections

with the Jesuits or the parti dévôt more generally. As a youth under his uncle's tutelage in Béthune Damiens may or may not have briefly been a pensionary at the Jesuit college in that town—probably not—and in Paris, as we have seen, he served as a busboy and part-time lackey for students at the Jesuit college of Louis-le-Grand in two separate installments from around 1737 to 1740.[74] But that had been a long time ago. Since then, he had remained in sporadic contact with the père de Launay, principal of the college, who apparently took a kindly interest in the college's former domestic servant and in 1752 procured him a place with the La Bourdonnaye family. It was possibly the père de Launay as well who in 1755 placed Damiens with his brother the abbé Le Corgne de Launay, a theology professor at the Sorbonne, whose service Damiens soon left because, he said, he grew "sick" of the *mauvais discours* he overheard while serving de Launay and some of his fellow professors at table. Asked to specify the nature of these discourses, he answered that they consisted in saying that the parlementaires were the "biggest knaves and scoundrels in the world" and that they, that is these professors, would readily "soak their hands in the blood of the parlement" and voluntarily serve as its "hangmen."[75]

Without doubt, then, Damiens had been exposed to the parti dévôt and its rhetoric. But this exposure was minimal, and its influence clearly negative. He had only served the Jesuits, he said on another occasion, "*par politique* and in order to have some bread" although he hated their "way of thinking." "If he were the master," he told his guards in prison, "he would expel the Jesuits within twenty-four hours." We have already noted what he thought of the archbishop of Paris and his refusal of sacraments.[76]

Yet despite these meager returns, Jesuitdom and its adjacent ecclesiastical domains remained the preferred hunting ground for Damiens' judges, whose interrogations fairly bristled with traps intended to reveal Jesuitical accomplices. Consider, for example, the following line of questioning: "Asked why he remained so long in the college of the Jesuits, hating, as he . . . declared, . . . the doctrine of their society, he had nothing to respond. Asked what he understood by the doctrine of the Jesuits," he had nothing more to say. To the objection that his "obstinate silence" was "very much opposed to his [previous] declaration . . . that only political considerations kept him in the said college, he said it was as well to eat bread in that house as in any other"; and in response to the argument that since life with the Jesuits had been "harder" than that in any of the other houses he had served, he must necessarily have remained there "with the intention of instructing himself in the doctrine of the Jesuits in order to live conformably to it," he had nothing to say. "Asked if he frequently approached the sacraments while he served in this college, he said he had approached them once in a while. Asked if he had been a member of the congregation of the domestics," he said he had not.[77] Despite the suspicions of Le Paige, Grosley, and the Gallican-Jansenist press, Damiens' interrogators were hardly soft on the Jesuits.

What if anything justified these suspicions in regard to the Jesuits and Jesuitically minded ecclesiastics was that the king's declaration of December 10 concerning religious affairs, although it had provoked the resignation of the greater part of the parlement of Paris and the ire of the parti janséniste, was not unequivocally in favor of the parti dévôt either. What it gave with one hand by denying the parlement's right to order the administration of the sacraments to appellants of *Unigenitus*, it took back with the other by explicitly denying that this papal document was a rule of faith, something that precisely distinguished Catholic dogma from error. It thereby implied that opponents of this bull were not necessarily heretics and therefore not always justifiably refused the sacraments, and it explicitly gave the parlement the right to *punish* ecclesiastics for doing so in some instances. The archbishop of Paris, leader of the parti dévôt and since 1755 in exile at Conflans for his sacrament-refusing pains, was not happy with these features of the declaration, which disavowed his own conduct as well as the parlement's, and rumor had it that he was about to make his unhappiness public with another of his anathema-snorting episcopal mandamuses. Other of his *Unigenitus*-enamored colleagues, such as Antoine de Brancas at Aix and Poncet de La Rivière at Troyes, remained exiled from their dioceses and for the same reasons.[78]

However downcast by the policies of Louis the *bien aimé*, the whole parti dévôt could nonetheless lift up its eyes toward the approaching reign of the Jesuitically oriented dauphin, the court's chief advocate for the parti dévôt, from whence it eagerly awaited its salvation. But could not this day of gladness be hastened a bit, for example by the death of the king? And who, if that were to be arranged, was better equipped for the task than the Jesuits, who since the sixteenth-century wars of religion were conspicuous among the theoreticians—and reputedly practitioners—of regicide or tyrannicide? Had not Juan de Marianna, one of their authors, gone so far as to assert that anyone at anytime possessed the right to assassinate a king turned tyrant? Were not Henry III and Henry IV among their many royal victims?[79] The history books continued to say so, and their assertions seem confirmed by some of the things that Jesuits reportedly said in the environs of the political crisis of December 1756. "The king will not live long, and his successor will change a lot of things," a Jesuit supposedly said to a certain Jacob, bookseller in Orléans, in the month of November. More ominously still, a Jesuit from Arras, of all places, was rumored to have remarked in Abbéville only ten days before the attempted assassination that "there are still some Ravaillacs." The remark was moreover made in the context of a heated discussion about the affaires du temps.[80]

The interrogators were especially alert, therefore, to the possibility that Damiens might have been exposed to the Jesuitical doctrine, or principle, that it is sometimes permitted to kill kings. January 29: "Asked if he had ever heard it taught that there are cases in which it is permitted to attempt the life of one's sovereign?" March 17: "Remonstrated" that since he knew that "obedience to kings is a principle of religion that Jesus Christ himself taught us, it therefore follows that someone taught him a contrary doctrine, and persuaded him that religion allows one to attack the life of his sovereign in certain cases." March 26: "Represented that it results from his responses that he believed his crime to be permitted, that it necessarily follows that someone taught him that it was permitted under certain circumstances," or that he "had read it in some books." March 28: "Asked if he believes that religion permits one under any pretext to assassinate kings."[81] Under this relentless barrage of loaded questions Damiens maintained his nay as nay. He did not even think that "anyone had ever dared to teach such a doctrine," or that "there were any books that talked about that." In any case, he had neither heard nor read about it.[82] The only minnow the interrogators could finally show for all their fishing was a remark that Damiens retained from a conversation about the affaires du temps that he had had with several ecclesiastics in Fies to the effect that "there is only one God, but kings are made every day."[83] Apart from the fact that the remark in question was an ecclesiastical banality, the sonorous stock-in-trade of court sermons and funeral orations, something very much like it was actually uttered by the cardinal de La Rochefoucauld in his episcopal mandamus published in celebration of the king's recovery, without its raising a single Gallican eyebrow. "It is a form that passes," he said, speaking of "human grandeurs" including that of Louis XV; "the Lord alone remains always the same."[84]

Yet this same lack of evidence of Jesuitical connections served only to fortify the convictions of the parti janséniste, which concluded that either Damiens and the Jesuits were adept at covering their tracks or that evidence was being actively suppressed by those secretly in charge of the trial. What about the two or three Jesuits disguised as laymen but recognized in both Paris and Versailles on the eve of the assassination? What about a conversation supposedly overheard in the Luxembourg Gardens between two Jesuits about a "blow" that would soon "finish everything," or the many reports, commented upon by both Le Paige and Grosley, of Jesuits' efforts to enlist penitents into a "holy league" or "the party of religion and the church" whose purpose was to "prevent the catholic religion from being banished from the realm." What about the many Jesuits, finally, observed entering the Bastille?[85] Toward the end of February and the beginning of March these suspicions reached the point of hysteria and broke the limits of all credulity. Grosley ascribed sinister meaning to the fact that on the day of the assassination itself five Jesuits were seen traveling in the direction of Conflans where the exiled archbishop of Paris was residing: "Were they going there to await news of success, and to concert measures with the prelate in case the coup were to fail?" Le Paige, for his part, perceived an infernal connection between the disappearance of a Jesuit named La Cour who had reputedly been in Saint-Omer simultaneously with Damiens, the affair of Marguerite Descouflet whose brother-in-law had a Jesuit relative in Arras, and the dismissal of the comte d'Argenson as secretary of war on February 1—together some beams and the dismantling, he thought, of a proud plot that would have placed the parti dévôt at the head of the realm. The dauphin himself might have been involved.[86]

Part of the reason for this hysteria was the entirely contrary turn, from the perspective of the parti janséniste, that the trial began to take when at Conti's insistence the entire procedure until that point was read before the assembled princes and peers beginning on February 12. It then became apparent that, though not precisely a Jansenist, as we have seen, the king's assailant was nonetheless imbued with the political and constitutional mentality of the parti janséniste and articulated his motivation in its terms. "It is no longer a question of the Jesuits nor of the clergy in general," reported Barbier in his journal, "it appears that one must grant that Damiens is a fanatic, and that this unfortunate blow is a consequence of the Jansenist system and the impressions with which this party has affected the public and troubled men's minds."[87] Worse yet, it developed that while still in the prisons of the prévôté at Versailles and at the prompting of one Henri Belot, an officer of the prévôté's guards, Damiens had written a letter to the king explaining his proparlementary motivation together with a small billet in which he named seven magistrates, among them Clément de Feillet, Rolland de Challerange, Guillaume II Lambert, and his former master Bèze de Lys—stalwarts of the parlement's parti janséniste, all. To be sure, Damiens consistently maintained that he had not named the seven as his accomplices, but simply as magistrates he knew particularly well; this was in response to Belot's question to this effect. It was Belot, he said, who had construed the list as one of his accomplices.[88] There is, moreover, good reason to believe him, because Rolland de Challerange and another whom he named, Jean-Nicolas de La Guillaumie, were simply Bèze de Lys' neighbors on the rue des Maçons where Damiens served; La Guillaumie had been the reporter of the Damiens inheritance lawsuit; and all except Challerange were members of the parlement's second chamber of enquêtes, that is, Bèze de Lys' closest judicial colleagues. But however innocent the explanation, the damage was essentially done by associating some of the most vociferous opponents of royal and ecclesiastical policies with the would-be assassin and his act.

The cup of Jansenist indignation ran over in reaction, submerging the evidence beneath a flood of anti-Jesuitical rhetoric. Belot, it was rumored, was a Jesuit agent, the brother of a well-known Jesuit professor in Toulouse.[89] Damiens, for his part, was cleverly playing the role of parlementaire for which the Jesuits, notorious students of the theatre, had prepared him. "This man poses as the parlementaire and almost the Jansenist," Le Paige wrathfully noted in a small journal he kept during the trial. "This is the diabolical turn he gives to his whole affair. Such is the mask with which he covers himself." The pamphlets repeated it after him; Damiens "perfectly enacted the personage of parlementaire"; he could "follow his system with all the art imaginable. . . ."[90]

And with all imaginable fortitude, it might have been added, for Damiens remained consistent in his role through his "question" and horrible execution. Indeed, for the parti janséniste as well as for the parlement as a whole, the evidence only worsened as the trial dragged on. On March 26, before the array of princes and peers, he asserted that had he never "set foot in the Palais [de justice]" or "served the councillors of the parlement" but remained instead with "men of the sword," "he would not have committed his crime."[91] Compromising evidence, this, but not perhaps as bad as Damiens' admission under torture two days later that the idea of "touching" or "hitting" the king had first been suggested to him way back in 1753 by a certain Dominique Gautier, "intendant" of the marquis Le Maistre de Ferrières, apropos of a deserted soldier who had frightened the king by throwing himself at his majesty's feet to demand his pardon. In judicial confrontation both the marquis de Ferrières and Gautier vehemently denied any knowledge of the incident in question much less any communication with Damiens on the subject, Gautier going so far as to say that he would never have stooped to talk in the street or drink wine with a mere lackey. In a social reaction comparable to the defense of *l'homme machine*—and at the behest, undoubtedly, of the marquis—all that was reputable in the rue des Maçons came forth in succeeding days to attest to the sterling character of Gautier.[92] But the facts that the incident involving the deserted soldier were very real and were discussed at the time, that Gautier himself had been embastillé in 1740 for distributing *nouvelles à la main* critical of the Jesuits, that one of the witnesses remembered Gautier being described to him as "very strong-headed in favor of the parti janséniste" and "decidedly against the Molinists," the whole Jansenist and parlementary ambiance, finally, of the rue de Maçons, including the familial tradition of Le Maistre de Ferrières—all this points to the probable truth of what Damiens said.[93]

An Abortive Trial

THE FULL IRONY of the Damiens' trial can perhaps now be savored. Damiens' interrogators, judges, and the articulate public generally but the clandestine Jansenist press especially set out with the assumption that Damiens could not have acted alone, that he had to have been the agent of accomplices. In the nature of things these accomplices had to be highly placed, aristocratic, part of the political nation, and therefore in a position to have quarreled with the king. Unable to locate specific, first order accomplices who paid Damiens to do the deed, however, his judges were forced to go fishing for a more elusive, second order conspiracy involving the influence of opinions, doctrines, principles, and in general the politico-ecclesiastical conflicts of the day. Yet once embarked upon this expedition, Damiens' parlementary judges not only drew back at the consequences of their own social logic—that anybody *they* knew would have had anything socially to do with Damiens—but as participants in and parties to the political conflicts they were judging, they were appalled at the direction in which these more slippery conspiracies moved. For no matter how far they cast their bait in a Jesuitical and devout direction, the bobbers floated perversely back toward the parlementary-Jansenist boat.

Damiens himself pointed toward the "rooms of the Palais," the remonstrances of the parlement of Paris, and especially toward Bèze de Lys and the parti janséniste. In a supposedly uncensored remark Damiens might have even described as "his God" the councillor Clément de Feillet, probably the most influential member of the parti janséniste at this time.[94] Assuming that the mysterious *l'homme machine* was the marquis de Montalembert, this personage would have led in the direction of the prince de Conti, patron of the parti janséniste, because Montalembert had once been his protégé and captain of his guards.[95] The Gautier affair not only led to the rue des Maçons and the magisterial parti janséniste but likewise to Conti, for the anti-Jesuitical nouvelles à la main that landed Gautier in the Bastille in 1740 he had distributed at the behest of the abbé Antoine-François Prévost, the prince de Conti's secretary.[96] In a related affair unmentioned thus far a seditious *propos* to the effect that France was in need of a "bloodletting" and that the race of the Bourbons should be "entirely destroyed" was traced from domestic to domestic until it returned, at least the "bloodletting" part, to the table talk of the parlementary lawyer Jean-Baptiste Le Gouvé, closely associated with Le Paige and Gerbier, that is, the legal entourage of the prince de Conti. In this instance it took all the prince's persuasive powers in the plenary session of February 12 to prevent the arrest of Le Gouvé, whose dinner companions also rushed to his rescue with visibly contrived renditions of what he had said. Le Paige was outraged that an "honnête homme" so narrowly escaped arrest "for having said at table what we say every day in our apartments," but not because the unfortunately talkative domestics in question spent three months in the prison of the Conciergerie. "After that," he sagely concluded, "prattle all you please in front of your lackeys."[97]

Not only was Le Gouvé never arrested, heard in deposition, or even informally sounded out but neither was Bèze de Lys or any of the other magistrates Damiens said he knew. More than anyone else, perhaps, Bèze de Lys might have enlightened the court on his former domestic's character and politicalization during the refusal of sacraments controversy, and the lack of at least a deposition on his part remains the most gaping omission in Damiens' trial. We catch a fleeting glimpse of him only on one occasion, fearfully inquiring of another former domestic whether the "Flammand" he had once employed was really the Damiens who attacked the king.[98] Otherwise he is not to be heard from. Nor to be sure were the brothers de Launay, principal of the college of Louis-le-Grand and professor of theology at the Sorbonne, who had both employed Damiens, or the Jesuit Simon de La Tour whom Damiens was also thought to have known. The principal of Louis-le-Grand in particular had known Damiens for a long time, perhaps since 1736 or 1737 and had been in touch with him as recently as 1755 or 1756. He was potentially the court's most authoritative witness on the subject of Damiens' ambitions, his professional hopes for himself and his family. It is difficult therefore to avoid the impression of an informal political quid pro quo, according to which the court could not judicially disquiet members of the parti dévôt if it were not to proceed against its colleagues in the parlement of Paris and the parti janséniste. What remained of the parlement of Paris could not pursue the Jesuits or the episcopacy without in all fairness pursuing itself.

This it might have been willing to do, however, at least as far as the seven magistrates whom Damiens named were concerned, because these began melodramatically beating their breasts and demanding some sort of judicial vindication. Innumerable scenarios were devised and considerable quantities of paper expended to this end, which tended toward a trial or summons to commence such a trial from which the seven councillors would emerge innocent and victorious, juridically cleansed of the taint of association with Damiens.[99] Conti, Le Paige, and others were in favor of such an arrangement because it would have entailed the trial of the officer Henri Belot, whom they regarded as a Jesuitical or devout agent—rumors even circulated to the effect that he had acted on orders from the dauphin—who had knowingly suborned Damiens into naming the seven. They wanted his blood in the worst way, Le Paige expending his ingenuity in devising the most appropriate criminal category—the *lex talionis*, he thought, which carried the death penalty—and Conti verbally sparring in the plenary sessions with Pasquier and Maupeou in an unsuccessful effort to get him arrested.[100]

Yet one major obstacle stood in the way of their plans. Even Le Paige had to recognize that Belot could not be tried without trying the seven magistrates, and that even the seven who had all resigned on December 13 could not in turn be tried without their recognizing the rump Grand' chambre as *the* parlement, which was alone competent to try its own members.[101] To what purpose, then, the lawyers' and attorneys' strike, which cost them dearly and which Maupeou and Pasquier were still trying to break, or the continuing resignation of the vast majority of the parlementary magistracy, if some of its most zealous and constitutionally articulate spokesmen such as Clément de Feillet and Lambert were to capitulate and make the essential concessions. Nothing would then remain to be done except to call off the strike, to accept the contested edict and declarations, and acquiese in the triumph of ecclesiastical domination and despotism masquerading as monarchical authority. The resultant victory of the king, or rather his ministers and the whole parti dévôt especially, would have far outweighed the loss of Belot, even supposing that he was in fact its agent. The parti janséniste would have snapped at a reflection only to lose its whole prey. In a larger, more globally political sense, then, the parlement could not have in this instance proceeded against the parti dévôt without at the same time proceeding against itself and its own constitutional position.

And so linked was the assassin's trial to the wider political conflicts of the day that the former could not be pursued without making unacceptable concessions in the latter.[102] The trial could break out of its vicious circle only by reaching a monumental dead end.

Damiens had therefore to remain officially alone, deprived of even the company that he himself acknowledged. He was a monster, a *scélérat*, a mutation in nature. Yet this view of him, which tended to place him outside the political conflicts of the day, was not altogether incompatible with pursuing these conflicts in ritualistic form. This was surely the meaning of the judges' decision to resurrect, for Damiens' final benefit, the horrible combination of tortures that were first brought together on the occasion of the trial of Henry IV's assassin in 1610, for to assimilate Damiens' case to that of Ravaillac who was still generally regarded as a creature of the Jesuits was ritualistically to assert in defiance of all the contrary evidence that Damiens was cut from the same leaguish and fanatical cloth, an agent, like his predecessor, of a Jesuitical and devout conspiracy.[103] This form of execution won the unanimous approval of the judges, who quibbled only about whether the sentence against Jean Chastel, who in 1594 had only wounded Henry IV, was in fact more appropriate.[104] Nothing important was at stake here because Chastel, too, was regarded as an agent of the Jesuits, his deed having provoked the expulsion of the society at the time. So the same retrospective, history-bookish mentality that characterized the politico-ecclesiastical conflicts of the day extended as far as this ultimate domain; and the judges were caught quite off their guard when four robust horses proved unable to pull Damiens apart, despite what the history books said to the contrary.[105]

Yet even on the place de Grève the parlement did not occupy the field alone; its enemies were too vigilant for that. Earlier, on March 11, the court on the recommendation of its four commissioners had nominated the abbé L.-François Gueret, curé of the parish of Saint-Paul in Paris, as Damiens' confessor. Though no longer officially an appellant of *Unigenitus*, Gueret had once vigorously rejected this bull, and even after formally accepting it, as he did around 1730, he staunchly opposed refusing the sacraments to those who did not follow his example, going so far as to provide a billet de confession to the Châtelet councillor Coffin, a notorious Jansenist, so that the latter could be administered the last sacraments in early January 1751, and to publish a pamphlet against the archbishop's policies in this matter a few years later.[106] He would almost certainly have found himself suspended from his functions as curé had not his *cure* been a privileged one dependent on the diocese of Rouen, "unmoveable" (*inamovible*) by the archbishop of Paris. To have permitted Gueret alone to be Damiens' confessor under these circumstances was quite unacceptable to the parti dévôt, which therefore protested in the form of a remonstrance by the Sorbonne to the attorney general, Joly de Fleury, on March 23. The Sorbonne had always, the memoir maintained, been in possession of the right to name two of its doctors as confessors to criminals at the time of their execution and had most notably exercised this right in the case of Ravaillac in 1610. The Sorbonne expressed even greater chagrin at the rumor that it had been bypassed in this instance because of a reputation for confessional laxity, an unwillingness to insist that the assassin name his accomplices. Yet the Sorbonne's concern over its reputation for indulgence in this matter did not prevent it, when a compromise solution was later reached, from appointing the doctor de Marcilly to accompany Gueret at Damiens' side. Marcilly, a representative in full of the theological and political position of the parti dévôt, had earlier been among the censors who approved the Jesuit père Jean Pichon's book precisely defending indulgent confessional practices.[107] Nothing perhaps more aptly encapsulates the character of Damiens' trial than this unedifying skirmish between the parti janséniste and the parti dévôt over the assassin's soul—or rather his confession, each hoping he would name adherents of the other side as his accomplices.

A certain rejoicing occurred in the Jesuitical camp when Damiens reportedly persisted in saying that had he never served any councillors in the parlement of Paris, he would not have finished his life in the place de Grève.[108] Damiens nonetheless escaped the retrospective and anachronistic categories with which his judges and politically engaged contemporaries sought to comprehend him, just as in spite of themselves they as well transcended these categories in the conflicts that divided them. As far as Damiens was concerned, the accused and imprisoned Dominique Gautier came inadvertently nearer the truth when he admitted that, having frequently observed from the window the "joy" and "satisfaction" with which Damiens spoke of "the affairs of the parlement, especially when it received favorable [royal] responses to its remonstrances," he had once remarked to his master Le Maistre de Ferrières that Damiens "appeared to be a good citizen."[109] For all Damiens' eccentricities and in part because of them, he aspired to be mainly that; his real "folly" consisted in thinking that someone like him could directly participate in the political conflicts of the day and in actually doing so in the only way available to him. Before long there would be many more like him.

The Unraveling of the *Ancien Régime*

Damiens' Masters as Magistrates:

The Refusal of Sacraments Controversy and the Political Crisis of 1756-1757

Christus and Fiscus

THE SET-TO between the king and the parlement of Paris in 1757 that Damiens aspired to influence represents the climax of a half-century of religious and ecclesiastical controversy that so dominated the French scene until about 1765 that the whole eighteenth century there might just as appropriately have been christened the century of *Unigenitus* as that of "lights." The beginnings of this drama stretch back to the various condemnations of Jansenism culminating in the bull *Unigenitus* in 1713; the denouement and conclusion may be said to extend well into the 1760s with the suppression of the Jesuits and the controversy over the general assembly of the clergy in 1765. At its center lies the great refusal of sacraments crisis, with its climax in 1757.

This is not, of course, to say that religious-ecclesiastical matters made up the exclusive conversation of Frenchmen during those years, or even that they were the only bone of contention between the parlements and the king. For many of the provincial parlements, the defense of provincial privileges, resistance to royal taxation, and jurisdictional rivalry with subaltern tribunals remained the overwhelming preoccupation; a few never embroiled themselves in battle with the king or clergy over religious matters at all. And in strictly quantitative terms the parlement of Paris itself engaged the king more frequently on fiscal and what might be called jurisdictional-constitutional fronts than on the religious one. A count by these categories reveals that although during the decade of the 1750s the parlement of Paris sent "representations" to the king on eighteen separate occasions on subjects relating to religion, as opposed to nine times on fiscal matters and two on jurisdictional and constitutional ones (Hôpital général, Grand conseil), it remonstrated six times concerning financial matters, four times in behalf of other parlements (Besançon and Rouen), two times concerning jurisdictional issues, and only three times in matters directly relating to religion. A similar count for the 1760s attests even more lopsidedly to the numerical superiority of financial and purely constitutional concerns: twenty-four representations and eleven remonstrances relating to finance, twenty-five representations and six remonstrances having to do with jurisdictional and constitutional issues (almost all in connection with the La Chalotais/d'Aiguillon affair), nine representations and six remonstrances on behalf of other parlements (mainly Brittany), and only three representations and two remonstrances concerning religion. The objects of the royal lits de justice held during these two decades would seem to confirm the distribution: only the one held on December 13, 1756, involved religion, whereas five others were held for the purpose of registering fiscal declarations.[1]

Yet these numbers are misleading for at least two reasons. First and simplest is the consideration that the fiscal contestations between king and parlement during these two decades produced nothing so traumatic as the three interruptions of ordinary justice (December 1751, May 1752, and May 1753), the two exiling of magistrates (May 1753 and January 1757), and one mass resignation of offices (December 1756), all occasioned by religious and ecclesiastical issues. Far from indicating the parlement's obstinacy in matters of royal taxation, the royal ministry's frequent use of the lit de justice in this connection is rather proof of the parlement's comparative docility. The ministry knew that after protestations of pure form the parlement of Paris would accept the forced registration and not push its resistance *jusqu'au bout*. But the experience of a whole century attests to the ineffectiveness of the lit de justice in matters of religion; far from resolving such conflicts, it only escalated them to more bellicose levels of confrontation. Quite indicative and partially explanatory of the parlement of Paris' docility in the one area and intractability in the other is the remark made by the councillor Philippe Thomé on May 29, 1751: "a distinction had to be drawn between one's conscience in religious matters and that in purely human affairs; that in religious affairs one ought never to do a thing that one believed to be evil, because one owed obedience to God rather than to men; but that in purely human affairs [such as taxation], one was quit after having made the appropriate efforts to enlighten the sovereign on the inconveniences of the measure he wished to adopt."[2] Bolstering such staunch religious consciences in the parlementaires was a vociferous public opinion that in the form of anonymous polemical pamphlets expressed itself much more voluminously during the 1750s and 1760s on the religious affaires du temps than it did on the crown's fiscal policies. No exact count has been attempted here, but the merest glance at the *Catalogue de l'histoire de France*'s sections on ecclesiastical history, religious orders, and *politique par règne* for the two decades in question is perhaps sufficient to indicate the crushing numerical superiority of the pamphlets listed under the former two categories over those under the latter. This distribution dramatically reverses itself, symptomatically, after 1770.[3]

A second consideration is that religious matters are only metaphysically distinguishable from constitutional and jurisdictional ones during this entire period. For example, religious issues lay not very far in the background of the parlement of Paris' remonstrances on the subjects of the administration of the Hôpital général in 1751 or the jurisdictional pretensions of the Grand conseil in 1755, just as the parlement's remonstrances on religious issues significantly advanced this institution's jurisdictional and constitutional claims. Indeed, it was first and foremost in the context of the *Unigenitus*-related quarrels that the parlement developed its constitutionalism, which in turn prompted it to see other royal initiatives in a much wider and more sinister light. Without the constitutional perspective forged in the crucible of religious dispute, it is highly unlikely that the parlement would have attached the dark significance it did to the king's declaration in favor of the Grand conseil in 1755, or his rough handling of the sundry provincial parlements during the 1760s.[4] The parlement's growing constitutional qualms also lay behind its stiffening resistance to the monarchy's financial exactions. First surfacing, as we shall see, in August 1756 in the form of questions about whether the parlement was even authorized by the "nation" to accede to the king's demand for additional wartime taxes, these qualms were in part responsible for forcing the ministry to hold a lit de justice on this and increasingly subsequent occasions.[5] Contrary to what a vulgar Marxism might have predicted, the progress of eighteenth-century French parlementary audacity went from religious to constitutional to fiscal resistance, not from economic to constitutional to religious concerns.

The connectedness between religious, constitutional, and even financial issues is well-illustrated by the king's edict and two declarations whose forced registration in a lit de justice of December 13, 1756, provoked the magistrates' combined resignations and Damiens' return from Arras. Of these measures, the least controversial was undoubtedly the edict eliminating sixty-five offices within the parlement of Paris.[6] More than forty of these offices were already vacant; the remainder were to be phased out only as their occupants died or voluntarily resigned. The parlement as a whole recognized the need to reduce the number of its purchasable offices in order to combat their steadily declining value on the market. The edict was moreover not unexpected and negotiations between members of the parlement and Minister of War d'Argenson had at least partially prepared the way.[7] Nonetheless, the edict's total suppression of the fourth and fifth chambers of enquêtes as well as the office of president in all five was excessively surgical for the tastes of most magistrates, who might also have not unreasonably suspected that this measure's unavowed purpose was to break the esprit de corps of precisely those parlementary units that had displayed the most zeal in the religious quarrels of the decade.

This purpose was less hidden in the declaration on parlementary discipline, which would have alone provoked the collective resignations. This declaration's principal provisions excluded councillors with less than ten years of service from plenary sessions of the assembled chambers and, further, prohibited the calling of these sessions—at least the ones concerning ecclesiastical affairs—except on the vote of the Grand' chambre. Otherwise, the Grand' chambre alone would judge. Under the pretense of reform, then, the declaration was calculated to bolster the strength of the older, generally more moderate members of the Grand' chambre at the expense of the recently growing influence, especially in religious affairs, of the younger and more radical parti janséniste whose numerical strength was concentrated in the lower chambers.[8]

Never far in the background of the declaration on parlementary discipline, ecclesiastical and religious affairs indeed constituted the direct object of the lit de justice's remaining declaration, that concerning the bull *Unigenitus* and the refusal of sacraments to those who opposed it. Opening with some vague references to the pope, this declaration first specified that the *Unigenitus* was not a "rule of faith" (*règle de foi*) but at the same time insisted that it receive the "respect and submission that are its due." Another of the declaration's articles authorized the refusal of sacraments to juridically notorious opponents of the bull, but also cautioned ecclesiastics against indiscreetly questioning penitents on this subject when they publicly requested the sacraments. The declaration's most crucial provision bristled with technical obscurities: all *civil* litigation concerning the sacraments was to be judged by the ecclesiastical courts, although the secular courts could take secondary and exceptional cognizance of such cases by means of the judicial review of ecclesiastical judgments known as the *appel comme d'abus*, as well as in instances involving a so-called privileged case (*cas privilégié*). What was abundantly clear, however, was that even in such exceptional cases the secular courts could do no more than punish ecclesiastics for infractions of the law; under no circumstances could they order the sacraments to be administered. The declaration's last article, finally, proclaimed a sort of amnesty for all ecclesiastics previously sentenced in connection with these controverted matters.[9]

What did this declaration mean? Was it as much in favor of the episcopacy as the parlement of Paris thought? Or was it really as proparlementary as the archbishop of Paris seems to have thought? And what was its fate? Was it executed after the return of the parlement of Paris and the resolution of the political crisis in September 1757? How was this crisis as a whole resolved, and in favor of which side, if any? How would Damiens himself have felt about the outcome?[10] To answer these questions entails a review of the entire refusal of sacraments controversy from 1749 to the early 1760s, the importance of which has perhaps never been fully appreciated. The breakdown of the Old Regime's institutional balance, the desacralization of the monarchy, the development of constitutional thought and the progress of secularization in France—in all this the refusal of sacraments controversy played a crucial if generally overlooked role.

Parlement against King and Bishops

NO SOONER did *Unigenitus* arrive in France than widespread alarm was sounded at the unnuanced character of its choice of propositions to condemn. To the chancellor Henri-François d'Aguesseau as well to many of the forty-nine bishops whom Louis XIV called in an extraordinary assembly to accept this bull, *Unigenitus* condemned many propositions that were innocent, orthodox, and even word-for-word translations of passages from the New Testament and the church fathers.[11] Accordingly, even the forty bishops who accepted the bull accompanied and in a sense qualifed their acceptance with a jointly adopted pastoral instruction explaining certain features of the bull. Shortly later, the parlement of Paris qualified its own (forced) registration of the bull by excepting everything in it that was contrary to the Gallican tradition, in particular its condemnation of the ninety-first proposition enjoining the performance of one's duty in the event of an unjust excommunication. Even the government qualified its acceptance of the bull by endorsing an explanatory "body of doctrine" (*corps de doctrine*) accompanying its declaration of 1720, which was registered, under duress again, by the parlement of Paris and which annulled conciliar appeals against the bull.[12] Acceptance of the bull in France was therefore anything but "pure and simple" and intransigent or "constitutionary" bishops who insisted on such acceptance were initially in a minority.

Insufficiently nuanced in what it condemned, the bull was nuanced to the point of principled ambiguity in its form of condemnation, for *Unigenitus* was an *in globo* condemnation, meaning that it applied none of its twenty-two condemnatory qualifications specifically to any of the 101 propositions from Quesnel, leaving the confused believer to wonder whether a given proposition was merely "shocking" and "offensive to pious ears" or rather "smacking of heresy" if not outrightly "heretical." This vagueness enabled even the most moderate of the bull's opponents to say that *Unigenitus* did not precisely distinguish dogma from error and was consequently not a rule of faith; hard-core opponents such as Le Paige went farther, saying it was a rule that "regulated nothing," at best a document that censured the use of certain expressions for a certain period of time.[13] It is difficult to deny that the bull's detractors stood on fairly solid ground here. In any case, the bull's reputation for doctrinal precision was not enhanced when one of its ardent defenders, Pierre-Guérin, the cardinal de Tencin, defined acceptance of it as an "implicit faith" in "indeterminate verities"; rare were those who agreed with the archbishop of Paris, Christophe de Beaumont, who in 1756 nonplussed the theological community with the assertion that if one wished to know precisely what truths the bull taught, one had only to take the contradictories of the propositions it condemned.[14]

The matter was important because if, as some French bishops insisted, the bull was indeed a rule of faith, then those who opposed it were heretics and refusal of the sacraments was in order. Unfortunately for the many ecclesiastics who had appealed the bull to an ecumenical council in 1717 or again in defiance of the declaration of 1720, the royal declaration of March 24, 1730, registered by the parlement in another lit de justice, called the bull a "law of church and state" and a "judgment of the universal church in the matter of doctrine." The latter expression especially seemed close enough to "rule of faith" to authorize its use.[15] Symptomatically, perhaps, after 1730 appellants of the bull found themselves increasingly the victims of the refusal of the sacraments of the Eucharist and extreme unction. Not even death necessarily ended the persecution; many of them were refused sacred burial and services for the repose of their souls.[16]

Although indeed the author of the declaration of 1730, Louis XV's chief minister, the cardinal de Fleury, was far from approving such extremes. Extant correspondence between Fleury and the zealously constitutionary bishop Etienne de La Fare of Laon during the 1730s and early 1740s makes it clear that whatever meaning he attached to "judgment of the universal church in the matter of doctrine," he did not think it the equivalent of "rule of faith," and that he used his very considerable personal authority to dampen constitutionary ardor and prevent refusal of the sacraments and the like in its name.[17] But when such refusals sometimes occurred in spite of his best preventative measures, he came down equally hard on those secular courts that entertained appeals in this matter, which from the outset the parlements were only too eager to do. Under his firm control the royal council consistently quashed all such secular interference in what the cardinal regarded as a strictly spiritual affair. It was a fine line to walk, but he did it well: church and state were kept more or less in their places and a Roman calm prevailed.[18]

The upsetting of this precarious balance after 1749 was to demonstrate the wisdom of having a churchman of the highest dignity as first or chief minister in the tradition of Richelieu and Mazarin. Though functioning in a secular capacity, to be sure, such a minister could curb the church's velleities toward turbulent independence far more effectively than could any lay personage. As it happened, Fleury's disappearance in 1743 left a vacuum that was never subsequently filled. On the ecclesiastical side Fleury was replaced in charge of ecclesiastical appointments by the zealously constitutionary Jean-François Boyer, bishop of Mirepoix, who indeed continued Fleury's policy of casting out the devil in the form of the episcopal foes of *Unigenitus*, but only to supplant them with the Beelzebub of bishops whose zeal for this bull and their sacrosanct jurisdiction knew no bounds whatever. In a mistake that Fleury would never have made, Boyer brought the ardently constitutionary torch in the person of Christophe de Beaumont to the volatile Parisian see in 1747. On the secular side the devout but ineffective Lamoignon de Blancmesnil replaced the venerable but aging d'Aguesseau as chancellor in 1749; and the parlement's offended first president, René-Charles Maupeou, who had thought himself in line for this promotion, retaliated by no longer restraining the parlement's more radical lower chambers and its dedicated parti janséniste. The king, unfortunately resolved to imitate the example of his predecessor by personally taking the helm after the death of "his" Mazarin, proved altogether unequal to the storm that soon broke. Continually buffeted by the conflicting counsels of the parti dévôt and the parti parlementaire, between the comte d'Argenson and his allies on the one side and the Machault/Pompadour axis on the other, he never succeeded in imposing his own will in the matter, however enlightened that may have been.[19]

It was in fact the clergy that took the offensive. Doubtless encouraged by Boyer and the parti dévôt at court and perhaps even with the initial blessings of a naive Louis XV, a militantly constitutionary and ultramontanist group within the episcopacy—Poncet de La Rivière at Troyes, Montmorency de Laval at Orléans, Caritat de Condorcet at Auxerre, and Orléans de La Motte at Amiens—began to systematize the previously diffuse practice of refusing the sacraments to appellants. The new and headstrong archbishop of Paris took their lead by requiring moribund penitents to produce a billet de confession, a written attestation that they had made confession to an orthodox priest, before receiving the viaticum or extreme unction. The billet de confession was as such not new; it had been previously used, in this diocese and that, mainly in connection with paschal communicants outside their own parishes. What was novel here was its bloodhoundish use as a means to track down and corner appellant priests who were confessing each other as well as laymen opposed to the bull.[20] What was particularly regrettable was that laymen too were directly affected, for if those suspected of Jansenist leanings refused either to produce a billet de confession or reveal the name of their confessors, they themselves were left to die without the sacraments. Along with the bureaucratization of the sacraments that this measure represented, its effect upon laymen is undoubtedly another factor in explaining why in this instance popular opinion and even crowds so noisily took the field against the archbishop of Paris and the priesthood in general.

At roughly the same time Christophe de Beaumont opened the offensive on another front by overriding the plurality vote of the administrative bureau of the Paris Hôpital général and installing his own candidate, a certain madame de Moysan, as superior of the Salpêtrière. This was at once a blow aimed at the administrative competence of the parlement of Paris and one aimed at Jansenism, in part because the bureau was stacked with parlementary lawyers, some of whom were Jansenists, and in part because the ecclesiastical staff of the Hôpital itself had long functioned as a Jansenist refuge. In protest the majority of administrators who had voted against the archbishop's candidate left the bureau. Matters remained in this exceptional state until Beaumont contrived to regularize them by means of a royal declaration dated March 24, 1751, which granted the archbishop unhampered control over the Hôpital's ecclesiastical personnel and reduced by nearly half the number of the administrative bureau's members, thereby eliminating most of those opposed to the archbishop's conduct. This time, however, the parlement struck back, retroactively quashing the election of Moysan and registering the declaration with such "modifications" as to restore the Hôpital's administration to its prior state. A royal-parlementary showdown ensued, the high noon of which witnessed the king's personal erasure of the parlement's judgments in this matter and the parlement's temporary suspension of justice. The contest ended in a victory for the king and the archbishop to which the parlement was far from definitively resigned.[21]

But the parlement's truculence on this secondary issue too easily obscures the moderation of its initial response to the refusal of sacraments campaign. The parlement did not so much as stir on behalf of Charles Coffin, the beloved but Jansenist principal of the college of Beauvais, whose deathbed efforts to procure the last sacraments did not prevail against the unbending refusal of Bouëttin, curé of Saint-Etienne-du-Mont—and behind him, the archbishop of Paris—in June 1749.[22] When more than a month later the parlement seemed belatedly inclined to proceed against the offending curé, it immediately desisted at the request of the king, who told the parlement on July 29 that the matter was "so important" that he wished to see to it personally. The same held true on March 20, 1750, when the councillor Antoine-Louis Chalmettes denounced six "new acts of schism," five of them refusals of sacraments, to the assembled chambers of the parlement. The parlement again docilely adhered to the king's wish as expressed on July 29 by bringing the matter to his attention, and the king in turn paternally complimented the parlement on its exemplary obedience, assuring it nonetheless that it was not his intention to deprive his judges of legal cognizance of such cases as could be subsumed—prophetic words—under the category of "public scandal." It was not until the deceased Coffin's nephew in turn fell ill and was denied the last sacraments by the same incorrigible curé of Saint-Etienne-du-Mont that the exasperated parlement went any further. Informed of Coffin's critical situation by Clément de Feillet on December 29, 1750, the parlement on this occasion arrested, interrogated, and briefly imprisoned Bouëttin; and upon learning that he was acting on instructions from the archbishop of Paris, sent its *gens du roi* to "invite" the archbishop to provide for Coffin's spiritual consolation. Receiving replies that were conciliatory in tone but adamant in substance, the parlement still *rejected* Durey de Mesnières' motion supported by Lambert to *enjoin* Bouëttin to bring Coffin the sacraments and decided instead to implore the king.[23]

The king's response, according to the councillor Rolland d'Erceville, "astonished everyone" and in a single stoke ended royal-parlementary cooperation in this matter. Far from praising the parlement's moderation the king castigated the parlement for precisely its lack of moderation with regard to the curé of Saint-Etienne-du-Mont and for not having come to him with the case in the first place. To understand the parlement's astonishment, it is well to consider that the obnoxious Bouëttin had spent a mere hour or two in prison, that when interrogated by the parlement he had indeed been insolent, and that for him to challenge, as he did, the parlement's competence in this case was to question the king's as well. The fact that the irenic curé of Saint-Paul, who would later serve as Damiens' confessor, rushed to the aid of the moribund Coffin and furnished him with the requisite billet de confession did not reassure the parlement, which perceived little prospect of the "public tranquility" that the king's response again promised. So the parlement set to work on remonstrances on the subject—March 4, 1751—which laid the legal groundwork for further action should the occasion again arise.[24]

A winter's freeze in Parisian appellant deaths gave way to a torrential descent from the Montagne Sainte-Geneviève with the spring of 1752. A certain abbé Le Merre, or Le Maire, an appellant priest originally from Marseilles, fell dangerously ill in March 1752 and found himself deprived of the last sacraments by the unrepentant curé of Saint-Etienne-du-Mont. On March 23, 1752, the second chamber of enquêtes brought the case to the attention of the assembled chambers, which after again interrogating Bouëttin, *forbade* him to cause another scandal of the sort, *enjoined* him to behave "charitably" toward his parishioners, and *invited* the archbishop to attend to Le Merre's spiritual consolation within twenty-four hours. These indirections were perhaps not quite the equivalent of an order to administer the sacraments. But what the parlement still viewed as its moderation in this matter remained again unrewarded, because on the one hand the king's council annulled the parlement's judgment of March 23 and on the other Le Merre continued unconsoled. In desperation the parlement sent its gens du roi to the king on March 27 and received the reply that he would personally provide for Le Merre's critical situation. Reassured by this response, the parlement desisted from further procedures, and the formality of its registers only imperfectly obscures the rage with which the assembled chambers received the news from a tearful solicitor general on March 28 that the unhappy Le Merre had died without the sacraments earlier the same day.[25]

No royal reassurances or even orders could thereafter restrain the parlement. Assembled until an unprecedented 4:00 A.M. on March 29—almost certainly one of the long nights in the Palais that Damiens so vividly recalled—the parlement ordered the arrest of the curé of Saint-Etienne-du-Mont who promptly went into hiding. Irritated to learn on April 10 that the king's council had annulled this judgment, the parlement ordered the composition of new remonstrances, and when in response to these remonstrances the king persisted in wishing "himself to judge in each circumstance the best means to employ," the parlement struck a decisive blow. Ignoring the moderate and tortuous recommendations of its gens du roi, the parlement on April 18 adopted a general rule that not only *forbade* ecclesiastics publicly to refuse the sacraments to anyone by reason of the absence of a billet de confession, failure to name his confessor, or refusal to accept the bull *Unigenitus*—entailing the right to punish in cases of the infraction of this prohibition—but also positively *enjoined* them "to conform themselves in the exterior administration of the sacraments to the canons and regulations authorized in the realm. . . ." In however general terms, this latter part of the arrêt was indeed an order to administer the sacraments.[26] Nor did the parlement hesitate to so order in particular when the occasion inevitably arose toward the end of the year. On December 13 the parlement ordered the two *vicaires* of the parish of Saint-Médard to "cause the scandal to cease by fulfilling in respect to the sick one the functions of their ministry," the sick one in this case being the seventy-nine-year-old Sister Perpétue of the religious community of Sainte-Agathe, deprived of last sacraments by reason of her refusal to accept the bull *Unigenitus*. The same day the parlement went so far as to attempt to convoke the princes and peers of the realm for the trial of Christophe de Beaumont du Repaire, duc de Saint-Cloud as well as archbishop of Paris.[27]

By this time the capital had descended into governmental anarchy, with the clergy and the parlement, church and state, engaged in a deadly exchange and the king and his ministry caught unprotected in the cross fire. The parlement persisted in prosecuting curés who refused the sacraments, and the royal council almost as doggedly annulled these procedures by means of conciliar judgments that the parlement refused to recognize. These contradictory judgments were "hawked every day," according to Barbier, and were "placarded on every street corner" where the "whole public" gathered to read them and seemed "much more disposed in favor of the arrêts of the parlement than those of the council."[28] Not only had the "greater part of Paris, the people, the bourgeoisie, and even that which is above them" become "Jansenist" in the sense of siding with the parlement against both the clergy and the ministry but a veritably Mosaic-scale plague of clandestinely printed pamphlets afflicted the capital, most of them sympathetic to the parlement.[29] In these, as well as in the parlement's remonstrances, which were similarly made public, the gravest constitutional questions were agitated and boiled inopportunely to the surface. What constituted obedience to the king? Was it docile adherence to his every whim, or was it not rather a steadfast obedience to his "real" will as expressed in the legislative monuments of his predecessors. In the latter case was it not really the parlement, as repository of the monarchy's—if not the nation's—collective memory or "fundamental laws of the realm," that better articulated the royal will than any particular monarch?[30] And what were the true boundaries between *sacerdoce* and empire, church and state? Was not the parlement overtly transgressing these by giving orders in so spiritual a domain as the administration of the sacraments?

This latter issue was seemingly decided in favor of the clergy by the edict of 1695, one of the great legislative tapestries of the late reign of Louis XIV.[31] Article 30 accorded jurisdiction over and judgment of doctrine to the bishops and archbishops and enjoined the parlements not only to defer to the prelates in this matter but to give them whatever help they needed in the execution of censures and other ecclesiastical judgments. Only in the case of a "scandal" occasioned by the "publication of the said doctrine" were the royal courts to intervene. Article 34 was even more to the point. It accorded "jurisdiction over cases concerning the sacraments, religious vows, the divine office, ecclesiastical discipline, and other purely spiritual matters" to the judges of the church and enjoined the royal judges and "even our courts of parlement" to leave such cases with the ecclesiastical courts and even send them there except in the event of an appeal "comme d'abus" entailing a secular review of the form or procedure of an ecclesiastical sentence. "Texts so clear," esteemed the legal historian Philippe Godard, "ought to obviate any commentary."[32]

Yet against these apparently unambiguous texts the parlement's magistrates and lawyers threw up a phalanx of commentary so impenetrable as nearly to stop their clerical opponents in their tracks.[33] Although no short summary can aspire to do justice to its sheer virtuosity, its general lines are clear enough. The major premise of its argumentation came from the conception of sacral kingship inherent in the Gallican tradition and held that the "most Christian king" as "eldest son of the church" as well as "exterior bishop" (*évêque du dehors*) exercised authority over all aspects of ecclesiastical discipline and even doctrine that were external and related to public order. As for doctrine, only the parlement's parti janséniste went so far as to deny that *Unigenitus* was a law of church and state, but even the moderate and certainly not Jansenist gens du roi agreed that the king—and hence his judges—was within his rights to judge from the bull's exterior form that it did not define doctrine, was not a "rule of faith," and that refusals of sacraments in its name were unwarranted. As for ecclesiastical discipline, the parlement contended that the king, although unable to formulate church order, nonetheless possessed the right to enforce the observance of what the church herself had canonically decided, and from here it was an easy step to argue that the practice of demanding billets de confession or asking impertinent questions about the bull *Unigenitus* of moribund penitents in quest of the "last act of Catholicity" was uncanonical, unauthorized by the standard rituals, and therefore punishable by the king's judges.

On the basis of this much argumentation the parlement might have chosen to send such cases to the ecclesiastical courts in the first instance and then to reform the resultant judgment and punish the clerical offender if ecclesiastical justice proved defective or not forthcoming. This course, moreover, would have more or less conformed to the edict of 1695. But this edict had not been promulgated on the supposition of an all-out war between empire and sacerdoce, and it proved inadequate to the parlement for several reasons. For one thing, experience had already demonstrated that however unjustly refused the last sacraments by his curé, a victim was not likely to get justice from the *officialité*, or bishop's court, since the curé was very probably acting on the orders of the bishop who also controlled the court. To be sure, the parlement or its *bailliage* court could then seize upon this ecclesiastical judgment by means of the appel comme d'abus and, more arguably, order the administration of the sacraments in consequence.[34] But all this would have taken considerable time, which in the case of someone in need of the last sacraments was very often in short supply.

To save this precious time, the parlement in effect abandoned the high but winding road of civil procedure and took the lower, judicially somewhat dubious but considerably more direct road of criminal procedure.[35] Distinguishing typically between the secretive and purely spiritual sacrament of penance, or *for intérieur*, which the church entirely controlled, and the public administration of such sacraments as the Eucharist, or *for extérieur*, in which the king as a purely secular or "political" magistrate had a legitimate interest, the parlement's lawyers argued that the public refusal of paschal communion, the viaticum, and extreme unction to a Catholic appellant constituted a public scandal of the sort referred to in article 30 of the edict of 1695, a gratuitous defamation of a personal and familial reputation in defense of which the victim was not without secular recourse. Affecting, as it did, public tranquility and order, such a public scandal fell into the category of a royal case (*cas royal*) over which the royal courts had exclusive jurisdiction, therefore also a privileged case in the sense that the royal court possessed the unique privilege of trying even ecclesiastical offenders if their crime merited "afflictive" or corporal punishments that the church and its courts could not dispense.[36] As such, finally, it was not a civil case but rather a criminal case to which article 34 of the edict of 1695 did not apply. That is why, after some initial hesitation, the parlements took the criminal route rather than the civil one, why they motivated their judgments (arrêts) by reference to scandals, and why from the outset they imposed rather severe corporal punishments such as deportations on the offending priests as "disturbers of the public peace."

The parlement's jurisprudence in this matter caught the ministry visibly off guard, and its response was correspondingly tardy and confused. The royal council might well lecture the parlement, as it did on August 21, 1752, against pronouncing "afflictive and degrading punishments in a case which is not susceptible to them," but without explaining why cases involving public refusal of the sacraments were not susceptible to afflictive punishments—why, in short, such cases were not "privileged"—these admonishments were ineffective.[37] Much worse was the outright incompetence displayed by the council just two days later in annulling the bailliage of Tours' procedure against a curé of that town by reiterating "word for word," as Lamoignon optimistically put it, the conciliar annullment of the bailliage of Bayeux's ordonnance of May 22, 1739.[38] This precedent was simply inapplicable because the bailliage of Bayeux's procedure was a civil one, Tours' a criminal one.[39] Indeed, not the least astonishing feature of the royal response was its failure ever to come directly to grips with the parlementary contention that a public refusal of sacraments by reason of opposition to *Unigenitus* was itself a cas privilégié.

Equally apparent was royal policy's vacillatory course: as Le Paige put it, "sometimes for the clergy, sometimes for the parlement, and sometimes in between."[40] From the outset until September 1754 the king and his council consistently opposed the parlement's initiatives in the refusal of sacraments controversy, but it did so sometimes decisively, sometimes apologetically. On April 8, 1750, for example, and again on August 17, 1752, the king assured his parlement that his intention "was never to deprive my parlement of all cognizance of the matter in question"; yet by his council's continual annullment of the parlement's arrêts and much more formally by his letters-patent of February 22, 1753, that is precisely what he did.[41] Even the king's de facto prohibitions were not consistent; after beginning by systematically annulling every parlementary judgment in the matter, he permitted the parlement to prosecute sacrament-refusing ecclesiastics uninhibitedly for most of the summer of 1752, only to recommence the annullments on August 21 of the same year.[42] In quashing two days later the bailliage of Tours' sentence already referred to, the royal council enunciated the most stringent imaginable interpretation of article 34 of the edict of 1695 and proclaimed unambiguously that the clergy possessed exclusive jurisdiction over all cases related to the sacraments. But when on November 21, 1752, the council belatedly got around to annulling the parlement's arrêt of April 18—which had said quite the contrary—it hedged and explicitly allowed for the possibility of criminal procedures and the cas privilégié, as well as the appel comme d'abus, in cases involving the refusal of sacraments for opposition to the bull *Unigenitus*.[43] It seemed to make a difference who exactly attended the council on a given day; Louis XV himself was apparently not always there.

These manifest twists and turns are evidence not only of alterations in direction but also of the fact that, just as in foreign policy, royal sacramental policy consisted not merely of one but of several separate strands not to mention a few loose ends. Although they might ultimately run in the same general direction, they occasionally tangled and knotted in confusing cross-purposes. One of the loose ends was undoubtedly the chancellor Lamoignon de Blancmesnil, backed by the dauphin, who agreed completely with the archbishop of Paris and could think of nothing better than to let the archbishop refuse as many sacraments as he pleased. Although he did not direct policy at Versailles, Lamoignon scored occasional successes and it is not implausible that the council's arrêt of August 23, 1752, against the bailliage of Tours was one of them.[44] One other major strand was of course the king himself, whose ideas on sacramental policy were in some ways unique. Still another was the advice of those councillors and ministers he especially commissioned to this effect; the rough concensus they reached might be called royal policy proper.

Consistent with his well-known penchants for secrecy and informality, Louis XV would have preferred a highly personal, case-by-case sort of justice, reached mainly outside the ordinary judicial machinery. In practice this amounted to putting literal distance between constitutionary curés and moribund appellants by fair means or foul, usually by means of lettres de cachet exiling excessively zealous curés or forcible transfers of appellants from parishes where they were likely to sustain a refusal of sacraments to others where they would not. Accordingly, he tirelessly ordered his parlement to alert him to each case in order "to judge myself of the best means to employ in each circumstance"; he did not think that the "ordinary procedure was the best suited by its éclat to maintain good order and peace." Closely related to these demands was the king's plea for moderation—the "moderation," he once reminded his parlement, "that I have so often recommended to you in the past."[45] In place of the parlement's public, righteously impersonal, and abrasive application of the laws, which only exacerbated the situation and provoked more refusals of sacraments, the king proposed the balm of his personal, hidden, though judicially irregular power.

It goes without saying that the parlement did not see matters in the same light, and an interesting debate developed between them concerning the legitimate exercise of monarchical authority. The parlement's objection was in part purely practical, for "however benign your intentions," Maupeou lectured the king on April 15, "the distance of the locations, the importance of your occupations, the difficulty of reaching the foot of your throne will impede their effect."[46] It might have helped if the king had gotten the last sacraments to Le Merre before he died, although he eventually exiled the intolerable curé of Saint-Etienne-du-Mont and punished another around the same time. But even if the king's intervention had always been prompt and efficacious, at least part of the parlement would have objected in principle. The king's "way" was that of capricious "authority" (*voie d'autorité*), which was "always dangerous" and under the cirumstances "less a punishment than a refuge against the severity of the parlement's arrêts."[47] To the parlement the monarchy was no stronger than its laws, whose strength in turn depended upon their constant, uniform application by the royal courts. For the king to play freely with them and thereby undermine the authority of his courts was to endanger both his own authority and the legitimate liberty of his subjects.[48] In the face of the hackneyed theme of a reforming, modernizing monarchy opposed by an archaic, tradition-bound parlement, it is worth noting in passing that it was the king's kind of justice that was here archaic and "charismatic" and the parlement's that was modern and "bureaucratic."

On a less eccentrically personal level, however, the direction of royal policy is more generally revealed by the correspondence between the secretary of foreign affairs, Antoine-Louis Rouillé, and the attorney general's father and retired predecessor in that office, Guillaume-François Joly de Fleury, who continued to function as the king's advisor. Secretly commissioned by the king to draft a royal declaration concerning the contested matters, the two men set to work in July 1752, then with the king's permission gradually took others into the "secret," including the pacific cardinal de La Rochefoucauld; the president Ogier d'Enonville; and the retired attorney general's two sons, Guillaume-François-Louis and Jean-Omer, the parlement's attorney general and solicitor general, respectively.[49] The drafts they considered came from various quarters—from Rouillé and the elder Joly de Fleury themselves, and from the prince de Conti, already playing a role in these affairs—and they differed importantly from each other in matters of detail.[50] But they unanimously tended toward the same mediating goal: to reaffirm the qualifications already accorded *Unigenitus* but to exclude that of "rule of faith," to authorize the refusal of sacraments in the most flagrant cases of opposition to the bull but to condemn any unnecessary pestering of people's consciences on the subject, and to restore the normal order of jurisdiction envisioned by the edict of 1695, that is, the ecclesiastical courts in the first instance and the secular courts only exceptionally, indirectly, and secondarily.[51] What monarchical policy was attempting to do at this level was what, given its obligatory respect to its own record and its arbitral position among the Old Regime's corps and corporations, it almost had to do: to continue the policies of the cardinal de Fleury, to uphold the legislation of the "sun king," to stay equidistant from both clergy and the parlements, and to keep church and state each in its proper place. Rouillé stated it succinctly when he wrote to Joly de Fleury *père*, on July 19, 1752, that "it would be pointless to try to satisfy both sides, and . . . dangerous to give total satisfaction to either one: we can only therefore try to formulate a policy that wins the approval of the reasonable members of both parties. . . ."[52]

Easy enough to state in general terms, this policy was mired with difficulties at the level of practice. If on the one hand *Unigenitus* was not a rule of faith, was it prudent, on the other, to call it a "judgment of the universal church in the matter of doctrine," especially since the constitutionary clergy construed the two denominations as synonymous and the parlement's parti janséniste rejected them both? Again, how in practice was one to distinguish, as these proposals theoretically tried to do, between an active sort of opposition to *Unigenitus* on the one hand, manifesting itself by means of unsolicited declarations at the moment of requesting the last sacraments, and a passive opposition on the other, which declared itself only in response to the administering priest's indiscreet questions? The proposals wished to authorize the refusal of sacraments in the first case and prohibit them in the second, but experience had already demonstrated that priest and communicant were not likely to agree about who had raised the issue in the first place. As for the billet de confession, the proposals tended to authorize their continued use in dioceses where they had traditionally been employed but to exclude their use as a pretext for refusing the last sacraments. But were not these proposals incompatible in practice? What was the point of requiring a billet de confession in any diocese if failure to have one resulted in no spiritual deprivation? Or who was to say that a priest's insistence on this score in any particular case had necessarily anything to do with the bull *Unigenitus*?

But the whole effort's lengthiest excursion into unreality lay in the attempt to restore the "order of jurisdictions" envisioned by the edict of 1695 for sacramental litigation, namely, the ecclesiastical courts in the first instance and the secular courts only by way of appel comme d'abus in civil cases or in the event of a cas privilégié in criminal ones. To have bothered at all about civil procedure and the appel comme d'abus in this context was wasted energy because "as long as the war lasts between the magistrates and the clergy," as Rouillé himself correctly observed to the council on November 21, "one will always take the criminal route, even should one wish to pursue only civil ends."[53] Yet "normal" criminal procedure in "spiritual" matters was rendered equally elusive by this war inasmuch as it envisioned a cooperative or conjoint instruction on the part of the ecclesiastical and royal courts. The criminal ordinance prescribed that if in the course of trying a clerical offender an ecclesiastical court encountered a privileged case, it should refer that portion of the case to the royal courts while pursuing only the *délit commun*, or common offense, which entailed purely canonical penalties. The royal court, instructing conjointly, was to judge the privileged case and apply the afflictive penalty. Conversely, if an ecclesiastic first tried by a secular court appealed his case to an ecclesiastical court, or if the latter laid claim to it, the secular court was supposed to relinquish it, except for the privileged case if any there were. But what was the common offense, and what was the privileged case, in the administration of the sacraments? Again, if under "normal" circumstances the former was the unjust refusal itself and the latter consisted of gratuitous insults accompanying the refusal, what was the distinction if the parlement claimed that the unjust public refusal was *itself* the insult, the defamation, and therefore the privileged case?[54] How could the cooperation of the ecclesiastical courts be expected upon such an hypothesis? How, finally, was the matter to be decided if the proposed declarations themselves did not? Despite repeated pleas by Rouillé and numbers of councillors of state for precise definitions of "common offense" and "privileged case" in relation to the administration of the sacraments, none ever materialized.[55]

Quite possibly the declarations left this vague in deference to the king's announced desire to decide each case individually. To that conjectural degree, a certain compatibility would have existed between the king's simultaneous secrets. But in all other respects an unresolvable tension existed between the desire to judge each case personally and the will to promulgate a judicially enforceable declaration on the subject. Interestingly enough, the one draft declaration of uncertain origin that tried to incorporate the king's reiterated order to his parlements to submit every case to him personally received a cold reception by Joly de Fleury père who had "difficulty subscribing to the sending of a procès-verbal to the king [who was] often distant by one hundred or perhaps two hundred leagues, which will make for an interval during which the sick person might die without the sacraments."[56] Even the devout Chancellor Lamoignon, on every other count sympathetic to the idea, warned that as an article in a declaration it would never make it through the parlement.[57]

Yet another incompatibility pitted the drafters of the king's declaration against the king's purely personal sacramental politics. This had to do with the king's apparently genuine fear that in officially pronouncing on such sensitive questions as the qualifications to be given the bull *Unigenitus*, the billets de confession, and the circumstances under which one might or might not legitimately be refused the sacraments, he himself would be transgressing the boundary dividing secular from ecclesiastical jurisdictions. That is of course what Christophe de Beaumont and the constitutionary clergy generally kept telling him, and apparently he took their preachments to heart.

Repeatedly in his memoirs and private reflections the chancellor Lamoignon referred to "the important questions concerning the refusal of sacraments and billets de confession . . . which the king himself does not believe he has the right to decide."[58] As the hour of the parlement of Paris' great exile approached, Antoine-Louis Rouillé too began warning the elder Joly de Fleury, much to the latter's chagrin, of "his majesty's scruples and fear of infringing upon ecclesiastical jurisdiction," of his horror "of thrusting his hand into the censer."[59] To the extent that these pious scruples prevailed, a royal declaration on the contested questions was quite out of the question—unless, of course, the king could claim to be acting with the blessings of the church.

That, in part, was the purpose of yet the third and most visible aspect of the king's sacramental politics, the specially appointed blue-ribbon commission consisting of laymen and, more importantly, clerics who began meeting toward the end of May 1752. Unlike the others, this facet of royal policy could hardly remain hidden, because its function was to provide public absolution for the king's guilt in advance of his violation of the tabernacle of ecclesiastical jurisdiction. The king accordingly announced the formation of this commission with a certain fanfare, both in the council's arrêt of April 29 and in response to the parlement's representations of May 5.[60] But partly, too, the commission was to work out the consensus uniting Rouillé's constituency of "reasonable members of both parties" who would rally around the king's declaration once it appeared. The clerical members were the cardinals de La Rochefoucauld and de Soubise and the bishops of Rouen and Laon; the lay members were the elder Joly de Fleury and the councillors of state Bidé de La Grandeville, Trudaine de Montigny, and Castannier d'Auriac, who was eventually replaced by Gilbert de Voisins. The commission's agenda was to advise the king on the utility and necessity of billets de confession, the proper sacramental conduct toward those who refused to present them, and the correct jurisdictional competence over the related litigation.[61]

This commission's task was not an easy one. Indeed, it would have been only somewhat more difficult for the negotiators of two warring states to agree upon peace terms while on the battlefield itself and at the height of the contest. The analogy is defective only in that the commission's lay members were not the representatives of the parlement and only partly sympathized with its stand, Bidé de La Grandeville in particular being almost wholly on the clergy's side. But despite a certain diversity of sentiments among the rest, they together defended the possibility of criminal procedure and a privileged case in sacramental matters and, more generally, the king's right to legislate on the questions submitted to the commission for its consideration. Not even this much was granted by the representatives of the episcopacy, who at least publicly presented a united front. Consistently, they contested both the competence of the royal courts over any facet of sacramental litigation except begrudgingly by way of an appel comme d'abus in civil cases and hence even the king's competence to legislate on the "spiritual" matters about which they were supposed to advise him.[62] "Why do we not have bishops such as we had at the time of the Declaration of 1682, when the bishops defended royal authority with such fanfare?" asked the seventy-seven-year-old Joly de Fleury in frustration. "Where are our Desmarets, Bossuets, Fénélons, Busanvals, and Arnaulds?" He was especially scandalized that these newfangled zealots would not even content themselves with an acceptance of *Unigenitus* relative to the episcopal pastoral instruction of 1714 and the "body of doctrine" of 1720 but insisted upon a "pure and simple" acceptance appropriate only to a rule of faith.[63]

The Gallican episcopacy was indeed unadorned at mid-eighteenth century by any Bossuets or Fénélons, but as the retired attorney general himself well knew, it contained many bishops with whom he could privately agree and who were as appalled as he by the "too extreme zeal" of the archbishop of Paris.[64] Frédéric-Jérôme, cardinal de La Rochefoucauld, who was "mildness itself," might privately concede that a refusal of sacraments accompanied by an "enormous scandal" might justify secular intervention, or that pestering people only reputedly Jansenist with questions about *Unigenitus* was uncharitable and indiscreet. But in meetings of the commission he would not part company with the "pretentious and brittle" Armand de Rohan, cardinal de Soubise, who would not in turn abandon the "iron-headed" Christophe de Beaumont, whose "cause," as Rouillé ruefully noted, "has become that of the whole episcopacy."[65] Rouillé was of a mind to blame the parlement's "excesses" for this, although these, if such they were, might just as plausibly have been laid at the unmoveable feet of the archbishop. In the parlement as well Rouillé's reasonable people were not lacking, such as the retired attorney general's two sons and much of the Grand' chambre. Through the president Ogier d'Enonville, the elder Joly de Fleury even established contact with Durey de Mesnières, one of the leaders of the parti janséniste, who showed himself receptive to the idea of a royal declaration.[66] But the archbishop's excessive zeal as well as some of the maladroit royal responses had seemed to justify the more surgical counsels of the parti janséniste, and by the end of the year the parlement's more moderate members had ceased attending the many sessions of the assembled chambers.[67] With such powerful corporate loyalties in full play, the extremes on either side tended to define normal relations between them, and Rouillé's reasonable people laid low or got out of the way. It was as though Christophe de Beaumont and Louis-Adrien Le Paige were locked in hand-to-hand combat with no one else between.

Under these circumstances nothing really remained for the commission to do, although the king maintained its agonized existence until the spring of 1753. But as early as October 1752 Trudaine, not demonstrating the same enthusiasm his father had brought to *ponts et chaussées*, was openly hoping "with all [his] heart" that the king would somehow "terminate this affair without waiting for our advice," and Bidé de la Grandeville was wishing that he could miraculously be deposited in "some far away country in order not to be an actor in a piece whose ending will not be agreeable." Alleging the gout, Castannier d'Auriac later bowed out and Gilbert de Voisins had to replace him.[68] On February 9 Joly de Fleury père described a meeting in which lay and clerical commissioners simply "looked at each other for a rather long time without saying anything" and which lasted for four hours without accomplishing more.[69] Finally, toward March, two strands of the king's sacramental policy intertwined when Rouillé and Joly de Fleury inflicted one of their draft declarations on the commission for its advice. True to form, the commission decided to give no advice, abandoning a unanimous opinion for eight individual reactions—or rather five, since the clerical members opined en bloc. The closest they could come to unanimity was to advise against any declaration at all.[70]

Things hardly went more smoothly in the royal council where beginning in October the ideas of Rouillé and Joly de Fleury suffered objection after objection: obedience to *Unigenitus* could not be expressly qualified by the pastoral instruction of 1714 and the declaration of 1720; the royal judge had no competence over sacramental matters in civil cases except by appel comme d'abus; the king could not pronounce on billets de confession without the advice of the commission, which however would give no advice; the parlements could do nothing about refusals of paschal communion at the holy table; the king could not "thrust his hand into the censer", and so on.[71] The naysayers were undoubtedly Lamoignon supported by d'Argenson. After ten months of arduous labor a defeated Rouillé confessed to a weary Joly de Fleury on April 22 that he was still uncertain if the king wanted to promulgate a declaration. His doubts were based on "the opposition of the bishops, the diversity of the commissioners' opinions . . . , the different sentiments [his majesty] hears in his council, the uncertainty over the effect a declaration will produce at a time when tempers are so heated, and above all his majesty's scruples and the fear he has of infringing upon the ecclesiastical jurisdiction in prescribing rules concerning the administration of the sacraments."[72]

These fears had not, it is true, prevented the royal council's arrêt of November 21, 1752, which though honoring the clergy's request to annul the parlement's arrêt of April 18, explicitly allowed for the possibility of criminal procedures and the privileged case in sacramental matters. In coming as close as anything had thus far to the royal declaration that Rouillé and Joly de Fleury contemplated, the arrêt "displeased everybody," as they themselves had anticipated, the parlement because it annulled its own arrêt of April 18, the clergy because the king appeared "to attribute to himself legislative power in spiritual matters" and "to approve the parlement's maxim that every public refusal of sacraments is a privileged case."[73] But the fact that the situation was already so polarized that no one could accept the crown's middle way was in no small measure due to the vacillatory and dilatory nature of the royal response from the beginning. Simple arrêts of the council unaccompanied by letters-patent could not take the place of a declaration formally registered by the parlement, and the fact that even at this late stage the monarchy could not engender one left the king legally defenseless in his duel with the parlement. Unarmed with any coherent royal policy, Louis XV was left to face the parlement with his none too considerable personal authority alone. This was a position of weakness that was bound sooner or later to masquerade as forcefulness and strength.

Hoping to gain time, the king on February 22, 1753, sent letters-patent ordering the indefinite suspension of all the legal proceedings then under way concerning the refusal of sacraments. The parlement had refused to register these letters, appending them instead to its already sizable list of grievances for the remonstrances upon which it had decided on January 4. Getting word, undoubtedly, that these remonstrances would be "without any measure" because their veritable authors were "the abbé Chauvelin and his party"—Clément de Feillet, Guillaume II Lambert, Robert de Saint-Vincent—the king first demanded to see the objects of these remonstrances, then decided upon this basis that he preferred not to see them at all.[74] In desperation, the parlement voted on May 5 to remain assembled, "all other service ceasing," until the king had "listened favorably" to its remonstrances. And when in response to the king's order to resume the administration of justice, the parlement decided two days later that it could not "obtemper the said letters-patent," a violent showdown became inevitable. Visibly counting on a division between the enquêtes and the Grand' chambre, the government exiled the former to various provincial towns on the night of May 8-9 but allowed the latter to remain assembled in Paris. But when the Grand' chambre too persisted in the arrêts of May 5 and 7 and continued to prosecute sacrament-refusing priests, it found itself "transferred" in turn to Pontoise and later exiled to Soissons.[75] The parlement of Paris' long disgrace had finally begun.

Bishops against Parlement and King

BESIDES the approximately thirty Grand' chambriers in Pontoise, comparable groups of magistrates took up residence in Angoulême, Bourges, Châlons-sur-Marne, Clermont-Ferrand, Montbrison, Poitiers, and Vendôme. The town of Bourges hosted the parlement's hard-core parti janséniste, or *chambre noire*, as they called themselves—Durey de Mesnières, Robert de Saint-Vincent, Clément de Feillet, Guillaume II Lambert, Lefebvre de Saint-Hilaire, Rolland de Challerange, Henri de Revol, Laverdy de Nizaret, but not the abbé Chauvelin, who was arrested and imprisoned at Mont-Saint-Michel. Three others demerited similar distinctions including Damiens' master Bèze de Lys, who was imprisoned in the château of Pierre-En-Cise in Lyons. In contrast, a favored fourteen were simply exiled to their properties.[76]

The Grand' chambre no sooner began its exile in Pontoise than negotiations got under way to end it, with or without the other chambers. The principal participants in these negotiations were, above all, the first president Maupeou and the prince de Conti; then the brothers Joly de Fleury; their retired father in Paris; and the presidents Gilbert de Voisins, Louis Chauvelin, Le Fèvre d'Ormesson, and Molé. Their chief object was to end the parlement's cessation of service and consequent exile by obtaining and registering a royal declaration on the contested matters along the lines sketched by Rouillé and the elder Joly de Fleury and in the spirit of the council's arrêt of November 21, 1752.[77] The envisioned scenario had the Grand' chambre resuming the administration of justice upon the king's promise to send a declaration, which after its registration by the Grand' chambre alone, would occasion the reunion of the whole parlement. The president Gilbert de Voisins and the abbé Du Trousset d'Héricourt calculated that if the Grand' chambre at Pontoise stood unanimously behind the declaration, the others would not object, either because "they would be content with it themselves" or because, having led or rather misled the Grand' chambre into exile, they would now "in turn defer to what those in Pontoise would have decided in favor of reconciliation."[78] But in the event of persistent objections on the other chambers' part, the solicitor general, for one, was prepared to contemplate a "blow of authority" from Versailles, which would result in a "general suppression" of the enquêtes followed by a "reform of the company." He acutely resented the "superiority" acquired by the enquêtes and requêtes in the assembled chambers as a result of the recent troubles.[79]

Things did not come to such a pass, however, because the projected declaration failed to materialize. Once again the king's troubled conscience was partly to blame. When the Grand' chambriers at Pontoise pleaded for a declaration, which among other things simply respected the council's own arrêt of November 21 to the effect that "causes" concerning the sacraments would go to the "judges of the church" except for the appel comme d'abus and the privileged case in criminal procedures, the government balked and offered only an authorized reprinting of the council's arrêt. "This clause of the council's arrêt is the common law of all the centuries, and can the king refuse to reformulate in the style of a declaration what he has already judged in his council?" asked an astounded Joly de Fleury.[80] There matters nonetheless remained. It is true, however, that the president Gilbert de Voisins and the abbé d'Héricourt were also holding out for clauses that would have enjoined "ecclesiastics to conform themselves to the canons received in the realm in the functions of their ministry" and punished refractories as "disturbers of the public peace."[81] These clauses clearly anticipated the key provisions of the Declaration of Silence, which eventually terminated the parlementary exile, but as they tended to vindicate the parlement's sacramental record and enshrine its contention that all *Unigenitus*-related refusals were privileged cases, the ministry was hardly ready for them in the spring of 1752. Not even the good offices of the prince de Conti, who expended himself in making trips between Vauréal and Versailles, could win acceptance of them at this time.[82]

Meanwhile, things went just as badly in Pontoise where corporate loyalties again dissolved Rouillé's consensus of reasonable people. As negotiations dragged on, the Joly de Fleury brothers became uncomfortably aware of the progressive defection of part of the Grand' chambre from the plan to register the royal declaration without the other chambers. By June 10 a hard-core opposition of fourteen votes had formed out of a grand total of roughly forty-five; four days later the attorney general estimated the division at more like half and half.[83] But even fourteen votes was enough to ruin the beautiful unanimity that the negotiations had until then assumed and without which registration by the Grand' chambre alone would be quite ineffective. Nothing remained to be done, given the Joly de Fleurys' failure effectively to "catechise" the fourteen, except to improvise another scenario postulating registration by all the chambers or the whole parlement reunited. All depended, therefore, on what the enquêtes' attitude toward the projected declaration would be. And since the enquêtes' leadership was concentrated at Bourges, the matter boiled down to what the chambre noire would think.[84]

The answer was not long in coming. In an effort to sound out Bourges, the "gentle" abbé d'Héricourt had sent the projected declaration and news of the negotiations to his friend and cousin Bèze de La Belouze, who perhaps indiscreetly revealed them to his colleagues in Bourges.[85] Enraged, the colony at Bourges responded with a barrage of bitter letters that began descending on Pontoise around the middle of July. These letters "raged with fury" against "not only the substance of the projected declaration but even against every means envisioned for getting it registered by the company": The Grand' chambre could do nothing without the others; no declaration registered by the Grand' chambre alone could have the force of law; the way of compromise envisioned by the projected declaration was no way at all because the conflict was not a petty quarrel between two *corps*, the parlement and the clergy, but rather an epochal struggle between the law, state, and nation on the one side and the independence and indocility of the clergy on the other.[86] Not only was *Unigenitus* no rule of faith but it was neither a "judgment of the universal church in the matter of doctrine" nor "law of church and state," and no one, not even the most indocile of its opponents, had any business being disquieted on its account.[87] However "unreasonable" and "false" such theses might have seemed to the attorney general, he and his brother nonetheless had to acknowledge that they and their adherents had effectively sprung the negotiations by the end of July.[88]

Negotiations were not seriously resumed for another eleven or twelve months. Meanwhile, the Grand' chambre at Pontoise persisted in its May 9 resolution to suspend its ordinary judicial functions, and a frustrated government further exiled its members individually to Soissons so that the Grand' chambre as such joined the other chambers in official oblivion. To ensure the administration of justice in the parlement of Paris' immense jurisdiction, the ministry improvised a *Chambre royale* consisting of councillors of state and masters of requests, which established its headquarters in the Louvre on November 11. But its efforts remained largely sterile, for the parlement's resistance was supported not only by the jurisdictions' subordinate tribunals, including the Paris Châtelet, but also by the capital's considerable population of lawyers, attorneys, notaries, and lesser judicial officials, who refused to do any work for the Chambre royale.[89] This abrupt and prolonged interruption of the capital's judicial business resulted in considerable hardship for the whole legal profession and even more numerous dependencies: Damiens, who lost his "condition" as Bèze de Lys' lackey at this time, was struck by how during the judicial strike "no procedure is judged, all business is stopped, and three-fourths of the people perish. . . ." In generally blaming, as Damiens did, the "too great clemence of the king" for the bishops and the advice of such ministers as d'Argenson and Machault, public opinion eventually put considerable pressure on the government to come to terms with the parlement.[90]

The event that finally heralded the resumption of negotiations was the first president Maupeou's secret trip to Versailles and interview with the king on the evening of June 4, 1754.[91] A few days later, signs of renewed activity are visible in the papers of the retired attorney general, who corresponded not with Rouillé on this occasion, but with the keeper of the seals, Machault. Did Joly de Fleury actually draft the royal declaration of September 2, 1754, or the Declaration of Silence, which finally ended the parlement's long exile and authorized its prosecution of sacrament-refusing priests? The duc de Luynes thought so, although the single draft of a law of silence in his papers with which he can undoubtedly be identified would have been emphatically rejected by the parlement inasmuch as it only partially imposed silence on the bishops and allowed for refusal of the sacraments in some instances.[92] Another draft sent by Machault to Joly de Fleury père around June 7 is much more similar to the one eventually registered by the parlement, but it is of uncertain authorship.[93] All that is sure is that, whether or not Joly de Fleury actually drafted the declaration, the prince de Conti was one of its chief promoters and perhaps the principal architect of the parlement's recall. It was his idea that the king talk to Maupeou on June 4, and he was the third person present when the king unveiled the general outline of the settlement he envisioned in his second secret interview with Maupeou on July 14.[94] In helping to formulate the declaration, Conti could have employed the expertise not only of the elder Joly de Fleury but also of his Jansenist legal advisors Pothouin and Le Paige, although judging from the latter's cool reaction to the declaration when it first appeared, he was certainly not its draftsman.[95] In any case, Le Paige's relation to Conti was then in its infancy; it was not yet as close as it was later to become.

Le Paige was soon to become an enthusiastic proponent of the Declaration of Silence and to sound off frequently in its behalf. But it seemed to take even him a couple of days to get past the preamble's harsh condemnation of the parlement's interruption of justice and penetrate the artful obscurity of the disposition's essential clause: ". . . and having recognized that the silence imposed for so many years upon such matters as can be agitated only at the equal expense of the good of religion and that of the state is the most appropriate means to assure the public peace and tranquility, we enjoin our parlement to make sure that in no quarter is anything done, attempted, undertaken, or innovated that could be contrary to this silence and the peace that we wish to see prevail in our States; ordering it to proceed against infractors conformably to the laws and the ordinances."[96] In the guise of censoring things said, this clause in effect authorized the parlement to prohibit and repress certain things done—in plainer terms, the public refusal of sacraments or the use of the billet de confession in connection with the bull *Unigenitus*. The reference to "laws and ordinances" legitimized the parlement's use of criminal procedure in sacramental litigation and could even be extended to embrace the parlement's law, or arrêt, of April 18, 1752. And in the event any doubts remained about its meaning, the reinstated parlement dissipated them in its September 5 registration of the law, to the effect that it be executed not only "conformably to the laws and ordinances of the realm" but to the "arrêts and regulations of the court"—read: the arrêt of April 18, 1752—and that "in consequence there be undertaken no innovation in the exterior and public administration of the sacraments."[97] "In the final analysis the parlement becomes the judge of ecclesiastical matters," commented a "sad" duc de Luynes. "Behold the bull *Unigenitus* humiliated and annihilated in France," more joyously responded the marquis d'Argenson.[98]

The silence, more narrowly defined, that the declaration of September 2 prescribed, was as much for the king's benefit as for the benefit of his subjects. Indeed, from Louis XV's perspective, the law's chief advantage was that it enabled him to side with his parlement and repress public refusals of sacraments without having to pronounce on or literally to say anything about matters that he continued to regard as outside his secular competence. Such, unfortunately, was also its chief disadvantage in that it did not enable him to distinguish formally between different kinds of cases or to say very clearly to his parlement how far and no farther it should go. To be sure, his response to the parlement's deputation of September 7, that he wished it to "maintain the laws of the realm without deviating from the respect due to religion," said clearly enough that he wanted it to observe the "moderation" he always preached, and rather less clearly, that it should restrict its procedures to priests and leave the bishops to the king.[99] But that left considerable room for misunderstanding.

This, however, became a problem only later. For the moment, and amidst tremendous popular rejoicing, the reinstated parlement set out with the king's arduously won good pleasure to repress the "schism," as it always called the refusal of sacraments to appellants. By now probably back to work for the liberated Bèze de Lys, Damiens could only applaud, as the intendant Gautier beamed down at him from the marquis de Ferrières' window, at the king's favorable response to the parlement's prosecution of Brunet and Meurizet, first vicaire and porte-Dieu of Damiens' parish, Saint-Etienne-du-Mont, who refused to administer the Eucharist and extreme unction on November 26, 1754, to one Marie-Gabrielle Lallemant, a laundress living on the rue Galland near the place Maubert. Her case perfectly illustrates the parlement's now well-established procedure in the matter as well as its new working relationship with the king. Employing criminal procedure, the parlement enjoined Meurizet and Brunet to "cause the scandal resulting from the said facts [of schism] to cease within the hour of the signification of the present arrêt, by fulfilling in regard to the said Lallemant the obligations that the canons received and authorized in the realm impose upon them"—in other words, as the parlement's first *huissier*, Henri Griveau, somewhat heavy-handedly explained on a different occasion, that they should administer the sacraments. Brunet and Meurizet of course did nothing of the sort, and when the parlement decreed their arrest, they promptly disappeared. The parlement then signified its arrêt to the parish's second vicaire, Ancel, who before similarly disappearing pleaded the orders of the archbishop. "Invited," finally, by the parlement to "cause the scandal to cease" and to "destroy at the same time [Ancel's] allegations tending to impute it to him," Christophe de Beaumont responded in the spirit of his previous rejoinders, to wit that the matter constituted none of the parlement's strictly temporal business. At this point, instead of proceeding against the archbishop and convoking the princes and peers, the parlement brought the prelate's response to the king, who on December 3 exiled him to his residence outside Paris at Conflans. Meanwhile the parlement exiled the three priests from the realm as "disturbers of the public peace" and started running through the list of priests simply resident in the parish in a continuing effort to get the moribund Lallemant administered.[100]

The rapid multiplication of such procedures in the years 1754-1756 produced not only populations of refractory and parlementary priests but a situation in some of the city's parishes that anticipated the experience of the Revolution. This was especially true in the parishes of Sainte-Marguerite and Damiens' parish of Saint-Etienne-du-Mont. In the latter the permanent disappearance from the scene of Bouëttin, despite the Declaration of Silence's general amnesty, did not readily improve the situation, as the Lallemant case amply demonstrates, and by the spring of 1754 the parish was quite without the services of beneficed clergy of any sort. All that remained, in fact, were two resident appellant priests who did the parlement's bidding. René Cerveau, undoubtedly engaged in research for the necrology of "friends of the truth" he was shortly to compile, administered Lallemant and a certain demoiselle Le Breton; and François Deshayes who though hardly a priest for all ecclesiastical seasons—he resided with his concubine and her daughter, who verbally and physically assaulted everyone else in the building—was sufficiently a priest to have administered yet another expiring member of the Coffin clan in 1755.[101] Predictably, the archbishop suspended Cerveau and Deshayes from their functions, whereupon the parlement received these ecclesiastical judgments appellant comme d'abus and, on the dubious principle that its appeal suspended the canonical suspensions, ordered these priests to continue their functions.[102] For those he deemed worthy to receive the last sacraments, the exiled but inflexible archbishop, for his part, sent a succession of ambulatory incognito priests no one of whom remained in the same place for more than a day or so at a time.[103]

Things were no better in the parish of Sainte-Marguerite, where six cases of the refusal of sacraments disturbed its peace in 1755-1756. More than his fair share, however, was caused by an appellant priest named Jean-François Gritte Coquelin, who having been interdicted from his priestly functions by the archbishop in 1755, took deathbed revenge by almost emptying the parish of the "approved" priests who remained.[104] In and out of death's revolving door for a period of about fifteen months, he demanded the last sacraments on three successive occasions, each of them giving rise to criminal procedures against the priests who refused him. On the last occasion, when Coquelin definitively expired, the parlement was reduced to proceeding against a doorkeeper of the empty residence for the parish's community of priests and of requisitioning a cooperative priest from the parish of Saint-Gervais to console the appellant priest.[105] In the process, it laid down the revolutionary principle that ecclesiastical boundaries are of human institution and can be altered or ignored by secular authority whenever circumstances require.[106] In this case as well, the parlement countermanded the archbishop's interdiction of the cooperative priest by means of the trusty appel comme d'abus.

In proceeding on the legal assumption that its appel comme d'abus immediately suspended the effect of an ecclesiastical censure until it was judged, the parlement was not so much circumventing as frontally assaulting the already battered edict of 1695, whose thirty-sixth article maintained precisely the contrary.[107] In consistently going beyond the moderate conclusions of its gens du roi and imposing the harshest imaginable punishments on the unfortunate priests who were in most cases only obeying the orders of their superior on pain of being interdicted if they did not, the parlement was hardly behaving with the moderation so close to the royal breast. The parlement even began extending its field of operations from the dying to the already dead when it proceeded in March 1755 against the curé of Saint-Médard for refusing to hold services for the repose of four of this Jansenist parish's deceased, and appellant, priests.[108] All of this was bound to be hard enough on Louis XV's sensitive conscience, but the literally crowning blow, for the king, undoubtedly came on March 18 when in the course of a particularly ugly case involving the refusal of last sacraments by the cathedral chapter of Orléans to one of its members, the parlement received its attorney general "appellant comme d'abus of the execution of the bull *Unigenitus*, notably in that some ecclesiastics pretend to give it the character and the effects of a rule of faith."[109] Under the pretense of maintaining the Declaration of Silence, this was quite clearly meant to break it by attacking the bull *Unigenitus* itself and by pronouncing on a question that the king continued to think himself incompetent to judge.

The explicit challenge to *Unigenitus* prompted the royal council to annul this part of the parlement's arrêt when it turned its attention to the task—the first time since the parlement's exile—on April 4. Seizing the occasion offered three days later by the first president Maupeou's visit concerning a recent secret conference at Conflans between the archbishop and Parisian curés, the king not only roundly condemned the parlement's forced interrogation of several curés in this connection but also disapproved of its appel comme d'abus against Beaumont's interdiction of René Cerveau as well as its intervention on behalf of the deceased curés of Saint-Médard. Thus ended the six-month honeymoon between king and parlement that had begun the previous September.[110] "How distressing, . . . that response! . . . and how different from the ones that have preceded it!" pathetically exclaimed Maupeou at the head of a parlementary delegation on April 20. Maupeou's harangue also somewhat insolently identified one of the sources of this new "surprise" perpetrated upon the king's "religion": a "negotiation" that malintentioned advisors "have presented to you as the most efficacious means to pacify everything, although its true object is to make the assembled bishops judges of what is manifestly decided by your declaration [of silence] and to submit the discussion of the extent of your authority to subjects who dare to disregard it openly."[111]

The king, indeed, was again attempting to obtain the cooperation of ecclesiastical authority and, in so doing, to grope his way back to that elusive *via media* between episcopacy and parlement that he had abandoned on September 2, 1754. The episcopal siege of the king's sensitive conscience had in the meanwhile found the secret of penetrating even the defense of the royal policy of silence; to impose silence, the bishops maintained, upon those whom Christ had instructed to "go teach all the nations" was just as much an infringement upon ecclesiastical authority as any more positive pronouncement would be.[112] With a small group of bishops resident in Paris, the king had therefore negotiated the abandonment of the billet de confession as such—that was what Beaumont's secret conference with the Parisian curés was about—on the condition, however, that the upcoming meeting of the general assembly of the clergy be allowed to discuss and explain itself on the subject of obedience due to the bull *Unigenitus* and the legitimacy of the refusal of sacraments on its account.[113] Even without the Declaration of Silence the general assembly would have needed the king's permission to do this, because it was not a church council, only a delegation of the clergy in its wholly temporal capacity as first order of the realm.

For that matter, it was also quite temporal concerns, not just his sensitive conscience, that had prompted the king to make this concession to the general assembly. From India, from the Ohio Valley, and from the high seas came rumors of impending war with England, especially during the months of March and April 1755.[114] Well before the general assembly was to meet on May 25, it was evident that Louis XV's pacific dispositions might not suffice to avert hostilities, in which case extraordinary subsidies would be needed. The king therefore requested from the general assembly an unprecedented sixteen million livres, which it promptly accorded on June

6.[115] But it is permissible to suspect that the assembly's act of prompt generosity is at least in part attributable to the "negotiations" that preceeded it.

On October 5, then, and with the king's blessing, the general assembly formally remonstrated against both the Declaration of Silence and the parlement's one-sided execution of this measure since its rehabilitation in September 1754. Drafted by Lefranc de Pompignan, the eloquent bishop of Le Puy, these remonstrances called for an interpretation of the declaration of September 2 compatible with the bishops' right and obligation (explicitly recognized by the declaration of March 24, 1730) "to instruct ecclesiastics and peoples confided to their care regarding their obligation to submit to the constitution *Unigenitus*"; for a strict application of article 34 of the edict of 1695 limiting secular interference in sacramental litigation to the appel comme d'abus; and for the nullification of all the royal courts' judgments, sentences, and still pending procedures against ecclesiastics "on the occasion of the late troubles."[116] The remonstrances trained their heaviest batteries on the royal courts' employment of the criminal procedure in cases of the public refusal of sacraments. Even assuming their injustice, such cases were not "privileged" but very "common" and deserved purely canonical penalties. A person thus deprived did not really suffer in his temporal capacity as citizen, and the only public scandal involved was the one that he himself caused by going to a secular court to obtain a spiritual gift. The unedifying spectacle of secular injunctions to administer the sacraments merited "sooner our tears," protested the bishop of Le Puy, "than an extended discussion."[117]

Although the assembly professed itself "penetrated with sorrow" at the noncommittal nature of the king's formal responses of October 23 and 27, less official evidence demonstrates that the king took the remonstrances very seriously.[118] The year 1755 was not out before the elder Joly de Fleury went tiredly to work on a royal project to annul the sentences incurred by ecclesiastics since September 1754; by the new year of 1756 this project had grown to include confirmation of article 34 of the edict of 1695 and the bishops' right to make *Unigenitus*-related noise—the other objects of the assembly's remonstrances. These drafts were probably submitted to the prince de Conti, who solicited similar projects from the president Murard and Le Paige.[119] Reluctantly, on January 1, 1756, Le Paige tried his hand at a declaration of annullment, but both he and Murard protested vigorously against any project that would except the bishops from the Declaration of Silence or exclude criminal procedure in sacramental litigation. What could be the continuing purpose of a law designed primarily "to prevent unjust and arbitrary refusals of sacraments," peremptorily asked Murard, if the bishops who were the primary authors of these refusals were to be excepted from its provisions?[120] And if the parlement were to be denied criminal procedure and confined to the appel comme d'abus, added Le Paige, the bishops had only to avoid canonical judgments and restrict themselves to simple acts and informal orders in order to refuse as many sacraments as they pleased.[121] In all probability, Conti agreed with these objections, since he asked both Murard and the elder Joly de Fleury for proofs of the legitimacy of injunctions to administer the sacraments.[122] In any case, the battle for the king's conscience was again on.

The concurrent Grand conseil affair stands as additional testimony to the government's attempt at this juncture to restore the upset balance between the parlement and the clergy and to pursue its perilous course between them. It is difficult to interpret otherwise the royal council's spectacular intervention in an affair that should perhaps never have emerged from its obscure and petty jurisdictional origins in the summer of 1755. But on September 13, 1755, the royal council supported the Grand conseil's claim to exclusive right to cases involving its own members at the jurisdictional expense of the Châtelet and the parlement of Paris. And when on October 2 the parlement ordered the Châtelet and its other subaltern tribunals to pay no further attention to any orders received from the Grand conseil, the king responded with a full-fledged declaration dated October 10, pronouncing the Grand conseil's judgments, ordinances, and orders enforceable throughout the length and breadth of the realm, independent of parlementary consent or registration. This held for the declaration itself, which the parlement's subaltern tribunals were supposed to register on the Grand conseil's orders alone, so that the declaration and the method employed for its registration together tended to bypass the parlement completely and make the Grand conseil into its equal if not its superior.[123] Together these provoked the parlement's monumental remonstrances of November 27, 1755, and eventually, a constitutional conflict of major proportions.[124]

If by these dubious means the king had hoped to distract parlementary attention from his dealings with the clergy, he must have been most bitterly disappointed, for the parlement simply redoubled its activity and vigilance. The government could usually hope for a short reprieve during the annual parlementary vacation from September 7 until November. But not in 1755. When in August the parlement requested permission to remain in session beyond September 7 in order to break the logjam of judicial business, the government hardly dared to refuse, even though it knew that at least part of the parlement's motivation was the desire to continue its close surveillance of the concurrently meeting general assembly of the clergy.[125] When this assembly's sessions continued beyond the scheduled closure of September 25, new disquietudes arose, and the relentless Clément de Feillet had to be publicly assured by the first president that the king had permitted the assembly to prolong its meeting until October 20.[126] This date too failed to bring political relief, because the clergy asked for and obtained yet another prolongation of its meetings until October 26, and the parlement in consequence decided not to take even the short break it had envisioned on the occasion of the feast day of Saint Simon. During this entire tension-ridden period the prince de Conti and the Joly de Fleury brothers exchanged panic-stricken notes in an effort to keep the precarious peace. "May God work a miracle," scrawled the normally skeptical prince de Conti, "to avert the fire that we fear."[127]

One of the reasons, it was rumored, for the repeated prolongations of the general assembly's session was a division—

the uncharitable might even have called it a schism—among its delegates. Alas, it was only too true. Unanimous enough in what it opposed, the assembly found itself sharply divided on the question of what positively to propose about *Unigenitus* and the refusal of sacraments to appellants.[128] All agreed that *Unigenitus* was a "dogmatic and irreformable judgment of the universal church" to which all Catholics owed a "sincere submission of heart and mind" and that those who too notoriously lacked this submission were unworthy to receive the sacraments, which were not to be procured by secular injunctions and the like. But on formulations of nuance the assembly broke down into a hard-line minority of sixteen, called *Théatins*, led by such bishops as Orléans de La Motte of Amiens and Montmorin de Saint-Herem of Langres, and a more moderate majority of seventeen, called *Feuillants*, led by the assembly's president, La Rochefoucauld, and enjoying the tacit support of Louis XV. For the Théatins, those who refused submission to the bull committed a mortal sin; for the Feuillants, they sinned only in "a grave matter." For the Théatins, a refractory was anyone with a public reputation as such; for the Feuillants, he had to be juridically convicted as such or to be so to the point of public scandal. For the Théatins, priests were publicly to "repair the scandal," even in dubious cases; for the Feuillants, they were to do so only privately and publicly stick to the rituals. For the Théatins, finally, priests who obeyed secular injunctions deserved ecclesiastical censures; for the Feuillants, they just sinned "gravely."[129] Unable on October 22 to resolve these differences, the general assembly went to the king for permission to consult the pope.[130]

This permission Louis XV gladly granted. However contrary to the Gallican tradition an appeal to Rome, the Rome of Pope Benedict XIV was in some ways more Gallican than much of the Gallican clergy itself. Personally moderate, kindly disposed toward France, and of theologically Augustinian orientation, Prospero Lambertini did not altogether share Christophe de Beaumont's admiration for the hundredfold excellencies of the bull *Unigenitus* or perhaps even the doctrine of papal infallibility. He could be expected to decide in favor of

La Rochefoucauld's Feuillant bishops.[131] In any case, Louis XV probably welcomed the division among the Gallican bishops. Until now the government had had to deal with an episcopacy that officially made common cause with the archbishop of Paris and therefore opposed even the mediating sacramental policy proposed by the king's advisors. With the episcopal phalanx now broken and Rouillé's reasonable people finally in evidence, royal policy could hope to profit from the breach by obtaining the hitherto elusive ecclesiastical backing for a royal declaration. The negotiations with Benedict XIV therefore became part of the larger royal effort to restore the lost balance between episcopacy and parlement and give birth to the royal declaration on the substance of the issues that had been so long and painstakingly in the making.

It was hence papal sanction for royal policy, not papal policy no matter what, that the French government proposed to obtain from the negotiations that got under way toward the close of 1755. Skillfully conducted by the new French ambassador at the court of Rome, Etienne-François, comte de Stainville, the negotiations eventually resulted in the papal encyclical *Ex Omnibus*, which appeared on October 27, 1756.[132] Predictably, and in the spirit of La Rochefoucauld's articles, *Ex Omnibus* so circumscribed the case for the refusal of sacraments on account of opposition to *Unigenitus* as to make this a more or less metaphysical possibility. The pope's judgment on this matter formed the basis of the royal declaration of December 10, which limted the refusal of sacraments to juridically convicted opponents of the bull. Carefully too the encyclical avoided describing *Unigenitus* as a rule of faith, thereby tacitly authorizing Louis XV's assertion to this effect in the same declaration. A papal brief dated January 5, 1757—fateful day—as well as references to Benedict XIV in the preamble to the declaration made it explicitly clear that it was with the pope's benediction that the king had so declared.[133] But the most astonishing thing about the making of *Ex Omnibus* is that according to both the abbé de Bernis and the comte de Stainville (by way of Durey de Mesnières), the pope's own drafts avoided calling *Unigenitus* anything at all and included only some vague injunctions concerning the respect and submission due papal judgments generally. The fact that *Ex Omnibus* finally called *Unigenitus* a "judgment" enjoying "so great an authority within the church" is attributable solely to the French government, which insisted that without such a qualification Christophe de Beaumont and his ilk were "disposed to put the whole realm on fire."[134] Doggedly, and in conformity with drafts of royal declarations dating from 1752, French royal policy plied its middle course.

"Royal policy" and "the French government" are of course abstractions. In the present instance, all fingers pointed to the keeper of the seals, Machault, with technical assistance from the councillor Gilbert de Voisins.[135] In terms of court alliances and alignments, "Machault" also meant madame de Pompadour, who had long been Machault's close friend. It is perhaps not accidental that at this precise moment the king's sometime mistress was undergoing her "devout" conversion and attempting to go straight at the court. The attempt to reconcile herself with her legal husband and to get absolution from the court's uncooperative Jesuit confessors, the walling up of the staircase leading from her red lacquered apartment to the king's upstairs, her contributions to the convent of Saint-Cyr and evolution into "dame of the palace of the queen," the abandonment of the public *toilette* for the humble activity of tapestry making, the fasts, the sighs, and the long prayers after mass—all this has been the stock-in-trade of anecdotal court history and need not detain us here.[136] But what has perhaps not been sufficiently appreciated is that Pompadour's "conversion" had serious political consequences, that in her attempt to gain the parti dévôt's favor, she transferred her influence to its side of the politico-ecclesiastical scale. "It is necessary, I believe, that the pope blend the articles from the two [episcopal] parties and take what is best from each . . . ," she wrote to her protégé, the future duc de Choiseul, while he was negotiating *Ex Omnibus* in Rome.[137] Such advice, to the extent it was followed, was bound to make *Ex Omnibus* more constitutionary than it might otherwise have been.

That Machault and madame de Pompadour were now playing roles of the first importance in the making of sacramental policy and that this policy was evolving toward the *juste milieu* it had abandoned in 1754 all represented a defeat for the prince de Conti. This defeat was highly personal in that Conti was one of the court holdouts who had never accepted the presence of Pompadour at Versailles, and Pompadour had always resented the impenetrable secrecy of the king's dealings with his princely cousin. This enmity dated at least to the War of the Austrian Succession when at Pompadour's solicitation Maurice de Saxe, not the less successful Conti, received the marshal's baton.[138]

Conti's defeat on the sacramental front, quite clear by the spring of 1756, was all the more stinging in that it coincided almost exactly with a resounding defeat on the foreign policy front at the hands of the same person and (to a lesser extent) the same parti dévôt. Since the 1740s Conti had been the king's confidant and the principal architect of the king's "secret" foreign policy, which outside of and in occasional tension with official foreign policy, aimed at supporting the "patriot," or pro-French, party in Poland and at aligning this realm with Sweden, Denmark, Turkey, and possibly Prussia in order to counteract the influence of Russia and France's traditional enemies, the Austrian Habsburgs, in northeastern Europe. The king's "secret" also had a dynastic goal: to place the prince de Conti on the Polish throne at the death of Augustus of Saxony, its perennially moribund occupant and father of the French dauphine.[139] In the course of the period from 1755 to 1756 the whole purpose of this secret found itself quite undone by another, which resulted in the famous "diplomatic revolution," aligning France with her traditional Habsburg enemy against her erstwhile ally, Prussia, now siding with the forever hostile England. Though not, strictly speaking, incompatible with Conti's eventual occupancy of the Polish throne, the new system tended in that direction because it brought in its train a rapprochement between Saxony and France and hence French support for Saxony's dynastic goals in Poland.[140] Given a choice in the summer of 1755 with approaching either Conti or madame de Pompadour with Empress Maria Theresa's diplomatic propositions, the Austrian ambassador, Count George Adam von Starhemberg, symptomatically opted for Pompadour; and the initial meeting between Starhemberg and the abbé de Bernis took place in the presence of Pompadour in her château of Bellevue in Sèvres on September 3, 1755.[141] Conti, the confidant of the old secret, was still totally unaware of the new one only weeks before the signing of the first Treaty of Versailles with Austria on May 1, 1756. But as early as March or April he was confusedly aware that on this front as well things were not going entirely his way.[142]

The diplomatic revolution represented a victory for the parti dévôt, for it united the two chief Catholic states of Europe against the major Protestant ones, achieving an old goal of the French parti dévôt dating from the days of Richelieu and the early seventeenth century. Despite the fact that the dauphin reacted coolly and the comte d'Argenson remained quietly hostile toward the diplomatic realignment, the confessional dimension of the new system was not unimportant to Maria Theresa or to Louis XV himself, who esteemed it the "only way . . . to maintain the Catholic religion" in Europe.[143]

Gradually replaced, then, in the king's secret counsels by an unequally yoked marriage of high religious considerations and purely personal rivalries, Conti's credit was declining rapidly by the spring of 1756. Nor was it bolstered at all by the senior Joly de Fleury's death and Rouillé's simultaneous descent into senility, for both would have counteracted the influence of Machault and Pompadour in parlementary-ecclesiastical affairs.[144] On April 3, 1756, the old maréchal de Noailles, another associate of Conti's party, stalked disgustedly out of the council, complaining that the king listened only to Machault or d'Argenson and always rode roughshod over the public-spirited counsels of his parlements.[145] The trace of Conti's activities as negotiator and honest broker between the parlement and Versailles are still numerous in the papers of the Joly de Fleury brothers as late as January and February 1756-1757.[146] But after that he disappears. Where he ominously resurfaces is in the papers of Louis-Adrien Le Paige, where around May or June 1756 we see Le Paige and Murard trying to persuade him of the importance of maintaining the Declaration of Silence. And it was at the end of March or the beginning of April that in his capacity as grand prior of the Order of Malta, Conti signed on Le Paige as the *bailli* of the temple. Le Paige touchingly warned Conti on that occasion of his personal "varnish of Jansenism" (*vernis du jansénisme*), which in a position as public and close to the prince as bailli of the temple, would inevitably rub off on his serene highness and possibly weaken his effectiveness at court.[147] What Le Paige evidently did not appreciate at this time was that Conti no longer possessed much influence to lose and that the ascendency he was beginning to assume over the radical parlementary-Jansenist opposition was in inverse proportion to his descendency at Versailles.

At this moment of rising grain prices, onerous and unprecedented taxes, widespread popular unrest, intense religious and political conflict, and all this against the background of a looming war, Conti's alienation and opposition was potentially dangerous, even frondish. Conti was imposing, decisive, persistent, quick-witted, a good general, and a surprisingly good orator, not the lockjawed dinosaur of a duc d'Orléans in 1789.[148] The president Jean-François Hénault remembered with amazement his political "perspicacity," legal acumen, and imposing stage presence in the plenary assemblies of the parlement, where he was "just as at ease as in his cabinet."[149] We dimly glimpse Conti encouraging the parlement of Paris' resistance to the second vingtième and other wartime taxes in the summer of 1756—or rather we do not quite see him, because he had taken to forming his letters by means of dots of the penpoint so that his handwriting could not be recognized.[150] The parlement's quarrel with the Grand conseil he readily adopted as his own, especially when this conflict issued into the larger one of whether the parlement could convoke the realm's princes and the peers to take part in its constitutional discussions without the express permission of the king. On this occasion and with his son in train, he stepped forward as a champion of the constitutional rights (not privileges) of the princes and peers, to the point of sustaining a "tracasserie" at the court.[151] In Le Paige, who in 1753-1754 had written a two-volume treatise on the historic constitutional rights of the princes and peers as constituent members of the parlement, Conti had found the perfect theoretician for his personal political ambitions.[152] And in the most astonishing initiative of all, Conti transformed his hitherto innocent and disinterested contacts with Paul Rabaut and the Protestants of Languedoc into a thinly veiled call to arms. Around March, again, of 1756 Conti engaged the Protestant leader Rabaut to have the upcoming May synod estimate how many men the Protestants could put into the field.[153] To what extent Louis XV was aware of these last developments before November 5 is unclear, but it is hardly surprising that he refused Conti the command of an army at that time, thus precipitating the break between the two Bourbons that lasted the rest of their lives.[154]

Meanwhile, the war between sacerdoce and empire was raging more fiercely than ever. Fearful of the king's negotiations with Rome and an imminent papal disavowal of his conduct, Christophe de Beaumont seized the occasion of his Sunday morning homily in the parish church of Conflans to promulgate, on September 19, the most incendiary mandamus and pastoral instruction of his already sufficiently explosive career. Expressly attacking the Declaration of Silence and defending the exclusive jurisdiction of the church over the articulation of doctrine and the administration of the sacraments, the mandamus indifferently threatened with excommunication, "incurred by the fact alone," anyone who had recourse to the secular tribunals to obtain the sacraments or even counseled such an expedient, the secular judges who issued such injunctions, as well as huissiers and others who notified them, and all curés, vicaires, and portes-Dieu who heeded these injunctions.[155] Beaumont's veritable *arrière ban* moreover rallied adhesions by the bishop of Saint-Pons on October 29; Troyes and Metz on November 1; Auxerre on November 7; and Amiens, Chartres, Meaux, Orléans, and Tours on November 14.[156] The episcopal counteroffensive began genuinely assuming the League-like aspect against which Le Paige and the parti janséniste had so insistently warned.

The exploits of several of these episcopal leaguers still merit attention if not admiration. Exiled for his sacramental stinginess to the town of Meung-sur-Loire in December 1754, Louis-Joseph Montmorency de Laval, bishop of Orléans, had watched helplessly as the parlement of Paris flung its infamous arrêt of August 29, 1755, in the face of the general assembly that was then in session.[157] This arrêt, in condemning the cathedral chapter of Orléans for having refused the last sacraments to one of its appellant members, Charles Cougniou, on October 13, 1754, had ordered the celebration of an annual and perpetual service for the repose of his soul in the parish church of Saint-Pierre-Lentin, as well as the erection of a marble plaque in the same church bearing the inscription of the parlement's very same arrêt.[158] It was with pious outrage, moreover, that he observed the marble plaque actually placed in the church thanks to the efforts of the local bailliage officers toward the beginning of February 1756.[159] But the prospect of the celebration of the service stipulated by this arrêt on October 30, 1756, was a cross he could not bear. Almost literally eaten up with his zeal for the Lord's house, he interdicted the church of Saint-Pierre-Lentin in an ordinance dated October 29, 1756, entailing the removal of the holy water, sacramental elements, sacred vessels, and the parish curé bodily to the chapel of the officialité in Orléans.[160] Others were not to be outdone. From his exile in Murbach the equally zealous bishop of Troyes, Poncet de La Rivière, reserved to himself, by means of a mandamus dated November 22, 1756, the right to absolve Troyes' bailliage officers of the sin of having condemned his holiness' November 1 adherence to Christophe de Beaumont's pastoral instruction of September 29.[161] Beaumont himself, finally, returned to the charge with another pastoral instruction on November 7 and a fresh refusal of sacraments to a sick nun of the Visitation on the rue Saint-Jacques.[162]

Although its hands were somewhat tied by the king's request that it not act in these matters until November 24, the parlement retaliated as best it could. It received its attorney general appellant comme d'abus of the various episcopal mandamuses and ordinances, had the Châtelet condemn others, and acting again on the principle that its appeal suspended their effects, most notably ordered the unfortunate curé of Saint-Pierre-Lentin in Orléans to celebrate divine services in the parish church despite his bishop's interdict.[163] But when all he obtained for his pains in obeying the parlement's orders was an episcopal *monitoire* threatening him with excommunication and a royal lettre de cachet exiling him to Angers, the parlement correctly sensed that the king was not contemplating an unequivocal gesture in its favor.[164]

In effect, with Rouillé's reasonable consensus less in evidence than ever before, the king had indeed chosen this rather unlikely moment to impose the royal via media, the long-discussed declaration on the substance of the contested matters. And yet, from the royal perspective, it must have seemed like the right or at least only possible moment. The long-sought ecclesiastical authorization of royal policy in the form of the papal encyclical *Ex Omnibus* had finally arrived in Versailles on October 27. Louis XV promptly sent copies to his bishops as a guide for their sacramental conduct. Before that, the king had obtained his huge *don gratuit* from the clergy and had gotten his wartime fiscal declarations through the parlement by means of a lit de justice held on August 21, 1756, at Versailles. The war with England had begun propitiously with the maréchal de Richelieu's spectacular storming of Fort Saint-Philippe guarding Minorca's Port Mahon on June 27.[165] Desperate last-minute entreaties by the parlement to the king and by both the attorney general and Le Paige to the politically disabled Conti were therefore powerless to head off the impending lit de justice.[166] For that matter, it was no longer Conti, who had already broken with the king, but rather Machault and Pompadour who were now calling the shots.[167] On December 13 and armed inadequately with an edict and two declarations Louis XV, the-no-longer-so-well-loved king, traversed a sullen Parisian population to preside over a lit de justice in his parlement of Paris.[168] On that day and the next most of the parlement's magistrates resigned.

The Political Crisis of 1756-1757

A SECOND LOOK is due the measures that provoked the crisis. It is by now evident that the declaration concerning religious affairs was the long-awaited offspring of the Rouillé/Joly de

Fleury drafts of 1752 and, in line with the council's arrêt of November 21 of the same year, a reaffirmation of the royal via media only temporarily abandoned in September 1754. In one breath, it accorded *Unigenitus* the "respect and submission that are its due"—read: law of church and state, judgment of the universal church in the matter of doctrine—but in the next it disavowed the denomination of "rule of faith." It authorized the refusal of sacraments in cases of juridically flagrant opposition to the bull but hastened to caution against pestilential questioning of penitents unauthorized by the rituals. And though it assigned civil sacramental litigation to the ecclesiastical courts, it also reserved both the appel comme d'abus and the privileged case to the royal judges. What was new in the declaration of December 10 reflected developments since 1752. The preamble's references to the pope and *Ex Omnibus* proclaimed the heretofore lacking ecclesiastical sanction for the declaration's more theological pronouncements. The emphasis upon article 34 of the edict of 1695, the outlawing of secular injunctions to administer the sacraments, and the partial exception to silence in favor of the bishops all responded to the general assembly's remonstrances of 1755. The absence of any reference to the billets de confession, finally, reflected the negotiated abandonment of their use in 1755.

If the declaration of December 10 shared its abortive predecessors' virtues, it also bore all of their vices. Chief among these was its inappropriateness to the polarized situation, its incapacity to placate virtually anyone. To take only the most obvious example, the inevitable alienation of the clergy at the mere mention of the privileged case was small consolation for the parlement, which found itself disbarred from the use of secular injunctions and thus without the chief advantage of criminal procedure, which consisted in actually getting the sacraments to someone unjustly refused them.[169] Where under these circumstances was the declaration to find Rouillé's reasonable people who desired both the letter of the law and the "respect due to religion"?

As far as the parlement was concerned, it was visibly to the purpose of finding these reasonable people and making them declare their colors, that the declaration concerning religious affairs was linked to the declaration on parlementary discipline and the edict eliminating parlementary offices. Even the relatively noncontroversial edict included several provisions that the ministry knew in advance to be favored by the "reasonable" Grand' chambre and rejected by the enquêtes; and the suppression of the last two chambers of enquêtes, although not overtly favored by the Grand' chambre, was calculated to break the esprit de corps in the former in order to augment the influence of the latter.[170] That such was more blatantly the purpose of the declaration on parlementary discipline, as we have previously noted, is also made evident by some of its secondary provisions: article 6's stipulation, for example, that the attorney general alone could make denunciations calling for plenary sessions unless the first president, on the advice of one of the councillors, deemed it appropriate; or article 4's provision that parlementary remonstrances be composed within fifteen days after the official presentation of the royal measures they concerned. Provisions such as these were almost personally aimed at the likes of the abbé Chauvelin, Clément de Feillet, Guillaume II Lambert, and Robert de Saint-Vincent, who had so often denounced instances of the refusal of sacraments provoking the assembling of the chambers and who had composed the immoderate and treatiselike remonstrances of April 9, 1753.[171]

We have it on the testimony of the abbé de Bernis, moreover, that a mere two days before the lit de justice Machault and madame de Pompadour were still counting on the fidelity of the whole Grand' chambre, which they thought would serve as a base for an eventually more docile parlement.[172] Had they but consulted the Joly de Fleury brothers, they would have learned about the defection of nearly half of this same chambre when the solicitor general had contemplated a similar coup only two and a half years earlier. Interestingly, the total number of Grand' chambre resignations in December 1756—seventeen—closely approximates the attorney general's estimate of fourteen or more in May 1754. Even more astounding is Bernis' report that the keeper of the seals and the king's sometime mistress had failed to reckon with the probable defection of the Châtelet and most of the lawyers and attorneys, to say nothing of the intervention of the provincial parlements. Urged by Bernis to consult the council, the king belatedly did so on December 12. But nothing remained to do at that late date except skeptically to wish success to an affair already engaged. The comte d'Argenson conspicuously washed his hands of the whole affair in succeeding days in front of anyone whose attention he could capture.[173]

So the predictable occurred, even though it evidently came as a considerable and most unpleasant surprise to his majesty. With only eleven loyal councillors plus the ten presidents to work with, the lit de justice had hopelessly missed its mark. The fact that Damiens only narrowly missed his own three weeks later hardly allayed the king's displeasure, which sent sixteen of the resigned magistrates into exile on January 27. Among these were predictably the hard core of the parti janséniste minus Damiens' former neighbor Rolland de Challerange and Lefebvre de Saint-Hilaire, despite the fact that it was the latter who had seen to the parlement's suppression of Benedict XIV's encyclical letter on December 7.[174] On the other hand, the king's blacklist included several magistrates such as Douet de Vichy and de Lattaignant de Bainville who had never distinguished themselves in the parlementary opposition or in any other way. "That policy is incomprehensible," commented Barbier at the time; and more than two centuries' leisure for retrospection has added nothing to its intelligibility.[175]

What might make a little more political sense was Louis XV's spectacular disgrace of his secretaries of war and the navy on February 1, however foolhardy this action undoubtedly was in the face of the beginning war with both Prussia and England. Court intrigue played its inevitable role, which was also the one that most captured the attention of contemporaries. Court memorialists insisted upon the rancors of madame de Pompadour who, counseled by Machault to leave court in the wake of Damiens' attempted assassination, employed her quickly regained credit to exact vengeance on her unfaithful friend as well as on her longstanding enemy d'Argenson with whom she had again noisily quarreled during the king's convalescence. The subject of their quarrel, interestingly enough, was whether the king should be shown all the seditious billets that d'Argenson's domestics found collected in front of his Paris hôtel every day or whether his majesty would best be spared, as Pompadour thought, this sort of exposure.[176] But as in the case of Conti personal rivalries intertwined with genuinely political considerations. In Machault the king undoubtedly dismissed the minister whom even Damiens correctly identified after his arrest as the architect of the disastrous lit de justice of December 13; the case of d'Argenson is less clear, but in the secretary of war, the king might possibly have disgraced an enemy of the recent Austrian alliance and the long-standing ministerial head of the parti dévôt at court and as such still identified with the parlement's exile of 1753-1754.[177] Damiens again spoke for much of the Parisian population when in prison on February 17 he said that "no matter what he does m. d'Argenson has to quit the camp [because] he ruins the people and France."[178] Although Damiens probably never knew it, he had fully accomplished his desire of ridding France of the ministers who badly counseled the king and "prevented him from seeing clearly."

It remains to be seen whether by Damiens' light the king subsequently saw more clearly. Did he in fact "cease heeding the pernicious advice of his ministers" and become "more disposed to listen to [his parlement's] remonstrances?" Did he, if not lop off some mitered heads, at least more politely dispose of Damiens' hated handful of bishops? Did he at least stop the refusal of sacraments and make the church obey the parlement? In a word, did Damiens successfully "touch the king?" A remark that the abbé de Bernis reportedly made to Rolland de Challerange and some other magistrates would seem to indicate that this was indeed the profounder political significance of the double disgrace of Machault and d'Argenson. You "ought to be satisfied," he told them, "with the exile of the two ministers," because "this disgrace had had no other cause than this very affair of the parlement. . . ." He added that the "new minister was going to act according to an entirely different plan; that instead of punishing and abasing the parlement he was going to second and honor it."[179]

The future cardinal de Bernis ought to have known, because he was by then the new minister in question as well as the architect, along with the president Molé, d'Ormesson, and the Joly de Fleury brothers, of the parlement's eventual rehabilitation. This finally occurred after long negotiations on September 1, 1757. Having been ordered by lettre de cachet to meet in the Grand' chambre on the morning of that day, all the parlement's magistrates except the exiled sixteen obeyed, whereupon they were further ordered to send a deputation to Versailles. There they listened to the chancellor read the king's conciliatory address as well as to the king himself, who ordered them immediately to register a declaration interpreting the least controversial of the December 10 measures, the edict suppressing the parlementary offices.[180] The following day the parlement made haste to obey after the "striking" magistrates had formally voted to take back their resignations; with some additional royal prodding, moreover, the parlement even registered the controversial declaration on *Unigenitus* and the refusal of sacraments on September 5. In return for these marks of obedience, the king agreed to make no use of his declaration on parlementary discipline, to modify further the edict suppressing the offices, and to allow the sixteen exiled magistrates, including the abbé Chauvelin and Clément de Feillet, to retain their offices and return a bit later.[181]

By means of a few concessions, then, the king appears to have obtained parlementary acquiescence in the declaration of December 10 concerning religious affairs. But these appearances are deceptive, as close attention to the following paragraph of the king's discourse of September 1 reveals: "If for superior reasons and in view of the general good his majesty has deemed it necessary to place himself above the ordinary laws, his parlement should not fear this as a precedent for the future." This passage refers to the declaration's general amnesty for ecclesiastics sentenced by the parlement for the refusal of sacraments. And what the king was saying, in plainer words, is that the parlement's application of the laws was justified, that for reasons best understood by himself he had decided to suspend their execution, but that he would not do so again. Attend now to the next paragraph of the king's response: "The king therefore commands you to execute his first declaration, conformably to the canons received in the realm, and to the laws and ordinances." The crucial reference here is to the canons, laws, and ordinances; it was a veiled invitation to the magistrates to register the declaration of December 10, 1756, according to the canons, laws, and ordinances as *they* had always interpreted these. The king could not have been ignorant of the fact that parlementary arrêts had enjoined priests "to cause the scandal to cease by conforming themselves" to precisely these "holy canons and laws of the realm," that it was in virtue of these that the parlement had forbidden priests "to refuse to hear in confession, and to administer the sacraments of the Eucharist and extreme unction."[182] The parlement was bound to understand "laws" as the royal declaration of September 2, 1754, and even—as the Jansenist weekly *Nouvelles écclésiastiques* carefully underscored—the parlement's own arrêt of April 18, 1752, which prohibited any refusals of sacraments on the grounds of opposition to *Unigenitus* or lack of a billet de confession.[183] "By means of obscure expressions," Le Paige shrewdly observed, "which each party nonetheless understands perfectly well, authority is reconciled with justice and peace reigns between them."[184] But just in case the message was not clear enough, the parlement added to its September 5, 1757, registration of the declaration the clause: "and to the usages and maxims of which the observation is necessary to the maintenance of the authority of the king and of his sovereign justice." The obviously Gallican ring of this clause announced to the world that the parlement intended to maintain the king's authority and sovereign justice precisely as it had in the past.[185]

And that is, moreover, what it did. Between 1758 and 1763, within the parishes of Paris alone, the parlement itself or the Châtelet instituted criminal proceedings in at least fifteen instances against curés, curates, or portes-Dieu who refused to administer the sacraments to appellants or to celebrate services for the repose of their souls.[186] The parlement continued to order that the sacraments be administered, or at least forbid that they be refused, and typically banished the offending priests from the realm for life as "disturbers of the public peace." The sole features that distinguished the new parlementary comportment from that earlier in the decade were a somewhat greater concession to the king's counsels of moderation and a more concerted effort to foresee and defuse potentially dangerous sacramental confrontations before they exploded in a public éclat. The new first president Molé and the gens du roi held frequent conferences with the abbé de Bernis upstairs and with their colleagues Chauvelin or Murard downstairs, the latter in the hopes that they could moderate the undiminished zeal of Clément de Feillet who seems to have been in contact with all of the moribund appellants in Paris.[187] When sacramental cases were engaged despite these precautions, the parlement often let the Châtelet do the dirty work in its stead—something, incidentally, that Louis XV had never permitted before—or sometimes failed to pursue them to the point of definitive judgment.[188] The gens du roi purposefully dragged their feet in the matter and had to be prodded by the ever vigilant enquêtes.[189] But the parlement as a whole could now afford to be occasionally moderate and incomplete because it had successfully sustained its case. By 1758 the state in the guise of the parlement had won ultimate jurisdictional control over the public dispensation of the church's most "august" sacraments, and the edict of 1695, one of Louis XIV's great legislative tapestries weaving church and state together, was completely in shreds.

The remonstrances of the general assemblies of the clergy in the years following the crisis of 1756-1757 further corroborate this conclusion. Far from regarding the declaration of December 10, 1756, as any kind of royal vindication of its jurisdiction, the clergy was still protesting its provisions as late as 1770: secular authority was unqualified to deny *Unigenitus* the title of "rule of faith"; the declaration did not sufficiently acknowledge the bishops' right to preach obedience to this bull from the housetops; it insinuated that every refusal of sacraments criminally contested was a privileged case; and so on.[190] Even more objectionable in the clergy's view was the parlement's execution of this declaration, which differed in no important respect from its execution of the Declaration of Silence of September 1754. The remonstrances of 1758, 1760, 1762, and 1765 all pointed out that in defiance of the declaration's explicit prohibition, the parlement continued to "trample under foot the most august of our sacraments by ordering under various formulae and on pain of the most severe punishments that they be administered without delay. . . ."[191] Nor did Louis XV, in his responses, really deny these charges. He contented himself with evasive promises to look into the matter and by characteristically insisting upon what he had *not* declared, namely, that every refusal of sacraments criminally contested was a privileged case.[192] The assembly's remonstrances of 1765 finally put the profane shoe on the royal foot. "Ah Sire," they asked with "sorrow but truth," "if the conduct of your parlements since 1756 have been contrary to the letter or the spirit of your declaration, how does it happen that none of their enterprises has been reprimanded by your sovereign power? Has not the silence of your council during these last nine years in some sense unhappily authorized the interpretation and the usage that the tribunals have made of your Law?"[193]

Indeed, the political crisis of 1756-1757 appears to have been the occasion for a rather massive reorientation of royal ecclesiastical policy in a parlementary direction. A religious community of women in Paris called the Hospitalières du faubourg Saint-Jacques, from whom Christophe de Beaumont had been withholding the sacraments and the right to elect a new superior, finally obtained both in 1758. The new ministry accomplished this by allowing the parlement to bypass the archbishop of Paris and go to the newly elevated and accommodating archbishop of Lyons, Melvin de Montazet, Beaumont's superior as primate of the Gauls.[194] As for the indomitable Christophe de Beaumont—whose conscience, observed the future cardinal de Bernis, "was a dim lamp that enlightened none but himself"—the king exiled him to La Roque in Périgord on January 4, 1758.[195] That was the best that could be done, because Beaumont would not resign his see. Although that might not have satisfied Damiens, he could only have approved of the forced resignation of some of Beaumont's like-minded, sacrament-refusing colleagues, especially Poncet de La Rivière at Troyes and Montmorency de Laval at Orléans. In the latter diocese the religious communities of Saint-Charles and Saint-Loup began receiving the sacraments after twenty years of de facto excommunication.[196] At the same time, the parlement succeeded in changing the corporate procedure by which the Orléans cathedral canons had administered the sacraments to each other, which had resulted in their colleague Cougniou's death without them on October 13, 1754. The annual service on this date, ordered by the parlement for the repose of his soul, actually took place in 1757, and the curé who conducted it in the once interdicted church of Saint-Pierre-Lentin was none other than the abbé Ducamel, exiled to Angers by royal lettre de cachet before the crisis of December 1756.[197]

Some very old scores were settled as well. By a declaration dated March 15, 1758, Louis XV revoked his council's arrêt of November 20, 1751, and restored the administration of the Paris Hôpital général to its state anterior to 1749.[198] On April 21, 1758, the parlement ceremoniously condemned a two-volume book published in 1755 entitled *La Réalité du projet de Bourg-fontaine, demontrée par l'éxécution*, for renewing a seventeenth-century "fable" about the original Jansenists and their consciously laid plans for the destruction of Catholicism in France. The importance of the arrêt far outstripped the object of its indignation, for it assured to all the world that in the estimation of the parlement the "great" Arnauld, Jansenius, and Saint-Cyran were "above all suspicion," "equally estimable by their piety, their light, and their attachment to religion."[199] What held for the forebears clearly held for their spiritual descendents as well.

But it is under the microscope of the Parisian parish that the evolution—or devolution—of royal policy can be perceived with greatest clarity. Take, for example, the parish of Saint-Médard, where from his tomb in the church cemetery at the foot of the rue Mouffetard the appellant deacon, François de Pâris, had produced the famous miracles and convulsions of the late 1720s and early 1730s. The king had closed the cemetery, as is well known, but to prevent the occurrence of any and all devotions and miracles related to the *diacre* Pâris, the government had further closed the church itself on May 1 and October 4 of every year, the dates of the diacre's death and the feast of his namesake, Saint Francis, respectively, when devotees of the local cult tended to congregate in and around the church. Those who persisted in coming to the church on these days were carefully noted by the police at the yearly behest of the archbishop of Paris.[200] Indeed, so hostile was Christophe de Beaumont to the memory and continuing cult of the diacre Pâris that he caused a small well located in the house where the diacre had lived to be filled in, in order to prevent local devotees from drawing the miraculous water; and his personally designated principal occupants of the building assiduously prevented, on his orders, any soil in its vicinity from being carted away.[201]

All this began to change after the Declaration of Silence of September 2, 1754. Already in 1755 the parish's churchwardens approached the parlement's first president and attorney general with a request for authorization to open Saint-Médard's doors on October 4. Though unenthusiastic about the diacre Pâris and his miracles, these magistrates admitted the request in consequence of the Declaration of Silence. Besides, nobody seemed able to find copies of the royal order in virtue of which the doors had been locked in the first place. To open the church doors was one thing, however; to allow mass to be said was quite another, and on the latter point the parish curé and his unfortunately named sacristan, Crevecoeur, proved recalcitrant. In 1755, 1756, and again in 1757 the sacristan regularly disappeared from the parish on the eve of both May 1 and October 4, taking the keys to the sacristy with him. The doors of the church were indeed open, but the sacristry remained locked and mass was not celebrated. The churchwardens seemed powerless to alter this state of affairs.[202]

The situation further evolved after the definitive parlementary triumph of September 1757. Sometime after this date the churchwardens somehow induced the sacristan to resign and appointed his more cooperative assistant to act temporarily in his place. Thus armed, they again approached the parlement of Paris on the subject, this time in the autumn of 1758, and through the good offices of Henri de Revol, one of the magisterial stalwarts of the parlement's parti janséniste, obtained the support of the *parquet*.[203] October 4 inexorably arrived, and at 5:00 A.M. the curé duly said mass. But when priests notoriously sympathetic to the diacre Pâris and his works arrived to say mass from other parishes, the cooperative sacristan found that the curé had taken the precaution of locking the armoires and drawers within the sacristry. So a locksmith had to be fetched, and near scuffles ensued between the curé and some of these priests, who celebrated mass all the same.[204] Happily, things transpired somewhat more smoothly in 1759—"with the greatest tranquility," according to the solicitor general Joly de Fleury—but by that date even Christophe de Beaumont was cooperating with the temporal authorities, although without zeal.[205] By 1759, in sum, the diacre Pâris' memory had in some sense been rehabilitated; devotees could at least go to the church of Saint-Médard on the feast of Saint Francis and solicit his intercession.

The parish of Saint-Nicolas-des-Champs presents a somewhat different, but equally instructive, example. In April of 1758 the curé of Saint-Nicolas-des-Champs—and one of Christophe de Beaumont's *grands vicaires*—one Jacques de L'Ecluse, refused to administer the viaticum or extreme unction to a moribund appellant priest residing in the parish, though he had received a summons to do so. The freshly triumphant parlement of Paris was uninclined to ignore this affront to its authority and, in its inimitably roundabout fashion, ordered L'Ecluse to administer the sacraments. L'Ecluse promptly disappeared, furniture and all, whereupon the parlement proceeded in similar fashion vis-à-vis the first curate, the third curate, and the porte-Dieu, who likewise took flight. Meanwhile the sick priest's nephew, who was fortunately a priest, came to the rescue by administering the sacraments to his dying uncle.[206] At about the same time, in June 1758, one of the parish's *vicaires en semaine*, the abbé Bonnet, refused to administer the last sacraments to a woman who failed to produce a billet de confession or name her confessor. When the parlement proceeded against Bonnet, he too disappeared from the parish.[207] On January 17, 1759, the parlement completed its contumacious procedures against these priests and banished all five from the realm for life.[208] To make the story complete, the parish's second curate, who had been carrying on as best he could in the absence of his colleagues, committed the indiscretion of refusing the viaticum and extreme unction to yet another appellant priest living in the parish in November 1759. The earlier appellant's nephew again came through, but not before the Châtelet had ordered the arrest of the second curate, who joined his colleagues in the martyrdom of exile.[209]

Having deprived the parish of its chief clergy, the parlement assured the continuation of divine services by appointing an officiating priest from among the remaining clergy. But it goes without saying that it was not really the priest, but rather the parlement, that thereafter ran the affairs of the parish, at least indirectly. This it did through the agency of the parish churchwardens among whom Clément de Feillet, perhaps the unofficial chief of the parlement's parti janséniste at this time, numbered some good friends. With parlementary backing, the churchwardens seized the control formerly exercised by the curé over parish poor relief and, moreover, ran it according to new principles, which effectively excluded "those addicted to wine or to debauchery, the lazy by profession, the swearers, and generally all those of bad life and morals."[210] Before long, the parish poor were openly regretting their curé.[211] A similar sort of conflict developed over the parish *écoles de charité*, which the churchwardens now also controlled. The former curé had obliged the parish poor by running them as glorified day-care centers, but the schools' sober new directors, after toying with the idea of eliminating these frivolous institutions altogether, elected to take them seriously and afflicted them with more than a thousand livres worth of mainly Jansenist catechisms and devotional books, each stamped with an extract of the appropriate parlementary arrêt.[212] In 1767, finally, the churchwardens humbly requested the parlement to provide them with a new curé; the parlement in turn magnanimously referred them to the patron of their parish, the prior of Saint-Martin-des-Champs. It was probably no accident, though, that the new curé turned out to be Jean-Etienne Parent, from an unimpeachably robe family, who thereafter consulted with the parlement at every turn.[213]

The parlement's power over the Parisian parishes did not diminish for becoming less formal and strictly judicial over time. The parlement had already cleared the appellant-filled parish of Saint-Sévérin of most of its beneficed clergy by 1756 when the new *desservant*, the abbé Bilhere, committed the indiscretion of refusing to administer the last sacraments to one Vale, an appellant and former professor of rhetoric, in 1769. Vale eventually obtained the viaticum and extreme unction from an appellant priest also resident in the parish, while the abbé Bilhere, for his part, received from Damiens' old neighbor Rolland de Challerange, one of the parish's honorary churchwardens, the advice "to retire and not reappear in the parish in order to avoid the troubles that were on the point of breaking out"—in effect, to get out of town. Bilhere promptly submitted his resignation to Christophe de Beaumont.[214] During the same year in the parish of Saint-Sulpice the curé was inclined to refuse the sacraments to the prince de Beaufremont because the prince's confessor, the *archidiacre* Tandeau, did not have the requisite powers. After a friendly chat with the parlement's first president the curé decided to administer, and the archbishop of Paris, who wanted to "get the said abbé out of view," was advised by the canon lawyers Claude Mey and Jean-Jacques Piales that he had best not try to do so.[215] It is somewhat surprising to note in passing that the archbishop could not find canon lawyers more sympathetic to his cause than these two notorious Jansenists.

Examples of this sort could be multiplied exponentially, but the point, I trust, is sufficiently clear. From 1757 until the Maupeou coup, there was little room for doubt about who was the ultimate ecclesiastical authority in the land. More than thirty years before the Civil Constitution of the Clergy ended the Gallican church's independence in France, the parlement of Paris was already running the parishes of Paris. Damiens himself could hardly have wished for more.

Christianization and Secularization

SPEAKING FOR the general assembly of the clergy in 1755, Lefranc de Pompignan, bishop of Le Puy, was surely correct in pointing out that the sacraments, "instituted by the entirely free grace of the Redeemer, do not belong to society" and that "citizens have no right to them by virtue of their birth." The language of "right" and "citizen," he sensitively observed, were wholly inappropriate to the sacraments.[216] But instead of logically concluding that the church itself ought therefore to be free by being separate from the state and its law, he chose only to insist in traditional fashion upon the church's freedom of action within the confines of the Christian empire and unjustly to downplay the reputational damage done to people in their capacities as citizens of such a state as a result of unjust public refusals of sacraments. Though he was later to inveigh against the "shameful slavery" of the "ecclesiastical ministry to the secular power," Pompignan did so mainly to the purpose of exalting monarchical power at the expense of the parlement.[217]

Similarly, considering especially their ecclesiology, the appellants and their allies stood on defensible ground when they insisted upon the unjust and arbitrary character of the refusal of sacraments in question. But far from concluding that the conciliar church they espoused might more attentively hearken to their appeal if it were free and separate from a state that in the persons of Richelieu, Mazarin, and Louis XIV had both anticipated and outdone the church in its condemnation of Jansenism, they chose instead to curry this state's favor by rationalizing the extension of its power in so spiritual a domain as the administration of the sacraments.

Both parties to the refusal of sacraments controversy therefore ironically contributed to the secularization of the realm in the very act of implementing their competitive visions of "Christendom." At their noblest, Christophe de Beaumont and his cohorts aspired to purify the sacraments by ridding the realm of unworthy or "heretical" communicants. In acting upon this principle, however, they unwittingly revealed the possibility of a citizenship no longer dependent upon the reception of the sacraments and, by implication, membership in the church. Less than forty years later the French Revolution would experiment with a completely lay state to which one's private confessional affiliations and loyalties were nothing to the point. At their best, again, and as we shall more clearly see in the following chapter, the appellants and their magisterial allies intended further to "Christianize" society by restoring a sort of pre-Gregorian state of affairs in which a pious but temporal head of Christendom on the model of Charlemagne would discipline schismatically inclined bishops while presiding over the purified and interiorized faith of his lay subjects. But by making the sacraments the object of profane litigation and justifying state intervention in their administration, they too unwittingly secularized the realm in the senses of temporalizing the meaning of the sacraments themselves and extending state power at the expense of the church within a cultural context very different from that obtaining in Charlemagne's day.[218] For after all was said and done, the day was long gone when a Charlemagne could consider himself as much the head of the church as that of the state and could indifferently employ counts and bishops as his *missi dominici* who performed both pastoral and judicial functions.[219] On the contrary, everything about the refusal of sacraments controversy—the distinction between *for extérieur* and *for intérieur*, the conflicting considerations of the holiness of the sacraments and one's reputation as a citizen—bespeaks the growing tension between the sacred and the secular, the church and civil society, thereby tending to sunder what the traditional concept of Christendom had barely distinguished.

Louis XV could not successfully reincarnate Charlemagne either. Nowhere, indeed, were the conflicts in question more poignantly embodied than in the person of the king himself, or more vividly illustrated than in the institution of the monarchy. Confronted with sharply contradictory visions of what it meant to be "the most Christian king" and between either of these models on the one hand and his obligations as purely temporal sovereign on the other, the king personally succumbed to a nagging conscience, schizophrenic "secrets," and a chronic indecision that anticipated his more unfortunate successor's literal flight from an analogous though more sharply posed dilemma in 1791. Surrounded by these incompatible alternatives, the monarchy as an institution succumbed to a process of desacralization to which all parties to the struggle made direct if unwitting contributions. The parti dévôt contributed by loudly proclaiming what the king and his judges could not do as purely *lay* persons; the parti janséniste contributed by insisting upon what the king—meaning his judges—could indeed do as a purely *lay* sovereign; and the monarchy itself made a contribution by its less than dazzling performance in the controversy as a whole. The quest for the decisive moment in the desacralization of the monarchy might well concentrate on the monarchy's lackluster attempts to avert the desacralization or at least politicalization of the sacraments themselves.

Desacralization seems not too strong a word in the light of such evidence as the decline in the number of communicants in Parisian parishes reported by the marquis d'Argenson, for the refusal of sacraments controversy was among other things a most unholy kind of tug of war between church and state, with the sacraments serving as rope. The severely frayed but unbroken sacramental bond yielded to the superior power of the state in parlementary form, presumably to Damiens' posthumous satisfaction. This unedifying contest therefore contributed not only to the process of secularization in France but also to what the French call "dechristianization," at least in the sense of a discontinuation of the outward practices of Catholicism if not the outright rejection of Christian dogma however construed.[220] The casualties of this reaction lay drooped over the rungs of the social and intellectual ladder, from a Conti or a Voltaire at the top to a Damiens near the bottom, and to that extent the Damiens sans religion—if not sans culotte—was not only the posthumous victor in the affaires du temps but among their many victims as well.

CHAPTER 4

Damiens' Masters as Theorists:

Constitutional Thought from 1750 to 1770

The Classical Synthesis

IN THE COURSE OF a homily delivered in advance of a solemn mass celebrating the king's recovery, Jean-Etienne de Caulet, the bishop of Grenoble, seized the occasion to expound upon the nature of "absolute government" that "made for the happiness of people." Distinguishing, in the spirit of Bossuet, between "arbitrary" and absolute government, the bishop of Grenoble defined the latter in terms of a prince who "owed an account to no one for what he ordained" and whose judgments, if abusive, had no other remedy than in "the authority itself that resides in his person." The subjects, in such a government, owed their prince "truth" as well as "obedience," but whereas the second obligation had to be "continual, without any interruption, and without exception as to time or persons," the first was limited to "certain cases and certain persons." This "very remarkable difference" moreover distinguished the two, that whereas a "merited distrust of one's own ideas" was always in order so far as the truth was concerned, no mistake was ever to be feared where obedience was involved. "Any subject who obeys his Sovereign is sure to have truth on his side."[1]

The parlementary-Jansenist press was probably not wholly mistaken in seeing in the bishop's remarks a covert condemnation of parlementary rhetoric and behavior, a part of an orchestrated attempt by "bishops and Jesuits" to "broadcast in every quarter that the attack on the person of the king was the effect produced by the remonstrances of the parlement, in heating people's heads with the subjects of the despotism of the government, the excessive taxes, and the disorders of the state."[2] Who, after all, was forever pretending to bring the "truth" to the foot of the throne and enlighten his majesty's "religion?" Who, if not the parlement had construed disobedience to the king's orders as a kind of obedience superior to blind adherence to royal whim and caprice. The bishop of Grenoble's insinuations found an echo, a month later, in the archbishop of Paris' belated episcopal mandamus of March 1, 1757. Inviting his parishioners to imagine "without prejudice" a punishment proportionate to the many sins committed by the French in recent years, the archbishop enjoined them to consider "in particular whether, since the weakening of the faith among us, there has not crept into our minds and into our books a multitude of principles that lead to disobedience, even to rebellion against the sovereign and his laws."[3] The application of these meditations to the parlement's rejection of the king's declarations of December 10 and the mass resignations that followed seemed not an uninvited transition.

The Jansenist press was not the sort to take such innuendos lying down. As if to confirm them, and despite its habitual reverence for the authority of Bossuet, the Jansenist weekly *Nouvelles ecclésiastiques* indeed censored the bishop of Grenoble's definition of monarchical or absolute government as excessively authoritarian. "Taken literally," objected the gazetteer, the bishop's definition "would establish the most complete and absolute despotism," as "in Turkey." But far from accepting the bishop's exhortations to unqualified submission to the monarchy at face value, the Jansenist weekly rather wondered aloud whether the bishop were willing to practice what he preached when it came to the Declaration of Silence concerning the bull *Unigenitus* and the refusal of sacraments.[4] Invoking a different Bossuet, the Bossuet who in 1682 had championed the principle that the temporal power owed no accounting to any ecclesiastical authority, an anonymous Jansenist rejoinder to the archbishop of Paris' mandamus of March 1 made the same point. Were not the archbishop's preachments against principles that had led to disobedience and rebellion a "public confession of his own errors?" Where were such principles more brazenly expressed "than in his different responses to the parlement—that is to say the king, since the parlement only exercises the authority of the king?" This pamphleteer invited his readers to pay particular attention to the mandamus' eccentric translation of Saint Paul's famous injunction to obey secular authorities in Romans 13:1: "Non est enim potestas nisi a Deo; quae autem sunt, a Deo ordinatae sunt." Whereas the Vulgate's Latin clearly conveyed the message that every power on earth was ordained by God, the archbishop's French translation had only "legitimate power as coming from God." The pamphleteer then challenged the archbishop and his like-minded episcopal colleagues to elucidate "the difference they see between legitimate authority and the authority of the king."[5]

Despite the fact that the distinction in question was also Bossuet's, at least one bishop, the very Gallican and almost Jansenist François de Fitz-James of Soissons, most emphatically denied its existence, and he seized the occasion of the Damiens affair to say so. Describing as "monstrous" and "diabolical" a doctrine that accorded the church the power to abrogate the tie of obedience binding subjects to sovereign—to distinguish, in effect, between legitimate and illegitimate secular authority—this bishop had no doubt that even heretical princes were entitled to his Catholic subjects' unqualified fidelity. "It is from God immediately that the civil authority holds its power," he proclaimed, setting the Pauline record straight; "to revolt against her [the civil authority] is to revolt against God himself, as Saint Paul has taught us." Not only was this the teaching of Saint Paul but also "the salutary doctrine that the church of France in particular has always gloried in professing, and which she has drawn from the pure sources of holy scripture and the tradition." The bishop's tacit appeal here to Bossuet and the famous Gallican articles of 1682, however, called to mind not just the first of them, which indeed proclaimed monarchical power free from accountability to the church, but also the others that Bossuet had likewise championed on that occasion, which elevated church councils above the pope. Was it perhaps the contrary doctrine of papal infallibility that Fitz-

James had in mind when he extended his condemnation of regicide to other "principles, from which the most frightening consequences follow rather naturally?"[6]

To call attention to the doctrine of regicide was also to point the finger at the Jesuit order, the traditional purveyors of this doctrine as well as partisans of the papacy's most extreme claims to temporal authority and spiritual supremacy. And what Fitz-James suggested obliquely, others, as we have noted, said very directly. The anonymous author of the *Lettre d'un patriote*, for one, was confident that the evidence would demonstrate that "the authors of [Damiens'] attack were the greatest enemies of the parlement and its remonstrances—the Jesuits themselves and those engaged in their interests."[7] But in a manner that would have horrified Bossuet and perhaps even Fitz-James, this polemicist expanded the category of those responsible to include ecclesiastics in general. The "true source" of France's troubles was not just the Jesuits or the papacy but "the spirit of domination and independence of the bishops and of ecclesiastics, that is to say, those who by virtue of their estate ought to be giving us an example of contrary virtues."[8]

Thus did the devout and Gallican-Jansenist parties in France attempt to unload the Damiens affair onto each other's doorsteps. Yet the whole exchange illustrates much more than that; it also throws into sharp relief the disintegration and polarized rearrangement, by the mid-eighteenth century, of the elements that once constituted the classical consensus in political and ecclesiastical conceptions, symbolized above all by the authority of Bishop Bossuet. The conflicting Bossuets, in this *dialogue des sourds*, are symptomatic of the disaggregation of a conceptual constellation that he among others in his generation had brought together and illuminated.

Take, for example, the conception of the monarchy. For Bossuet, to be sure, monarchs were "ministers of God and his lieutenants on earth" to whose persons adhered he knew not "what of the divine" and whose authority was both "sacred" and "absolute."[9] Since they were like gods and accounted to God alone, no earthly remedy existed against an abuse of their authority except that authority itself, no form of resistance available except that of "prayers and respectful remonstrances."[10] Yet, less noticeably surrounding such glistening superlatives, how many dikes did not Bossuet erect to prevent the "running waters" of monarchical power from bursting forth in an undisciplined flow.[11] Not only must "absolute government," which Bossuet indeed distinguished from "arbitrary government," be reasonable, in accordance with divine and natural law, and therefore respectful of liberty and property but it ultimately strains in vain against certain "fundamental laws that cannot be changed," even against particular rights accorded by monarchical predecessors and "laudable customs" that "stand in the place of laws."[12]

Such a synthesis of potentially inimical elements should not be thought unique to churchmen of the day, however; a glance at the political thought of one of Bossuet's younger and magisterial contemporaries, the chancellor Henri-François d'Aguesseau, demonstrates otherwise. For the parlementary magistrate, to be sure, the emphasis predictably falls on what the monarch cannot or should not do, such as abrogate the parlement's right to remonstrate. To abolish this right would be "in some manner to separate reason from authority" and to court the risk of "degrading the monarchy into a tyranny, odious name that is often given arbitrary and despotic power. . . ."[13] Yet none of this prevented d'Aguesseau from recognizing in language reminiscent of Bossuet's that the French government was "purely monarchical, and that the kings exercise an absolute dominion, which resides in their persons, for which they render account to God alone." Any limitations on monarchical power were ultimately self-imposed, and when push came to shove, the king "remained always the master not to observe them" (*y avoir égard*).[14]

In the conception of the church, the same basic unity subsisted beneath superficial diversity. Both Bossuet and d'Aguesseau staunchly held to the ultimate superiority of the whole Catholic church over the bishop of Rome and to the right of the Gallican church in particular to judge doctrine concurrently with Rome, Bossuet of course playing a conspicuous role in the celebrated assembly that put the Gallican church on record in favor of these "liberties."[15] Both, too, understood the governance of the conciliar church in terms of an episcopal aristocracy, d'Aguesseau even explicitly distancing himself from the rather more democratic emphases in the works of the sixteenth-century Sorbonne conciliarists Jacques Almain and Edmond Richer.[16] Beyond this point, the inevitable differences of emphasis crop up. The churchman Bossuet miraculously contrived to compliment the papacy in the very act of circumscribing its power—"even the ocean in all its plenitude has its limits"—while the magistrate d'Aguesseau naturally maintained an attitude of wary circumspection toward that "foreign power always attentive to extending the boundaries of its power and encroaching upon our liberties."[17] Nonetheless, even he retained a "profound veneration" for "the most august although not the unique judge of our faith."[18]

A similar pattern prevailed, finally, in Bossuet's and d'Aguesseau's conceptions of sacerdotal-imperial relations. What Bossuet most emphasized, among the many limitations to monarchical power he opposed, were the specifically ecclesiastical ones. As the "Lord's annointed" and "vice-regent" over temporal affairs, the king's power indeed "lays down the law, and leads the way as sovereign. Yet in ecclesiastical affairs it only serves and assists." In matters "not only of faith but of ecclesiastical discipline the decision belongs to the church while to the prince belongs the protection, defense, and the execution of the canons and ecclesiastical regulations."[19] Yet this emphasis did not inhibit Bossuet from playing a leading if somewhat exaggerated role in the general assembly that conversely proclaimed the independence of temporal authority from any ecclesiastical—specifically papal—accountability.[20]

With d'Aguesseau again the emphasis is different, falling instead on the church's subordination to monarchical authority. Much more than "the Lord's annointed" or "the eldest son of the church," titles that pointed to the king as member of the church and therefore subject to its discipline, d'Aguesseau preferred "protector of the church" and "exterior bishop," which connoted a much more enterprising role in church affairs.[21] The king was to "add that which is lacking in the authority of the church" and "to do for God everything that can only be done by a king," even in the face of opposition by the clergy, one suspects, if matters came to that.[22] On the other hand, churchmen who exercised temporal judicial authority in "mixed matters" did so only by way of the king's revokable concession, while they themselves remained entirely subject to temporal authority, because the "church was in the state, not the state in the church."[23] Yet the same d'Aguesseau could stubbornly defend the church's spiritual independence, both against the king, as when he braved Louis XIV's wrath by defending some recalcitrant bishops' right not to accept *Unigenitus* in their dioceses, and against his beloved parlements, as when he scolded the parlement of Bordeaux in 1731 for wishing to intervene in a case of the refusal of sacraments in connection with this same bull.[24] "If there are any orders to be given in a matter so spiritual and important," he wrote to the parlement on that occasion, "it is from the bishop alone that they should be solicited."[25]

The classical balance of potentially antithetical elements, the conceptual counterpart of the cardinal de Fleury's balancing act in sacerdotal-imperial relations until 1750, combined constitutional limitations with absolute monarchy, ecclesiastical conciliarism with veneration for the papacy, and an insistence upon the state's independence of ecclesiastical supervision with a recognition of the church's spiritual integrity. The continued survival of this balance was precariously dependent upon an unclassical fuzziness in jurisdictional and constitutional boundaries, however, and on a jarringly asymmetrical coupling of its political and ecclesiastical conceptions. On the one hand, it made a most un-Cartesian virtue of obscurity and imprecision in such questions as where the authority of the prince stopped and the rights of his subjects began, or where the domain of the temporal retired and that of the spiritual took over. Speaking of the latter, d'Aguesseau repeatedly warned of "many things that one must never try to define too exactly between two powers jealous of each other; peace is preferable to a useless discussion of their rights, which infallibly becomes an occasion for war."[26] On the other hand, the Gallican Declaration of 1682, another of the great legislative tapestries of Louis XIV's late reign, unequally yoked an absolute conception of the monarchy to a conciliar or aristocratic conception of the church;

and d'Aguesseau again made the asymmetrical character of this linkage a matter of high principle by strenuously opposing any attempt to conceive of the government of the church in terms analogous to a monarchy.[27] For the chancellor, the pope was most emphatically not the "monarch" of the church but rather its "chief" and in that capacity its "first although not only bishop."[28]

A half-century of *Unigenitus*-related controversies served to correct and dispel this conceptual imbalance and obscurity. In the process, however, the unstable classical compound of political and ecclesiastical conceptions came undone, collapsing into two antithetical combinations of elements opposing constitutionalism against absolutism, Gallican conciliarism against not only the papacy but paradoxically against much of the Gallican episcopacy itself, and embroiling the church more deeply than ever with the state. The newer compounds, moreover, included some elements unknown to the old: the appeal to the "nation," for example, in constitutional discourse, an emphasis on the lower clergy and even the laity (the *congregatio fidelium*) in ecclesiastical discourse, and the presence of ultramontanism in the opposing conception of the church. In the resulting combinations, a Gallican-Jansenist side sponsored a monarchy controlled by the parlement and ultimately by the nation exercising almost complete control over a democratically constituted and participatory church, while the "devout" side posited a veritably absolute monarch in relation to his lay subjects, encountering his equal only in relation to a similarly authoritarian and monarchically structured church. These divisions, already clearly illuminated by the controversy surrounding the Damiens affair, moreover unmistakably prefigure the two France's of the Revolution and the early nineteenth century: nation and constitution on the one side, throne and altar on the other.

The Participatory Church

IF ANY LOGIC presided over this process of conceptual disintegration and recrystallization, it was that of persecution. Condemned by the papacy, Jansenism turned conciliarist and sought refuge beneath the Gallican conciliarism of the parlement of Paris, which viewed with suspicion the condemnation of Frenchmen in Rome. As early as 1717 thousands of French clerics had appealed the bull *Unigenitus* to an ecumenical council.[29] Persecuted by the monarchy, Jansenists then embraced parlementary constitutionalism; they eventually gave it an antimonarchical coherence it had hitherto lacked. Persecuted by an ever larger proportion of the Gallican episcopacy, which the monarchy inexorably purged of opponents of *Unigenitus*, Jansenism reached beyond the purely episcopal conciliarism of Bossuet and 1682 to the more democratic lower clerical and lay conciliarism of the Paris school and the late Middle Ages. They became champions of the rights of the lower clergy and even laymen to a share in the governance of the church.[30] And when the monarchical and ecclesiastical establishments remained hostile and only the parlements continued to defend them, Jansenists adopted and willingly expanded upon the parlement's brand of Gallicanism, which subjected the church and its functions to close supervision and even control by the state, at least in parlementary form. Jansenists became champions of secularization in spite of themselves. By this stage, however, the movement was by no means exclusively Jansenist; combining parlementary constitutionalism, Gallicanism, and Jansenism, it had come to include all those who by reason of any of these considerations opposed the monarchical and ecclesiastical establishments.

By virtue of their role as persecutors, Jansenism's French enemies within the Jesuit order and the episcopacy had to rely heavily on the authority of Rome and the monarchical "secular sword." For this reason, too, they tended from the outset to exalt these authorities, their posture only stiffening in this regard when in the 1750s the persecutors became persecuted in their turn. Pursued by the parlements, episcopal zealots exalted the monarchy, divesting it of whatever constitutional restraints their predecessors had acknowledged. They became more royalist than the king. Increasingly beset by a brand of Gallicanism they could not accept, they more than ever glorified the authority of the papacy within the church, going so far as to renege on the declaration of 1682. A part of the episcopacy became more pontifical than the pope, at least Pope Benedict XIV. Harassed by constant secular infringements upon their sacrosanct jurisdiction, they tempered their royalism by stridently insisting upon the church's sovereignty and spiritual independence, to the point of de facto disobedience and the theoretical justification of ecclesiastical interference in temporal affairs. In this as well, they turned their backs on 1682.

This process was not accomplished in a day. On the clerical or "devout" side, d'Aguesseau was already complaining at the turn of the century about "the prodigious tendency of certain Frenchmen to forget the engagements of their birth and the interests of their nation, to become the zealous partisans and blind instruments of a power that our fathers never acknowledged in the popes."[31] On the other side, Jansenism and Gallicanism had already effected a tentative union before the coming of *Unigenitus*; expressions of lay or Richerist conciliarism were already among the propositions from Quesnel's book condemned by that bull; and in 1732 Jansenists connived at the publication of the *Judicium Francorum*, a pamphlet modeled upon one written during the Fronde, which articulated the parlement's most extravagant constitutional claims until that date.[32] Lest too much be ascribed to the vacillatory character of Louis XV, we should note that his steadier predecessor was already having trouble toward the setting of his reign in keeping ultramontanist episcopacy and Gallican parlement from each other's throats, and was seemingly not altogether of tranquil conscience in the matter himself.[33]

Something decisive nonetheless marks the century's midpoint, dramatized by the successive disappearances from the scene of the cardinal de Fleury and the chancellor d'Aguesseau, by the controller general Machault's unsuccessful attempt to impose the vingtième tax on the clergy, and the onset in deadly earnest of the refusal of sacraments controversy. By tugging in opposite directions upon the fabric of church and state, the latter especially tended to unravel the close texture of conceptions hitherto governing thought about these entities.

The 1750s are not unimportant for even the Jansenist-Gallican view of the church, although the basic lineaments of this conception existed long before this decade. From the very outset Jansenists' exaltation of episcopal dignity at the expense of the religious orders—in particular, the Jesuits—tended to draw them into the orbit of episcopal Gallicanism, an attraction that papal condemnation only augmented.[34] Yet by 1682 Jansenism's adherence to Gallicanism was so tenuous that the episcopacy's four Jansenist bishops sided with the papacy against Louis XIV in the very (*régale*) controversy that culminated in the meeting of the clergy's extraordinary assembly and its declaration of Gallican liberties.[35] But in the long run the government's systematic purge of the episcopacy and the resultant episcopal persecution of Jansenism inexorably drove this movement beyond purely episcopal Gallicanism toward a more radical, democratic sort of conciliarism that vested the church's "keys," or ultimate sacerdotal authority, with the *whole* church or *congregatio fidelium*, not bishops with the pope alone.

The sources of this conciliarism went back immediately to Edmond Richer, syndic of the Sorbonne from 1608 to 1612, and ultimately to the philosophers John Major and Jacques Almain of the early sixteenth-century Sorbonne, who had laid down the principle that every community whether political or ecclesiastical retained possession of its sovereignty and only delegated its exercise to its chiefs.[36] Initially restricted in its practical application to parish priests, whom Richer regarded as successors to the seventy-two disciples commissioned by Christ (and therefore equal, in point of sacerdotal dignity, to the bishops), the principle was gradually extended, by the Jansenists Pasquier Quesnel, Vivien de La Borde and Nicolas Le Gros, to include a measure of active participation by even laymen in the formulation of excommunications. This *Richérisme*, as it is sometimes called, achieved its most audacious and systematic expression in the work of the Nantese curé Nicolas Travers, whose *Pouvoirs légitimes du second ordre dans l'administration des sacrements et le gouvernement de l'église* (1744) obliterated all but the most honorific distinctions between the clergy's first and second orders.[37]

If it failed to elicit any strikingly original contribution to this corpus, the refusal of sacraments crisis at least provoked some eloquent restatements of a sort to diffuse its message to an ever wider public. Two of these statements stand out from the rest: Le Paige's *Lettres pacifiques au sujet des contestations présentes* (1752), ostensibly written for the instruction of Louis XV's specially appointed commission; and the abbé Claude Mey's and Gabriel-Nicolas Maultrot's monumental *Apologie de tous les jugements rendus par les tribunaux séculiers en France contre le schisme* (1752).[38] The latter was in fact more than an *ex post facto* justification or apology for what the parlements had done in the refusal of sacraments controversy; it also visibly influenced the parlement's own justification of its conduct as expressed in its remonstrances of April 9, 1753.[39]

Appalled at the tendency toward "true tyranny" and a "government fully despotic" on the part of the Gallican episcopacy, which increasingly resorted to "ways of violence and fiat [*autorité*]" to force submission to *Unigenitus*, Le Paige sought guidance and consolation in the true "spirit of the church in these different sorts of contestations," a spirit of "peace and equity" or that of a "tender mother for her children."[40] This spirit he found displayed most clearly in the course of the doctrinal disputes of the first several centuries, those of the church's greatest purity. Or were they really doctrinal quarrels after all? Many, upon closer examination, turned out to have been contestations not so much about the substance of the faith as about "chimeras" and "little bagatelles," many of them bearing a suspicious resemblance to the question of what relation obtained between *Unigenitus*' twenty-two qualifications and any one of the propositions it condemned.[41] What did honor to the early church's record was of course not the existence of such controversies—that much it had in common with the Gallican church in the eighteenth century—as in her way of resolving them: not by means of censures, anathemas, the refusal of sacraments, and mutual excommunications, but by means of a "charitable condescendence" and even "tolerance," which, concerning itself uniquely with clarification of dogma, maintained a benign neglect of everything else.[42] "In a word, the dogmas of the faith once assured, the peace has always been deemed by the [church] as meriting priority over all the rest."[43] It was an elegant plea for what appellants and opponents of *Unigenitus* had long been asking of the papacy: namely, a positive and explanatory body of doctrine that, if they could subscribe to it, would nullify all the previous decisions against them.[44]

So loose, however, was Le Paige's definition of chimerical disputes, so hard his condemnation of "false zeal," and so all-embracing his advocacy of "toleration," that his *Lettres pacifiques* might have won the muffled plaudits of a Voltaire and most certainly gave pause to some of Le Paige's appellant comrades.[45] Was it the term "consubstantial" that the venerable council of Nicea had used to describe the relation between the first two persons of the Trinity but which for a time divided church fathers such as Athanasius and Jerome who accepted it from Eusebius and Cirille who did not? Once they discovered that they shared a belief in the divinity of the Son, their division over "consubstantial" was recognized as a "useless dispute over words," and the council of Alexandria permitted those who still opposed this term to omit it from their theological vocabulary.[46] Was it a question of Nestorianism, condemned by Saint Cirille and the council of Ephesus but seemingly defended for a time by John of Antioch and the Eastern bishops? As soon as they succeeded in signing the same positive profession of faith, "all the rest and the decision of the council concerning the anathemas" were forgotten as "vain questions of fact."[47] The church, moreover, had been tolerant where genuine heresies were involved, as in the case of Saint Cyprien's anticipation of Donatism, her rule having always been "to tolerate those who were in error until the decision of the general council."[48] Not even the most solemn conciliar decisions necessarily ended the church's patience and condescendence, for as Le Paige perversely observed, the Gallican church accepted the councils of Constance and Basle as ecumenical and with them the dogma of conciliar supremacy over the pope as decided, yet continued "to admit to public participation in the sacraments such notorious ultramontanists as the nuncio and other Italians" and to maintain peace and unity with Rome.[49]

Le Paige visibly strayed too far in his advocacy of tolerance and condemnation of excessive zeal to suit some of his Jansenist cohorts. One of his correspondents objected that he had put the appellants in a false and unfavorable light by comparing their situation to that of groups legitimately suspected of heresy in the past; another accused Le Paige of taking inadmissible liberties with the history of Saint Athanasius and the council of Nicea, whose "inviolable attachment to an expression so essential for distinguishing heretics is represented as a too ardent zeal. . . ."[50] Le Paige was sufficiently reproved by such critics to insert numerous footnotes and textual additions in the 1753 edition, which went out of their way to assure such critics that in the long run the church "can never abandon formulations consecrated to express her doctrine" and that "in suffering for a time of diversity of doctrine, . . . the church . . . never loses sight of . . . the reign and triumph of the truth."[51] Yet despite the qualms of his cohorts, Le Paige's ecclesiology was at basis authentically Jansenist, as indicated by his *Lettres*' offhanded observation that it was frequently "by the mouth of the smallest number, and often by that of the oppressed, that [the church] judged most sanely."[52] The practical Le Paige was painfully aware that however much the oppressed appellants might have "truth" on their side, they represented a small and still dwindling number within the ecclesiastical hierarchy and that they could benefit from whatever tolerance they could get.

The ecclesiology half-visibly undergirding Le Paige's *Lettres pacifiques* was almost simultaneously exposed to full view by Mey's and Maultrot's two-volume *Apologie de tous les jugements*, which began appearing in 1752. Taking their axe to the very root of the problem, namely, *Unigenitus* and its condemnation of Jansenism, the authors undercut the authority of this document by insisting that even if its form allowed one to regard it as a rule of faith or judgment in the matter of doctrine, which of course it did not, it could never be so regarded without the express consent of the entire church or "the applause of the entire corps." "From whatever authority therefore proceeds a judgment in the matter of doctrine," concluded the authors, meaning pope and church councils, "it can only become an unchangeable rule of our faith, when it is no longer doubtful that it is consecrated by the acceptance of the universal church, when no clouds remain to obscure her submission, when *all attentive persons* are in a position to recognize that she herself has spoken; that her witness is so public as not to be overlooked by anyone, and that its notoriety has attained such a degree of evidence, that obstination alone is capable of hiding it and impeding its evidential force." Any "cri publique" against a recent doctrinal judgment or even fresh doubts about an ancient one were sufficient to neutralize this force, without which the public refusal of sacraments amounted to "a tyrannical vexation" and a "visibly schismatic conduct." "The rule of our submission must not be uncertain," concluded the authors, quoting Bossuet.[53] Certainly it was not.

That took care of the bull *Unigenitus*—and much else besides. But Mey and Maultrot did not shrink from even the most drastic of their already surgical criterion's consequences. The authority of general councils? All depended on their ecumenicity, which, however, the whole church alone could ascertain because the councils' "power resides only in that they exercise the rights of the universal church, that they act in her name, that they represent her, and that she ratifies what they do."[54] Take away or so much as effectively challenge any of these conditions and the councils' decisions become problematical, as were in fact those of any number of councils "now regarded as truly ecumenical" but which "long sustained oppositions suspending the obligation to submit."[55] The decisions of particular councils or the pope? Much less reliable, these, than the decisions of general councils, and hence it was all the more important that the church's consent "take the form of a judgment rendered after an examination and a deliberation" and that it be "clear, constant, and notorious."[56] The power of individual ministers, say, to fulminate censures, to excommunicate? To do so legitimately, they "ought at least to presume the consent of their particular church," but in the last analysis, they should have the consent of the whole church. Not even the pope's anathemas if fulminated without the church's consent presented anything "veritably frightening," because "the power to excommunicate belonging firstly and principally to the entire society, the pope cannot employ any censures except in her name."[57]

These audacities presupposed a representational relationship between clergy and laity that Mey and Maultrot made bold to spell out. Explicitly appealing to "the doctors of Paris"—Jean Gerson, Jacques Almain, John Major, and Edmond Richer—the authors maintained that "although the [church's] keys have been *entrusted* to Saint Peter and the apostles, it is to the church that they were *given* in their persons because they were, so to speak, her deputies. The authority of the keys therefore belongs at once to the whole body and to its ministers, but in different senses: to the body as to the property, to the ministers as to the *usage* and *exercise*." This did not mean, in the authors' estimation, that the ministers actually received their power from the body of the faithful or the "choice of the people"; this power, on the contrary, they received directly from Jesus Christ.[58] In their own minds this somewhat metaphysical proviso sufficiently distinguished their position from that of the "last heretics" whose "errors" they duly professed to detest. Their position nonetheless entailed that ministers only *exercised* a power that *belonged* to the whole church and that they were accountable in the manner of deputies to the church for the way they performed.[59] The authors did not hesitate to employ the analogy of a republic in expressing this relationship: "In republics the judgment of the magistrate constitutes the judgment of the society, because the people consent by those who are charged to govern them. It is the same," the authors boldly added, "with the church. The ecumenical councils possess an infallible authority because they sufficiently represent the universal church: these holy assemblies carry with them the consent of the corps."[60]

Despite frequent nostalgic appeals to the "happy centuries" of the "primitive church" when the laity participated actively in the exercise of ecclesiastical discipline, Mey and Maultrot do not seem to have been contemplating any such revolutionary reorganization of the church of their day.[61] Had they been given the opportunity, it is doubtful that at this stage they would have gone much beyond the rehabilitation of the curé in the governance of the diocese.[62] The role they assigned the laity in the curbing of the episcopacy's schismatic conduct was indirect, operating mainly through the channels of canon law accepted in France and regarded by them as embodying the will of the ecclesiastical collectivity. By forbidding the public refusal of sacraments for reasons of factual notoriety alone and discouraging impertinent questions about particular papal decisions, these canons and usages could "ensure the ministers who conformed [to them] of the public's well-wishes and approbation, because it rarely happens that those who have been convicted within the terms of the law are not regarded as veritably guilty."[63] If however the minister violated these usages, the aggrieved layman could take his case directly to the secular courts, whose interventions in so spiritual a domain the book was primarily at pains to uphold.[64]

The main effect of this line of argument was the gradual transformation of the bishops into "simple dispensers of the holy mysteries," where the least spontaneous deviation from the "holy canons"—and ultimately, the presumed will of their lay congregations—were so many examples of "despotism" and the "spirit of domination."[65] Mey's and Maultrot's *Apologie* itself led the way by invidiously comparing the ministers' "tyrannical" despotism and a spirit of domination, with the "charity and mildness" thought appropriate to the church; and the parlement's monumental remonstrances of April 9, 1753, more than followed suit with thirteen references to the bishops' "arbitrary domination" or "spirit of independence," plus a reference apiece to their "tyrannical domination," "arbitrary will" and aspirations to become "absolute masters."[66] The bishops were not to be "sovereign in [their] diocese," for their authority was "a ministry and not an empire, a ministry of rule, reason, tenderness, and charity" whose purpose was "to dispense the spiritual goods of which they are the depositories."[67] But to comb through these two treatises for expressions of this ilk is to create a distorted impression, because the whole staggering corpus of polemical literature of Jansenist-Gallican inspiration is peppered with such language from at least 1750 onwards. Its theoretical basis lay in the subjection of the bishops to French canon law conceived of as a sort of ecclesiastical common law representing the profound will of the Gallican if not the universal church.

Yet another polemical and popular manifestation of Gallican-Jansenism's theoretical laicism took the form of an appeal to the unlearned but right-minded layman over the heads of the ecclesiastical hierarchy and theological "experts." The commonest of these appeals was to "the public" in general or to the anonymous "every good Frenchman" or "any reasonable person" who, conspicuous especially in the pages of the *Nouvelles écclésiastiques*, patriotically detested the Jesuits, the ultramontanist bishops, and despotism in all its forms. Though still confident in 1762 in the capacity of any "man who reasons, and who is attentive" to detect the "league between the bishops and the Jesuits to effect the triumph of an anti-Christian morality within the church," the Jansenist press was by 1770 nervous that this same league was successfully inculcating an "ignorant faith among the laics" the better to exercise over them an "arbitrary domination."[68] But the anonymous denouncer of the despotism of the bishops remained confident that at least the women could never be seduced. "The very dullest of women would not sign a billet whose content she ignored," as the bishops were asking the faithful to do. Or put forty women in one room and forty bishops in another and ask each group what it thought about the proposition, "The fear of an unjust excommunication should not deter us from doing our duty," and the women would unanimously agree, while in the bishops' room one would "not even hear French."[69] But in the event even the women should succumb, there stood united against the forces of ultramontanism and Jesuitism a mixed but impregnable array of "men of quality," "damsels of consideration," "knights of the Order of Malta," along with other assorted "militaries," including even a "philosophical" variety, hard-working people with "only three minutes to spare," all manner of "patriots," "friends in the provinces," a "great number of the faithful," plus a cloud of magisterial and lawyerly witnesses.[70]

But Gallican-Jansenism's parochialism and laicism did not remain restricted to polemical purposes alone. It was in virtue of the principle of the fundamental equality between bishop and curé—in the event, the right of a priest to administer the sacrament of penitence anywhere without the bishop's express permission—that in the 1750s the parlement of Paris effected the administration of the sacraments by priests simply resident in the parish or by a curé from a neighboring parish in defiance of both the parish's absent ordinary and the diocesan archbishop.[71] It was in virtue of the same "republican" conception of the church that the parlements of France suppressed the Jesuit order in the 1760s.[72] And it was in virtue of Gallican-Jansenist lay and ecclesiastical republicanism that in 1790 the famous Civil Constitution of the Clergy subjected bishops to the counsel of their parish priests and both to election by their lay congregations.[73]

Long before that, however, as early as the 1750s, Gallican-Jansenist ecclesiology began to impinge upon and reshape the conception of the state.

National Sovereignty and Integral Absolutism

For the flow of political thought, the century's midpoint marks a more decisive transition. Earlier it remains effectively confined within Bossuet's bounds; later it diverges into increasingly separate streams before merging with the ideological currents of the Revolution. The transition did not go unnoticed by contemporaries. Writing in 1753, the councillor of state Gilbert de Voisins noted with alarm that the "public" had begun "to occupy itself seriously with matters of state" and that whereas formerly the French had reasoned "frivolously and without consequence concerning the conduct of the government," it was now "the very foundations of the constitution and the order of the state that they called into question."[74]

Taking a more favorable view of the matter, the Jansenist councillor Henri de Revol pointed to 1752 as the date of the rending of the "veil" concerning the "mysteries of the monarchy" and the advent of "light" upon "these matters too little studied until now."[75] In d'Argenson's judgment this questioning tended toward the conclusion that "the royal authority was false law and tyranny."[76]

In accounting for this phenomenon, d'Argenson repeatedly pointed to a "philosophical wind of free and antimonarchical government" of specifically English provenance, but the other observers, and even d'Argenson in moments, were more inclined to blame the performance of the monarchy and the episcopacy in the *Unigenitus*-related controversies and especially the refusal of sacraments quarrel, which, "in exciting [the public] to explore these profundities, turns curiosity into a need."[77] In retrospect, it seems clear that the refusal of sacraments controversy provided the occasion for a cautious transferal of Jansenist-Gallican ecclesiastical conceptions to the state. This transferal had perforce to be hesitant because, unlike in the church where the Gallican tradition lent it a semblance of orthodoxy, Gallican-Jansenist thought when applied to the state produced results less easily disguised as traditional. By 1753 the process was in any case sufficiently advanced for d'Argenson to observe that for many of the magistrates then exiled at Bourges the "nation is above kings just as the universal church is above the pope."[78]

The publication of Montesquieu's *Esprit des lois* in 1748 was not specifically related to these controversies, but Le Paige's *Lettres historiques sur les fonctions essentielles du parlement, sur le droit des pairs, et sur les loix fondamentales du royaume* certainly was; appearing during the parlementary exile of 1753-1754, this publication was unmistakably intended as a justification for the parlementary conduct that had provoked this exile. The parlement's tactic of permanently assembling its chambers in pursuance of "public affairs" to the detriment of all private justice, its refusal to obey the letters-patent of February 22, 1753, its prosecution of ecclesiastical "independence" in the refusal of sacraments affair, its right to convoke the realm's princes and peers for public affairs independently of royal initiative, even the parlement's claim to monopolize criminal litigation at the expense of the king—all these found precedents, by means of Le Paige's dubious erudition, in the monarchy's historical record.[79] More immediately and palpably influential than Montesquieu's masterpiece, in part because of its very lack of subtlety, the work's central message was unambiguously clear. As lineal historical successor to the Germanic and Merovingian *parlements généraux* and *cours plenières*, the parlement of Paris as well as its provincial "emanations" (*démembrements*) was "just as old as the monarchy itself."[80] Inheritor as well of the Merovingian assemblies' legislative functions, the eighteenth-century parlement's authority, "the same today as at the time of Clovis," consisted in "never doing or registering anything contrary to the laws of the realm, to the veritable interests of the monarch . . . and to the cry of its own conscience; in knowing how to say with courage: Sire, that is not just, you cannot do it nor ought you to do it; and in sacrificing everything and even dying if necessary rather than in contributing to it in any way." By this means, Le Paige justified the parlement's disobediences of May 5, 7, and 9, 1753—or rather, obedience in the guise of disobedience, because in refusing to consent to something unjust, the parlement "executes the command that the kings themselves have given to resist them, and in disobeying they fulfill the law which they have likewise imposed, not to obey them."[81]

Or was Le Paige's message so unambiguous after all? Read one way, Le Paige's thesis seems quite conservative and in no way goes beyond the *Judicium Francorum* upon which it was based, or what even d'Aguesseau had been willing to say. On such a reading, the parlement was passively "to be the repository and conservatory of the state's constitutive laws"; its constitutional task, like that of a supreme court, "to oppose like an iron wall everything that could weaken the authority and the tradition of these laws."[82] These constitutive or "fundamental" laws were those legislative pillars so basic to the existence of the monarchy that they could not be altered without endangering the whole monarchical structure itself—the famous Salic law, for instance, which designated the nearest male relative as the successor of any deceased king; or the "law" deemed by Le Paige as fundamental, which reserved criminal justice to the parlement in order to leave the more endearing role of pardoner to the king.[83] In occasionally safeguarding this constitutional treasury against the momentary whims and caprices of individual and all-too-human monarchs, the parlement was only conforming to the monarchy's more authentic wishes as expressed in the threatened laws themselves and obeying the indeed thankless but royally imposed task of doing precisely that. The parlement's destruction would therefore veritably entail the monarchy's, not to be sure in an actively revolutionary sense, but in the quite conservative sense that the monarchy would thereby divest itself of its self-imposed restraint upon its most suicidal impulses and flirt openly with despotism.[84]

For Le Paige's immediate political purposes this modest claim sufficed, and we may moreover suppose it to be the one he had chiefly in view. What adds additional weight to this conservative interpretation of the *Lettres historiques* are the very Bossuet-like utterances midway through the first book, that the "king reunites in his person all the legislative and coactive power; that he is eminently the principle and source of all justice and all the authority that exist in the realm: that they are only an emanation of his power and that those who exercise it hold it from him alone."[85]

This much granted, Le Paige's argumentation nonetheless overshoots his own modest conclusions because it makes popular consent one of the monarchy's fundamental or constituent laws.[86] Unlike Montesquieu but like Henri de Boulainvilliers, Le Paige distinguished no special nobility among the primitive Franks; all were originally free and equal. Unlike Boulainvilliers but like Montesquieu, Le Paige allowed for early assimilation between the conquering Franks and the defeated Gauls, thereby bringing the latter into the Frankish nation. The resultant nation regularly gathered, according to Le Paige, in the form of parlements généraux, and "without the counsel of the nation itself," including even the women, the Merovingian—even Carolingian—kings could do nothing of any consequence.[87] Lest counsel, moreover, be construed as simple advice that the king was free to heed or disregard, Le Paige made it abundantly clear that by "counsel" he meant *assent* or "the suffrage of all," for an adverse "murmur" by the assembled Franks sealed the fate of a proposed law on the spot.[88] Now if, as Le Paige insisted, this "constituent" or "primitive" law that was "born with the monarchy" had never lapsed or been invalidated, and if, as he equally insisted, the parlement had inherited the old parlements généraux's functions by a kind of Salic succession, then did it not follow that the modern parlement continued to consent or dissent as mandatory or representative of the nation as distinct from the king? Le Paige repeatedly described the parlement as "representing" the medieval assemblies, which had at one time consisted of all the people: it was in virtue of the same "primitive" law of consent that "no edict, ordonnance, or other acts have the force of public law in the realm before they have been deliberated in parlement, which represents today those princes and those assemblies."[89] Even if, therefore, Le Paige himself did not explicitly enunciate the principle of national sovereignty in his *Lettres historiques*, it remains true to say that the book's premises "invite" if not "convoke" such a conclusion, which others were less timid to draw.

What lends credence to the hypothesis that this might not have been an altogether unwitting business on Le Paige's part is the studied ambiguity of his phrase, "the founders of the monarchy," or the "state." This curious phrase crops up three times in rapid succession in the course of his first "recapitulation," and in each of these instances it is followed by the phrase, "as also by the kings," or "of the monarchs themselves," as if to let it be understood that the founders of the monarchy and monarchs were not the same historical actors.[90] The phrase takes on added significance in view of the exchange between the parlementary presidents Murard and Durey de Mesnières during the political crisis of 1756-1757. In the course of some draft remonstrances that never saw the light of day, Murard employed the phrase, "our kings the founders of the monarchy." When Mesnières, Le Paige's close collaborator on the *Lettres historiques*, encountered this phrase, he objected that "this expression will not suit the taste of many parlementaires, for they pretend that it is the nation that established the law of [parlementary] registration, that it is just as old as the monarchy, and that it is part of the contract, etc."[91] If, as seems almost certainly the case, Mesnières was speaking both for himself and Le Paige in this instance, then the curious disjuncture between "monarchs" and "founders of the monarchy" in the *Lettres historiques* is hardly an oversight, for like these "many parlementaires," Le Paige had also repeatedly insisted that the fundamental law of consent that had evolved into that of parlementary registration was "just as old, just as unshakable, as the monarchy itself."[92]

The phrase, "monarch founder of our government," rings therefore in a most discordant fashion when one encounters it in a footnote at the beginning of the second volume of the *Lettres historiques*, where it is closely succeeded by the Bossuet-like pronouncements that "kings can do everything, without doubt . . . if they only consider the force of their power, because it is never permitted to oppose them otherwise than by representations and prayer." What weight should be accorded this profession of absolutist orthodoxy should in part be determined by its eleventh-hour inclusion in response to adverse criticism by a "temerarious writing" between the publication of the two volumes.[93] This is not necessarily to suggest insincerity on Le Paige's part, because Le Paige, and much of the parlement with him, were perfectly capable of reading themselves and their self-annointed constitutional roles into their very definition of the monarchy on the one hand, thereby enabling them to profess unlimited dependence on the king, while on the other claiming to act in behalf of the nation in relation to the monarchy, conceived in this instance as an entity quite distinct from themselves. The resultant confusion, in any case, was not so much akin to the salutary imprecision bordering on silence so warmly recommended by d'Aguesseau as it was to the irritation infallibly engendered by conclusions bearing conspicuously little relationship to their forgoing premises. It inspired, not so much a sense of religious awe in the presence of the unfathomable mystery of the monarchy as an altogether profane desire to iron out the book's logical inconsistencies at the demystifying expense of either monarchy or parlement or both.

Le Paige's recipe for d'Argensonian curiosity was all the more provocative in that it was served up in much the same form by the parlement of Paris. Almost completely, albeit in more cautious phraseology, the parlement repeated Le Paige's fundamental theses in its remonstrances of November 27, 1755, and August 22, 1756. "Sire," the first of these informed the king, "it has been for thirteen hundred years that the monarchy has existed, and it has been for thirteen hundred years that your parlement, under whatever denomination it has been known, has formed the same tribunal and exercised the same functions in the state." And if he chose to read any further—the remonstrances were too long to have been delivered—the same king might have been puzzled to learn that while on the one hand the parlement was virtually indistinguishable from his majesty, with his person forming "but a single body" whose "chief" was the king and whose "members" were the magistrates, the very same parlement was on the other hand the lineal descendant of the ancient "general assembly of the [whole Frankish] nation," which the kings had been obliged to consult on every important occasion.[94] Appealing in a footnote to (of all people!) Bossuet, these remonstrances further described the parlement as "the state concentrated, where the law is prepared, determined, consummated, laid down, and executed." The ambiguous designation of the founders of the monarchy as the "ancient conquerors"; the further stylization of the parlement as "the tribunal of the nation," the "center of the state," and the "national and essential repository of the laws"; the Delphic reference to "the sacred engagements that constitute the monarchy"—these would have given him further cause for mixed puzzlement and alarm.[95] On August 22, 1756, moreover, in the second set of remonstrances having to do with the government's treatment of the parlements of Bordeaux and Rouen, Louis XV actually heard with his own ears another of

Le Paige's recently propounded theses, that the provincial parlements were not discrete and unrelated bodies but rather the various "colonies and divers classes of a sole and unique parlement, the divers members of a sole and unique corps. . . ."[96]

One way of resolving these apparent contradictions was early marked out by Henri de Revol, one of the parlement's indisputably Jansenist magistrates and Le Paige's good friend and regular correspondent. Writing to Le Paige shortly after the parlement's reinstatement in the autumn of 1757, Revol complained of "equivocal expressions" and the want of "circumspection" in some of the parlement's recent remonstrances, especially those of August 22, 1756.[97] The theory of a single parlement embracing various "classes" in particular enabled the "ministerial cabale," the Jesuits, and the "black cluster of royal confessors" successfully to insinuate that the entire magistracy was forming itself into an antimonarchical "League" and that if the king did not suppress the parlements, "soon there would be no more royalty." Had it not indeed been for the king's own suspicions and "jealousies of authority" to this effect, the parlement might have already destroyed the Jesuits and "very probably prevented the horrible blow [Damiens'] of which France had just been the victim." The place to dissipate these calumnious impressions, Revol thought, was in the "sequel so desired to [Le Paige's] letters on the origin of the parlements." There, he was sure, Le Paige could reassure the royalist public how little redoubtable to the monarchy was this "true confraternity between the peers and magistrates of Paris and the parlements of the provinces," because "far from these corps being able to form an active league capable of usurping a legitimate portion of the royal prerogative, they would be on the contrary always reduced to the pure defensive relative to their repository." To conserve this repository consisting of the realm's maxims and laws constituted the parlements' only "procuration from the rest of the nation"; and even though they could be said to have arisen from and to represent "in a certain manner" the ancient Frankish assemblies, or *champs de mars*, they most certainly possessed "no mission to change the principles of the monarchy."

A conservative reading of Le Paige's intentions in the *Lettres historiques*, guarded criticism of some of its more radical implications, and an invitation to the author to undo the damage he had done—all would seem fairly to characterize Revol's reaction so far. At precisely this juncture, however, Revol's letter takes an unexpected twist. Far from merely concluding that the parlement should stick more modestly to its conservatively defined business or that the constitution of the monarchy should be left unchanged, he pleaded instead for a "meeting of all free citizens," which alone could "faithfully" represent the old Frankish assemblies and consequently "effect some veritable change in the constitution of the monarchy and in the legitimate power of the ruling house. . . ." This seemed to imply the convocation of the estates-general, despite Le Paige's snubbing of that institution in his *Lettres historiques* as only an "imperfect copy" of the ancient parlements or assemblies, and Revol indeed employed the term "Etats-généraux" in his letter.[98] But he made it clear that "since the Third Estate had come to share with the nobility in the rights of frankness" (*ingénuité*), the only way to replace the ancient assemblies would be by means of an estates-general of an altogether new order, "where each town or canton would give to its deputies a special procuration in which the nature of the innovation desired by the nation would be stipulated." Presumably Revol would not have voted in 1788 to constitute the estates-general in exactly the same manner as before.

What Revol had done, then, was to disentangle the conservative from the more radical threads in Le Paige's argumentation and to take each to its properly logical conclusion. From Le Paige's (mainly) conservative description of the contemporary parlement's function as passively to preserve and safeguard a certain legacy of traditional maxims and laws, Revol concluded that its "primitive mission" had never been larger and for the parlements to claim descendance and pedigrees from Frankish general assemblies, whose role had been much more active than this, was both fraudulent and unnecessarily provocative. From Le Paige's insistence, however, that genuinely national consent operating through general assemblies had once been part of the monarchy's constitution, Revol drew the conclusion that it ought to be still but that its practical implementation entailed the convocation of an estates-general adapted to eighteenth-century conditions. That Revol was altogether serious about this is indicated by his insistence that, however justifiably the parlement claimed the right to "concur in everything that is true legislation in order to conserve all the fundamental principles and having no primitive mission and national representation except to that effect," the parlement had no real right to consent (or even not to consent) to the innovations represented by royal fiscal edicts. In registering these, as it most recently had in a lit de justice held in August the previous year, the parlement "accords only the *provisoire* to the king and cannot dispense him from requesting the suffrage of the nation. . . ."

What precisely Le Paige thought of all this is not known, although Revol assumed throughout that his correspondent was in essential agreement and that he would manifest this agreement in a projected third volume of the *Lettres historiques*. "He to whom I take the liberty to address myself already possesses many pages from the same hand relative to all this and he has had them since 1753 and 1754. In truth if he really deigns to make something (*faire quelque cas*) of these ideas, which are said to be reserved for the conclusion of the *Lettres*, . . . it is more than ever time to develop for the public the veritable consequences of this estimable work. . . ." The projected third volume never appeared, although its existence was attested to by the abbé Rondeau who at the time of Le Paige's death in 1802 remarked that a third volume of the *Lettres historiques* on the right of people to tax themselves had been written but not printed.[99] In 1772 during the Maupeou crisis, Le Paige privately recognized to Murard the principle of national sovereignty, at least in the matter of taxation, and the necessity of an "assembly of states" for the reformation of the realm.[100] But by then, it is true, even the parlements had included the convocation of the estates-general as part of their swan songs and numbers of pamphlets had gone further.[101] What is worth noting, however, is that by the year of Damiens, and long before this fact surfaced more clearly in the wake of Maupeou's "revolution" of 1770, a troop of mainly Jansenist magistrates and lawyers within the parlement of Paris—Le Paige, the abbé Claude Mey, Revol, Durey de Mesnières, Lambert—had gone beyond the mere constitutional exaltation of the parlement and were seriously thinking in terms of the estates-general and national sovereignty.[102]

During the 1750s and most of the 1760s, such expressions of "republican" sentiment remained either private or sufficiently obscured by traditional phraseology as to convince many historians even today of the politically uninnovative and essentially conservative character of mid-century Jansenist-parlementary thought.[103] Not so, however, for the party's "devout" antagonists, who with an unnuanced but perspicacious brutality disregarded the Jansenists' hesitant steps and backward glances and called attention to the fundamentally radical direction of their constitutional thought. The abbé Bertrand Capmartin de Chaupy in his *Observations sur le refus que fait le Châtelet de reconnoître la Chambre royale* and *Réflexions d'un avocat sur les remontrances du parlement, du 27 novembre 1755*; Lafiteau, bishop of Sisteron, in his *Entretiens d'Anselme et d'Isidore sur les affaires du temps*; and François de Paul Lagarde in his *Traité historique de la souveraineté du roi et des droits en dépendant* all accusingly pointed their fingers at the principle of national sovereignty implicitly undergirding Jansenist-parlementary constitutionalism.[104]

For the bishop of Sisteron, the Jansenist heresy was ultimately the culprit, but his working definition of heresy was of a peculiarly political sort. Jansenism consisted not so much in adherence to any of the propositions condemned as heretical by *Unigenitus* (whichever these were) as in "opposition itself to the Bull."[105] Beginning with this original sin of contestation of papal authority, the Jansenists were led by degrees to challenge one set of authorities after another until "not even the monarch found himself protected from their blows."[106] Never, however, had "a sect been more opposed to royal authority than this one," albeit a mere "castoff from the sect of Calvin," for "it aspires everywhere to a republican liberty."[107] From Luther and Calvin, but more immediately from Edmond Richer, Jacques Almain, and John Major, those Jansenists entrenched in the parlements had drawn the principle that the political or ecclesiastical community alone possessed sovereignty and only delegated its usage to its chiefs.[108] From here the parlements had proclaimed "our kings . . . dependent upon their subjects," theoretically surrendered their "supreme authority to the corps of the nation," and then anointed themselves as the nation's mouthpiece.[109]

The abbé Capmartin de Chaupy, for his part, aimed his batteries more particularly against the parlement's remonstrances of November 27, 1755, and, indirectly, Le Paige's *Lettres historiques*. In painstaking and irrefutable detail he compared the texts of the *Judicium Francorum* and the parlement's remonstrances of 1755 to show that not only had the parlement officially adopted the same principles it had condemned in 1730 but that, additionally inspired by Le Paige's *Lettres historiques*, it had gone beyond them in audacity.[110] The *Judicium Francorum* had claimed the parlement's right of registration as a concession by the monarchy motivated by considerations of public utility; the remonstrances of 1755 claimed it as a possession essential to the constitution.[111] The *Judicium Francorum* essentially divided legislative sovereignty and accorded the parlement only a share; the remonstrances essentially transferred sovereignty undivided from the king to the parlement acting in the name of the nation.[112] With surgical precision he dissected the artful ambiguity of the remonstrances' language to expose its most subversive implications. If the king and the parlement were indeed indivisible, as the remonstrances asserted, and if the king was only the parlement's "chief" (*chef*) and the magistrates its members, then the parlement was in fact superior to the king because a "chief," like the first president, was obliged to follow the vote of the plurality. If, moreover, the king was reputed "habitually residing in the parlement," whether he was physically there or not, there was nothing the parlement could not do without the king, while there was nothing the king could do without the parlement.[113] And at the same time that the parlement attributed to itself monarchical sovereignty with respect to the nation, it gave itself national sovereignty with respect to the king, for how else could "the laws the instant they left the throne [that is, the parlement] already represent the free wishes of the nation?"[114]

In their zeal to confirm the king and the court in their darkest suspicions regarding this evolving parlementary constitutionalism, however, these "devout" pamphleteers either forgot or did not see fit to recall the constitutional limitations with which even a Bossuet was willing to hedge about the royal majesty. Taking issue with the remonstrances' use of the term "protector," with which "a celebrated usurper . . . of a neighboring state had affected to content himself with modesty," Capmartin de Chaupy insisted that in France the kings were "masters" and "possessors"; going in fact beyond anything that Louis XIV had said of himself, Chaupy maintained that in "pure monarchies," of which France was an example, "the king is the state" and "the will of the king is the will of the state."[115] For Sisteron as well, "the property of government resides in the king alone"; the monarch was the "sole master, absolute and independent to command in the state."[116] Both, too, rang the tocsin of monarchical violence against the upstart parlement, whose sole legitimate function was to administer justice between particulars. Chaupy compared the parlement's "vain words" with the king's potentially "terrible blows," which could "dumbfound, transfer, or disperse the parlements entirely," while Sisteron affected regretfully to foresee the day when, however inevitably it might hurt the king's goodness, his majesty would be forced to "sever the head of this monster." Just in case the French Herod might not know what to do with the disembodied head, Sisteron took it into his own to suggest the substance of what Maupeou did fifteen years later.[117]

The conceptual dismantling of the monarchy might have ceased at that point if the volcanic religious-ecclesiastical controversies that had occasioned it could have mercifully died.

Such, however, was not to be; they soon erupted anew in connection with the parlement's suppression of the Jesuit order in the early 1760s. Once again in the course of this controversy the parlementary parti janséniste and episcopal parti dévôt pulled violently in opposite directions at the Old Regime's delicate fabric of institutional definitions and relationships. Once again, although less wholeheartedly in this instance, the monarchy and Louis XV personally tried to maintain a via media in the form of the edict of March 8, 1762, which attempted at once to preserve and reform the Jesuit order along Gallican lines. And once again, as in the refusal of sacraments controversy, financial necessity forced the monarchy to acquiesce—this time even formally—in another parlementary and Jansenist triumph, which lacked only the right to pursue ex-Jesuits individually to be accounted complete.[118]

But it was as much the accompanying pamphlet debate as it was the additional defeat of its ecclesiastical policy that dealt the monarchy the severest blows, for under the apparent rubric of the Jesuit order and the nature of its constitutions the debate more profoundly concerned the French monarchy and the nature of *its* constitution, and in the end it rent it further asunder. It all began when, following Le Paige's and the abbé Christophe Coudrette's lead in their four-volume *Histoire générale de la naissance et des progrès de la compagnie de Jésus en France*, yet other pamphleteers and the parlements themselves described as "despotic" the unlimited character of the Jesuit general's authority within the order and as "slavery" the "blind obedience" owed to him by the order's ordinary members.[119] In response, Jesuit apologists defended their order as only monarchically structured—innocent enough, they thought, in a monarchical state—and accused their parlementary-Jansenist detractors of harboring "republican" maxims of suspiciously English provenance. Thrown on the defensive, parlementary-Jansenist pamphleteers were forced to define their conception of monarchy, which they did in markedly constitutional terms, and in turn accused the Jesuits of scheming to transform the French monarchy into a despotism, or of placing a "scepter of iron" in "the hands of the Bourbons."[120]

The tempest over the Jesuits thus again threw to the surface both devout and parlementary-Jansenist conceptions of the monarchy, only to separate them by means of a trough wider and deeper than ever. Speaking for the devout side, the Jesuit Claude Frey de Neuville thought the king of France's authority more untrammeled than that of his order's general, because unlike the latter's, the king's admitted of "neither inspection nor limitation." It was "born entirely with him, lives only in and through him, and only dies or rather does not die at all with him. . . ."[121] If this description of monarchical authority failed to irritate parlementary and Jansenist sensibilities, the Jesuit author of a memoir to the attorney general was ready with another, which equated the king's "will" with the "sovereign depository and the authority of the laws," terms that to the parlement were antithetical. And in case all else failed, the Jesuit André-Christophe Balbani was waiting in the antechambers with a definition of a king as "absolute" and "legislator."[122] "As absolute," he explained, "there is nobody in his state who ought to resist him; . . . as legislator, he alone makes new laws and abrogates old ones"; both of these royal prerogatives, as Balbani well knew, the parlements were then precisely contesting with Louis XV.[123] Parting company, here, with Bossuet, Henri de Fumel, the bishop of Lodève, would not even disavow the term "despotism" and allowed that such a government was "only the wiser for that, more apt to maintain peace and subordination. . . ."[124] "The hatred that you have sworn against the parlements," correctly observed the enraged anonymous author of the *Réplique aux apologies des Jésuites*, "has its source in the diversity of opinions about monarchical authority."[125]

If it were to avoid this Jesuitical trap and escape guilt by contamination with "republican maxims," the parlementary-Jansenist response to these monarchical effusions had to fall back on the classical distinction between monarchy and despotism and proclaim loyalty to the former. This it typically did by identifying a checklist of attributes—the inviolability of private property, the availability of the formalities of justice, the complete security of public officers, the existence of Montesquieuean "intermediate powers" and a body of "fixed" or "fundamental" law—that it thought characteristic of monarchies such as France but totally absent in the "despotic" Jesuit order.[126] Among these attributes, however, it was predictably the security of crown offices and the existence of fundamental laws—both precious, of course, to the parlement of Paris—that parlementary-Jansenist pamphleteers and parlementary *comptes rendus* most accented. The essentially parlementary character of their conception of the monarchical constitution became clear when, in response to the rhetorical question of why the king sometimes encountered a "firm but respectful suspension of obedience," a "noble resistance always accompanied by the most devoted filial love" to "new laws too little reflected upon, or orders surprised by treason against the generosity of the master," the anonymous *Réplique* replied that it was because in monarchies "dignities cannot be lost without crime and . . . punishments are not inflicted without judgment. Take away these two barriers," he warned, "and you would only be left, as in Turkey, with dumb slaves in the place of magistrates who, when it is necessary, make audible to the best of princes the voice of reclamation, the prayers, and interests of a people whom they love tenderly."[127]

As in the refusal of sacraments controversy, however, so also in the debate over the Jesuits, parlementary-Jansenist constitutionalism went beyond mere institutional exaltation of the parlement and appealed ultimately to the nation. Explicitly taking to task Balbani's definition of the French monarch as "absolute" and unique "legislator," the anonymous author of *Questions proposées à l'auteur de l'Appel à la raison* wagered that a "Frenchman who understands the monarchy would never say . . . that there is no corps within the state that can and ought in certain cases resist the will of the king, still less that that will alone ought to bend the law." This right, of course, he accorded the parlement, but a parlement whose "duty" consisted in representing "the true interests of the nation, which ought never be separated from those of the king." The parlement had therefore to oppose the registration and execution of new laws, not only if they contradicted existing ones or the sacrosanct fundamental laws, but if in any way they "appeared prejudicial or useless to the general welfare"; and if Jesuits such as Balbani thought this resistance a usurpation of monarchical power, the "general sentiment of the nation" bade them anathema. The monarch's true wishes were by definition "the true interests of his people, which are always his own," and the "*true* [my emphasis] monarch's wishes are that his power be recognized as absolute and irresistible [only] for the public good and justice."[128] Applying these criteria to a particular case, the anonymous author of *Réflexions sur le despotisme des évêques* chose to dispose of the "famous edict of 1695" as no edict at all because it had visibly "not been dictated by a love for the common good, . . . not registered by the assembled chambers, . . . not applauded by the realm, . . . and not accepted by all of France. . . ." Even the clergy's frequent complaints about this edict's nonexecution was proof to this author of its nullity, because its very inexecution was evidence of its rejection by the nation.[129]

Ultimately, then, the classical distinction between absolute monarchy and despotism proved unequal to the exigencies of the parlementary-Jansenist retreat, provoking a reevaluation of these constitutional concepts as distinguishing genuinely different governmental types. Hallowed by Bossuet and d'Aguesseau and accorded lip service by Le Paige in the mid-1750s, the term "absolute" left an increasingly foul taste in parlementary-Jansenist mouths in the 1760s. For Ripert de Monclar, attorney general of the parlement of Aix, what was precisely objectionable about the Jesuit general's authority was its "perpetual, immediate, and *absolute*" character, nor was his authority any the less despotic for his being susceptible to deposition, because such was the only "counterweight" in "despotic Empires" to "*absolute* power."[130] By regarding this Jesuitical "despotism" as "the most *absolute* that has ever existed," one of messieurs of the parlement of Toulouse similarly tended to equate the two terms, as did also one of messieurs at Besançon who, speaking for his fellow commissioners, pronounced the Jesuits' general a "despot in the most odious sense of the expression," his authority being at once "absolute" and "tyrannical," the "most absolute and the most unlimited."[131] Following Montesquieu, the Toulouse commissioner thought that fear was characteristic of despotism, but the Jesuits' voluntary obedience to their superiors, far from getting their regime off this typological hook, produced rather the spectacle of a fear that had penetrated "all the way into the heart," producing a "voluntary and absolute obedience" without precedent even "in a despotic state."[132]

It was not long before this new equation reached the king's ears directly in the form of remonstrances by the parlement of Paris. Here, moreover, it was applied to royal authority itself, taken to task for its rough handling of sundry provincial "classes" of France's unique and unitary parlement. First appearing in the remonstrances of April 4, 1759, which complained of the "irregular, illegal means of absolute power" in its punishment of certain magistrates of the parlement of Besançon, the expression caught the attention of the king, whose rebuke chastened the parlement into referring to "your absolute authority" in an orthodox sense in its reiterative remonstrances of July 3.[133] But with the culmination of the Jesuit affair in 1763-1764, the equation of "absolute" with "arbitrary" or even "despotic" entered the remonstrances' vocabulary massively and to stay. The remonstrances of January 18, 1764, perhaps expressed the equation most forcefully in warning the king against "those who dare counsel your majesty to employ the ways of absolute authority against the divers classes of your parlement" and who "want to substitute for a monarchical government a despotic and absolute government."[134] But elsewhere "absolute power" was pronounced "incompatible with the rule of law" and compared with a "yoke" that, if borne, would "entail the overthrow of the joyous constitution of the French government," as well as "undermine the foundations and the support of monarchical authority."[135] The remonstrances of June 1, 1766, employed the terms "absolute will" or "absolute power" in these unfavorable senses no less than twenty times in the course of as many printed pages.[136]

Just as Gallican-Jansenist denunciations of episcopal despotism antedated the denunciations of particular monarchical acts as despotic, so the breakdown of the distinction between the despotic and the absolute occurred first in an ecclesiastical context and then spread to relations between king and subjects in other domains. In this latter instance it was less the refusal of sacraments controversy than the expulsion of the Jesuits that proved decisive.

Sacerdoce and Empire

THOUGH constitutionally reserved toward absolute monarchy in relation to the parlement and the lay citizenry it "represented," Gallican-Jansenist thought came forward as its enthusiastic advocate where its relation to the church was concerned. Or perhaps for "monarchy" the more neutral term "state" should be preferred, for beneath parlementary-Jansenism's ritual appeal to the "prince" in sacerdotal-imperial relations it is more accurately the power of the parlement and behind it the nation that is half-consciously being invoked. Thus understood, the "prince's" heavy-footed transgression upon the church's sacrosanct ecclesiastical and spiritual independence stands out as one of the more salient features of the eighteenth-century Jansenist and Gallican agenda. With the parlement's victory in the refusal of sacraments controversy in 1757 and the outright dissolution of the Jesuits' religious vows in 1762, it had practically anticipated much of what the Revolution later accomplished.

But theory by no means yielded the palm to practice. Mey's and Maultrot's *Apologie de tous les jugements rendus par les tribunaux séculiers en France contre le schisme*, Le Paige's *Réflexions . . . sur les lois que les souverains sont en droit de faire pour rétablir la paix dans leurs états, quand ils sont troublés par les disputes de religion*, the anonymous *Autorité royale justifiée sur les fausses accusations de l'Assemblée générale du clergé en 1765*, and François Richer's *De L'Autorité du clergé, et du pouvoir du magistrat politique sur l'exercise des fonctions du ministère écclésiastique* are some of the works whose titles alone announce an orientation shared by most of this literature to one degree or another.[137] This tendency was never more clearly articulated than in polemical reaction to an "exposition of the rights of the spiritual power" drafted by Damiens' sometime "devout" master Le Corgne de Launay and promulgated by an exasperated general assembly of the Gallican clergy as part of its *Actes* in 1765.[138]

This document began innocuously enough with Bossuet-inspired banalities: two powers had been established to govern man, "the sacred authority of priests and that of kings"; both came from God, from whom emanated all "well-ordered power on the earth." The goal of the second of these powers was man's well-being in the present life; the object of the first was to prepare him for eternity. In establishing these two powers, God had not intended their strife, but their cooperation, so that they might lend mutual aid and support. But neither power was to be subordinate to the other, for each was "sovereign, independent, and absolute" in its own domain. For that reason, "the clergy of France" had always taught that the church's power was confined to "spiritual things" and that kings were "not subordinate to any ecclesiastical power . . . in temporal things," because they held their power from God himself. But if kings commanded in temporal affairs, "the universal church" had always taught that kings were "obliged to obey priests in the order of religion," to whom "alone the government of the church belongs."[139]

But it was not so much the glittering teeth of its principles as the tail-end whiplash of their applications that constituted the *Actes'* chief force. "Silence," the *Actes* for example proclaimed, "can never be imposed upon those whom God had instituted as His mouthpiece." This was a not very covert condemnation of Louis XV's Declaration of Silence of September 2, 1754. Again, "the civil power . . . cannot . . . be permitted to contradict the doctrine received by the church, to suspend the execution of her judgments, or to elude their effects"—read: the parlement of Paris flagrantly exceeded its authority on April 18, 1752, when it declared that no one could be refused the sacraments by virtue of opposition to *Unigenitus*. Moreover, "the laws of the church can receive no qualifications except from the authority that pronounced them." In other words, even Louis XV exceeded his authority in his declaration of December 10, 1756, by saying that *Unigenitus* was not a rule of faith. And finally, "the refusal of the most august of our sacraments can never be the object of the competence of the civil authority." This passage speaks clearly enough for itself.[140]

The general assembly's *Actes* were no sooner published than they fell victim to the parlement's condemnation, setting off the sort of jurisdictional and corporate slugfest to which the realm had grown accustomed since 1750.[141] The resultant controversy slowly melted away during the spring and early summer of 1767 and subsequently disappeared altogether beneath the avalanche of the La Chalotais/d'Aiguillon affair, but not before precipitating a minor avalanche of its own in the form of mainly proparlementary pamphlets plus a few full-scale treatises. Among these were some *Observations sur les Actes de l'Assemblée du clergé de 1765* by the relentless Le Paige. But the *Actes* were also the object of *Réflexions, Remarques diverses, Anathèmes, Plaintes légitimes*, and a *Préservatif contre*, to say nothing of numbers of *Lettre*[s], including one by a *philosophe militaire*.[142]

This literature scrutinized the *Actes* with a malevolent thoroughness, even finding yawning cavities beneath the pearly white of the principles themselves. To what mischievous end, for example, did the author of the *Actes* place the comma in Romans 13:1 after *Deo* rather than *sunt*, where the Vulgate put it? Whereas Christophe de Beaumont had only mistranslated the passage in his mandamus apropos of the Damiens affair, the *Actes* tampered with Holy Writ itself by cajoling the Latin into saying that only "well-ordered" powers had God's blessing. Who, in the latter case, was to decide whether a given polity was well-ordered or not? The bishops? The pope? And if not well-ordered, was obedience suspended?[143] The fact that Boniface VIII had punctuated the verse in this eccentric fashion in *Unam Sanctam* (1302) could scarcely be expected to allay suspicions. These were instead reinforced by the *Actes*' failure to imitate the assembly of 1682 in explicitly condemning Cardinal Bellarmin's theory of indirect ecclesiastical authority, which allowed for papal intervention in temporal affairs in cases where sin was clearly involved.[144]

To be sure, the *Actes* in principle concurred with the "divine right" theory of the Gallican Declaration of 1682 in teaching that kings were not accountable to any ecclesiastical authority in temporal matters and that they received their power from God directly. But this high principled dust thrown into the eyes of the inattentive citizen was not sufficiently dense to prevent the perspicacious editor of the *Nouvelles écclésiastiques* from noting that "even the independence of the crown is only presented in the *Actes* as the sentiment of the *clergy of France*; whereas all the pretensions of the spiritual power . . . are presented as the teaching of the *universal church*."[145] Other pamphleteers were quick to concur. The declaration of the assembly of 1682, explained Maultrot in *Les Droits de la puissance temporelle défendus*, had proclaimed the independence of the temporal authority "as a truth conformed to the word of God, the tradition of the fathers, and to the examples of the saints. In 1765 this doctrine is no more than the teaching of the clergy of France. The reader is therefore entitled to conclude that it is a national opinion concerning which doubts are legitimate. . . ."[146] And if the *Actes*' pronouncements on the subject of the first Gallican article lacked constancy, the consistency of its commitment to the others was that of the purest sponge rubber. Its description of the bull *Unigenitus* as an "irreformable judgment" and its publication of Pope Benedict's encyclical letter of 1756 without protestation against this document's presumption of papal infallibility—both these and more, complained Le Blanc de Castillon of the parlement of Aix, breathed an "ultramontanist spirit" in blatant disharmony with the conciliarist tradition of the Gallican church.[147] Taken together, concluded the *Nouvelles écclésiastiques*, these traits entitled one "to regard the *Actes* of the assembly of 1765 as a revocation of the declaration of 1682."[148]

The whole range of issues dividing rival conceptions of the church and her relation to the state were engaged in this polemicizing. On the episcopal side, a rigidly authoritarian and hierarchical structure dominated by the episcopacy in cooperation with the pope stood proudly on an equal footing with the state. On the Gallican-Jansenist side, a more malleable and egalitarian structure allowing parish priests and laymen a role of active participation maneuvered exclusively within the confines of the state. Among these features, however, it was the latter, the degree to which Gallican-Jansenist polemicists were willing to subordinate even the most "spiritual" of the church's functions to the supervision of the state, that emerges most strikingly in this controversy.

The authorities they most frequently cited in doing so were in this instance treatises on canon law written around the turn of the last century, especially those by Van Espen and Pierre de Marca, and the example of the early church, especially under the emperors Constantine and Theodosius, as presented in the ecclesiastical histories of Noël Alexandre and Claude Fleury. Perhaps the chief principle they invoked and claimed to have found in these sources was that the church was within the "empire," and not the empire within the church, which, however, they took much further than had d'Aguesseau, extending it to mean that the state, or "prince," alone possessed coercive power on earth, that the church's ministry was in contrast exclusively spiritual, and that such authority as it did possess could be regulated by the prince in the interests of the temporal welfare of his subjects.[149] Even pagan or heretical princes were entitled to do this by virtue of their God-conferred capacity as "political magistrate," but since the regular establishment of Christianity after the conversion of the Roman emperors and the Germanic kings, the "Christian prince" was further authorized by his role as "outside bishop" and "protector of the canons," enabling him to enforce and uphold the church's own laws and constitutions—even against churchmen, they stressed, should this become necessary. The very active role of a Constantine, Theodosius, or Charlemagne in decisions of ecclesiastical discipline and even doctrine were the historical examples they had in mind; they seemed imperfectly conscious that the cultural context was no longer the same.[150]

Yet the principles could not have produced the radical consequences they did except in alliance with the corrosive and closely related distinctions between externality and spiritual internality, fact and principle. The latter represents one of the more authentically Jansenist contributions to the Gallican, Jansenist, and parlementary mix and goes back to "the great" Antoine Arnauld's division between the questions of whether the five famous propositions supposedly extracted from Jansenius' *Augustinus* were *in fact* to be found in this treatise, and whether these propositions should *in principle* be regarded as heretical. Arnauld argued that the papacy was indeed infallible in matters of principle (*droit*) and hence entitled to declare the propositions heretical, but that it was quite fallible in matters of fact (*fait*) and therefore incompetent to say that Jansenius' treatise contained these propositions.[151] Arnauld himself was not very Gallican, as his concessions to papal infallibility demonstrate, but after the merging of Gallicanism and Jansenism in the wake of *Unigenitus*, his distinction was extended to ecumenical councils, indeed to the church universal, which was similarly held to be infallible in matters of doctrine but not in matters of fact. All the territory annexed by the realm of *fait* and externality at the expense of *droit* and internality was territory opened up to the intervention of the prince and "reason," which could as competently judge matters of fact as any prelate, pope, or ecumenical council. As it turned out, moreover, there were few if any matters so vaporously spiritual that they could not be condensed into matters of temporal fact and thereby rendered accessible to profane inspection.

Not only were councils quite fallible in matters of fact, according to these pamphleteers, but whether they were ecumenical or not was itself a matter of fact, which only the prince was competent to judge. "Once the universal church has pronounced, the laity has no choice except that of submission," conceded the self-annointed defender of *Les Droits de la puissance temporelle*. "But the prince, the magistrates, even the simple faithful," he added, "have the right to examine the exterior character of the judgment that is attributed to the church in order to see if she has really spoken, if it is not just a small number of bishops who have usurped her name." They moreover "have the right to examine if the judgment has been reached freely and unanimously," that is, canonically, "and whether it has been formulated clearly, in such a manner as to abate the controversy."[152] And should any of these criteria remain unfulfilled, the prince, as "protector of the canons," was obliged to reject the judgment; or even if it met them all, as did the Council of Trent, the prince as "political magistrate" had the right to see that nothing had "slipped by" under the name of doctrine that was "contrary to the rights of the prince, to the interests of his crown, to the tranquility of his realm" and to accept or reject the judgment "according to the utility or the danger of which it is susceptible in his states."[153]

If such were the rights of princes with regard to decisions by ecumenical councils, how much more amply entitled was Louis XV in imposing silence on the subject of *Unigenitus*, that mere product of Jesuitical intrigue, and in declaring that it was not a rule of faith. By imposing silence, this prince was not, as the *Actes* implied, infringing upon the bishops' sacred right to teach, but merely forbidding them to make reference to the "exterior character" in which certain teachings were embodied.[154] In rendering the bull this dubious "honor . . . , one can in truth no longer speak about it," elucidated Le Paige, speaking about it, "yet one can continue to teach the great and beautiful verities it has reputedly decided." In declaring that *Unigenitus* was not a rule of faith, on the other hand, the king, as both political magistrate and protector of the canons, had only decided whether it taught "without ambiguity what should be believed and what should be rejected" and whether it was "more apt to augment the disputes than to terminate them."[155] "Such an examination," assured the *Requête d'un grand nombre de fidèles* "has no article of doctrine as its object, but rather pure and palpable exterior facts of which the eyes are natural judges, and of which princes and magistrates can rightfully take cognizance."[156]

The same held for the *Actes'* other particular claims to independent ecclesiastical jurisdiction. The sole and infallible right to make moral judgments? "Who doubts that in certain doctrinal matters the prince cannot go much further" than what is purely factual and exterior, argued the defender of *Les Droits de la puissance temporelle.* "There are certain points of doctrine"—namely, moral ones—"that have an intimate connection with the state. Is all cognizance of them to be denied to the prince because they fall into the category of a spiritual matter?"[157] The sole right to judge religious vows? One must distinguish (Le Paige again) between *"le droit et le fait."* If it is a case of a simple vow validly contracted with God, "it is for the ecclesiastical power alone . . . to decide concerning its substance, to commute it, even to dispense someone from it. . . ." But whether the vow was validly contracted at all was a matter of fact, which the prince could judge "by the light of reason" alone.[158] The exclusive jurisdiction, finally, over the Eucharist and extreme unction, the church's most "august" sacraments? One must again distinguish, with Le Paige, between the "interior dispositions required to approach the sacraments worthily"—altogether spiritual, this, and the business of the confessor—and the "conditions required to refuse them publicly," another matter entirely. In the latter case, canon law was the guide, and the prince—read: the parlement—as protector of the canons, could "bend a bishop to the laws of the church when he has violated these overtly."[159] As political magistrate, moreover, to believe the relentless defender of *La Puissance temporelle*, he had the right "to maintain a citizen in the possession of the exterior advantages assured to all Christians, because the legal possession [*possessoire*] of even spiritual things is a purely profane matter."[160]

Despite these and other audacities all these pamphleteers stopped short before what they condemned as the heresy of "Anglican supremacy." Self-consciously Catholic, they sincerely believed that by granting the church jurisdiction over matters "purely spiritual," they were safeguarding what was essential to ecclesiastical authority; the "capital error of the *Actes*," complained Le Blanc de Castillon, was "to have excluded the authority and even the prince's right of inspection over everything that is not entirely profane, instead of restricting the innate power of the church to what is purely spiritual," thereby resurrecting, in his opinion, the dreaded ultramontanist theory of indirect power.[161] Yet by restricting the church to what was ethereally and internally spiritual and in fastening upon the temporal dimension all that remained, these polemicists ran close to the opposite extreme of temporalizing the spiritual and thereby ironically tempting the spirit (if not the matter) of the future Civil Constitution of the Clergy.

But these anticipations were perforce material as well, for how were pamphleteers, so willing to factualize the spiritual, to keep hands off something so matter-of-fact as ecclesiastical property? Victimized by occasional sniper attacks by appellant and Gallican irregulars from the time of Machault's unsuccessful attempt to impose the vingtième on the clergy in 1749—the recognizably Jansenist *Voix du prêtre* in 1750, the abbé Etienne Mignot's *Traité des droits de l'état et du prince sur les biens possédés par le clergé* in 1755—ecclesiastical property became the object of a regular literary siege in response to the 1765 general assembly's assertion that the clergy could "hold property and honors that had been given to them by the piety of the kings and emperors" and that "these temporal goods and titles, which had been legitimately acquired, ought to be carefully preserved."[162] François Richer's *De L'Autorité du clergé, et du pouvoir du magistrat politique*, the marquis de Puységur's *Discussion intéressante, sur la prétention du clergé d'être le premier ordre d'un état*, and the anonymous *Lettre* from a *philosophe militaire* all stressed the inherent incompatibility between the clergy's purely spiritual functions and the possession of temporal goods and honors, the latter getting so specific as to suggest that the state help itself to a third of the church's revenues every year.[163]

They were all outdone by the anonymous author of *Du Droit du souverain sur les biens fonds du clergé et des moines, et de l'usage qu'il peut faire de ces biens pour le bonheur des citoyens*, who in 1770 imagined precisely the situation in which the monarchy and the revolutionary assemblies successively found themselves in 1789. The state owed three billion livres, and the payment of the interest on this debt, which consumed nearly half of the annual revenues, did not leave enough to meet the state's ordinary expenses. Taxes could not be augmented because of the "*cherté* of nearly all sorts of goods. . . ." What was then to be done? After considering and dismissing sundry alternatives, such as bankruptcy, economy measures, and additional loans, the author opted for the "surgical, decisive," and "simple" solution also adopted in 1789, namely, the confiscation of all ecclesiastical property and its sale to private citizens, together with the transformation of ecclesiastics into paid "pensionaries of the state." Nowhere, not even in the literature immediately preceding the Revolution, was the revolutionary solution to the state's financial problems more clearly anticipated than here.[164]

Quantitatively, at least, the episcopal cause mustered no more than a Noah's ark-like response to this deluge of writings submerging its *Actes*. With the exception of Lefranc de Pompignan's monumental *Défense des Actes du clergé de France concernant la religion*, moreover, the response tended to be uninspired as well. Particularly distinguished by its erudite aridity was a *Dissertation* by Jean-Etienne de Caulet, the same bishop of Grenoble who distinguished between despotism and absolute authority on the occasion of the king's recovery from Damiens' coup.[165]

Not that this situation was unprecedented in 1765. The comparative sterility of the clergy's polemical endeavors is attributable less to a dearth of legal and theological talent than to the various tactical positions from which it successively fought the century's battles. As long as the episcopacy was clearly on the offensive, it had only to appeal to the letter and even the spirit of the existing legislation, which in the case of the edict of 1695, appeared overwhelmingly in its favor. But however effective in terms of results, simple appeals to the letter of the law were unproductive of memorable prose. When beginning in 1754 the fortunes of battle shifted decisively against them, the bishops and their allies found themselves defending inherently untenable terrain. Only on the subject of the nature of the monarchy, where orthodoxy seemed clearly on their side, could the bishops continue to thrust aggressively and force their opponents into vulnerable positions. But on questions of ecclesiology and church-state relations it proved intrinsically difficult to parry their opponents' flat-footed but devastating offensive, for here it was their opponents who fought under the ensign of orthodoxy, accusing the bishops of disloyalty to all the tenets of the Gallican declaration so solemnly proclaimed by their predecessors in 1682.

The episcopal rejoinder to these accusations was superficially easy, consisting of another appeal to the letter and spirit of this same declaration. It was not difficult for the bishops to reply that in insisting that there were certain spiritual domains in which the secular power could not tread, they were hardly challenging the prince's independence in temporal affairs, and that not only had the declaration of 1682 assumed this to be so but the mouthpiece of the assembly that had adopted it, Bossuet himself, had repeatedly and explicitly affirmed this in his celebrated inaugural "sermon on unity."[166] Nor was it impossible to argue that deference to papal authority, even in the form of *Unigenitus*, was not incompatible with historic Gallican conciliarism, which according to both the assembly of 1682 and Bishop Bossuet was limited to bishops alone, exclusive of priests and laymen.[167] Everyone knew that any national or even ecumenical council composed of bishops alone would accept *Unigenitus*; it was moreover arguable that if tacit assent was all that was needed, both the Gallican and universal episcopacy had already accepted it.

Both these points were made with uncommon eloquence and ingenuity by Lefranc de Pompignan, the bishop of Le Puy, in his *Défense des Actes du clergé de France concernant la religion*, which appeared in 1769.[168] Just as he had done fourteen years earlier as author of the general assembly's 1755 remonstrances, Pompignan effectively challenged the criteria of factuality, externality, and relatedness to public order with which his Gallican-Jansenist opponents justified the intervention of the state in spiritual concerns: "In point of fact . . . this so-called power of the political sovereign, which only impinges, they say, on what affects the state in the affairs of religion, becomes the judge by [this] means . . . of everything that is most spiritual, for what is there in religion," he asked, "including its ceremonies, its cult, its discipline . . . that . . . does not possess the most important sorts of connections with public order and the tranquility of a state?"[169] Pompignan made this point most tellingly in relation to the prince's loudly trumpeted right to inspect and pass upon the ecumenicity of general church councils. Defining true or "divine" faith in unimpeachably Catholic fashion as "reliant upon the motive of the authority of the church," he concluded that "whoever is the master to apply or to withdraw this motive"—whoever, that is, is able to say whether the church has really spoken or no—"is the master of the faith of Christians. He is even more so than if he entered the immediate discussion of the dogmas. When one disposes of the spring that makes a machine move, one controls all its movements."[170]

What happens, then, to the distinction between the two powers, temporal and spiritual? In responding to this question, the bishop of Le Puy drove home his point by observing the close similarity in means between his Gallican-Jansenist opponents and the ultramontanists they despised:

> One side [the ultramontanists], favoring excessively the spiritual authority, and seeking a pretext for subordinating temporal affairs, thinks it has found it in their relatedness to spiritual objects. The other side, devoted without measure to the temporal power, and wishing to submit to it all of religion, establishes the rights that it attributes to this power upon the interest that the state might have in religious affairs. Here, it is the indirect power of the pope and the church over the temporal; there, it is the indirect power of the sovereign and the political magistrate over the spiritual.[171]

Against these opposite but equally reductionist indirections the bishop of Le Puy opposed his classical "juste milieu," consisting in "the immobile boundary separating spiritual from temporal," even if that entailed insisting that "princes, as members of [Christian] society and children of the church, obey the holy authority instituted by the Son of God in all that concerns religion," or that within its domain this authority "subjugates crowned heads along with those that are not."[172]

It was the same "juste milieu" that the bishop claimed to defend against Gallican-Jansenist ecclesiastical laicism. "It is a formal heresy," the bishop asserted, with perhaps the abbés Mey and Maultrot in mind, "to construe as republican the government of the church." "In a republic the laws draw their authority from the people who are the veritable sovereign; . . . in the church, on the contrary, the public laws, . . . called canons or holy decrees, emanate only from the corps of first pastors." In obeying these canons, the bishop obeyed only his corps, "not the society of the faithful, who can never become his superior in this regard, however numerous they be."[173] As uncompromisingly, then, as Damiens' short-term master Le Corgne de Launay in his *Défense des droits des évêques dans l'église*, but with a force uniquely his own, Pompignan hammered the point home: "It is absurd, it is repugnant to the nature of things, that the members, who have only been placed in the church to hear and follow, participate in the property of a power that consists in conducting and teaching."[174] The property of the power, and not its exercise only, the bishop of Le Puy placed squarely on the ermined shoulders of his peers, to the exclusion as well of simple parish priests, for unlike a republic, again, "where it could be said that the substance [*fond*] of political power belongs to the nation and the chiefs and magistrates enjoy only its exercise," the church's "fundamental law"—a phrase he undoubtedly employed with malice and aforethought—was "that the multitude be submissive."[175]

Pompignan hastened to add, in the spirit of 1682, that the bishops were no more the "vicars of the pope" than the "agents and mandatories of the people." The government of the church, he thought, was a "monarchy essentially tempered by an aristocracy, a monarchy of an entirely singular sort, where there is a king and also princes . . . whose dignities and functions are all necessary, whose origin is common, and where power in its divers degrees flows from the same source."[176] Yet his whole emphasis seemed rather to demonstrate how difficult it was becoming to maintain this classically Gallican "juste milieu," the articulation of which d'Aguesseau would have already found too ultramontanist. If choose he must, Pompignan admitted, between being the pope's vicars and the people's mandatories, accountable to laymen to say nothing of women, he would unhesitatingly embrace the former. For most practical purposes, at least, the "ultramontanist theologians" maintained the church as a "mixture of aristocracy with monarchy" instead of reducing it to the "tumults" and "discords" of "popular tribunals."[177]

A compromising admission, this, confirming his enemies' darkest suspicions. These suspicions were nonetheless self-fulfilling, especially after 1754. Increasingly thrown on the defensive by a Gallican declaration construed to mean the democratization and laicization of a church wholly under the thumb of the state, whose contents were described, in the bishop of Soissons' words, as "holy Truths, which belong to revelation, which form part of the sacred *dépôt* that Jesus Christ confided to his disciples, which has come down to us by the tradition of all the centuries," the Gallican episcopacy was bound to suffer a sort of identity crisis.[178] On a practical level, this crisis took the form of the appeal to the papacy to resolve Feuillant-Théatin doctrinal differences in October 1755, and the attempt by each side to appropriate *Ex Omnibus* to its own purposes thereafter. On a more theoretical level, the crisis assumed the form of a guarded challenge to the high status accorded the four Gallican liberties, their relegation to that of mere and problematical "opinion."

In response, for example, to the accusation that the general assembly of 1765 had avoided the expressions consecrated by that of 1682, Lefranc de Pompignan pleaded guilty to the opinion that "whatever the respect" that subsequent assemblies of the clergy had paid to the one held in 1682, they had "never considered its authority as equal to that of the universal church or an ecumenical council."[179] Such was also the judgment of the archbishops of Narbonne, Lyons, and Toulouse and the bishop of Orléans, who, appointed by Louis XV to examine the renegade Jansenist bishop of Soissons' high view of the

Gallican declaration, rather inclined to view it as a venerable but debatable "opinion" or "sentiment," which, however compatible with revelation, did not really belong to the realm of faith or dogma.[180] All, however, were preceded and outdone by Henri-Jacques de Montesquiou, bishop of Sarlat, who in 1764 had informed his diocesan clergy in an *Instruction pastorale* that God's word was "not the foundation of our [Gallican] liberties, for the word being unchangeable and uniform, all the churches that do not possess such liberties would then be governed against the word of God."[181] At about the same time, the bishop of Langres, Montmorin de Saint-Herem, ventured the opinion that the declaration of 1682 was more than just an opinion. But in the same breath he told his diocesan clergy that the "particular certitude" attributable to the article concerning the independence of the temporal power was "much superior to that of the other articles," leaving his clergy to wonder what precisely he thought of these.[182]

They might well have wondered what he and certain of his colleagues thought of the first article as well, for however inclined, as we have noted, the parti dévôt" was toward a despotic or anticonstitutional monarčhy in relation to lay subjects, it was by 1765 more than ever inclined to stress the limitations of the monarch's power in relation to the church. Recall the *Actes*' dubious but calculated punctuation of Romans 13:1; its spirited defense of the spiritual power as "sovereign, independent, and absolute"; its strident insistence that kings themselves should obey priests; its ominous admonition, finally, that priests were to obey "God rather than men."[183] Unlike the assembly of 1682, after all, which had defended the temporal power against the church, the assembly of 1765 rather defended the church against the temporal power.

On this high ridge as well, Pompignan's precarious "juste milieu" proved difficult to execute, and one easily slid from the proclamation of the temporal and spiritual powers' equal and complementary jurisdictions into a fall from obedience to the former. In practice, this disobedience assumed the form of a Christophe de Beaumont's or a Montmorency de Laval's belligerent disregard for the Declaration of Silence or even the general assembly's publication of the *Actes* in defiance of Louis XV's tacit but sufficiently known wishes. On a theoretical level, it took the shape of open exhortations to disobedience. "One might oppose me with the silence prescribed by the king's last declaration," conceded the bishop of Boulogne in a letter to the attorney general on October 1, 1754; "but you surely know, monsieur," he added, "that according to that of 1730 this silence that concerns the obedience due to the constitution *Unigenitus* . . . does not extend to the first pastors whom the holy spirit has commissioned to govern the church, and who have been charged with preaching the verities of the gospel from the rooftops. . . ." But just in case the declaration of 1754 differed from that of 1730 in this regard, which he very well knew it did, he reminded the attorney general that it was "better to obey God than men" and that he and his colleagues were prepared for "reproaches and persecutions."[184] Similarly, the bishop of Sisteron could proclaim in 1756 that "it is the king and not the parlements that we should obey," and that "to obey the parlements in sacramental matters would on the contrary be to disobey the king."[185] But just in case the parlement really represented the king's authority in this instance he flatly denied its competence: "I add that however sovereign and independent royal authority might be in relation to anyone except God, it could never have authorized the inclusion of the bishops in the silence that it has imposed." He likewise announced himself prepared for fire, dungeon, and sword.[186] If something frondish hovered about Gallican-Jansenist opposition during this period, something leaguish clung to that of their devout and episcopal foes.

Yet this leaguishness no more prevented episcopal publicists from coming forward as monarchy's last and truest defenders on the question of sovereignty than had the Gallican-Jansenists' frondishness inhibited them from posing as the monarchy's faithful vassals in matters of church-state relations. Joining his voice to those of his colleagues, Lefranc de Pompignan himself devoted considerable portions of his *Défense* to a defense of monarchy—with the aid of Bossuet, even the term "absolute"—against his opponents' unavowed principle of national sovereignty.[187] Moreover, he did not permit an opportunity to escape for insulting the magistracy. "A monarch," he asserted, "whose right is hereditary and absolute, reigns alone in his states," while "the governors, the generals, the magistrates he institutes are his first subjects *and nothing more.*"[188] But in a move already reflexive to the episcopacy, the bishop of Le Puy ahistorically linked the cause of the monarchy to that of his hierarchical and increasingly ultramontanist church and defended the absolutism of both. If it were really true, he said, that the bishops "in their chairs" were only "mandatories" and "representatives" of the people, then "the most absolute monarchs should be and are as much on their thrones."[189]

Many of his colleagues were more forthright. As early as 1753 the marquis d'Argenson complained of an "insane and fanatical" mandamus by the bishop of Montauban, which attributed France's good fortune to "papism" and England's misfortunes to heresy. England's revolutions of the previous century and consequent exile of her legitimate rulers were presented as the direct consequence of her earlier loss of "the true faith and Catholic unity."[190] It is not likely that the mandamus was a product of the marquis' unaided imagination, because only a couple of years later the bishop of Sisteron said much the same thing. Heresy's attacks upon the spiritual power of popes and bishops had always been the preludes to attacks upon the temporal powers of emperors and kings.[191] It was therefore to be hoped that the present king would soon perceive that "under the pretense of desiring to place himself triumphantly on the altar," the authors of the Declaration of Silence of 1754 were the "secret enemies of his own glory" who "tended toward nothing less than the immolation of his [royal] authority."[192] These enemies who could abide "neither king nor pope at their heads," had forcedly to be taught to leave "throne and altar as they have always been, that is, the bishops as sole masters with their chief to command in the church . . . and the monarch as sole absolute and independent master to command in the state."[193] By the time of the trial of the Jesuits, even the general assemblies had taken up the refrain. "Episcopal authority is the rampart of monarchical authority," its remonstrances solemnly informed the king. "The example of a neighboring realm teaches us that the independence of the people is a necessary consequence of the supremacy of the prince [over the church]." By violating ecclesiastical jurisdiction, "the tribunals might acquire some rights, but your majesty loses his own."[194]

The clergy's reaction to the suppression of the Jesuit order and to criticism of its *Actes* finally hardened this refrain into a full-scale litany. The *Réflexions d'un François papiste et royaliste*, the title of a pro-Jesuit pamphlet published in 1764, by itself speaks volumes, as does a *Lettre d'un cosmopolite*, published the same year, which announced the formation and growth of a conspiracy against throne and altar.[195] Yet another clerical pamphleteer contested Gallican-Jansenism's hitherto unchallenged quasi-monopoly of what one Jesuit had already dubbed "the jargon of patriotism," and in his "double title" of "Catholic" and "Frenchman," raised a "cry of indignation" in reaction to Le Blanc de Castillon's *Réquisitoire*, especially its disrespectful attitude toward the papacy.[196] Well before it described a political reality of the counterrevolution or became a watchword of the Bourbon and Catholic Restoration, Bourbon "throne" and papal "altar" began huddling together, if not in fact, at least in the minds of the emerging clerical party in France.

Ultramontanism and monarchical absolutism, or the Civil Constitution of the Clergy—that was how matters stood by 1765. Whatever the original intentions of the celebrated assembly of 1682, they were irrelevant now; whatever bridge classical Gallicanism yet maintained across the widening chasm was rapidly collapsing. Symptomatically, the royal council's judgment of May 24, 1765, which attempted to articulate and reinforce this bridge, was beset by both sides, as increasingly these sides had beset almost everything the king had attempted to do affecting their relations since 1750. The Gallican Declaration of 1682, that great legislative tapestry from the age of Louis XIV, weaving conciliar church and divine right monarchy together, now joined the edict of 1695 in shreds.

CHAPTER 4

A Literary Damiens

SEVENTEEN hundred and fifty-seven, the year of Damiens, narrowly missed witnessing a notorious literary blow to royal authority as well. About a year and a half after Damiens' assault, Claude-Adrien Helvétius, sometime tax farmer, the queen's maître d'hôtel, and would-be philosophe, published a book that exhibited a marked preference for the republican institutions of contemporary England or ancient Athens and Rome, proffered a few kind words for regicides such as Cromwell, and resounded with declamations against despotism.[197] "Know O King," he quoted the ancient Persian maxim with evident approval, "that your authority will cease to be legitimate the moment you cease to render the Persians happy."[198]

Coming as it did on the heels of the Damiens affair, Helvétius' *De L'Esprit* aroused the vigilance of both episcopal and parlementary watchmen, among them some of the chief protagonists in the conflicts we have here described. From his ancestral home in La Roque in Périgord, whence Louis XV had recently relegated him for his unrepentant disobedience to the Declaration of Silence, Christophe de Beaumont fulminated his anathemas in a mandamus dated November 22, 1758. Sensitive, no doubt, to Jansenist accusations of his having seditiously distinguished between legitimate and illegitimate monarchical authority in his previous mandamus on the occasion of the Damiens affair, the archbishop severely censured the book's "temerarious discussions," which "always manifest only too clearly the sentiments of independence and even of revolt" against "everything that bears the character of supreme power." In enjoining upon his parishioners the spirit of "humble and Christian subordination," the "most perfect submission toward all the powers," the archbishop on this occasion even correctly translated the Vulgate's rendering of Romans 13:1 and recalled in addition the preachments of Bossuet: "There is no power that does not come from God; it is he who has established all those on earth: hence he who opposes these powers resists God's command and brings upon himself His condemnation . . . ; it is therefore necessary to submit to them, not only from the fear of punishment, but also as a dictate of conscience."[199]

It took Le Paige much longer to detect the "republican" venom in Helvétius' book, not improbably because his own was sufficiently akin to *De L'Esprit*'s to ensure nearly total immunity. Invited by a mysterious "B" in December of 1758 to help review the political portion of Christophe de Beaumont's mandamus for the *Nouvelles écclésiastiques*, Le Paige could not find anything in *De L'Esprit* to substantiate the archbishop's strictures as late as January 16, 1759.[200] The archbishop's accusations against *De L'Esprit* in this regard were nothing less than "exaggerated," "exorbitant," even bordering on the "calumnious." It was the same old archepiscopal performance again, "rather too tardily and without real necessity" barking up the wrong tree, in part to regain the royal good favor, in part to throw the true guardians of royal authority off the track of the Jesuits and their episcopal devotees, the real culprits in the matter.[201] Not until February 13 did Le Paige see the light—or the darkness—when, peripherally blinded in either event, he lost sight of the *champs de mars* and national consent and remembered only the *Politique tirée des propres paroles de l'Ecriture sainte*. The Persian maxim that royal authority was legitimate only inasmuch as it rendered people happy Le Paige found "seditious and always false"; royal authority itself remained inviolately legitimate, its exercise alone occasionally not. The maxim that a puissant corps of magistrates kept a prince in line by inspiring in him not only a sense of justice but also fear Le Paige likewise found objectionable; however abusive the exercise of his authority, the prince never needed to doubt the fidelity of his magistrates.[202] No less than the archbishop, the parlement and Le Paige as its spokesman deemed it imperative to make a point of their monarchical orthodoxy.[203]

But even without the pressure of the Damiens affair, Le Paige and Christophe de Beaumont would probably have sooner or later reacted as they did to the political philosophy of *De L'Esprit*, for linked as they were to a purely sensationalistic epistemology, a relentlessly hedonistic ethics, and an implicit denial of the soul, Helvétius' "republican" effusions were bound to elicit the most conservative elements in the political thought of both. In spite of their differences, sincere Catholics both, the Jansenist lawyer and the Jesuitical archbishop together retreated from some of the radical implications of their own political thought when these boomeranged in the form of a challenge to their faith. It is hardly surprising to find even the most embroiled of neighbors cooperating or at least dousing in tandem with the house between them on fire.

The neighbors in question nonetheless contrived to spill more than half the water on each other, for the Helvétius affair presented all too natural an opportunity to tax each other with its responsibility. Le Paige took the lead in this by identifying the Jesuits as the true authors of the seditious maxims that Helvétius had only repeated in considerably less virulent form. Had not the Jesuits been "a thousand times convicted of traditionally having a doctrine murderous of kings for every occasion where such action is called for and of which they have appointed themselves as judges?" Had not the year 1757 itself witnessed a new edition of the Jesuit Busembaum's *Theologia Moralis*, which defended this doctrine? Even Helvétius' "materialism" was laid at the feet of the order's Molinistic and *Unigenitus*-consecrated theology, which by abstracting the supernatural and hypostatizing a purely natural man, had laid the foundations for the impious edifice the philosophes were then in the act of raising. Le Paige took up considerably more of the *Nouvelles écclésiastiques*' space in flagellating the archbishop's mandamus and its "veritable authors"—the Jesuits, of course—than in refuting Helvétius' *De L'Esprit.*[204]

But Le Paige was perhaps not being altogether paranoiac in suspecting the archbishop of a similar maneuver. In showily waving his finger at deism and the "proud philosophy of our century," was Beaumont not subtly indicting appellants and the parlement of Paris?[205] Is that not what his mandamus on the occasion of the Damiens affair had already done, by maliciously associating the encyclopedic "weakening of the faith among us" with a parlementary "disobedience and even rebellion against the sovereign and his laws" and then attributing to this fictitious ensemble the responsibility for Damiens' blow of January 5?[206] Certain it is, in any event, that Capmartin de Chaupy's *Observations sur le refus que fait le Châtelet* had earlier accused the parlement of being riddled with unbelievers and deists, and that the Jesuits were soon to employ the same tactic more subtly and massively by lavishing all their attention, in the debate accompanying their expulsion, on the relatively "enlightened" *Compte rendu* of the attorney general of the parlement of Brittany while feigning ignorance of the hundred or more pamphlets of purely Gallican-Jansenist inspiration that were delivering them the most damaging blows.[207] To concentrate all their polemical energies in corralling the most conspicuously "enlightened" opponents the better to brand them all with the stigma of unbelief was a tactic not infrequently employed among Old Regime defenders of the ecclesiastical establishment.

It would therefore be most naive to judge Le Paige's or Beaumont's political thought, much less that of parlementary-Jansenist or devout milieux in general, exclusively by reference to their reactions to Helvétius' *De L'Esprit* or any other literary production of a distinctively "enlightened" hue.[208] It was in dialogue with each other, where the most fundamental givens of Catholicism were not at stake, that they most candidly spoke their political minds. What clearly emerged as early as 1757 from their century-long and hostile exchange were the ideological contours of both Revolution and counterrevolution—and that, moreover, quite independently of what one might call typically "enlightened" thought. Is it so fanciful, on the one hand, to recognize the lineaments of revolutionary "liberalism" in the ecclesiastical laicism, political constitutionalism, and guarded appeal to the nation typical of the Jansenist, Gallican, and parlementary syndrome of mid-century? The confiscation of ecclesiastical property, the redrawing of ecclesiastical boundaries, the transformation of the church's ministers into the state's salaried officials, even their election by the nation—all these provisions of the Civil Constitution of the Clergy were in one way or another specifically anticipated in the Gallican-Jansenist literature of the century's middle decades. Or does it, on the other hand, stretch the imagination unduly to discern within the "devout" camp's mid-century synthesis between ultramontanism and anticonstitutional royalism one of the hallmarks of later counterrevolutionary thought and action? Most conspicuously missing, at this stage, is aristocracy as such as a bone of contention.[209] But the anti-aristocratic egalitarianism that played so important a role in the revolutionary mentality of the 1790s was a late-comer to the eighteenth-century scene; it was nowhere to be found in concentrated form during its middle decades.

As for Helvétius, it has been as easy for historians as it was for his contemporaries to exaggerate the radicalism of *De L'Esprit*'s political message. How far does its fire really extend, once the billowy smoke of its Anglophilism and nostalgic hankering after the ancient "warrior republics" is finally cleared, beyond a vaguely Montesquieuean division of power between the people, the great, and the king, or more specifically in a "puissant corps of magistrates" protecting the people from "the cruelties of tyranny" and the king from the "furors of sedition?"[210] It is nothing, in any case, that is not derivative and banal or that goes much beyond the average parlementary remonstrance of the 1750s. In locating national consent closer to home within French constitutional history specifically and in linking it by clear implication to real and contemporary institutions, Le Paige had in his way been more subversive. Moreover, it is not easy to see in his quibbling objections to Helvétius' maxims anything other than a straining at gnats, a belated and not very convincing attempt to distinguish between himself and a compromising bedfellow. The distinction between the legitimacy of royal authority itself, in case of abuse, and that of its abusive *usage*, was metaphysical enough; whether in practice the one justified for Helvétius more than the dutiful disobedience that the other justified for Le Paige is moreover far from evident. And as for the "fears" that Le Paige objected to in principle as a magisterial weapon against the prince, it entered routinely into his political calculations at the level of practice, at least in the form of the fear of going broke. His calculations in this regard during the parlementary "strike" of 1756-1757 were fully as Machiavellian as any that took place.[211]

In the last analysis, Helvétius was a sort of literary Damiens, another castoff from the college of Louis-le-Grand, his blow the literary counterpart to Damiens' physical one of January 5. What made either blow so unacceptable to ecclesiastical and Jansenist-parlementary antagonists alike was in part the socially or intellectually alien nature of its *source*, Damiens representing the "vilest dredges of the people" and Helvétius that of materialistic and hedonistic unbelief. Yet neither blow would have been as unacceptable as it was had its *content* not been embarrassingly close to the positions represented by the same censorious antagonists. Damiens unmistakably articulated his motives in terms of the language of the Jansenist-parlementary rhetoric of opposition; and to whatever dubious extent Helvétius' opposition to "despotic" monarchical authority went beyond the dutiful disobedience of the Jansenists and parlementaires, it could be and was in fact said to have gone there with the help of precedents still closely associated with their devout antagonists. Le Paige and Christophe de Beaumont therefore fairly stumbled over each other in their zeal to make sacrificial victims of Damiens and Helvétius, literally avoiding doing so only because the archbishop was a bit laggard in the first case, Le Paige a bit so in the second. But their zealous stumbling is a measure not so much of their conservatism as of the extent to which each had separately strayed from the monarchical-ecclesiastical synthesis once articulated by a Bossuet or a d'Aguesseau.

CHAPTER 5

Damiens' Peers

The Mauvais Discours Janséniste

BOTH PARTIES, then, to the politico-religious disputes of the 1750s and 1760s tended diversely to oppose and undermine the royal good pleasure in the very act of exalting it. Although magnifying the "prince's" right in relation to ecclesiastical "independence," Jansenist and parlementary polemicists also telescoped it together with that of the parlement and the nation at the first sign of independence by the person of the prince himself. And while raising the royal will to new levels of irresponsibility in relation to its lay subjects, episcopal apologists melted it down as it approached the sun of their own sacrosanct jurisdiction. Each side cried "despotism" in the event of a royal transgression of its particular version of constitutional limitations, although Jansenists and parlementary partisans more readily charged into battle with this war cry on their lips than did their opponents. But did either or both of these forms of elite political opposition provoke echoes among the lower Parisian or more generally French populace? If so, did they remain echoes only or were they resonances also, contributing something of their own? More specifically, did the elites' theoretical undermining of the constitutional bases of divine-right monarchy in any way affect popular attitudes toward this venerable and quasi-sacral institution? On the parlementary and Jansenist side of the lines, Damiens' own oppositional odyssey has already affirmatively answered the first of these questions.[1] But even here, a greater precision can perhaps be attained by an examination of the approximately one hundred cases of yet more numerous unfortunates who found themselves arrested and interrogated in the wake of

Damiens' deed by reason of "seditious remarks," or "mauvais discours," supposed foreknowledge of or participation in a regicidal plot, or mere acquaintance with or proximity to the king's assailant.

Scattered among the archives of the Bastille, the Châtelet, and the parlement of Paris, as well as in the papers of the Joly de Fleury brothers and the marquis de Sourches, grand provost of France, these dossiers prove less than transparent as indices of popular political consciousness. The regicidal plots turned out to exist in the imaginations of their denouncers alone; the instances of foreknowledge disintegrated upon closer examination into either foreknowledge about something quite different or humdrum after-knowledge after all; and the mauvais discours often proved unverifiable, distorted by rumor, or calumniously attributed to their utterers. One readily shares Lieutenant of Police Berryer's sense of frustration upon ascertaining that a certain *discours* that had seemed very *mauvais* when reported by the vigilant widow Makkinsy of the Jesuitical rue Saint-Jacques dwindled into something quite innocent when tracked down to the lawyer Sache de Bellevaux of the Jansenist and parlementary rue des Maçons: "It is almost always the same in these verifications . . . in which one discovers that the contents of the propos change in the measure that they pass from person to person."[2] It is also hard not to share the attorney general's sense of outrage over the fact that "it suffices these days to acquire an enemy in order at once to be accused of a mauvais propos," as well as his desire to make an example of the huissier Jacques Mirlavaud of the town of Gonnat, false accuser of his neighbor, in order to "put a stop to these calumnies" to which "vengeance and animosity alone have given birth."[3] What makes this evidence all the more difficult to construe is that it cannot be simply dismissed. Even if calumniously attributed, the mauvais discours was nonetheless uttered; even if originally innocent, the distorted discours nonetheless became mauvais; and even if unexecuted, the regicidal plot was nonetheless imagined. All may therefore be indicative of unavowed political opposition.

But a good part of the evidence's limitations is attributable to the magistracy and the police themselves, who for obvious reasons were unenthusiastic about tracking down mauvais discours of a distinctively Jansenist-parlementary stripe. The attorney general and the lieutenant of police assiduously followed the trail of the mauvais propos reported by the stockbroker Langlois de Beaumont—that the king would do better to "look out for himself" instead of sending troops to Austria—until it led to the mouth of the lawyer Sache de Bellevaux, who reportedly only said, in a conversation on the rue de Bièvre, that it might be dangerous for the king to create a civilian militia of forty-two thousand men. At this point, the magistrates deemed it unnecessary to ask the parlementary lawyer what he himself could recall having said, even though they had at least informally interrogated everyone else in the matter, including—formally, in his case—the abbé Blanche de Valfontaine, an almoner resident on the Jesuitical rue Saint-Antoine.[4] We earlier noted how the propos about the need for a "bloodletting" in France was tracked from domestic servant to domestic servant until it alighted at the dinner table of the parlementary lawyer Jean-Baptiste Le Gouvé, who was then not even so much as extrajudicially questioned about what he had said.[5]

Yet more startling is the magisterial response to a deposition by one Noël de Lailly, a royal procurator at the salt storehouse at Arnay-le-Duc, who after the assassination recalled to the subdelegate of the Parisian généralité that on November 19, 1756—a mere month and a half, that is, before Damiens took the coach from Arras to Paris—he himself had taken the coach from Arras to Paris accompanied by a "young man" of perhaps eighteen or nineteen years. This passenger, an Arras alderman's son on his way to begin the study of law in Paris, had spoken freely while on the coach concerning the "affairs of the parlement and the clergy," more particularly "praising the prince de Conti for having greatly contributed to the recall of the parlement" and blaming "the clergy and above all the Jesuits" for causing all "the troubles that agitate the state." The Jesuits, he said, were "wretches of whom he knew things that would destroy them if they were widely known." Lailly remembered that the *jeune homme* had intended to lodge with a Châtelet attorney who lived near the place Maubert and bore the surname of a bird. A little research in the *Almanach royal* turned up a sieur Letourneaux (*l'étourneau*), an attorney at the Châtelet, residing in the rue des Rats near the place Maubert, and the attorney general went so far as to write to Arras for a copy of the November register of the Arras-Paris coach. But on February 17 the parlementary commissioners decided not to pursue the matter further because the propos in question were "too vague to merit attention."[6]

Lest they be deemed too vague to merit our attention as well, what of the deposition of the domestic servant Jean Persy, corroborated by that of the greffier Larquois de Courboissy, who on March 1 reported to the police commissioner Rochebrune concerning the sayings of a certain sieur Le Blanc, a resident of the same building with Persy? Both before and following the December 13 lit de justice this Le Blanc, according to Persy, had said "before all the world and without any precaution" that "without the parlement there was no king," that "the parlement existed before any royalty," that the king behaved irresponsibly in "not following the counsels of the prince de Conti," that this prince would do well to retire to Languedoc where there were plenty of [Protestant] malcontents ready to take his side," but that the king could yet prevent such a revolt by "abasing the heads of d'Argenson, Bellisle, and the archbishop of Paris," after which the Jesuits should be "burned and hung."[7] Sufficiently precise and undeniably seditious, these remarks! Yet no trace exists of any judicial follow-up to Persy's deposition, even though Le Blanc still resided at the same address on the rue de la Croix-des-Petits-Champs. Or what, again, of the propos of the master locksmith Chaumet who, according to the tapestry worker André Aubryé, allowed shortly after the event of January 5 that Louis XV was a tyrant who treated his people like "dogs," that the actual (or rump) parlement was a "band of robbers authorized by the king," and that after the "honnêtes gens" who truly comprised the parlement had "flung their resignations in the face of the king" (*avoit jetté leur bonne casse au roi*) there remained only the "Jean F[outres] to compose it?" Despite the antiparlementary twist, the propos were nonetheless basically proparlementary—or pro-parti janséniste—and although they were more or less corroborated by the watchmaker Philippe-Henri Bery who lived in the same building on the rue Saint-André-des-Arts, there again seems to have been no judicial follow-up or prosecution.[8]

But in other cases the parlement simply could not ignore such compromising discourses and had to cope with them as best it could. Such was the case with Dominique Gautier, intendant of the marquis de Ferrières, whom Damiens accused of anti-archepiscopal remarks and having suggested to him the idea of "touching" the king. The fact that in this instance Damiens himself was the accuser made it imperative to arrest Gautier and at least question the marquis de Ferrières, although apparently not to wait for a formal verdict before declaring them both innocent in a semi-official fashion. "Gautier appeared first with the countenance of a surprised man, but who knows himself to be innocent," declared the parlement's greffier Le Breton in his preface to the published trial record: as for Ferrières, the confrontation with the assassin was a "painful" though victorious ordeal "for a man of his birth."[9] Such was also the case with the famous "France needs a bloodletting" propos involving the lawyer Le Gouvé, which the parlement unavoidably inherited when it took over the Damiens trial from the not so discriminate *prévôté de l'Hôtel du roi* on January 18. Once this deposition had been accepted as part of the case's *information*, there was no judicial alternative except to see it through, and wait patiently until the end of the trial in order to "disjoin" it from—and in this way declare it irrelevant to—the case of Damiens.[10] Nor could the parlement do anything to prevent Jean-Antoine Lefevre, a huissier in the Paris Cour des aides whose family had been reduced to penury because of the parlementary "strike" of December 13, from going to Versailles on February 10 and requesting from both Richelieu and the comte de Saint-Florentin the permission to harangue the king personally with a memorized "rhapsody drawn from all the remonstrances of the different parlements" against ministerial despotism, ecclesiastical independence, and the king's authoritative blows in favor of the Grand conseil. Nothing, that is, except to work hand-in-glove with the police in keeping the affair out of the courts and strictly "extrajudicial."[11]

Still other cases perversely revealed their parlementary colors only after they had been engaged. The huissier Jacques Mirlavaud of the town of Gonnat near Moulins, calumnious accuser of his neighbor Claude Horsel, a bourgeois of the same town, initially charged this neighbor with having opined over dinner that Damiens had intended to "over-die (*surmourir*) in wishing to destroy a king pitiless toward his people, and that in knifing his majesty he had gained paradise." Only while languishing in the prisons of Moulins while his case was being instructed did he remember that Claude Horsel had also "sung verses in the middle of the street" to the effect that "the king was no longer anything and the parlement would not concede to him anything, along with other words he could no longer recall."[12] The final judgment in the Mirlavaud/Horsel case, which indeed made it into the published supplement to the Damiens trial, mentioned only the mauvais discours initially attributed to Horsel and remained reticent concerning the parlementary ones that his accuser had later imagined.[13] Similarly, the Parisian hatter Jean Aveque, originally arrested as a participant in a regicidal plot falsely denounced by a certain Alexandre-Louis Maréchal, turned out upon further investigation by the police to be (in their words) a "gossip" and a "born malicious tongue," who could "not help himself from speaking thoughtlessly and randomly" in favor of the parlement, Cromwell, and Ravaillac and against the king and Pompadour.[14] And in a different yet somewhat parallel vein, Charles-Solamon de Sourdeval's accusation that a certain blacksmith in Dampierre named Hérault had not only uttered "seditious and insolent propos against the king" but had also fabricated empoisoned arms with which to assassinate him made some kind of formal investigation imperative. This investigation predictably revealed Sourdeval as Hérault's calumnious neighbor, earning him perpetual galley labor as his reward. Yet the Châtelet's sentence of October 4, 1758, neither specified that one of the seditious propos in question involved Hérault's loudly taking the side of the parlement against the king on the occasion of the lit de justice of December 13, 1756, nor does it seem that Hérault himself was ever inconvenienced on the subject, even though one of the witnesses in the case, a tonsured cleric named François Le Vacher, partly and rather reluctantly corroborated the verbal portion of Sourdeval's accusations in the course of an extrajudicial interrogation.[15]

Despite the magistracy's obvious reluctance to pursue leads too close to home, the evidence, then, unquestionably points to the existence of a parlementary-Jansenist species of mauvais discours circulating in diverse degrees of distortion, at various levels of society and in the provinces as well as in Paris. Under the same category perhaps, although the *discours* in question were not especially *mauvais*, we can group a couple of the cases mentioned earlier of supposed foreknowledge of the event. The shopboy Fidelle-Amable Chauveau's "something terrible," which he predicted would "soon surprise" his cousin in Péronne turned out to be "a revolution in the state" occasioned by the king's expected suppression of the parlement; and the "very surprising news" promised by the wife of Prussian-born Parisian shoemaker Guillaume Kattman in a letter to a curé in Hargest-en-Santerre became among other things the expected "return of the parlement and the disgrace of the archbishop of Paris."[16] Both could be construed as mildly sympathetic to the parlement and further attest at least to the popular interest in the politico-ecclesiastical quarrels embroiling the parlements and appellants with the episcopacy and the monarchy in France.

A marquis, a lawyer, a huissier, a greffier, a law student, a master locksmith, a master blacksmith, a journeyman and an apprentice hatter, a shoemaker and his wife, five or six domestic servants plus a jeweler's shopboy—these, it is true, do not make for a very homogeneous crowd, despite the predictable presence of venal officialdom and the domestics in its service. Nor does it quite qualify as a crowd. Yet it would more nearly approach the dimensions of one if we could only discover who precisely threw a folded piece of paper into Jean-Thomas Herrissant's bookstore in the rue Saint-Jacques on

January 12, 1757, prophesying that "if we do not burn the Jesuits all Paris is lost"; or who left a similar billet found in the Palais de justice at about the same time with the threat that "as long as we have the Jesuits in France, the parlement and the people will be unhappy, and since the king does not want to get rid of them we must burn them in their houses."[17] They seem in any case to have been of the same political persuasion as the person who sent a packet to the consular court of Paris advising the parlement as "head of the people" to "give our remonstrances, the people will obey you"; or who periodically peppered Paris with seditious placards and billets.[18] Some of these latter exude a distinctively Jansenist and parlementary aroma, such as the one found in October 1758 in the Châtelet courtyard against the archbishop of Paris' return from exile, while others reveal a more antiroyal pungency, such as the following billet found circulating at the time of Damiens' trial:

Bed of justice at Versailles (Aug. 21, 1756)
Bed of justice at Paris (Dec. 13, 1756)
Bed of justice at Saint Denis (French kings' burial place)

Louis-Adrien Le Paige reported and commented upon similar placards and billets found in January 1757 in the Luxembourg Gardens, the doors of the Hôtel de Ville, and on various street corners elsewhere in Paris.[19]

At least one fabricator of placards was found out, and since he was also a mauvais discourser, having committed the indiscretion of voicing the substance of some of his placards over dinner in polite company, he may be added to our list. His name was Moriceau de La Motte, a huissier in the Paris prevotal court, who placarded the rue Saint-Germain l'Auxerrois and the door of the Tuileries with the suggestion that the villain Damiens had been judged by men fully as villainous as he. His imagination, he confessed, "had been fired against the king by various writings and by the divisions between the parlement and the bishops; and that in his heat he had tried to make the truth reach the king by means of these placards."[20] The fact that his placards were in a limited sense directed against the parlement—the nonresigners who stayed on to try Damiens—probably made it easier for the parlement to make him into an example. On September 6, 1758, it upheld the Châtelet prosecuting attorney's *a minima* appeal to the effect that Moriceau de La Motte deserved to be hung after sustaining the question and performing an *amende honorable*. This sentence was executed on the place de Grève five days later.[21]

The Mauvais Discours Dévôt

THE EXISTENCE of Jansenist-parlementary mauvais discours at the popular level does not of course preclude popular support for the opposing party in the century's ecclesiastical and religious disputes, that which Damiens designated as the ecclesiastics'. Were there "devout" counterparts to the parlementary-Jansenist seditious remarks circulating in connection with or proximity to the Damiens affair? Did it proceed from the mouths of others besides ecclesiastics? In neither case would we expect the parlement to have passed by such an opportunity to compensate for its partially blindfolded one eye by means of some equally partial perspicacity by the other. And indeed, numbers of such cases caught its attention.

Among them, those involving ecclesiastics predictably dominated, although these cases fall into several distinct categories. Heading this list—and the kind that the parlement pursued most seriously—was the seemingly threatening mauvais discours with regicidal overtones that their denouncers recalled having been uttered shortly before Damiens' deed of January 5. One such discourse was that of a Lazarist priest of Artesian birth residing in the port of Rochefort, one Canson, who on the occasion of a discussion about the bull *Unigenitus* in the house of the naval lieutenant Cherotel shortly before the assassination had supposedly said that "it was not too much to employ [the means of] iron and fire [against appellants of the bull *Unigenitus*], and that one would see plenty of other [means] as well." When rendered by the intendant's subdelegate as "one will see plenty of other *events* before long," this discourse struck the attorney general and the parlementary commissioners (although not Rouillé to whom it was originally reported) as sufficiently seditious to warrant judicial proceedings on the part of the local criminal lieutenant. These duly took their course until it became apparent that only a single witness could directly attest to what Canson had said.[22] The parlement itself commenced proceedings in the case of a Jesuit from Arras who in the context of a conversation about the affaires du temps occurring in Abbéville ten or twelve days before the assassination had reportedly remarked that "there are still Ravaillacs." Decisive as this seemed, it nonetheless developed that the remark in question had only been remembered by a certain Godart de Thurion, a treasurer of France, in a conversation that took place a week *after* the assassination, and that Thurion had had it, not from the Jesuit directly, but only secondhand from the abbé de Hodens, a local abbé who in turn had heard it in a conversation with this Jesuit, not toward the end of 1756, but possibly as many as two or three years earlier.[23] The abbé de Hodens was still in Abbéville and available to testify to what the Jesuit had said, but the discourse's distance from the event sufficiently blunted its seditiousness as to slacken the zeal of the attorney general.

Another type of "devout" mauvais discours had to do with ecclesiastics' after-the-event reactions to the news of Damiens' deed. These usually consisted in public expressions of the conviction that Damiens' assault was of parlementary inspiration or provenance. "Yes, monsieur, nothing is more certain than that the king has been assassinated, and that it is the parlement that commissioned the assassin because the king did not want to exile three bishops," reportedly opined a Capuchin friar of Issoire in response to the local *procureur du roi*'s request for news. Needless to say the procurator lost no time in bringing the matter to the attention of his superior in Paris.[24] A similar remark by a Jesuit in Lyons, that "that could only have come from a parlementarian," was vigilantly noted and reported by the procureur du roi of the same city.[25] A variation on the same theme was struck by the curé Tournial of La Chatre, an ex-Jesuit, who in the course of his January 9 Sunday sermon announced that the church and her ministers, though they had "long groaned under the weight of their enemies' persecutions," would soon be "more triumphant than ever." The attorney general's substitute in La Chatre was probably not mistaken in detecting in the remark the curé's hopeful prediction of royal policy's eventual reaction to Damiens' parlementary associations.[26]

Yet none of this was sufficiently seditious, in the sense of threatening the king, to warrant prosecution; however indignant he might have been, therefore, the attorney general could do little more in response to such denunciations than to scrawl "nothing to be done, at least for the present" in the margins.[27] The only possible exception to this rule concerned a priest names Jean-Baptiste Mesguet from the diocese of Bayeux, one of the participants in a bizarre but revelatory exchange that occurred on Thursday, January 6, at the café Procope. In the midst of a lively discussion about Damiens' "horrible attempt" someone ventured that it could only have been the work of a fanatic, whereupon this ecclesiastic, according to one witness, responded that "assuredly this blow could not have been struck by a royalist."[28] Other witnesses recalled the response differently, maintaining that Mesguet had virtually accused his conversant of being a royalist, thereby giving his hearers to understand that he, Mesguet, was not. But in either case the abbé's curious remark was taken to imply the existence of "two parties in France," one royalist and the other not, and the Procope's clientele had little doubt about which one the abbé belonged to. "You see how all of those types [ecclesiastics] think," one of them loudly concluded after the abbé left.[29] The incident illustrates how widespread was the distrust of ecclesiastics as un-French, even though the unfortunate abbé most probably intended to suggest quite the contrary, that it was he and his kind who were royalists and advocates of the parlement who were not. Arrested and embastillé on January 14, he denied any subversive intent or even having uttered the remark attributed to him. Berryer deemed him "sufficiently punished" by six months of imprisonment to release him on July 23.[30]

Genuinely antiroyal remarks by ecclesiastics had to wait

until the epoch of the expulsion of the Jesuits to find utterance. Then a small cluster of denunciations crop up in the papers of the attorney general. In Cirray in Poitou, a woman informant complained of a Capuchin friar named Pacifique who, hardly in keeping with his namesake, preached a sermon full of "the most scandalous and atrocious traits with regard to the prince, saying that he was a tyrant both by himself and in his administration."[31] From Melun in Brie came the complaint that a certain père Arnoult of the Picpus religious said to the curé of Mormons over dinner in October 1764 that "if there were two eyes the less in France the Jesuits would soon be reestablished," a reference to the dauphin's well-known pro-Jesuit sympathies.[32] More seditious still were the sayings attributed to a vagabond priest who appeared near Chaource in December 1766 demanding bread at the curé's house and announcing that whereas the people had sincerely mourned the dauphin's death they would not have been aggrieved by his father's because "the king wanted to take all his subjects' property," including the Jesuits', "for fear that the latter might give him battle." He added the prediction that the king "would die in the month of February" and although "Damiens had said that he could not kill him . . . others soon would. . . ."[33]

In none of these cases were any arrests made, either because the denunciations proved impossible to corroborate or (as in the case of the vagabond) the denounced too elusive to catch. It was otherwise with the unfortunate Jacques Ringuet, ex-Jesuit and priest of the diocese of Cambrai, who demanded hospitality at the house of a monastic order on the evening of September 1, 1762. Over dinner and wine, this embittered ex-Jesuit "overflowed with insults and invectives against the parlement of Paris and in particular against m. de Chauvelin," physically threatening the latter and allowing that "only the *putainisme* could have destroyed the order of Jesuits." He was on his way to Paris, he said, where he would work for the restoration of his society, failing which he would retire to Holland in the company of a married Jesuit with whose help he would compose books against France and her government. Repeatedly boasting that he had been "present when the king was wounded by Damiens," he said that "he would have been very unhappy had his society not known he was there." The parlement did not take this matter lightly. On December 29, 1762, it upheld the Châtelet's sentence of December 9 condemning him to hanging in the place de Grève after performing an *amende honorable* before Notre Dame, the Tuileries Palace, and the Hôtel de Ville.[34]

Yet a fourth category of "devout" mauvais discours took the form of a condemnation of the king's unedifying moral example, together with expressions of sympathy for his unfortunate queen and their scandalized heir. One might more logically expect to encounter such a complaint in Jansenist-parlementary guise, given Jansenism's long-standing moral rigorism and the Jansenizing bishop Fitz-James' spectacular insistence, as Louis XV's confessor at Metz in 1745, that the gravely ill king dismiss his mistress madame de Châteauroux as a condition for receiving the viaticum or extreme unction.[35] On the contrary, however, it was the Jesuits and especially the king's Jesuit confessors who despite their equally long-standing reputation for moral laxism most strenuously condemned the king's promiscuous sexual example, going so far as to deny either the king or madame de Pompadour absolution so long as the latter merely remained at court.[36] The fact that the offended queen, embarrassed *mesdames de France*, and the scandalized dauphin also paraded their pro-Jesuitical and archepiscopal sympathies further reinforced this association, the reaction to which explains, perhaps, the Jansenist press' silence. At least the king's moral misconduct plays no role in the antigovernmental case of the Jansenist-parlementary polemical literature of the period.

An ecclesiastical example of this "devout" moral concern in the form of mauvais discours is perhaps provided by Lesnier, curé of the duchy of Piney near Troyes, who on the Sunday following January 5 sermonized against "Herods on the throne who made no scruple about helping themselves to their subjects' women" and further ventured that "nothing is more common today than adulterers among the court great." Or was the reference so unmistakably pointed as that? All agreed that the curé had spoken in his sermon about King Herod and John the Baptist, but only four of his parishioners—the *procureur fiscal* and his wife, another procurator, and a huissier—insisted that he had made any implicit reference to Louis XV and his court. The four witnesses in question, representatives of local justice all, had moreover been long notoriously *brouillé* with the curé, in view of which the attorney general and Saint-Florentin on the advice of the intendant of Champagne decided that inaction was in this instance the better part of vigilance.[37]

Whatever the truth of the matter, a mauvais discours of that variety on the tongue of a curé was not at all the rule. Paradoxical as it may again seem, expressions of moral indignation over the king's private conduct was more typically a lay rather than an ecclesiastical mauvais discours. The veteran soldier Jean-François Le Clerc, the same who christened the king a "bougre" in a La Vilette cabaret on January 5, might be such an example, because according to one of the witnesses Le Clerc also complained of France being governed "by two *p[utains]*," a sufficiently clear reference to the king's mistresses. The prediction that the same fate would befall Louis XV as his ancestors—presumably Henry III and Henry IV—might also indicate leaguish or devout sympathies.[38] But much clearer cases abound. Take, for example, seventy-eight-year-old Pierre Thomas, a sometime vinedresser turned beggar from Auxerre, who was arrested in March 1757 in Clamecy near Orléans for having wagered that the king would die before Easter at the hands of the queen, dauphin, and unspecified "*grands*." These wished it, he reportedly explained, because the king "had made himself hated by too much oppressing his people and by giving his soul to the devil in the exile of several bishops."[39] Or consider Pierre Liebert, retailer of beer and tobacco on the Ile de la Cité, who found himself embastillé on October 31, 1757, for having proclaimed a few weeks earlier while in a drunken rage and playing at quoits in a cabaret that the king was a "Jean Foutre" and that although he "greatly respected the queen," "all the rest were B[ougres] to hang." (Indicatively, perhaps, his curé pleaded on his behalf.)[40] Or consider, finally, the woman Renard, cabaret-keeper and tobacco retailer in

Rheims, who was arrested in December 1765 in that city and later embastillé for having remarked to an excise tax collector a month earlier that "the dauphin was very sick, and that for her part she preferred the death of the king to that of the dauphin because if the latter were king he would restore the Jesuits in France." "The king and the parlement were both atheists," she had further opined.[41]

One of the most interesting of such cases is that of Michel Le Roy, the pious but deranged son of a Dreux huissier, whom we encounter for the first time in the Châtelet prison on January 2, 1757, having been arrested by the Paris guet in a cabaret on the rue aux Ours upon the request of his mother who was afraid of his "esprit aliéné."[42] Whether his alienation had political content at that time is not clear, but he resurfaces as a potentially "devout" Damiens and an object of governmental concern in the spring of 1759. Long noted for his "piety and devotion of a superior degree," Michel Le Roy's religious fervor attained unacceptable heights when he threw himself onto a stone figure of Christ in the parish church of Saint-Pierre, claiming that he had no other father and like-mannered "propos of extravagant devotion." The fact that he had lost his real father, his mother remarrying after the death of the elder Michel Le Roy, had undoubtedly contributed to his condition, which steadily worsened after the incident in the church. Its most alarming feature was that during his seizures, which began ominously to outnumber his moments of lucidity, he was overwhelmed with the desire to go to Versailles and attend to the "conversion of the king."[43] Urged on April 14 by an apothecary to take some *eau de mélisse*, he refused unless "Louis Quinze converted himself and made a general confession," indeed came personally "before him and say himself that he had been converted. . . ." Bled the same day by the surgeon Collette, he specified that "it was necessary to kick out (*mettre dehors*) madame de Pompadour," that the king's conversion "would not be sincere" if he "approached the sacraments without kicking her out."[44] Neither the attorney general nor his local substitute thought Le Roy constituted any real threat to the king, but they feared an "éclat, and a disagreeable éclat at that." The preferred solution was to lock him up with the Brothers of Charity at Pontorson.[45]

A veteran gunner, two cabaret keepers, a beggar and sometime vinedresser, and a convulsive huissier's son do not make a formidable army, but it is nonetheless clear that the parti dévôt was not without a certain lay constituency, even in Paris. Recall the two procurator's clerks who fought a duel over *Unigenitus* in 1752, one of whom thought that the parlement was "sticking its nose (*s'ingéroit*) into matters that were none of its business" and that "monseigneur the archbishop was right in acting as he did because the constitution [*Unigenitus*] had been declared a rule of faith."[46] Remember as well Mazcout Chérault, the drunken bourgeois of Paris, who on August 6, 1754, provoked cabaret clients in the rue de la Harpe by declaiming against the parlement's persecution of true religion.[47] Or witness the antics of one Dollisson, secondhand clothing salesman established in the rue de Louvine, faubourg Saint-Médard, who on the occasion of a colporter's attempt to hawk copies of the parlement's anti-*Unigenitus* rulings, emerged threateningly from his shop brandishing his *balai* and yelling in a "loud and intelligible voice" that "the parlement would do better to keep quiet and mind its own business, and that what it was doing was as good as mud" (*n'étoit que de la boue*). "The party of the king," he added—one thinks of the priest Mesguet's royalists—"would know how to shut the parlement up together with its arrêts." This *fripier* and his wife, according to the unsympathetic shoemaker who made this report, were supported by the curé and the priests of Saint-Médard, who classified the street's parishioners as Molinists and Jansenists and made life miserable for the latter.[48]

The rue de Louvine incident allows us a glimpse of the parish curé in the background and suggests that one's relationship with the local curé might be the determining factor in some cases of lay enlistment in the devout cause. This seems to have been true, for example, of Mazcout Chérault, who before becoming a bourgeois of Paris had served the abbé Guerbois of the parish of Saint-Sulpice as a domestic servant and who had acquired his late high status by means of the financial generosity of his deceased former master.[49] It was more certainly true of Elizabeth Chauvin, a launderess native to the rue du Temple in the parish of Saint-Nicolas-des-Champs, who in May 1758 publicly insulted the abbé Charles de Willemsens in the parish church apropos of this priest's obedience to a parlementary injunction to administer the last sacraments to his dying appellant uncle a week or so earlier.[50] Chauvin, it later developed, lived in the same building as did one Dubertrand, a master surgeon and brother of one of the parish curates whom the parlement had exiled in connection with the Willemsens affair. Chauvin was moreover a relative of the Dubertrand family and a frequent recipient of the exiled curate's generosity. So popular, in fact, had similar generosities made the parish curé in the quarter generally that the Châtelet's prosecuting attorney deemed it prudent to take advance precautions against "movements that could take place" when Chauvin's sentence of "blame" was placarded on the neighborhood carrefour on March 29, 1759.[51] Beyond such dependency on, relatedness to, or affection for this or that curé as factors in lay "devout" allegiances, the evidence unfortunately does not allow us to go.

Political Folly

THE CASE of the appropriately named Michel Le Roy, the convulsive would-be converter of the king, points to the potential value of hallucinations and other less than lucid utterances as possible indices of the affaires du temps' diffusion. Indeed, the extent of the political content present in such utterances might even function generally as a reliable barometer of the intensity of political conflicts in a given society as well as of their diffusion through the population. Paris commissioners of police, for example, were occasionally called upon to go "ascertain the insanity (*démence*) of so and so" at the request of his annoyed neighbors and as a necessary prerequisite to consignment to Bicêtre. The resultant interrogations are scattered throughout the voluminous papers of forty-eight different commissioners, and locating them is like looking for needles in proverbial haystacks. Still, chance encounters with such interrogations are often suggestive enough. Was it a distant echo of the affaires du temps, specifically the refusal of sacraments controversy, that Claude Le Roy, appropriately "the King of France and the King of Christendom," had not gone in mass for four years because all the masses in Paris were said "in the name of the devil" and refused to go to confession because "there were no confessors in Paris, their all being sorcerers by baptism?"[52] A clearer case is that of Pierre Arnault, sometime shoemaker from Champagne interrogated by Rochebrune in October 1757, who was happily "getting younger every day." Asked why he had allowed so much time to elapse since last approaching the sacraments, he replied that "as he had worked to abase the constitution [*Unigenitus*] he had seen that the constitution did not validate the souls (*ne validoit pas sur les âmes*) of which the Roman church made profession, that he perceived this by means of a great vision (*grand coup de ciel*) while doing penance the night of Ash Wednesday . . . 1756, that this vision from heaven appeared as a white cloud, as a resurrection mother (*resurrection mater*), that he saw serpents, toads, and immobile laws at his feet, and a foal race like a skeleton across the paving stones near the curial house of Montierender, etc." The response trailed off into unintelligible Latin except for the declaration that he had "never adored Molinists in the conservation [constitution?]"[53]

But the Damiens affair itself brought the like-minded out of the woodwork. A small army in Bicêtre, seizing the affair as an occasion for momentary and perhaps purely internal release, besieged the authorities with denunciations of plots and claims to privy knowledge of Damiens' conspirators. Sometime tax farm officer Pierre-Paul Boucher de La Timonière, for example, his career cut short by too frequent visitations by the Virgin, denounced a convulsionary-Jansenist conspiracy whose participants readied themselves in a little wooded hideout by knifing a waxen figure representing the king while uttering terrible imprecations.[54] Similarly, François d'Arguetil, a master tailor from Rouen, originally imprisoned because of a theft of two pewter plates from a cabaret, revealed an antiroyal plot of probably Jansenist-parlementary complexion inasmuch as the archbishop of Paris was also one of its intended victims.[55] On the other hand, the archbishop was one of the prominent movers behind the "devout" conspiracy of which Damiens was the abortive agent in the imagination of Louis-Guillaume Artus, former blind inmate of the royal hospital of the Quinze-Vingts but transferred to Bicêtre in 1756, then to its section for the "insane" in 1758. Whether insane or not, Artus "aveugle" seemed especially well informed concerning current events and the political prejudices of the parlement of Paris. The conspiracy he revealed to the attorney general was nothing less than a full-blown League organized by the archbishop of Paris with one of his cathedral canons and directed "against the person of the king because his majesty does not favor or support the authority of the Church against the parlements." The conspirators regularly met at the archepiscopal residence in Conflans and other places where they had gone so far as to import "savages from the isles" to teach Damiens how to work the bow and arrow. Although Protestant, even England and Prussia were involved, furnishing money with which nine or ten thousand adherents were to be recruited to "put Paris to the torch" and create confusion in Versailles while Damiens made good his escape.[56]

But Bicêtre and the Bastille were not alone in refracting the affaires du temps through the minds of the mentally afflicted, or those treated as such. The fields and the open road also contributed to the cacophony. François Lépine or l'Epine, a forty-year-old migrant laborer from Colombe near Montreuil, was originally denounced in July 1757 for having boasted, in a cabaret near Vitry, that he could if he wished kill the king, the dauphin, and the "entire royal family" as well as "destroy all the goods of the earth."[57] Although he avoided arrest on this occasion, his unabated loquaciousness as a vinedresser near Melun aroused the vigilance of the local authorities the following spring. This time it was the "constitution" and "spells" that preoccupied him; he said on the one hand that "he holds to the constitution [*Unigenitus*] and that one could do nothing without it," but on the other, that the dauphin, the bishop of Meaux, and other constitutionaries had been "seduced" by means of a "spell" into embracing the constitution, which for his part—or rather his "good spirit's" part—he thought they should "renounce." Again denounced and on this occasion arrested, Lépine himself described his mind as "disordered" (*dérangé*), and it was not long before the authorities shared his opinion.[58] In contrast, the priest Denis Pansin made no reference to the affaires du temps until after his arrest for suspicious conduct and the possession of a knife in the vicinity of Versailles toward the end of January 1757. Forced to resign his cure in Gap around 1754 because of "mental pains" (*peines d'esprit*), headaches, and a black melancholy," he led an itinerant existence until he was taken in by the *Missions étrangères* in Paris, where the medical doctor de Bordeu diagnosed his illness as hypochondria and recommended the sea air of the Indies. Two times Pansin boarded the coach for Rennes, and both times he got out in fear of the other passengers, on the second occasion taking refuge in an inn, which called the constabulary at his own request. Asked why he had fled to the horse stables and had thrown a knife on the ground when the constabulary in turn arrived, he responded that he feared that his possession of a knife would arouse suspicions that he had intended to kill the king but also that he might be taken for "a Jesuit, a spy of the Jesuits," "one of the priests exiled by the parlement of Paris," or again as "emissary of the bishops."[59]

More enigmatic is the case of Louis-Dominique Hidou, sometime Parisian schoolmaster turned beggar, who turned up in Béthune in July 1758 loudly proclaiming his identity as "king" and "master of the universe" and his intention of returning to Paris "in order to ascend the throne." This latter feat he expected to be facilitated by "the combustion that existed between the flowers of the lily." While in prison, according to the local prosecuting attorney, Hidou also "declaimed sometimes against priests and sometimes against women." One would like to know more, but the unfortunate man died before further interrogation.[60] More ominous as well was the case of J. A. Thorin, a domestic in the service of the governor of the duc de Chartres, who began in December 1758 to maintain in writing that his recently deceased mistress, madame de Fonçemagne, had ordered him to assassinate the king until which time he would remain deaf and dumb. The authorities were persuaded that he was "counterfeiting the imbecile and the fool" in order to pass himself off as a "little saint in whose person God had performed a miracle," and indeed, miracles of all sorts soon began to punctuate the monotony of his detention in the Bastille. Whether an act or not, he was "adhering to his first system"—albeit orally—in 1759, after which he was transferred to the château of Vincennes. In 1779 an uncle obtained his release on condition of placing him in the charge of brothers in Switzerland, the country of his birth.[61]

The Desacralization of the Monarchy

THE GREAT MAJORITY of the approximately twenty-five antiroyal plots and conspiracies denounced to the authorities in the years 1757-1758 took root in the imaginations of people whose sanity was never called into question. The confessed motivations in these cases tended toward score-settling among the embroiled, liberty for the imprisoned, or royal pensions for the ambitious. Some of these plots possessed political content, for instance the plot to destroy the "whole royal family" involving (among others) a curé, a curate, and a Jesuit postulant denounced in January 1757 by an imprisoned soldier named Durand in Rouen; or, to go a bit beyond the period 1757-1758, the armed attack upon the king at Versailles in 1762 by an ecclesiastic and a man dressed in green intent upon restoring "annihilated religion" and only thwarted by the heroics of Paul-René Du Truche de La Chaux, one of the king's guards, who covered himself with wounds in an unsuccessful attempt to convince the court of this story and thereby merit a pension with which to pay his crushing debts.[62] But more often, the plots were of a simple antiroyal type, in the sense of being unencumbered by much politico-ecclesiastical baggage, and directed primarily against the king's person—the deserter soldier Félix Ricard's assertion, for example, that he had been offered three hundred louis by the Hargest-en-Santerre textile merchant-manufacturer Claude Lefort to shoot the king at close range, or the story concocted by Jean Breton, an out-of-work stonecutter from Bourges recently migrated to Paris, to the effect that on March 11, 1757, while "tending to necessities" beneath one end of the Pont Neuf, he saw and heard two men dressed in black, equipped with swords and gold-rimmed hats, discussing the readiness of their pistols for shooting the king and the comte d'Argenson.[63]

Is it permissible to treat such politically uncomplicated antiroyal plots and conspiracies as unavowable "projections" on the part of their inventors, and to group them together with straightforwardly antiroyal mauvais discours, whether calumniously attributed or not? It is the latter, in any event, which are especially interesting and fairly numerous as well, comprising a score or so of cases in the years 1757-1758. These most often consisted in a spontaneous, unwholesome, and sometimes inebriated commentary upon either Damiens' coup of January 5 or execution of March 28. Note has already been taken of how, upon hearing an account of Damiens' execution, the apprentice tanner and deserted soldier François Bellier de La Chauvellais opined in a cabaret near Château-Gontier that in Damiens' place he "would have stuck his knife into the heart of the sacred bugger (in speaking of the sacred person of his majesty)." Witnesses thought he was drunk at the time, but when reproached by them for what he had said, he maintained that on the morning after he would be of the same opinion still.[64] Similarly, a "peasant" conversing with two others in a cabaret near Gisors in Normandy, declared that in Damiens' place "he would not have missed the king and would have pierced his guts with an awl" (*percé les boyaux avec une aleine*); and in the same spirit the nailsmith turned beggar Rémond Dupont declared in two different cabarets in Sézanne in Brie that "it would have been better for the king and queen to have been reduced to ashes instead of Damiens. . . ."[65] In Clermont-Ferrand an indigent tailor, seeing a "woman of his estate" in tears and hearing that they were apropos of Damiens' coup, consoled her with the reflection that "the misfortune was not great enough to sadden her that much." And in Mayenne a petty judicial employee named Marin Gonnet, drunkenly quarreling with a certain Pipellier about paying his share of the wine, announced that he intended to kill not only Pipellier but also "the king and the judge of Mayenne."[66]

One thing that emerges very clearly from the evidence is the humbler socioeconomic status of the perpetrators of these simple and violent antiroyal mauvais discours compared with that of those guilty of mauvais discours with a more distinctive political coloration. Besides the apprentice tanner, tailor, peasant, nailsmith turned beggar, and small-time judicial employee already mentioned, this category of verbal offense boasts four additional peasant day laborers, a mendicant deserter, an unemployed cloth shearer, a "sinister" woman without profession (except possibly the oldest one), a schoolmaster, an itinerant chanter, an itinerant church clock repairman (and jack-of-all-trades), an innkeeper, a farmer (*laboureur*), and a jeweler in prison for debts. The addition of the remaining denouncers of antiroyal plots fails signally to embellish this list. Besides the unemployed stonecutter Breton and the deserted soldier Félix Ricard whom we have previously encountered, this latter category contributes three domestic servants (one of them unemployed), two *gagne deniers* (one of them in prison for theft), a journeyman hatter, the impecunious and imprisoned widow of a pin maker, a minor employee of the General Farm, a provincial notary's clerk, a pensioner fallen upon hard times, an unemployed carter crushed by debt, and a person of uncertain profession in prison for debt. The denouncers of politically motivated conspiracies and sayers of politically slanted *discours* look socially stellar in comparison.

The humbler circumstances of these subjects are, not surprisingly, apparent in the content of their mauvais discours themselves. Like Damiens, but unlike most of the politically oriented discoursers so far considered, these seditious discoursers often pointed to the high price of bread, excessive taxes, and in general the misery of the people as reasons for why the king ought to be slain. Among those already encountered, Rémond Dupont thought the king and queen deserved Damiens' terrible punishment and execution more than Damiens himself because the royal pair "served only to ruin the people. . . ."[67] But others were even more specific. A certain Gambit, a farmer in the parish of La Ferte sur Perron near Laon, was reported to have said that the attempted assassination was "not so bad, that that was well done," and that if it had succeeded "the people would have been much relieved."[68] Joseph Le Cocq, an itinerant cloth shearer originally from Lyons and lately unable to find work in Rheims, admitted to venting his frustrations on the king directly. It was "Louis XV," he said, "who was the cause of his misery" and "the state of indigence in which he found himself," to which he appended, according to some witnesses, that the king was a "bugger" or a "f[outu] gueux" who "would not be alive in eight days."[69] Under interrogation, Marie-Marguerite Gadibois, a day laborer from Rambouillet near Orléans, was just as candid about what she had said. That "the grains were extremely dear" and that most likely the dauphin "would be a better king" she cited as sufficient reasons for her having ventured, in a conversation about the exportation of wheat, that Damiens "had done badly to have missed his coup, since the said Damiens would have been just as dead in the one event as in the other." "The whole *menu peuple* spoke as she did," she added.[70] The day laborer Filassier reportedly went so far, while working in the vineyards of Saunoy near Argenteuil, to opine that Damiens was a "saint" and a "martyr" who "appeared daily at the [place de] Grève demanding vengeance for his execution."[71]

It is indeed tempting, in view of this evidence, to conclude that the violently antimonarchical—or anti-Bourbon—element likewise distinguishes the popular from the more elite and politically specific type of mauvais discours, for by no means can all of these *discours* be dismissed as mindless or drunken effusions or as directed only against the throne's particular occupant. Take the example of the itinerant church clock repairman, François Roger, calumnious accuser of one of the churchwardens of the parish of Savonnière near Tours with whom he became embroiled concerning the price of his services to the parish. The *discours* calumniously attributed to this churchwarden, named Jean Mirault, scorned not only Louis XV personally—"how did the sacred bugger survive?"—but challenged monarchical legitimacy in general. On January 7 or 8 and in the company of Roger and a locksmith named Bauge, Mirault supposedly cited the passage in Samuel where Jehovah reproached the Israelites for requesting a king, and in response to the question of who would administer justice in a royal vacuum, in turn asked "who administered it before?"[72] In Boufflers a noncommissioned officer named L'Herbier—admittedly, not too humble a situation—reportedly said to a number of cavalrymen in the course of a conversation about Damiens on March 19 that "if the king had been missed one time he would not be missed on another" but also that the "Bourbons are f[outu] beasts and never wise up until they are fifty-five or sixty years old—witness Louis XIV."[73] And in Dijon on January 12 a certain Borjon de Scellery concluded from the overheard conversation of two domestic servants that they wished not merely to do away with the king, the dauphin, and all the ministers but even "to change the form of government since according to these same remarks men were supposed to be . . . in a position to cry 'liberty' as soon as it was known that the blow had succeeded."[74]

What makes the association of bluntly personal and dynastic, if not institutional, antiroyalism with the popular milieu more plausible as an hypothesis is that even in cases of *discours* of identifiably Jansenist-parlementary derivation, their popular respondents often appended an antimonarchical or anti-Bourbon note before sending it back as an echo. To the unimpeachably parlementary maxim "no parlement, no king," the Parisian journeyman hatter Jean Aveque tacked on the dubious observation that "Cromwell was one of the great men of his century who never wanted to assume the title of king but [preferred] that of protector of England, with which he had the power to lay low the head of his king."[75] The elusive and mysterious Le Blanc, the same who thought that "the parlement existed before any royalty," did not let his loudly expressed enthusiasm for the prince de Conti prevent him from also opining that "the branch of the Bourbons had reigned long enough."[76] And the Parisian master locksmith Chaumet, who had erupted into imprecations against the rump parlement or "band of robbers" left after the lit de justice of December 13, 1756, also thought that "Frenchmen would always be unfortunate (*malheureux*) so long as the Bourbon branch subsisted" and wished "that the Protestants would take up arms and join the enemies [of France] in order to dethrone the king. . . ." The "people would be a thousand times happier," he thought, in such an eventuality.[77] The part about the Protestants might very well have been derivative, having a basis in reality, as we have noted, in the prince de Conti's relationship with Paul Rabaut and the Protestants of Languedoc. The part against the Bourbon family, however, could hardly have originated in that very Bourbon quarter.[78]

But the most spectacular example of the popular echo effect is provided by the famous "bloodletting" propos, which became part of the Damiens trial itself and was "disjoined" from it only toward its conclusion in March. It all began with the sort of recollection that suddenly seemed significant in the light of what happened on January 5. On New Year's Eve, it seems, when Damiens himself had returned to Paris, a certain domestic servant known in the quarter as Saint-Jean had stopped in at the apartment of a Parisian stocking merchant named Jean Gabriel in the rue Saint-Sauveur in order to pick up some socks for his master's guest. Queried about news by Gabriel and his wife, he responded that "things were going very badly because the king could hardly undo what he had recently done," and upon Gabriel's objection that things might be accommodated by means of another lit de justice, Saint-Jean blurted, "Good God, you are not on top of things (*vous n'y etês pas*); people say we need a bloodletting in France, and that the Bourbon house must be destroyed." A certain prior named Alexandre Ingoult, then boarding with the Gabriels and to whom the couple had later recounted the incident, deemed the matter serious enough to inform the prévôté de l'Hôtel in a formal deposition on January 12. Having received this testimony, the prévôté had no alternative except to follow it up, so Jean and Pierrette-Victoire Gabriel confirmed Ingoult's story with minor rectifications on the same day.[79]

That much done, the procedure next called for arrests and interrogations, the first victim being the domestic servant Jean Aubrais, better known as Saint-Jean, whose master was Fossier Du Bourneaux, an exempt of the One Hundred Swiss living in the rue du Paradis. In the resultant interrogation on January 15, the unfortunate Aubrais owned up to having uttered the substance of what the Gabriels reported but credited the "things are going badly" part of his discourse to "women of the *menu peuple*" and "several fishwives" he had heard in the courtyard of the Palais de justice the day of the lit de justice (December 13), and the part about the "bloodletting" and "destruction of the Bourbon house" to two of his fellow domestics in the Fossier household.[80] Arrested and interrogated in turn, these latter two pointed their fingers at a domestic servant of a Châtelet notary named Jacques Lenoir who had visited the Fossier household not long before.[81] The bottom line was finally reached when this domestic servant, one Noël Roi, better known as Roi, pointed his finger at the parlementary lawyer Jean-Baptiste Le Gouvé whom he had heard at dinner while serving his master and thirteen other guests. The *discours* as recalled by Noël Roi was that "the king was good, and that what he had done in holding his lit de justice did not reflect his own mind, but it was to be feared that the troubles of the affaires [du temps] might occasion a revolution in France similar to that which occurred 250 years earlier, and there would be a similar bloodletting in France as there was at that time."[82]

This discourse as reported by Noël Roi is wholly believable, for it is precisely the sort of thing that people in Le Gouvé's milieu were saying at the time, and which was moreover appearing in print in only slightly milder form. The efforts of a few of Le Noir's other guests to explain away the incriminating remark as Le Gouvé's misunderstood recommendation of a "purging" to a mildly ill dinner companion are unconvincing if not visibly contrived.[83] Moreover, it was in substance this same discourse that Jean Aubrais or Saint-Jean repeated fourth-hand to the Gabriel family on December 31—except, significantly, for the highly seditious part about the desirability of the destruction of the Bourbon family, which Noël Roi and the other two domestics working for Fossier du Bourneaux emphatically denied having either heard or repeated.[84] The problem is therefore to determine at precisely what juncture in its mouth-to-mouth progress Le Gouvé's originally rather anodyne remark took on the highly explosive baggage of the destruction of the Bourbon family. Either terminus seems excluded, because on the one hand, it is highly unlikely that Le Gouvé would have thought such a thing not to mention actually mentioning it in polite company, and on the other, the domestic Jean Aubrais admitted that the Gabriel family had indeed gotten it from him. That leaves the possibility that one of the four domestics was lying and had appended it himself, or that it was a vintage contribution of the women of the *menu peuple* or fishwives at the Palais de justice, and that Jean Aubrais was mistaken about what he had heard from whom. In view of the considerations that all the other domestic servants denied having so much as heard about the destruction of the Bourbons—by itself not a terribly compromising admission—and that Jean Aubrais was apparently mistaken about having gotten the comments about the king's December lit de justice from the *poissardes*—that was already part of Le Gouvé's discourse—the hypothesis of the fishwives as the original would-be destroyers of the Bourbon family seems most plausible and moreover comports well with what we know of the fishwives generally.[85] In any event, it is transparently a case of a popular transformation of an originally purely Jansenist-parlementary mauvais discours.

The Damiens affair, then, reveals that by 1757 the popular mauvais discours was affecting the monarchy directly. This holds true for mauvais discours of "devout" as well as of Jansenist-parlementary derivation: the discourses of Le Clerc, Thomas, Liebert, Renard, and the vagabond priest in Chaource all ended in predictions of the king's death, if not explicit desires for this event's imminent occurrence. Though the Damiens affair *reveals* this to be so, the evidence suggests that this phenomenon did not long antedate 1757, and that the

1750s were in general decisive in this respect.[86] It was in 1750 during the "children's kidnapping" riots that a police spy heard someone say that the fishwives of the Paris Halles would do well to go to Versailles, "grab the king by the hair," and "pluck out the eyes from his head."[87] It was in 1753 at the height of the refusal of sacraments controversy that d'Argenson first noted "seditious billets" in public places proclaiming "Long live the parlement! Death to the king and the bishops"; and in 1754 during the parlement's long exile that he observed people being arrested for "having spoken of the present troubles."[88] Damiens' own biography microcosmically recapitulates this sequence and suggests much the same chronology.

That it was the Jansenist-parlementary but also the "devout" popular mauvais discours that turned antiroyal both points to and partly explains the gradual desacralization of the monarchy in mid-eighteenth-century France. Although overtly respecting the person of the king, elite Jansenist-parlementary rhetoric tended on the one hand so to constitutionalize the monarchy, so to identify it with the parlement and ultimately with the nation, as to leave the flesh and blood monarchical person quite superfluous if not conspicuously in the way. For example, the king could no longer intervene directly and personally in cases of the refusal of sacraments because the parlement represented the king better than the king himself. In terms of the theory of the "king's two bodies" developed in the later Middle Ages, this was to divorce the king's immortal or mystical body (representing the body politic) so totally from his mortal and individual body as to desacralize the latter.[89] And by paying homage, on the other hand, to an excessively sacrosanct conception of the Christian monarchy quite divorced from the sexually insatiable person who represented it, elite parti dévôt sermonizing only reinforced this same tendency. What was admired on the part of Henry IV and tolerated on the part of Louis XIV was no longer licit for Louis XV. But whether removed from an increasingly nationalized or Christianized ideal of the monarchical institution, the king's consequently secularized person was left vulnerable and exposed, on the popular level, to the sort of scurrilous, sometimes sacrilegious abuse—the "sacred bugger," for example—of which Damiens' bodily assault was but the physical representation. Damiens' desire "to touch" and wound the king can be construed as a sort of sacrilegious reversal of the king's traditional power to touch and heal his scrofulous subjects. And had not Louis XV already failed to heal these subjects on at least three occasions because of his abstention from the Eucharistic sacrament?[90]

The fact that it was the high price of bread rather than deprivation of the sacraments that figured as the avowed motivation behind some of the popular mauvais discours need not detract from the centrality of the refusal of sacraments controversy, which by desacralizing the monarchical person tended to liberate popular tongues, whatever their particular grievances. Nor does it seem surprising that a traditionally quasi-sacramental monarchy should have become desacralized in the course of revealing its ineptitude—in the popular view, its ill will—in a controversy that tended to desacralize or at least politicize the sacraments themselves.[91] Moreover, the deprivation of sacraments and the high price of bread seem to have been closely related in the popular mentality, as this mixture in Damiens' own articulated motivation strongly suggests. The search for the ideological origins of the French Revolution must therefore not restrict itself to the volcanic heights of elite polemical literature, which, in Jansenist and parlementary forms, anticipated the national constitutionalism compatible with the monarchy of 1789. It must also hearken to the popular ground tremors first discernible beneath the refusal of sacraments controversy, which anticipate the seeming ease with which the French dispensed with their monarch in 1792.

Lèse-Majesté Verbale

THE MONARCHY's response to these rumblings hardly enhanced its image, for it consisted uniquely in muffling their sound and preventing their reaching the proportions of an éclat. In a quandary about what to do with a schoolmaster-beggar named Hidou and his projected ascent to the throne, the attorney general's first thought was to send him by mail coach from Béthune to Paris, but further reflection disclosed the inconvenience that "this imbecile might repeat on the road the [same] discourse he held at Béthune, which would create a bad effect in a vehicle where there are ordinarily many other voyagers."[92] Better to let him die in the prisons of Béthune, which he obligingly did in January 1759, than to take risks of such proportions. Although unsatisfied, again, with the lenient sentences that the Châtelet pronounced in the cases of Gaspard Ferlin and Toussaint Courtin, the first accused by the second of having threatened the king's life, the attorney general and his Châtelet counterpart decided not to appeal the case to the parlement "in order to make no further éclat of the affair at this time."[93] The attorney general was above all summing up the experience of the Damiens affair and its aftermath when he wrote to his substitute in Béthune apropos of a developing case of mauvais discours in 1765 that "it seems [to me] that in these sorts of matters we have always sought to avoid an éclat, especially in the first moments. We have always begun by informing the ministry of affairs of this genre, in order to enable it to choose between the different alternatives available in such occasions."[94]

The avoidance of éclat all but excluded formal, judicial procedure from among these available alternatives because of its noisy, conspicuous character. Not surprisingly, therefore, we find the "extrajudicial" alternative being generally preferred, which is to say that in most cases their subjects were indefinitely imprisoned without benefit of judicial accusation (*plainte*) or sometimes even interrogation. Barentin, intendant of Orléans, was inclined toward leniency in the case of beggar-vinedresser Pierre Thomas, seventy-eight-year-old prophet of the king's doom, on the grounds that he was feeble-minded besides being inebriated at the time. No reason, therefore, to conduct his trial, he generously reasoned, "but at the same time I deem it apropos to sequester him from society."[95] The attorney general heaved a sigh of relief to learn that the presidial court of Rheims had initiated no judicial procedure in the case of the out-of-work cloth shearer Joseph Le Cocq, who had loudly identified Louis XV as the cause of his misery. In consequence "we have thought," he informed Police Lieutenant Berryer, "that the best course would be to lock this wretch up forever."[96] And on March 5, 1757, in the town of Ribemont near Soissons the constabulary arrested a beggar and sometime soldier named Marc Legris for having said, among other things, that he was Damiens' maternal cousin, whom he had last seen working as a tailor in the town of Rancourt in Flanders. The Damiens that Legris knew was obviously not the one who had wounded the king, but the attorney general with the parlement's commissioners decided to keep him in prison anyway, because "he might be of use in the course of our procedure"—they retain the secret of how—and besides "does not appear to be a very good subject, having admitted to begging and being once imprisoned for that reason in the Châtelet. . . ."[97]

Even among cases initially launched with the christening and fanfare of judicial *plainte* and *information*, how many mysteriously shipwrecked only to reemerge much later in extrajudicial waters! The cases of Rémond Dupont, Bellier de La Chauvellais, and Marin Gonnet all began as judicial inquiries (*informations*) in the towns of Sézanne, Château-Gontier, and Mayenne respectively, but none successfully reached a judicial conclusion. In the case of Gonnet in particular, the attorney general uncharacteristically sermonized Mayenne's fiscal procurator on how he could "not dispense himself from conducting [Gonnet's] trial, and to teach him by the sentence you will pronounce . . . never again . . . to fail in the respect due to his sovereign."[98] Yet in October we find Gonnet precisely where the other two have ended: in Bicêtre, never a destination in virtue of any judicial sentence.

A more flagrant example is that of itinerant chanter Nicolas Lagrené, arrested in February near Orléans for having propositioned a pregnant woman on the road between Orléans and Saint-Lauraut-des-Eaux and for having spoken to her on the same occasion about Damiens whom he claimed to have known.[99] Eager to prosecute Lagrené on the spot, the Orléans bailliage and its procurator, Le Clerc de Doüy, obtained the attorney general's permission to do so in March 1757, but with the proviso that the bailliage solicit new orders before proceeding to a definitive judgment. This it did by March 15, in response to which the bailliage's procurator received instructions to render a definitive judgment but not to let Lagrené out of prison regardless of what his sentence was. Over the shoulder, however, of the attorney general who sent these instructions loomed the figure of the secretary of the king's household, Saint-Florentin, who, informed of the affair by the intendant of Orléans, Barentin, was equally concerned about its outcome. The bailliage's sentence was a lenient three months in prison pending a "more ample investigation" (PAI), converted into a PAI with liberty at the expiration of this term, in spite of which the bailliage could not obtain the elder Joly de Fleury's permission to free Lagrené in accordance with this sentence in July 1757. The attorney general in turn acted—or rather, neglected to act—under some pressure from Saint-Florentin, who, persuaded that the chanter was "a very bad subject wandering all around the country despite having a wife and children," suggested Bicêtre as ballast. No decision was however reached, and the attorney general had to admit to a frustrated Doüy no less than two years later that he had quite "lost sight of this affair." Had not Lagrené been punished enough, inquired the Orléans procurator on visit to Paris? Yet further huddles between the attorney general and Saint-Florentin produced nothing more than a revival of the plan to transfer Lagrené to Bicêtre, which was actually accomplished, this time, in September 1759. Entreaties from his unhappy wife unable to support several children went unheeded.[100]

Examples of this sort also demonstrate that where vainly taking the king's name was involved, the parlement of Paris did not violently object to ministerial-royal diversion of the normal course of justice. Parlementary flexibility on this front contrasts strangely with its simultaneous and rigid opposition to ministerial interference in refusal of sacraments cases, where the issue of éclat was likewise at stake. True, the parlement in this instance boiled down mainly to the attorney general, who was all the freer to act as he did because the firebrands were all on "strike" at the time. The impression is nonetheless difficult to resist that not even they would have reacted very strongly, and that their objections to "the secret ways of authority," "all too suited to the taste of our government," were inextricably bound up with their conviction that a conspiracy on the part of their politico-ecclesiastical enemies was afoot.[101] No less a personage than the prince de Conti, very much their mouthpiece in this whole affair, allowed in the plenary judicial session of February 25 that this was indeed a "case where the ways of authority merited nothing but praise—above all," in truth he added, "when the whole is later returned to the way of judicial order and the rules."[102] Not only do we therefore find Saint-Florentin, the comte d'Argenson (before February 1, 1757), the new minister of war, the marquis de Paulmy, Rouillé, the chancellor Lamoignon, the police chief Berryer, and various intendants getting into the act, but the king himself personally intervened, precisely as he wished to do in the refusal of sacraments affair. It was due to his majesty's "goodness" alone, according to Saint-Florentin, that the judicial procedures against Dupont, Bellier, and Gonnet were not followed up, and that these representatives of the "dredges of the people" were transferred to Bicêtre instead.[103] It was his majesty as well who judged that a "regular accusation" was not appropriate to the case of Gisors peasant Besnard, whom "his majesty had locked into a prison."[104]

Royal judges, intendants, and ministers were therefore free literally to stumble over each other in their zeal to protect the king's life or vindicate his offended majesty. Some cases, such as those of the four Parisian domestics, Mirlavaud/Horsel in Moulins, Mirault/Roger in Tours, and Félix Ricard in Montdidier, took the judicial highway from start to finish, with only an occasional detour in the form of an extrajudicial interrogation or two. Other cases that began judicially were permanently rerouted onto the backroads of extrajudicial treatment, as the examples of Gonnet, Bellier, and Dupont have shown. A third kind of case began in clandestine extrajudiciality and subsequently sustained judicial scrutiny only in response to a peremptory demand for information: it was from Berryer, for example, that the attorney general had to obtain the extrajudicial interrogations of the two Kattmans and Chauveau, in order to satisfy, in turn, the rumor-piqued curiosity of judges in the Grand' chambre.[105] Yet a fourth category bypassed justice altogether; no evidence suggests that either the attorney general or any other member of the parlement so much as suspected the existence of the cases of, say, Marie-Marguerite Gadibois, Jean Aveque, Jeanette Bironneau, and Jean-Baptiste Mesguet, which were handled by the police with Saint-Florentin alone. Finally, a couple of cases, like that of Pierre Thomas, hardly crossed paths with even the police, remaining the prerogative of a minister and an intendant in the field.

The resultant jurisdictional anarchy did not always operate for the benefit of the accused. Take the veteran gunner Jean-François Le Clerc, to whose overly exploited case we now turn for the last time. It was on March 4, 1757, that the attorney general got word from a magistrate in the Grand' chambre that someone had been arrested near Arras or Compiègne for having predicted "troubles" and "great events" around the time of the king's assassination. As fully in the dark about the matter as anyone in the Grand' chambre, the attorney general turned to Saint-Florentin on March 5, who responded that he too had heard the same thing but that since he had not been informed of any arrest on the subject, he had concluded that the rumor lacked foundation in fact. But on March 16 Saint-Florentin wrote again to report that one of the king's guards had informed him that the war minister de Paulmy had indeed ordered the arrest of a veteran soldier accused of uttering a mauvais propos around the time of the assassination while on his way to Douay, that this soldier was still in prison, and that the intendant would be able to furnish additional information. In consequence, the attorney general wrote to Bertier de Sauvigny, intendant of Paris, who responded that he knew absolutely nothing, and a frustrated Joly de Fleury returned empty-handed to Saint-Florentin on March 21 demanding to know why he had been instructed to write to Bertier de Sauvigny. But it was not the intendant of Paris, came the answer, but the intendant of Lille that he had had in mind. Queried in turn, m. de Caumartin, intendant of Lille, responded on March 26 that, yes, he had both arrested and interrogated a veteran soldier named Le Clerc for having predicted "trouble" and "big events" at the Versailles court, but that he had sent all the documents including Le Clerc's confrontation with his accusers to de Paulmy in Versailles where the attorney general would do better to address himself. Finally, on April 5 or 6, Joly de Fleury received the documents from an obliging de Paulmy, who assured the attorney general that the affair merited no sequel. The attorney general and the parlementary commissioners indeed thought likewise, which however did not prevent Le Clerc from still languishing in prison on June 19. Did the attorney general see any "inconvenience" in setting Le Clerc free, asked de Paulmy on that date? No, the leisurely reply arrived on July 3, the attorney general saw no "inconvenience." Presumably Le Clerc was in consequence set free, no doubt to the considerable relief of his twelve-year-old daughter and pregnant wife, who had experienced a difficult time of it these past seven months.[106]

Yet a six- or seven-month stint in prison was hardly rigorous by Old Regime standards, nor had Saint-Florentin's tongue been wholly in his cheek when he ascribed to the king's "goodness" the decision to imprison the aged Pierre Thomas. Except in connection with a PAI, imprisonment as such did not at all figure in the Old Regime's armory of judicial punishments, which in cases smacking of verbal *lèse-majesté* tended to be infinitely more draconian. Among those we have mentioned Jacques Mirlavaud and François Roger got "amende honorable" and perpetual galley labor; Jacques Ringuet and Du Truche de la Chaux got amende honorable and the gibbet; while Félix Ricard was broken on the wheel after performing amende honorable in Montdidier.[107] By comparison, most of those subjected to extrajudicial imprisonment scraped by with fairly short stays in the Bastille or Bicêtre. Jean Aveque and Jean-Baptiste Mesguet got seven to eight months; Pierre Liebert and Jean-Antoine Lefevre, ten to eleven months; Joseph Le Cocq and Toussaint Courtin, about twenty months each; while Jean Bosquet and Marie-Marguerite Gadibois remained for five to six years.[108] What clearly worked to the advantage of those extrajudicially handled was the very secrecy of their affairs, for unlike cases more exposed to public view theirs were hardly the stuff of which "examples" were made.

The chief danger for the person extrajudicially imprisoned was that he would simply be forgotten, as Lagrené discovered to his chagrin in the bailliage prisons of Orléans. The risk of this happening not surprisingly rose in inverse proportion as one descended the social ladder, the gagne denier Bosquet or the "wretched woman of nothing" Gadibois tending to stay much longer than the huissier Jean-Antoine Lefevre, who could muster family and friends to subject Saint-Florentin and Berryer to a steady barrage of *placets*.[109] Indeed, the mere fact of not being reclaimed by anyone could itself constitute grounds for continued imprisonment, as the retired soldier-become-beggar Marc Legris found in 1757.[110] It was not until February 1771 that Saint-Florentin prodded Joly de Fleury into fresh consideration of the case of Bellier de La Chauvelais, whose dossier the attorney general had lost but whose fourteen years at Bicêtre Saint-Florentin deemed adequate leisure "to have made some serious reflections."[111] And by June 1762 the police had all but forgotten the original reason for the detention of Marie-Angélique (Jeanne) Bironneau, who had never been so much as interrogated about the "immoderate joy" she had supposedly expressed at the news of the king's misfortune in 1757 on the authority of one witness alone.[112] What tended to take its place as a rationale for her continued detention was her physiognomy and objectionable comportment as a prisoner in the Bastille and the Salpêtrière: she was a "notorious liar" and "intriguer" of a "dangerous disposition," a woman "without modesty although ugly," and furthermore over forty years old.[113]

Given this judicial system, or rather antisystem, some spectacular miscarriages of justice were inevitable, no matter how justice be construed. Firman-Olivier de Rome, thirty-five-year-old native of Amiens, had come to Paris in 1740 and married a girl whose deceased father's fancy goods business procured him a living until bad health and bankruptcy forced him to relinquish this business around 1754. It was then that he turned versifier, publishing the anticlerical *Préjugés démasqués* with the connivance of the prince de Conti and some magistrates in the parlement the same year.[114] The king's "accident" and prompt recovery moved him to compose some mediocre verses on the subject, which he subsequently contrived to sell to the Parisian coach renters who were looking for ways to win royal favor toward this confraternity's litigation with the General Farm. Firman de Rome and two of the confraternity's delegates therefore brought these verses to Versailles on the eighteenth of January and received Richelieu's compliments on behalf of the king on the twentieth, only to be arrested and embastillé on the way back to Paris the following day. While on their second trip to Versailles, it seems, they had stopped off in a Sèvres cabaret, and in response to a postilion's remark that Damiens was a "monster risen from hell," the three had smiled knowingly among themselves thinking they recognized one of de Rome's inspired lines and concluding that their poem's renown had already traveled as far as Sèvres. The mystified postilion, however, construed their mirthful satisfaction as sympathy for Damiens and promptly denounced them, whereupon the three were recognized and arrested when they stopped off at the same cabaret on their way back to Paris.[115]

That much was unfortunate enough, but worse was soon to follow. The two carriage hirers, Joseph Jérôme and Jean-Baptiste Meusnier, remained three months in the Bastille for "their imprudence in being found in the company of Firman de Rome," who was guilty for his part of being "a kind of poet and a bad subject." Overcrowding in the Bastille forced the transfer of this unhappy author to Bicêtre on March 21, 1757, where "sick and swelled from scurvy," he still languished in the spring of 1758. He was only freed at this time in response to incessant *placets* from his indigent wife and on condition that he track down every last copy of his *Préjugés démasqués*.[116] Speaking for de Rome as well as for themselves, the two carriage hirers found the courage to protest in their awkwardly formal French against the "injustice vexation" of "groaning" in "the irons of the severest captivity" for having tried to express their "zeal and good wishes" for the "most powerful monarch in the world and so worthy of being loved." "Besides, what weight," they asked, "should be given to nonjuridical declarations rendered inconsiderately and without any examination. If they are received, who is the citizen whose liberty could not be attacked. . . ."[117]

Meusnier and Jérôme were not the only victims of political "justice" to have haltingly articulated a conception of civil rights and due process. Another was Jean-Paul Anne, a journeyman shoemaker in Troyes known there as Languedoc, whose master, Nicolas Patin, told him on the morning of June 25, 1758, that the "month would perhaps not end before the king was assassinated." Deeply upset by the thought of a second attack on the king, Languedoc dutifully reported Patin's prediction to the curé Dubois who in turn informed m. Jourdain, provost of the constabulary. Jourdain promptly rousted Languedoc out of bed on the evening of the same day to receive his deposition, then arrested and interrogated Patin and four others on succeeding days before getting to the bottom of the matter on the thirtieth. It seems as though Jacques Goulard, local commissioner of the *taille*, met a couple of individuals on the road to Sens who told him that twenty hangmen had gathered in Paris to execute someone for having said that the king would not make it through the month without being assassinated. From Goulard this already distorted rumor went to the journeyman weaver Jean-Baptiste Houssian, who told his wife, who told one of their cotton spinners, who told her daughter, who told Patin until, minus its connection with someone executed in Paris for having *said* that the king would soon be assassinated, it reached Languedoc in the disturbing form we have noted.[118]

That might have ended the rumor's history, but it was only the beginning of Languedoc's, for on the very same day that Jourdain finally interrogated Languedoc, he found himself newly arrested and taken to the prisons of the bailliage and *sénéchaussée* of Troyes and from there transported in turn to the Bastille. What had happened is that the royal procurator of the bailliage and sénéchaussée had laid claim to the affair as a *royal* case, thereby belatedly quashing the procedure in the prevotal constabulary court and effecting its transferal to the bailliage, whence Languedoc's trip to its prisons on the thirtieth. Meanwhile the attorney general in Paris, unaware of the bailliage's action, had informed Saint-Florentin, who promptly ordered the prevost Jourdain to bring Languedoc to the Bastille. So by the time Joly de Fleury got word of the bailliage's *revendication*, it was too late to prevent Saint-Florentin's orders from reaching Jourdain, who, though no longer in charge of Languedoc's case, managed to obtain his release from the bailliage's prisons only to see to his reimprisonment in Paris where the two of them arrived to everyone's chagrin on July 1. Nothing remained to do by that date except to put Languedoc up in the Bastille for a few days while Jourdain, the attorney general, and Saint-Florentin tried to untie this jurisdictional Gordian Knot. On July 4, finally, the attorney general sent Jourdain back to Troyes with Languedoc and orders to relinquish his case to the bailliage and sénéchaussée courts, which began instructing it anew on July 6.[119] When, still in prison, Languedoc reiterated his original deposition, he could not restrain himself from appending to it the comment that "he would never have thought that his love for his prince, of which he gave proof by his declaration to the curé Dubois, would have merited the disgrace of being detained as a prisoner and thus transferred from one place to another as if he had been a criminal . . . in spite of which he does not repent of the declaration that he gave since it concerns so seriously the person of the king."[120] Like Damiens, although in an opposite sense, Languedoc had tried to perform his duty as citizen; and a more ingenuous indictment of the reign of Louis le Bien-Aimé can hardly be said to exist.

Conclusion

THE SAME Ravaillac and Châtel precedents that condemned Damiens to his horrible and anachronistic execution in the place de Grève carried with them draconian consequences for his family. These required that the assailant's parents and children "leave the realm with the injunction never to return on pain of hanging and strangulation without formality or trial" and that his brothers and sister change their family name or incur the same penalty.[1] So important to Damiens' judges was the matter of this arrêt's precise conformity to the precedents in question that the attorney general had to be urged by his chief substitute Pierron "to find a way in repeating the name of Damiens to add the name of his birthplace, for the arrêt [against Damiens] is already being criticized for not recalling the birthplace as did the arrêt against Châtel and Ravaillac. It is being said," he further warned, "that this is an affected reticence"—to precisely what effect, it must be confessed, is not easy to conceive.[2] Under such circumstances, the only inventiveness the prosecution dared to exercise was in assimilating the case of Damiens' wife to that of his lineal relatives; neither Jean Châtel nor François Ravaillac had been married.[3]

Damiens' aged father accordingly took the road to Poperingue near Ypres in the Austrian Netherlands, where a Benedictine priory provided asylum a short eight leagues from his home in Saint-Omer. The assailant's wife betook herself and her daughter to Luxembourg in German Lorraine not far from Metz where she was born. None of her family there had survived, however, nor did she say how she and her daughter intended to.[4] A question arose regarding their passports, whether they should bear some name other than Damiens lest their bearers suffer from the "insults of the public"; the solution finally arrived at was to persuade father, wife, and daughter to change their names to Guillemant so that their passports could legitimately omit the name Damiens. To each party

Saint-Florentin and the parlement's commissioners generously gave three hundred livres to cover the costs of food, lodging, and travel and a passport valid for a month.[5] Damiens' sister and brothers with their wives likewise adopted their mother's name of Guillemant and faced their individual fates.[6] Louis may have gone back to work as the councillor Charles Aubin's domestic, but judging by the infamy that dogged Renée Macée from condition to condition, scented though she was with only the most passing connection with the affair, this hypothesis seems unlikely.[7] Catherine and the pious Antoine-Joseph must surely have returned to Saint-Omer or thereabouts, for an inquiry from the latter concerning his 140 bound volumes of confiscated devotional, catechetical, and theological works reached the desk of the attorney general in January 1761.[8] Guillaume-François Joly de Fleury's many and weighty duties, on the eve of the expulsion of the Jesuits, had undoubtedly not permitted him the leisure to think of how to dispose of them before that date.

The unholy stigmata of association with Damiens' trial did not confine their damnation to the lowest of the lowly alone. Doubtless the arrival of monseigneur de Brunes de Monloüet at the head of the diocese of Saint-Omer had made some nasty Flemish weather predictable for the Jansenist curé and vicaire of the parish of Sainte-Marguerite. "Devoted to the bull," according to the *Nouvelles écclésiastiques*, "and to the Jesuits who had promoted him to the episcopacy," the new bishop could neither "view with pleasure the affluence of auditors who assiduously frequented this church to nourish themselves with precious truths that zealous constitutionaries do not like" nor "leave unpunished the blows that the teaching of the ancient and perpetual doctrine of the church delivered indirectly to [the bull]."[9] But it was surely the dubious publicity given the Fenes' brothers' garden catechetical conventicles by Damiens' trial that transformed the episcopal storm watch into an imminent certainty. Two royal lettres de cachet accordingly descended on the Fenes brothers in the summer of 1757, one exiling the curé to the convent of the Penitents of Nazareth near Louviers in upper Normandy, the other relegating the vicaire to the monastery of the Brothers of the Christian Schools at Saint-Yon in the same province. Detained in bed by the gout, the curé could only acknowledge the lettre de cachet and receive the condolences of his tearful parishioners during his remaining ten days of freedom. His physically more vigorous brother fled the parish before receipt of the lettre de cachet, thus avoiding formal disobedience to the king, then appropriately resurfaced in the Parisian parish of Saint-Etienne-du-Mont in 1758 where he successfully obtained the last sacraments before dying there the same year.[10]

Calloused though it may seem to say so, life went on as "normal" for these and other unfortunates, just as it soon did in court routine and in politics. Catastrophic changes had indeed overwhelmed them, but it can justly be said of these changes that the more they occurred, the more things remained the same. But change in the profounder sense of the structurally new can also be detected among the refractions of the Damiens affair, most discernibly at the level of language and perception. Outraged over the treatment of the Fenes brothers, the same Le Paige who thought Belot deserving of the Tallion law reclaimed the general rights of "a Frenchman, a priest, a citizen" in behalf of these persecuted Jansenist clerics.[11] Reacting to Damiens' execution, the same Le Paige who thought the Ravaillac and Châtel precedents altogether appropriate for the occasion and who only faulted the parlement of Paris' traditional "question" of the *brodequins* for being insufficiently torturous could also reflect that the gory nature of the spectacle was perhaps "too contrary to the gentleness of our manners and to the amenity of our century."[12] In the same strokes with which Dominique Gautier's lawyer Doillot sketched Damiens' monstrosity in the most Gothic shades, he could also depict the procedure employed in cases of lèse-majesté as the "universal violation of every principle" and blot out as immaterial any avowal uttered under torture.[13] Even the steely Pierron, roughing out the attorney general's prospective "conclusions" against the Damiens family, could not suppress the thought that the threat of "hanging and strangulation without formality or semblance of trial" if they returned to the realm was "very savage in our customs."[14] The point that bears emphasis is that these novel sounds represent a metamorphosis from within, not an "influence" from without, the parlement of Paris, the parti janséniste, and their mixed but distinguishable milieux.

Not that official policy remained indefinitely unreceptive to these fertile linguistic and perceptual changes, in which the Damiens affair played a role as pollinator. To be sure, the emptying of the Bastille and other state prisons of most political prisoners and the gradual abandonment of the use of lettres de cachet waited until the accession of Louis XVI and the reformist nonactivity of Lamoignon de Malesherbes, the old chancellor's son, as secretary of the king's household in 1775-1776.[15] And an authentic veteran of the Damiens roundup by the name of Auguste-Claude Tavernier was among the six prisoners who greeted the liberators of the Bastille in 1789.[16] Nonetheless, the thoroughly disillusioning lesson afforded by the Damiens affair in the matters of calumnious denunciations and elusive mauvais discours probably played its role in the preparation for this limited and belated reform. Less conjectural and more immediate is the momentous shift in royal ecclesiastical policy with regard to appellants of the bull *Unigenitus*, which we have located at September 1757. If, moreover, the clergy's remonstrances of 1770 are correct in pointing to the onset of the Seven Years' War (1756-1757) as the beginning of the Protestants' new assertiveness and the nonenforcement of the declaration of 1724 against them, then the year of Damiens marks a sacramental moment of the greatest significance in France.[17] Not only would the monarchy have ceased supporting the clergy in its attempt to withhold the sacraments from those who persisted in regarding themselves as orthodox Catholics but it would have also begun to distance itself from the campaign to foist the sacraments of baptism and marriage upon those who in spite of a century of persecution persisted in their refusal to regard the second of these as a sacrament at all. A de facto policy of sacramental live-and-let-live seems to have taken root at this date, and the declaration of 1724 (with the revocation of the Edict of Nantes, another of the "sun king's" legislative landmarks) seems to have begun to wither with the edict of 1695.

Of greatest import nonetheless remain the changes in language, feeling, and perception of which the Damiens drama provides a revelatory if fleeting glimpse. The slow parting of the paths between the sacred and secular, together with the Jansenist internalization of religion; the disintegration of the Gallican synthesis of 1682 and its rearrangement as antithetical constitutional systems; the rise of the principle of national sovereignty among Gallican-Jansenists and their growing perception of absolutism as despotism; the waxing ultramontanism and authoritarianism of episcopal apologists and their tendency to externalize religion—these changes occupy center stage, although some of them are more easily felt than seen. But also decidedly on stage in this drama, and as represented by Damiens even playing a leading role, a popular chorus of sorts constitutes more than a group of passive respondents and articulates more clearly than the literate elites the growing desacralization of the monarchy.

Yet this whole prologue to the Revolution is nonetheless difficult to recognize as such because of its anachronistic, history-bookish staging. Soon, the language of national sovereignty will shed its ecclesiastical-religious chrysallis and take flight toward the Revolution; soon, as early as the Maupeou "revolution," the parti janséniste will effect its metamorphosis into the "patriot party," as a perspicacious observer noted at the time.[18] What has so memorably been said of the waning of the Middle Ages can perhaps also be said of the period from 1750 to 1770 in France: "The tide is turning; the tone of life is about to change."

Notes

Notes to the Introduction

1. Bibliothèque Nationale (hereafter BN), Collection Joly de Fleury (hereafter JF) 2070, fols. 122-23, 125, depositions by François Gorgu, Feb. 7 and 25; and fols. 121-22, interrogation of Le Clerc by Pierre-Antoine Dervillers, subdelegate of the intendant of Flanders, Feb. 3. The year is understood to be 1757 unless otherwise specified.

2. *Pièces originales et procédures du procès fait à Robert-François Damiens, tant en la prévôté de l'Hôtel qu'en la cour du parlement* (hereafter *PO*) (Paris, 1757), "Précis historique," pp. xix-xx; and Charles-Philippe d'Albert, duc de Luynes, *Mémoires du duc de Luynes, sur la cour de Louis XV, 1735-1758*, eds. L. Dussieux and E. Soulié, 17 vols. (Paris, 1860-1865), 15:355.

3. *PO*, 3rd continuation d'information, deposition of Louis-François Armand Duplessis, duc de Richelieu, Jan. 9, p. 75.

4. *PO*, "Précis historique," pp. xx; and depositions of Pierre-Charles Selim, information, Jan. 6, pp. 49-50, of Louis-Charles de Brionne, Louis de Noailles, duc d'Ayen, and Henri-Camille de Beringhen, continuation d'information, Jan. 7, pp. 62-64; and of François Duras and Claude-Louis-Victor de Vigny, 3rd continuation d'information, Jan. 9, pp. 73-74.

5. *PO*, continuation d'information, deposition of Charles-François Césard Le Tellier, marquis de Montmirail, Jan. 7, p. 64.

6. In addition to testimony cited above, see *PO*, continuation d'information, depositions of André Fiefré and Charles-François Badelart, Jan. 7, pp. 60-61; 3rd continuation d'information, deposition of David-Léonard Bertou, marquis d'Hendreville, Jan. 9, pp. 74-75.

7. Luynes, *Mémoires* 15:356-58; and *Mémoires de m. le baron de Besanval, . . . contenant beaucoup de particularités et d'anecdotes sur la cour, sur les ministres et les règnes de Louis XV et Louis XVI et sur les événements du temps*, ed. A.-J. de Ségur, 3 vols. (Paris, 1805), 1:304-305.

8. Luynes, *Mémoires* 15:356-58; *PO*, 2nd continuation d'information, depositions of Jean Senac and Germain de La Martinière, Jan. 9, pp. 70-71.

9. Luynes, *Mémoires* 15-357; *Mémoires de madame Du Hausset, femme*

de chambre de madame de Pompadour, avec des notes et des éclaircissements historiques, ed. Quentin Crauford (Paris, 1824), p. 139; Edmond-J. F. Barbier, *Chronique de la régence et du règne de Louis XV, 1718-1763* (hereafter *Journal*), 8 vols. (Paris, 1857-1866), 6:433, 439.

10. Madame de Campan, *Mémoires sur la vie privée de Marie Antoinette, reine de France et de Navarre, suivis de souvenirs et anecdotes historiques sur les règnes de Louis XIV, de Louis XV, et de Louis XVI*, ed. F. Barrière, 3 vols. (Paris, 1822), 3:22-25.

11. *Mémoires sur les règnes de Louis XV et Louis XVI et sur la Révolution, par J.-N. Dufort, comte de Cheverny, introducteur des ambassadeurs*, ed. R. de Crevecoeur, 2 vols. (Paris, 1886), 1:184. The duc de Luynes added, "Il est très certain qu'il [Louis XV] a dit qu'il voudroit qu'il lui en eût coûté un bras et que ceci ne fût pas arrivé; et l'on assure que lorsque l'on lui sonda sa plaie et qu'on lui dit avec plaisir qu'elle n'étoit pas profonde, il dit: 'Elle l'est plus que vous ne le croyez, car elle va jusqu'au coeur.' Il est très certain aussi que depuis qu'il est guéri et habillé, quelqu'un lui ayant marqué sa joie de sa santé, il dit: 'Oui, le corps va bien, mais ceci va mal, en mettant la main à sa tête, et ceci est impossible à guérir." (*Mémoires* 16:281-82.)

12. René-Louis de Voyer, marquis d'Argenson, *Journal et mémoires du marquis d'Argenson*, ed. E.-J.-B. Rathery, 9 vols. (Paris, 1859-1867), 9:390.

13. Luynes, *Mémoires* 16:281-82, but also 15:373, 380; *Mémoires et lettres de François-Joachim de Pierre, cardinal de Bernis, 1715-1758*, ed. Frédéric Masson, 2 vols. (Paris, 1911), 1:364; see also Barbier, *Journal* 6:464.

14. Barbier, *Journal* 6:433; Luynes, *Mémoires* 15:361.

15. D'Argenson, *Journal et mémoires* 9:385, 392. Strictly speaking, the archbishop of Paris could not order a *Te Deum* to be celebrated without violating the terms of his exile (see Barbier, *Journal* 6:490).

16. Paul Rabaut, *Lettre adressée aux protestants du Languédoc, à l'occasion de l'attentat commis sur la personne sacrée du roi* (n.p., 1757); and Rabbi Athias, *Prière faite par les juifs portugais de Bordeaux, à l'occasion de l'attentat commis sur la personne sacrée du roi, et action de grâces pour son heureuse convalescence* (n.p., 1757). On celebrations and rejoicings, see Pierre Rétat et al., *L'Attentat de Damiens: Discours sur l'événement au XVIIIe siècle* (Lyons, n.d.), pp. 101-44.

17. On the crisis in Paris, see Jean Egret, *Louis XV et l'opposition parlementaire* (Paris, 1970), pp. 79-86, and this volume, pp. 149-63. On the conflict in Brittany, see Barthélemy Pocquet du Haut-

Jussé, *Le Pouvoir absolu et l'esprit provincial: Le Duc d'Aiquillon et La Chalotais*, 3 vols. (Paris, 1900-1901), 1:30-65; and Marcel Marion, *Le Bretagne et le duc d'Aiquillon, 1753-1770* (Paris, 1898), pp. 43-66.

18. On Paris, see Barbier, *Journal* 6:431-38, 452; Luynes, *Mémoires* 15:359-60; and Bernis, *Mémoires et lettres* 1:361. On Brittany, see Luynes, *Mémoires* 15:363, 366, 374-75, 379, 382-83; and A. Le Moy, *Le Parlement de Bretagne et le pouvoir royal au XVIIIe siècle* (Angers, 1909), pp. 195-210.

19. *PO*, "Précis historique," pp. xxi-xxii; information, depositions of Pierre-Charles Selim and other of the king's bodyguards, Jan. 6, pp. 49-55; Damiens' letter to the king in 3rd interrogation at Versailles, p. 69; and interrogation of Jan. 18, no. 144, p. 132.

20. Esp. *PO*, 3rd continuation d'information, deposition of Jean-Marie de La Brou de Vareilles, Jan. 9, p. 72.

21. *PO*, 1st interrogation at Versailles, pp. 43-44; "Précis historique," pp. xxi-xxii.

22. Roland Mousnier, *L'Assassinat d'Henri IV*, no. 13 in "Trente journées qui ont fait la France" series (Paris, 1964).

23. Richard Waddington, *Louis XV et le renversement des alliances: Préliminaires de la Guerre de Sept Ans, 1754-1756* (Paris, 1896).

24. On the influence of Pompadour, see Henri Carré, *Louis XV, 1715-1774*, in Ernest Lavisse, *Histoire de France illustrée depuis les origines jusqu'à la révolution*, 9 vols. (Paris, 1911), 8 (2nd pt.):263; and Pierre de Nolhac, *Madame de Pompadour et la politique, d'après des documents nouveaux* (Paris, 1930).

25. See pp. 154-55.

26. Dale Van Kley, *The Jansenists and the Expulsion of the Jesuits from France, 1757-1765* (New Haven, 1975), pp. 62-89; and Rétat et al., *L'Attentat de Damiens*, pp. 267-94.

Notes to Chapter 1

1. *PO*, 2nd interrogation at Versailles, no. 44, p. 59; 5th interrogation at Versailles, no. 95, p. 85; interrogation of Jan. 25, nos. 368-69, p. 142; "Précis historique," p. v; and "Supplément au recueil des informations faites par le prince de Cröy . . ." (hereafter "Supplément au recueil"), p. 7.

2. *PO*, 1st interrogation at Versailles, no. 1, p. 44; 2nd interrogation at Versailles, no. 38, p. 58; and 3rd interrogation at Versailles, no. 54, p. 66.

3. *PO*, interrogation of Jan. 18, pp. 123-32; Jean Michel's declaration and Damiens' interrogation of Feb. 18, pp. 350-61. Damiens had confessed to this theft as early as Jan. 11 (see 4th interrogation at Versailles, nos. 82-84, p. 80).

4. See, for example, the greffier Alexandre-André Le Breton's "Précis historique," pp. viii, xx-xxi.

5. *PO*, "Recueil des informations faites par le prince de Cröy . . ." (henceforth "Recueil des informations"), p. 2; "Supplément au recueil," p. 7; and interrogation of Jan. 18, nos. 1-24, pp. 123-24. Damiens himself specified that "ses parents se sont chargés de ses frères et soeurs, et que lui s'est retiré chez un parent à Béthune" (no. 21, p. 124).

6. *PO*, interrogation of Feb. 15, nos. 3-5, p. 221; and interrogation of Mar. 26, no. 3, p. 383. For the prince de Cröy's discovery, see "Supplément au recueil," p. 7.

7. *PO*, "Supplément au recueil," p. 7; and interrogation of Jan. 18, nos. 24-38, pp. 124-25. Damiens said in his 2nd interrogation at Versailles on Jan. 7 (no. 48, p. 59) that he had been a pensionary of the Jesuits at Béthune, but an aged Béthune widow who remembered Damiens denied this in "Supplément au recueil," p. 7. Damiens also asserted in this same interrogation (no. 48, p. 59) that he had briefly served as an apprentice wig maker with Domguisse in Arras. On the provincial origins of more than ninety percent of Parisian domestic servants, see Daniel Roche, *Le Peuple de Paris* (Paris, 1981), pp. 26-29.

8. *PO*, interrogation of Jan. 18, nos. 39-51, pp. 125-26; nos. 129-32, pp. 130-31; and "Recueil des informations," p. 1. On later relations with Jesuits, see 6th interrogation at Versailles, no. 167, p. 104; and nos. 264-67, pp. 141-42.

9. Jeffrey Kaplow, *The Names of Kings: The Parisian Laboring Poor in the Eighteenth Century* (New York, 1972), pp. 50-51; Jules Michelet, *Histoire de France*, new ed., revised and expanded, 19 vols. (Paris, n.d.), 18:319.

10. BN, JF 2069, fol. 229, interrogation of Marie-Elizabeth Damiens by the police commissioner Miché de Rochebrune at Bastille, Jan. 10. See also the court's interrogation of Damiens' wife on Feb. 5 in *PO*, no. 19, p. 202.

11. Ibid.; also "Eclaircissements sans datte donnés à m. le grand Prévost par m. de Maridor concernant Robert-François Damiens" in BN, JF 2069, fols. 64-65; and anonymous note (probably by the curé of Saint-Sulpice), BN, JF 2070, fols. 284-85.

12. *PO*, interrogation of Feb. 5, nos. 15, 23, 26-27, pp. 201-202; also BN, JF 2069, fol. 223, interrogation at Bastille on Jan. 10 by the lieutenant of police, Nicolas-René Berryer. On the frequency of such double accommodations for married domestic servants, one for the husband under the roof of his employer and the other for his wife and children, see Roche, *Le Peuple de Paris*, pp. 107-108.

13. *PO*, interrogation of Jan. 25, nos. 259-60, p. 141; and of Mar. 26, nos. 55-85, pp. 372-75; also, BN, JF 2070, fol. 158, "Extrait de ce que le prisonnier a dit et qui a paru mériter attention, aux douze sergents du régiment des gardes françoises chargés de la garder à vüe," Feb. 18.

14. *PO*, interrogation of Jan. 18, nos. 33-77, pp. 125-28. Elsewhere Damiens remembered having served the comte de Raymond for only six months (see *PO*, 5th interrogation at Versailles, no. 126, p. 88).

15. BN, JF 2069, fol. 216, extrajudicial interrogation by the police commissioner, Hughes-Phillippes Duchesne, on Jan. 9, at Ripandelly residence.

16. *PO*, interrogation of Feb. 5, no. 19, p. 202; and of Jan. 25, nos. 198-202, p. 137. Damiens' wife also mentioned his service at Le Corgne de Launay in the course of Berryer's extrajudicial interrogation of her at Bastille (BN, JF 2069, fols. 222-23); and his brother Louis remembered the service for Barré (BN, JF 2068, fols. 123-24, interrogation by Rochebrune at Bastille on Jan. 12).

17. *PO*, 1st interrogation at Versailles, no. 10, p. 45; and Le Breton's "Précis historique," p. vi.

18. *PO*, recollement, the testimony of Charlotte-Elizabeth Combault d'Autueil, veuve de La Bourdonnaye, Feb. 21, p. 257. For Maridor's recollections, see BN, JF 2069, fols. 64-65.

19. Ibid.; and *PO*, information par addition, Mar. 13, p. 194.

20. *PO*, information par addition, Feb. 4, p. 183; confrontations of Mar. 3 and 13, pp. 282, 305.

21. *PO*, interrogation of Louis Damiens on Feb. 15, nos. 1-3, p. 223; and Damiens' 3rd interrogation at Versailles, no. 66, p. 67.

22. See, for example, the lawyer Doillot's assertions to this effect in *Supplément au procès et procédures de Robert-François Damiens* (henceforth *Supplément au procès*) (Paris, 1757), p. 21.

23. Cissey Fairchilds, "Masters and Servants in Eighteenth-Century Toulouse," *Journal of Social History* 12 (Spring 1979):368-93. For Parisian domestics in particular, this high rate of mobility prob-

ably holds for the first half of the century as well. See Roche, *Le Peuple de Paris*, pp. 70-71.

24. Extrajudicial interrogation of Elizabeth Molerienne, wife of Damiens, at Bastille on Jan. 10 in BN, JF 2069, fol. 221; and of Elizabeth Schoirtz, wife of Louis Damiens, at Bastille on Jan. 12, BN, JF 2068, fol. 128. See also *PO*, interrogation of Louis Damiens on Feb. 15, nos. 1-3, p. 223; of Jean Aubrais on Jan. 15, pp. 95-96; of Noële Selim on Jan. 16, p. 107; of Quentin Ferard on Jan. 16, p. 110; of Noël Roi on Jan. 17, pp. 114-15; and of Julien Le Guerinays dit Saint-Jean on Jan. 14, p. 92.

25. *PO*, interrogation of Jan. 17, p. 115.

26. *PO*, information par addition, testimony of Félicité Bezin, wife of Charles de Sainte-Rheuse, Feb. 3, p. 182; on Damiens' service to Bèze de Lys, see *PO*, testimony of Marguerite Lafaye, Jan. 27, p. 178. On Damiens as domestic servant, see also Michelet, *Histoire de France* 18:321-26.

27. *Arrest de la cour de parlement, qui condamne Pierre Pizel dit La Pierre, domestique sans condition, au carcan et au banissement, pour avoir été insolent envers son maître. Du 14 août 1751*, in Archives Nationales (henceforth AN) AB III, 8. For Damiens' denial of Sainte-Rheuse's accusations, see *PO*, confrontation of Mar. 3, p. 283.

28. AN, AP 177mi (Chartrier de Tocqueville), 118, fols. 227-28, Sept. 16-18.

29. AN, Y 13105 (Commissioner Bricogne), Apr. 4; and Y 15633 (Commissioner Sirebeau), Mar. 14.

30. *PO*, addition d'information, testimony of Louis-Auguste des Tournelles, lieutenant of the king's bodyguards, Feb. 8, pp. 189-90. Damiens, however, denied he had said this to Machault (*PO*, interrogation of Feb. 18, no. 533, p. 165). See also Barbier, *Journal* 6:434, 438.

31. *PO*, "Précis historique," p. xxxiv.

32. *PO*, interrogation of Mar. 26, no. 89, p. 374, and no. 157, p. 380; as well as Luynes, *Mémoires* 15:481. For remark addressed to the duc de Noailles, see *Mémoires authentiques du maréchal de Richelieu, publiés d'après le manuscrit original pour la Société de l'histoire de France*, ed. A. de Boislisle (Paris, 1918), p. 14.

33. Michelet, *Histoire de France* 18:318-20.

34. *PO*, 3rd interrogation at Versailles, no. 62, pp. 66-67. Damiens undoubtedly exaggerated, however, when he told his prison guards in the conciergerie that he was "connu du quarts du monde de Paris. . . ." (BN, JF 2070, fol. 158, Feb. 4).

35. *PO*, 3rd interrogation at Versailles, no. 74, p. 67.

36. See again the lawyer Doillot's defense of Dominique Gautier in *Supplément au procès*, p. 21: "Il passe jusqu'à quatre grands vols connus, et il avoue ne pas se souvenir d'une foule d'autres faits à ses camarades."

37. *PO*, addition d'information, testimony of Pierre-François Desvaux, Feb. 4, p. 183; for Damiens' denial, see *PO*, confrontation of Mar. 3, p. 282. On the Desvaux affair in 1783, see Porphyre Petrovitch, "Recherches sur la criminalité à Paris dans le seconde moitié du XVIIIe siècle," in A. Abbiateci, F. Billacois, Y. Castan, et al., *Crimes et criminalité en France, 17e-18e siècles*, Cahiers des Annales, no. 33 (Paris, 1971), p. 214.

38. Petrovitch, "Recherches sur la criminalité à Paris," pp. 212-13. On domestic servants as cultural intermediaries between elites and popular milieux, see Roche, *Le Peuple de Paris, passim.*

39. BN, JF 2069, fol. 230, extrajudicial interrogation of Marie-Elizabeth Damiens by Rochebrune at Bastille on Jan. 10; also *PO*, interrogation of Elizabeth Molerienne, Feb. 5, nos. 72-75, pp. 205-206. For Michel's deposition and order for Damiens' arrest in consequence, see *PO*, pp. 350-52.

40. BN, JF 2069, fol. 274, Louis Damiens to Antoine-Joseph Damiens, Aug. 31, 1756.

41. AN, Y 12743 (Commissioner Roland), "Procès-verbal au sujet du vol des 250 livres fait au Sr. baron de Traverse. Du 27 mars 1757."

42. *PO*, interrogation of Feb. 18, no. 3, p. 356; and confrontation with Michel, Mar. 1, p. 359.

43. BN, JF 2069, fol. 230, extrajudicial interrogation of Marie-Elizabeth Damiens by Rochebrune at Bastille, Jan. 10.

44. On lawsuit, see BN, JF 2069, fol. 266, Louis Damiens to Antoine-Joseph Damiens, Feb. 20, 1754; fol. 272, Mar. 11, 1756; fol. 278, Dec. 18, 1756; and fol. 270, Robert-François Damiens to Catherine Damiens, widow Collet, Oct. 28, 1754. See also *PO*, interrogation of Jan. 18, nos. 87-93, p. 128; and "Recueil des informations," pp. 2-3, 7-9, 15, 29.

45. BN, JF 2069, fol. 49, Courtaillon to provost of Saint-Omer, Jul. 14, 1756.

46. *PO*, "Supplément au recueil," pp. 7-9.

47. Ibid., pp. 9-10; and *PO*, interrogations of Antoine-Joseph Damiens, Feb. 16, pp. 231-34; of Marie Pauvret, wife of A.-J. Damiens, Feb. 16, p. 230; and of Marie-Catherine Damiens, Feb.

15, pp. 226-29. See also BN, JF 2068, fols. 99-101, interrogation of A.-J. Damiens by Vanden Driesche, Jan. 11 and 13; and fols. 123-24, interrogation of Louis Damiens by Rochebrune at Bastille, Jan. 12.

48. *PO*, "Supplément au recueil," p. 10; and interrogation of Damiens, Feb. 18, nos. 449-50, p. 156. See also BN, JF 2068, fols. 115-16, interrogation of Marie-Catherine Damiens by Vanden Driesche at Saint-Omer, Jan. 11.

49. BN, JF 2068, fol. 110, interrogation of Antoine-Joseph Damiens by Vanden Driesche at Saint-Omer, Jan. 11.

50. BN, JF 2068, fol. 94, Jan. 13; and fol. 119, interrogation of Marie-Catherine Damiens by Vanden Driesche at Saint-Omer, Jan. 11. See also *PO*, 6th interrogation at Versailles, no. 171, p. 105; interrogation of Antoine-Joseph Damiens, Feb. 16, no. 20, p. 233; and "Supplément au recueil," p. 11.

51. BN, JF 2068, fol. 91, interrogation of Antoine-Joseph Damiens by Commissioner Chenon at Saint-Omer, Jan. 13; and *PO*, "Supplément au recueil," p. 12; interrogation of A.-J. Damiens, Feb. 16, no. 36, p. 234; and of Robert-François Damiens, Feb. 18, nos. 457-58, p. 157.

52. *PO*, "Supplément au recueil," p. 12; interrogation of Catherine Damiens, Feb. 15, no. 22, p. 228; and of Antoine-Joseph Damiens, Feb. 16, no. 7, pp. 231-32. The order of Good Sons was founded with this purpose in view. See Michel Foucault, *Madness and Civilization: A History of Insanity in the Age of Reason*, trans. Richard Howard (New York, 1973), p. 42.

53. *PO*, "Supplément au recueil," pp. 12-13, 18-19; interrogation of Catherine Damiens, Feb. 16, nos. 24-27, p. 233. On desire to see the sea, interrogation of Feb. 18, nos. 459-60, p. 157.

54. *PO*, 6th interrogation at Versailles, no. 106, p. 86.

55. *PO*, "Deuxième et dernière Supplément, au recueil des informations faites par m. le prince de Cröy" (henceforth "Deuxième Supplément"), pp. 22, 25.

56. Ibid., pp. 21-22; and *PO*, interrogation of Feb. 18, nos. 466-68, p. 158.

57. "Deuxième Supplément," pp. 25-26; *PO*, interrogation of Feb. 18, nos. 469-73, pp. 158-59. BN, JF 2068, fol. 95, interrogation of Antoine-Joseph Damiens by Vanden Driesche in Saint-Omer, Jan. 13.

58. "Deuxième Supplément," pp. 26-27; *PO*, interrogation of Feb. 18, no. 474, p. 159.

59. "Deuxième Supplément," p. 24; *PO*, interrogation of Feb. 18, no. 482, p. 160; and in general nos. 475-86, pp. 159-60.

60. "Deuxième Supplément," pp. 27-28; *PO*, interrogation of Feb. 18, nos. 489-90, pp. 160-61.

61. "Deuxième Supplément," p. 28; *PO*, interrogation of Feb. 18, no. 491, p. 161.

62. "Deuxième Supplément," p. 29; *PO*, interrogation of Feb. 18, no. 494, p. 161.

63. "Deuxième Supplément," p. 29; *PO*, interrogation of Feb. 18, nos. 496-97, p. 161.

64. "Recueil des informations," p. 2; *PO*, interrogation of Feb. 18, no. 498, p. 161.

65. "Recueil des informations," p. 3; "Supplément au recueil," pp. 16-17; *PO*, interrogation of Jan. 25, nos. 160-67, pp. 133-34; and Feb. 18, nos. 500-502, p. 162.

66. "Recueil des informations," p. 5; *PO*, interrogation of Feb. 18, no. 507, p. 162.

67. "Recueil des informations," p. 3. On procuration, see *PO*, interrogation of Antoine-Joseph Damiens, Feb. 16, nos. 32-33, pp. 233-34; and BN, JF 2068, fol. 119, interrogation of Marie-Catherine Damiens by Vanden Driesche in Saint-Omer, Jan. 11. On the limited possibility of such a social aspiration among better-off Parisian domestic servants, see Roche, *Le Peuple de Paris*, p. 83.

68. "Supplément au recueil," p. 14; BN, JF 2068, fols. 117-18, interrogation of Marie-Catherine Damiens at Saint-Omer, Jan. 11.

69. Testimony of Nicolas Breuvart in "Recueil des informations," p. 1; and of Saint-Julien Le Guerinays in *PO*, interrogation of Jan. 14 at Versailles, no. 12, pp. 93-94.

70. *PO*, continuation d'information, deposition of Louis-Claude-Marie Madeleine Perier, first in charge (commis) of the buildings of the king, Jan. 7, p. 62; and addition d'information, deposition of Félicité Bezin de Sainte-Rheuse, employee at the bureau of war, Feb. 3, p. 182.

71. *PO*, addition d'information, deposition of Nicolas Playoust, stocking-maker and vendor, Mar. 13, pp. 191-94.

72. *PO*, deposition of François-Joseph Bourbier, blacksmith, Mar. 13, p. 196.

73. Foucault, *Madness and Civilization*, pp. 117-35.

74. BN, JF 2068, fol. 251, Foubert to attorney general, Feb. 22.

75. *PO*, addition d'information, deposition of Félicité Bezin de

Sainte-Rheuse, Feb. 3, p. 182; Foucault, *Madness and Civilization*, pp. 136-58, 162-77.

76. Emmanuel prince de Cröy, *Journal inédit du duc de Cröy, 1718-1784*, ed. vicomte de Grouchy and Paul Cottin, 4 vols. (Paris, 1906-1907), 1:382.

77. AN, Y 15813 (Commissioner Rochebrune), "Déclaration de François Boussin, maître de flûte allemande, le 15 janvier, 1757."

78. "Supplément au recueil," p. 13; *PO*, interrogation of Damiens on Jan. 18, nos. 71-75, pp. 127-28; on Feb. 18, nos. 477-79, p. 159; and on Mar. 17, no. 6, p. 328; confrontation with Louise-Henriette Deuser, Mar. 3, pp. 283-84; interrogation of Louis Damiens, Feb. 15, nos. 9-10, p. 224; of Marie-Catherine Damiens, Feb. 15, nos. 5-7, pp. 226-27; of Antoine-Joseph Damiens, Feb. 16, nos. 20-23, p. 233. See also BN, JF 2068, fol. 95, interrogation of Marie-Catherine Damiens in Saint-Omer, Jan. 13; and fol. 111, the same by Commissioner Chenon in Saint-Omer, Jan. 13.

79. Roland Mousnier, *L'Assassinat d'Henri IV* (Paris, 1964), pp. 28-29.

80. *PO*, 1st interrogation at Versailles, Jan. 5, no. 2, p. 44; interrogation of Jan. 18, no. 144, p. 132; Mar. 17, nos. 19, 22-26, pp. 330-32; Mar. 26, nos. 171-73, p. 381.

81. *PO*, interrogation of Mar. 17, no. 26, p. 331; see also Luynes, *Mémoires du duc de Luynes, sur la cour de Louis XV, 1735-1758*, ed. L. Dussieux and E. Soulié, 17 vols. (Paris, 1860-1865), 15:482, 491.

82. BN, JF 2069, fols. 64-65.

83. "Supplément au recueil," p. 15; *PO*, interrogation of Jan. 29, nos. 333-35, p. 147.

84. The investigation of these events and trial of *meneurs* conducted by the parlement of Paris (AN, X^{2B} 1367) turned up four veritable child arresters: Joseph Faillon, Sebastien Le Blanc, Julien Danguisy, and Jacques de Brucelles. All were sergeants or exempts in the Paris *guet* with the exception of Brucelles, who was an inspector of police; all functioned as disguised arresters of children in virtue of a special commission from the lieutenant of police, Nicolas-René Berryer. Faillon said that Berryer's order was "pour arrester les vagabonds, libertins, gens sans aveu, qui jouent à la halle aux cartes et qui jettent des pierres pour casser les lanternes publiques." (Interrogation of June 13, 1750.) The one reference to an attempt to arrest girls is in deposition by eleven-year-old François Copin, May 30, as part of *information* of May 27, 1750. The statement concerning precisely where in Paris the children were arrested is based on an examination

of the trial record as well as on A. P. Herlaut, "Les Enlèvements d'enfants à Paris en 1720 et en 1750," *Revue historique* 139 (1922):43-61, 202-223.

85. In his deposition before the court on Mar. 13, Maridor described himself as "demeurant ordinairement en son Château de Saint-Ouen, Province du Maine" and remembered having dismissed Damiens "de sa campagne . . ." (*PO*, addition d'information, p. 194).

86. AN, X² 1367. The list of those either arrested in connection with these disturbances and subsequently interrogated or specifically denounced as participants (but not arrested) by witnesses heard in deposition during the parlement of Paris' trial is as follows: three persons who described themselves as "masters" (a locksmith and his wife and a roastmeat-woman), a journeyman carpenter and two apprentices, three apprentice (*garçon*) locksmiths, two apprentice stirrup-makers, one apprentice butcher, eight domestic servants (including one coachman), four unspecified porters (*crocheteurs*), two port workers (*bouttes à port*), two chairmen, one stonemason, one coal-heaver, one colporter, one pastry cook, one errand boy (*décrotteur*), two laundresses, and one vagabond. Another way of describing the apprentices, however, is simply as boys between the ages of nine and fifteen, most of them guilty of throwing stones at Commissioner La Vergée's hôtel on the rue Saint-Honoré. The proportion of domestics involved would probably increase if we could take unspecific denunciations into account. The rioting crowd at Croix-Rouge, for example, where there were no arrests, was said to have been composed "principalement de domestiques" or to have consisted of "principalement la livrée." Another witness remarked that "y avoit un grand nombre de domestiques et beaucoup d'autres." See depositions of two *guet* sergeants in AN, X² 1367, addition d'information, June 12, 18, and 20, 1750. In any event, the whole "crowd" involved here seems socially and professionally a cut or two below that portrayed by George Rudé in *The Crowd in the French Revolution* (London, Oxford, and New York, 1959).

87. *PO*, 1st interrogation at Versailles, nos. 11-12, p. 46; 6th interrogation at Versailles, no, 158, p. 103; and Maridor's deposition, addition d'information, Mar. 13, p. 194.

88. BN, JF 2069, fols. 58-60, prince de Cröy to the marquis de Sourches, Jan. 19, 1757.

89. *PO*, interrogation of Jan. 18, nos. 135-36, p. 131; of Jan. 29, nos. 320-21, p. 146; of Mar. 26, no. 150, p. 379; and of Mar. 28 (the question), p. 402.

90. BN, JF 2070, fol. 158, Feb. 6.

91. Ibid., Jan. 18; *PO*, interrogation of Mar. 17, no. 25, p. 331.

92. Jules Flammermont, ed., *Remontrances du parlement de Paris au XVIIIe siècle*, 3 vols. (Paris, 1888-1898; reprint ed., Geneva, 1978), 1:116-17, 121.

93. "Remontrances sur la déclaration établissant la levée du dixième des revenus. Du 6 septembre 1741," in ibid., 1:381-82; and "Remontrances sur la Déclaration du 21 octobre 1749. Du 7 juin 1759," in ibid., 1:407-408.

94. *PO*, interrogation of Jan. 25, nos. 180-81, p. 135.

95. Best illustrated in figures 36-40 in Ernest Labrousse, Pierre Léon, Pierre Goubert, et al., *Histoire économique et sociale de la France*, vol. 2: *Des Derniers Temps de l'âge seigneurial aux préludes de l'âge industriel, 1660-1789* (Paris, 1970), pp. 401-403, but in general, pp. 529-63. See also Ernest Labrousse, *Esquisse du mouvement des prix et des revenus en France au XVIIIe siècle*, 2 vols. (Paris, 1933), 1:94, 98, 239; and C. Verlinden, *Documents sur l'histoire des prix et des salaires en Flandre et en Brabant, XVe à XVIIIe siècles*, 2 vols. (Bruges, 1959-1965).

96. *An Inquiry into the Price of Wheat, Malt, and Occasionally of Other Provisions. . . . As Sold in England, from the Year 1000 to the Year 1765* (London, 1768), pp. 90-93.

97. Cröy, *Journal inédit* 1:413n.

98. Bibliothèque de Port Royal (hereafter BPR), Collection Le Paige (hereafter LP), 532, unnumbered fol., de Saget to Lefebvre to Saint-Hilaire, Apr. 12, 1757.

99. BN, JF 2072, fol. 257, "Olive" to attorney general, Flixcourt near Amiens, undated; accompanied by a whole memoir, fols. 255-56; and an anonymous letter from Lyons, Mar. 19, 1757, fols. 298-99. See also fol. 300, attorney general to Saint-Florentin, Apr. 7, 1757, on the subject of this letter.

100. BN, JF 2069, fol. 239, letter found in the possession of Noële Selim, wife of Chevalier, Jan. 1, 1757, and signed by "La Brun" from Amiens; and fol. 243, letter in the possession of Quentin Ferard dit Condé, July 18, 1756, sent to Condé by his father who admonishes: "Vous qui parle de la misère dans Paris. . . ."

101. BN, JF 2071, fols. 241-42, Bataille to attorney general, Arras, undated; and fols. 149-51, same to same, Arras, June 15, 1757.

102. Steven L. Kaplan, *Bread, Politics and Political Economy in the*

Reign of Louis XV, 2 vols. (The Hague, 1976), 1:53-56; and Petrovitch, "Recherches sur la criminalité à Paris," p. 213.

103. On the Félix Ricard affair, see in general *PO*, pp. 497-610; and *Supplément au procès*, pp. 29-47. For Ricard's reactions, see *PO*, interrogation at Montdidier, Mar. 3, pp. 520-21; and Feb. 22, pp. 507-510; interrogation at Paris, Mar. 6, pp. 531-37; and Luynes, *Mémoires* 15:444. Le Fort was a wool and stocking merchant at Hargest, employing more than two hundred people in a putting-out industry; Dangest was a wine, *eau de vie*, and stocking merchant, a farmer (*laboureur*), a judge, and both a royal and seigneurial tax collector. *PO*, pp. 564, 569.

104. *PO*, "Recueil des informations," p. 2; BN, JF 2068, fols. 92-93, interrogation of Antoine-Joseph Damiens by Vanden Driesche in Saint-Omer, Jan. 13. Antoine-Joseph says here that Damiens "a dépensé comme de la paille pendant les huit jours qu'il a resté icy, qu'il en avoit donné beaucoup au pauvre. . . ."

105. *PO*, interrogation of Mar. 26, no. 150, p. 379; and information, Jan. 6, depositions of Jean-François Dubois, p. 50, and Jean-Louis-N.-C. de Hédouville, p. 51; 3rd continuation d'information, Jan. 9, deposition of Jean-Marie de la Brou de Vareilles, p. 73; addition d'information, Feb. 8, deposition of Louis-Auguste des Tournelles, pp. 189-90.

106. *PO*, interrogation of Jan. 18, no. 137, p. 131; of Mar. 17, no. 5, p. 328; of March 26, no. 143, p. 378; and of Mar. 28 (the question), pp. 402-403.

107. BN, JF 2070, fol. 158, Jan. 18.

108. See Chapter 2, pp. 102-104, 149-58.

109. *PO*, interrogation of Mar. 28 (the question), p. 402; see also Flammermont, *Remontrances* 1:489-90.

110. Damiens described himself as having been Bèze de Lys' "seul laquais . . . son seul domestique" in *PO*, 1st interrogation at Versailles, no. 10, p. 45. See also *PO*, interrogation of Mar. 17, no. 5, p. 328; of Mar. 26, no. 115, p. 376; no. 160, p. 380; and of Mar. 28 (the question), p. 401.

111. *PO*, pp. 403-404.

112. BN, JF 2070, fols. 283-84. This anecdote is also reported in Edmond Georges d'Heylli, *La Cour et la ville pendant le procès de Damiens, 1757: Lettres du poète Robbé de Beauvesal au dessinateur Desfriches* (Paris, 1875), letter xvi, Mar. 7, 1757, pp. 72-73.

113. AN, AB XIX 3192, dr 7, file 3, May 5, 1752.

114. BN, JF 2069, fols. 264-78, Louis Damiens to Antoine-

Joseph Damiens, Apr. 7, 1753; Feb. 20, 1754; Mar. 11, 1756; and Dec. 18, 1756. Daniel Roche's *Le Peuple de Paris*, p. 225, also acknowledges the politicalization of the Parisian popular milieux by way of the various Jansenist controversies.

115. For disruption of procession, see AN, AB XIX 3192, dr 7, file 3, Apr. 27, 1752; for clercs' duel, see BN, JF 1566, fol. 67, "Déclaration faite au commissaire Charles-Daniel de La Fosse, May 7, 1752"; and for near riot in rue de la Harpe, see BN, JF 1566, fol. 27, Aug. 7, 1754. The bourgeois of Paris was Mazcout Cherault, formerly the domestic servant of the abbé Guérbois, and his case also left traces in BPR, LP 532, unnumbered fol., Rolland de Challerange to Lefebvre de Saint-Hilaire, Aug. 8, 1754.

116. AN, AB XIX, dr 7, file 2, Mar. 29, 1752.

117. BN, JF 2070, fols. 283-84. A somewhat diminished echo of Lafaye's extrajudicial recollections is heard in her official deposition in *PO*, addition d'information, Jan. 27, p. 178. For Damiens' own vocabulary, see *PO*, interrogation of Jan. 29, nos. 283-88, p. 143.

118. *PO*, 6th interrogation at Versailles, nos. 155-56, p. 103; interrogation of Jan. 18, no. 138, p. 131; of Jan. 25, no. 246, p. 140, and nos. 271-73, p. 142; of Jan. 29, no. 286, p. 143, and nos. 330-32, p. 147; of Mar. 26, no. 40, p. 371; and of Mar. 28 (the question), p. 399.

119. AN, AB XIX 3192, dr 7, file 2, Feb. 5, 1752; and René-Louis de Voyer, marquis d'Argenson, *Journal et mémoires du marquis d'Argenson*, ed. E.-J.-B. Rathery, 9 vols. (Paris, 1859-1867), 9:390. Historians of the dechristianization movement during the French Revolution have long discerned, if they have not altogether understood, a certain connection between popular anticlericalism and subsistence concerns. See Marcel Reinhard, *Histoire de l'Ile de France et de Paris* (Toulouse, 1971), p. 396; Richard Cobb, *Les Armées révolutionaires*, 2 vols. (Paris, 1963), 2:634-90; and S. Bianchi, "De La Déchristianisation de l'an II, essai d'interprétation," *Annales historiques de la Révolution française*, 233 (July-September, 1978), pp. 352, 358-59.

120. *PO*, interrogation of Feb. 5, nos. 102-103, p. 209; interrogation of Julien Le Guerinays dit Saint-Julien, Jan. 22, no. 28, pp. 170-71; and addition d'information, depositions of Pierre-François Desvaux and Charlotte-Elizabeth Combault d'Auteuil, widow of La Bourdonnaye, Feb. 4, pp. 183-84.

121. *PO*, interrogation of Elizabeth Molerienne, Feb. 5, nos. 102-103, p. 209; and BN, JF 2070, fols. 283-84.

122. *PO*, interrogation of Mar. 17, no. 29, p. 331; and of Mar. 26, no. 159, p. 380.

123. For other evidence of *popular* "dechristianization," see Albert Soboul, "Sentiments religieux et cultes populaires pendant la Révolution: Saintes patriotes et martyrs de la liberté," *Archives de sociologie religieuses* (1956), p. 73, and S. Bianchi, "De La Déchristianisation de l'an II, essai d'interprétation," *Annales historiques de la Révolution française*, 233 (July-September, 1758), pp. 341-71.

124. D'Argenson, *Journal et mémoires* 8:12, 35. The quotation is from p. 35.

125. BN, JF 1493, fols. 144-45, the elder Joly de Fleury to Rouillé, Aug. 28, 1752.

126. For the rue des Prouvaires incident, see BN, JF 2070, fol. 111, Moreau to attorney general, Jan. 25, 1757 (see also fols. 118 and 120); for the Sainte-Marguerite incidents, see AN, AP 177mi 118, no. 37, Feb. 8, 1757; and 108, nos. 10 and 38, Aug. 9 and 10, 1758.

127. "Recueil des informations," p. 4; "Supplément au recueil," pp. 8, 10, 16.

128. *PO*, interrogation of Jan. 25, no. 197, p. 136.

129. "Recueil des informations," p. 4. See also *PO*, addition d'information, deposition of Nicolas Breuvart, Mar. 13, p. 196; and interrogation of Feb. 18, no. 504, p. 182. Damiens, it is true, denied having said some of these things in confrontation with Breuvart (p. 306), but it is not likely that his memory would have been very reliable about things he mumbled in a state of evident desperation.

130. *PO*, "Deuxième Supplément," p. 25. See also *PO*, addition d'information, depositions of Nicolas Playoust and François-Joseph Bourbier, Mar. 13, pp. 192, 196-97; interrogation of Feb. 18, no. 480, p. 159; and of Mar. 26, nos. 28-29, p. 371. In confrontation with these witnesses, Damiens again denied having uttered these things, *PO*, Mar. 13, pp. 304-306.

131. Damiens himself pointed to the news of the Dec. 13 lit de justice as decisive. See *PO*, interrogation of Jan. 25, no. 196, p. 136; and of Feb. 18, no. 520, p. 164.

132. *PO*, 3rd continuation d'information, deposition of Jean-Marie de La Brou de Vareilles, Jan. 9, p. 73; and 6th interrogation at Versailles, no. 155, p. 103.

133. *PO*, addition d'information, depositions of Jean Bonot, Louis-

Joseph Chouet, and the frère Simon-Joseph Duparcq, Feb. 7, pp. 186-88; and recollement, Feb. 23, pp. 263-64.

134. *PO*, addition d'information, deposition of Louis-Joseph Chouet, Feb. 7, pp. 187-88; interrogation of Louis Damiens, Feb. 15, pp. 223-26; and interrogation of same by Rochebrune at Bastille, JF 2068, Jan. 12, fols. 124-25.

135. *PO*, information par addition, deposition of Charles Hurillon, Mar. 1, pp. 246-47; interrogation of Perine-Joseph-Renée Macé, Feb. 16, pp. 235-36.

136. *PO*, information par addition, declaration of Marie Dorgebray, dishwasher, Jan. 22, pp. 236-37; and deposition of same, Feb. 1, p. 242; depositions of Charles Hurillon, Mar. 1, pp. 246-47; and of Marguerite-Denise Michel, wife of François Ripandelly, négociant, Feb. 16, p. 274; interrogations of Damiens, Feb. 18, no. 7, pp. 356-57; and of Mar. 26, no. 69-70, 83, pp. 373-74. See also interrogation of Elizabeth Schoirtz, wife of Louis Damiens, by Rochebrune at Bastille, Jan. 12, in BN, JF 2068, fol. 129.

137. *PO*, information par addition, deposition of Marie-Madeleine Mary, widow of Wattebled, Mar. 1, pp. 245-46; and BN, JF 2069, fols. 230-31, interrogation of Marie-Elizabeth Damiens by Rochebrune at Bastille, Jan. 10.

138. Elizabeth Schoirtz remembered that Marie-Elizabeth Damiens had told her this (*PO*, interrogation of Schoirtz, Feb. 15, no. 10, pp. 222-23). But Marie-Elizabeth denied it, and Damiens' wife claimed not to have heard him announce such an intention (*PO*, interrogations of Elizabeth Molerienne, Feb. 5, nos. 98-99, p. 208; and of Marie-Elizabeth Damiens, Feb. 5, nos. 50-51, p. 213). See also *PO*, interrogations of Damiens, Mar. 26, no. 82, pp. 373-74; of Marie-Elizabeth the same day, no. 9, p. 383; as well as confrontations between Damiens and Elizabeth Schoirtz, Mar. 8, p. 314; and Marie-Elizabeth, Mar. 12, p. 316. Rochebrune's interrogations of Damiens' wife and daughter at Bastille on Jan. 10 (BN, JF 2069, fols. 223, 230) complete the documentation.

139. Damiens said each of these things in turn. See *PO*, 5th interrogation at Versailles, no. 117, p. 87; interrogation of Mar. 18, nos. 5-7, p. 333; Mar. 26, nos. 88-89, p. 374; and Mar. 28 (the question), p. 404.

140. *PO*, information, deposition of Joseph de La Barré dit Labrie, coachman at the bureau of court carriages, and of Jacques-Guillaume Canée, commissioner of transport at the bureau of court carriages, Jan. 6, pp. 53-55.

141. *PO*, deposition of Antoine Fortier, in keeper in the rue Satory, Jan. 6, pp. 55-56.

142. *PO*, 5th interrogation at Versailles, no. 120, p. 87.

143. *PO*, information, deposition of Antoine Fortier, Jan. 6, pp. 55-56.

144. *PO*, deposition of Marie-Françoise Delisle, wife of Fortier, Jan. 6, pp. 56-57.

145. *PO*, 3rd continuation d'information, deposition of François Bonnemant, king's sentinel, Jan. 10, p. 77; and interrogation of Mar. 26, nos. 105-110, p. 375.

146. *PO*, interrogation of Jan. 18, no. 144, p. 132.

147. *PO*, "Précis historique," p. xx.

Notes to Chapter 2

1. Edmond-J.F. Barbier, *Chronique de la régence et du règne de Louis XV, 1718-1763*, 8 vols. (Paris, 1857-1866), 6:443, lists fifteen, whereas the Jansenist lawyer Louis-Adrien Le Paige (BPR, LP 547, no. 85) insists upon seventeen or eighteen resignations with only ten or eleven councillors remaining. My own count reveals both to be correct: fifteen, if counting only counseillers laics et clercs, seventeen if counting conseillers d'honneur as well. After Damiens' attack, however, the two conseillers d'honneur and two of the fifteen other councillors returned to the Grand' chambre, leaving thirteen resignations and thirteen ordinary councillors loyal to the ministry. For king's refusal to take back the resignations, see Charles-Philippe d'Albert, duc de Luynes, *Mémoires du duc de Luynes, sur la cour de Louis XV, 1735-1758*, ed. L. Dussieux and E. Soulié, 17 vols. (Paris, 1860-1865), 15:359.

2. *Déclaration du roi. Donnée à Versailles le 10 décembre 1756* (Paris, 1757).

3. Works on Jansenism are myriad, but the best and most recent introductions are Alexander Sedgwick, *Jansenism in Seventeenth-Century France: Voices from the Wilderness* (Charlottesville, Va., 1977); Walter E. Rex, *Pascal's Provincial Letters: An Introduction* (London and Sydney, 1977); and René Taveneaux, *La Vie quotidienne des jansénistes aux xviie et xviiie siècles* (Paris, 1973). Taveneaux's *Jansénisme et politique* (Paris, 1965), Jean Orcibal's *Jean Duvergier de Hauranne, abbé de Saint-Cyran et son temps* (Louvain and Paris, 1947), and Louis Cognet's *Le Jansénisme* (Paris, 1964) remain indispensable, and nothing is likely entirely to supplant Augustin Gazier's *Histoire générale du mouvement*

janséniste depuis ses origines jusqu'à nos jours, 2 vols. (Paris, 1923), or Charles-Augustin de Sainte-Beuve's *Port-Royal*, ed. Maxime Leroy, 3 vols. (Paris, 1952).

4. On Gallicanism, Bossuet, and the assembly of 1682, see Victor Martin, *Le Gallicanisme politique et le clergé de France* (Paris, 1929); and Aimé-Georges Martimort, *Le Gallicanisme de Bossuet* (Paris, 1953). The best treatment of seventeenth-century parlementary constitutionalism remains Paul Rice Doolin's *The Fronde* (Cambridge, Mass., 1935). For the eighteenth century, see Roger Bickart, *Les Parlements et la notion de souveraineté nationale au xviiie siècle* (Paris, 1932); Jean Egret, *Louis XV et l'opposition parlementaire, 1715-1774* (Paris, 1970); and Elie Carcassonne, *Montesquieu et le problème de la constitution française au XVIIIe siècle* (Paris, 1926).

5. That it was contingent circumstances rather than an intrinsic affinity between the Jansenist outlook and the socioeconomic situation of the nobility of the robe that brought these two together is argued in my *The Jansenists and the Expulsion of the Jesuits, 1757-1765* (New Haven, 1975), pp. 6-36; and Albert Hamscher, "The Parlement of Paris and the Social Interpretation of Early French Jansenism," *Catholic Historical Review* 63 (July 1977):392-410. It is also the view adopted by René Taveneaux in *Jansénisme et politique*, pp. 17-34. For the Marxist view, see Lucien Goldmann, *Le Dieu caché: Etude sur la vision tragique dans les Pensées de Pascal et dans le théâtre de Racine* (Paris, 1955), esp. pp. 304-314.

6. For text of *Unigenitus*, see Gazier, *Histoire générale du mouvement janséniste* 2:305-41. On *Unigenitus* more generally, see Jacques-François Thomas, *La Querelle de l'Unigenitus* (Paris, 1949).

7. On these conflicts in general, see Léon Cahen, *Les Querelles religieuses et parlementaires sous Louis XV* (Paris, 1913); Egret, *Louis XV et l'opposition parlementaire*; Georges Hardy, *Le Cardinal de Fleury et le mouvement janséniste* (Paris, 1925); Robert Kreiser, *Miracles, Convulsions, and Ecclesiastical Politics in Early Eighteenth-Century Paris* (Princeton, 1978), pp. 3-69 and Jacques Parguet, *Le Bulle Unigenitus et le jansénisme politique* (Paris, 1976).

8. For two more extended attempts to describe this mentality, see my *The Jansenists*, pp. 6-36; and "Church, State, and the Ideological Origins of the French Revolution: The Debate over the General Assembly of the Gallican Clergy in 1765," *Journal of Modern History* 51 (December 1979):635-38.

9. René-Louis de Voyer, marquis d'Argenson, *Journal et mémoires du marquis d'Argenson*, ed. E.-J.-B. Rathery, 9 vols. (Paris, 1859-1867), 9:256.

10. On composition of parti janséniste in the parlement in Paris, see my *The Jansenists*, pp. 37-61. Henri de Revol figures prominently in this analysis and only parenthetically in that one because he had retired from active service before the period of the expulsion of the Jesuits.

11. Barbier, *Journal* 5:221; D'Argenson, *Journal et mémoires* 7:270.

12. On the composition of the *dévôt* or *zélanti* party within the French episcopacy, see Emile Appolis, *Entre Jansénistes et zélanti: Le 'Tiers Parti' catholique au XVIIIe siècle* (Paris, 1960), pp. 70-109, 217-48, 441-64.

13. Van Kley, "Church, State, and the Ideological Origins of the French Revolution," pp. 652-62; and this volume pp. 196-200, 213-19.

14. Van Kley, "Church, State, and the Ideological Origins of the French Revolution"; and this volume, pp. 196-225.

15. Legier Desgranges, *Madame de Moysan et l'extravagante affaire de l'hôpital générale, 1749-1758* (Paris, 1954).

16. [Jean-Pierre Grosley], *Lettre d'un patriote, où l'on rapporte les faits qui prouvent que l'auteur de l'attentat commis sur la vie du roi a des complices, et la manière dont on instruit son procès* (n.p., "ce 11 mars"), p. 4.

17. BPR, LP 547, no. 3, "Première Mémoire ou lettre de moi à mr le prince de conti, 9 décembre 1756."

18. Paul-Alexandre de Gérénet, *Mandement de monseigneur l'évêque de Saint-Pons, par lequel il adopte le Mandement et instruction pastorale de monseigneur l'archévêque de Paris, par lui publié le 19 septembre de la présente année 1756, et en ordonne l'éxécution* (n.p., 1756), in BN, Manuscrits Français (henceforth MSS FR) 22093 (90), pp. 2-3.

19. Christophe de Beaumont du Repaire, *Mandement et instruction pastorale de monseigneur l'archévêque de Paris, touchant l'autorité de l'église, l'enseignement de la foi, l'administration des sacrements, la soumission due à la constitution Unigenitus, portant défense de lire plusieurs écrits* (Paris, 1756), p. 19; and letter from Orléans de La Motte to Dom Léon, Jan. 26, 1758, quoted in Emile Regnault, *Christophe de Beaumont, archévêque de Paris*, 2 vols. (Paris, 1882), 1:420.

20. Henri-Marie-Bernardin de Rosset de Fleury, *Mandement de monseigneur l'archévêque de Tours par lequel il adhère au Mandement et à l'instruction pastorale de monseigneur l'archévêque de Paris* . . . (n.p., 1756), in BN, MSS FR 22093 (107), p. 2.

21. AN, AP 177mi 75, no. 40, the abbé de Nicolas to Lamoignon,

Oct. 31, 1752. Another example is Poncet de La Rivière, *Mandement et instruction pastorale de monseigneur l'évêque de Troyes, par lequel il adhère au Mandement et à l'instruction pastorale de monseigneur l'archévêque de Paris* . . . (n.p., 1756), in BN, Mss Fr 22093 (115), pp. 9-15.

22. "Mémoires de Pierre-Augustin-Robert de Saint-Vincent, 1725-1799" (henceforth "Mémoires"), pp. 195-205. According to their owner, m. Michel Vinot-Préfontaine, who kindly granted me permission to consult them, these memoirs should soon be available in published form. See also [Grosley], *Lettre d'un patriote*, pp. 6-7, 15-17.

23. On this conflict, see Egret, *Louis XV et l'opposition parlementaire*, pp. 72-76. For an example of how contemporaries construed royal demarches in the Grand conseil's favor, see d'Argenson, *Journal et mémoires* 9:256.

24. BPR, LP 548, unnumbered fol. On the composition of Conti's legal council, see BPR, LP 549, "Remarques sur l'arrêt contre Damiens et sur la séance du 29 mars lendemain de l'arrêt," where Le Paige speaks of "m. de murard, m. gerbier, et moi." On Conti's evolving relationship with the king and the parlementary opposition, see this volume, pp. 143-47.

25. *PO*, 3rd continuation d'information, deposition of Jean-Marie de La Brou de Vareilles, Jan. 9, p. 72.

26. [Jean-Pierre Grosley], *Réflexions sur l'attentat commis le 5 janvier contre la vie du roi* (n.p., "ce 5 mars"), pp. 5-6, 18. The anonymous *Lettre d'un patriote*, p. 46, likewise assured the public that "il n'est pas vraisèmblable, que le projet d'attenter à la vie du Roi vienne dans l'esprit d'un laquais et d'autres gens de cette espèce: ils s'interessent trop peu à ce qui peut faire le sujet des troubles et des mécontentements dans un Etat."

27. *PO*, interrogation of Mar. 17, no. 14, p. 329.

28. BN, JF 2072, fols. 219-26, depositions of Marie Goupil, Urbain Guiter, and Julien Le Clerc, May 20; fol. 233, of Gabriel Bienvenu, June 5; and fols. 230-38, interrogation of Bellier by Joseph Fronchon, lieutenant criminal judge, etc., June 6.

29. Archives de la Bastille (hereafter AB) 11, 968, fols. 176-79, interrogation of Apr. 15, 1758, by Rochebrune.

30. *PO*, information, depositions of Guillaume Bonot, Robert-Michel Le Forestier, and Jean-François Filhoc, royal bodyguards, Jan. 6, pp. 52-53; continuation d'information, deposition of François de Saint-Julien, royal commandant of the town and citadel of Stenay, Jan. 7, pp. 61-62; 3rd continuation d'information, deposition of

François Duras, exempt of the king's bodyguards, Jan. 9, p. 74; and information par addition, depositions by Antoine Richer, the king's locksmith, and François Corbonnois, bodyguard, Jan. 27, pp. 180-81.

31. *PO*, 1st interrogation at Versailles, no. 17, p. 46; interrogation of Mar. 17, no. 8, p. 328; and interrogation of Mar. 26, no. 124, p. 377.

32. Robert de Saint-Vincent, "Mémoires," pp. 195-96; BPR, LP 548-49; and Pierre Rétat et al., *L'Attentat de Damiens: Discours sur l'événement au XVIIIe siècle* (Lyons, n.d.), pp. 177-86, 425n5. Le Paige's "Indiculus" (BPR, LP 548, unnumbered fol.) was written for the prince de Conti. For one of Conti's autograph responses to Le Paige, see BPR, LP 549, unnumbered fol., Conti to Le Paige, Feb. 25.

33. *Arrest de la cour de parlement, qui condamne différens libelles à être lacérés et brûlés dans la cour du palais par l'éxécuteur de la haute justice. Extrait des registres du parlement. Du 30 mars 1757;* and *Déclaration du roi, portant défense à toutes personnes . . . de composer, ni faire composer, imprimer et distribuer aucun écrits contre la règle des ordonnances. . . . Donnée à Versailles le 16 avril 1757*; in BN, JF 333, file 3570, fol. 840-41, and file 3579, fols. 374-75.

34. Following Antoine-Alexandre Barbier in *Dictionnaire des anonymes*, 4 vols. (Paris, 1872), and with the additional testimony of Grosley himself in his manuscript additions to his published *Vie de m. Grosley* (Bibliothèque Municipale de Troyes, RR 330, pp. 41-42 n97, and p. 158n1), Pierre Rétat probably rightly credits these pamphlets to Grosley and contests my tentative attribution to Le Paige (Rétat, *L'Attentat de Damiens*, p. 425n5; and Van Kley, *The Jansenists*, p. 70n27). To my mind, however, the matter is still less than certain. Not only did d'Hémery attribute some of these pamphlets to Le Paige (BN, Collection Anisson-Duperron 22094, fol. 354) but Le Paige himself, at least equally in-the-know as Barbier, attributed the *Réflexions sur l'attentat* to one Pierre Batbédat, "born in March 1714 and deceased in April 1762 in Bayonne" (BPR, LP 761). And Le Paige's private admission that "il faut avouer que cet écrit [*Lettre d'un patriote*] n'est pas mesuré" sounds a bit like a confession of guilt (BPR, LP 549, his resumé of sessions of April 2 and 4). For one person, in any case, to turn out three or four pamphlets in one or two months seems an excessively high level of activity by even the eighteenth century's pace-setting standards. Is it just possible that Grosley was something of a *fanfaron*?

35. BPR, LP 548, no. 43 bis, and unnumbered fol., entitled "Indiculus," nos. 2, 3, 7, and 8; and [Grosley], *Lettre d'un patriote*, pp. 18-19, 21-22.

36. BPR, LP 548, "Indiculus," nos. 1, 11, 12, 14, 18, and 21; [Grosley], *Lettre d'un patriote*, pp. 22, 24-26.

37. Robert de Saint-Vincent, "Mémoires," pp. 198-203; [Grosley], *Lettre d'un patriote*, pp. 4-5, 14-15, 16-17, 29-30, 47-48, 68-69; and Le Paige's diary-like account of the judicial sessions of the princes and peers in BPR, LP 548, no. 43 bis; and 549, unnumbered "lettre(s)," esp. his remarks concerning sessions of Feb. 12, 19, 25, Mar. 9 and 29. The "negligence" accusation is in 548, no. 43 bis, session of Feb. 19. For a more neutral but basically corroborative account of Conti's suggestions in judicial sessions, see Luynes, *Mémoires* 15:409, 412, 421, 437-38, 472, 474, 486, 488, 495.

38. [Grosley], *Lettre d'un patriote*, p. 14; Robert de Saint-Vincent, "Mémoires," p. 196; and for suspicion regarding Pasquier and Berryer, see BPR, LP 543 bis, session of Mar. 11.

39. [Grosley], *Lettre d'un patriote*, pp. 68-69; [Grosley], *Déclaration de guerre contre les auteurs du parricide tenté sur la personne du roi* (n.p., "ce 5 mars"), p. 87. On Jesuits, BPR, LP 548, "Quelques faits," nos. 2, 3, and 4.

40. Emmanuel, prince de Cröy, *Journal inédit du duc de Cröy, 1718-1784*, ed. vicomte de Grouchy and Paul Cottin, 4 vols. (Paris, 1906-1907), 1:399; Luynes, *Mémoires* 15:422. For the attorney general's admission of haste, see BN, JF 2070, fol. 314, attorney general to Paulmy, Feb. 26: "Nous vous prions, monsieur, de vouloir bien prendre à ce sujet les mesures que vous croirés convenables, en vous observant cependant que nous souhaiterions fort qu'elles puissent être prises promptement occupés comme nous le sommes d'accélérer autant qu'il sera en nous l'instruction et par conséquent le jugement du criminel."

41. On the destruction of Damiens' native house, see *PO, Supplément au procès*, pp. 1-16; on Damiens' supplice, see *PO*, "Relation de l'éxécution de Damiens, qui a été faite le lundi 28 mars 1757 . . . ," pp. 1-10, before index. On concern with éclat, see the chancellor Lamoignon's comment concerning "mauvais propos . . . qu'il faut tascher d'étouffer plustost que de faire des poursuites qui ne servent qu'à faire de l'éclat," in BN, JF 2078, fol. 15, Lamoignon to attorney general, Mar. 9.

42. See original letters in BN, JF 2070, fols. 149-51, one dated Jan. 3 and the other undated but obviously after Jan. 5. For inter-

rogations of the Kattmans and Jean-François Frédéric, public letter writer, by Rochebrune at Bastille on Jan. 21, see BN, JF 2070, fols. 137-38, 141-42. For Le Paige's reaction to these anticlimactic revelations, see BPR, LP 548, no. 43 bis, session of Mar. 2.

43. BN, JF 2073, fol. 120, copy of letter from Chauveau to Sabinet, chanoine à Péronne, Jan. 3; and fols. 135-36, interrogation of Chauveau by Rochebrune on Jan. 14 at Bastille. The original letter is in AB 11979, fol. 79.

44. BN, JF 2072, fols. 122-23, 125, depositions by François Gorgu, Feb. 7 and 25.

45. BN, JF 2070, fol. 111, Moreau, prosecuting attorney at Châtelet, to attorney general, Jan. 25.

46. *PO*, interrogations of Feb. 19, 22, 26, and Mar. 3 in Montdidier, pp. 501-513, 518-21; interrogation of Mar. 6 in Paris, pp. 531-37.

47. *PO*, "Précis historique," pp. xxiv-xxx; and information par addition, deposition of Louis-Gabriel Lainé, Jan. 27, pp. 179-80; also BPR, LP 548, no. 43 bis, session of Wednesday, March 9. For one of the abbé de La Chapelle's earlier revelations, see BN, JF 2070, fols. 178-79, "Déclaration de l'abbé de La Chapelle, ce 29 aoust 1755."

48. *PO*, "Précis historique au sujet des propos tenus en la communauté de Saint-Joseph, faubourg Saint-Germain, à Paris," pp. 449-54; deposition of Marie Geoffroy, Jan. 13, p. 456; declaration by Marguerite Descouflet, Jan. 13, pp. 456-57; interrogations of both on Mar. 5, nos. 14-23, pp. 480-81; and no. 9, p. 482; interrogation of Geoffroy on Mar. 17, nos. 3-4, pp. 489-90. For imprisonments, see *PO*, pp. 476-77, 484-85.

49. *PO*, interrogations of Jan. 18, no. 145, p. 132; of Jan. 25, nos. 247, 256, pp. 140-41; of Mar. 17, no. 13, p. 329; and of Mar. 18, no. 7, p. 333.

50. *PO*, 5th interrogation at Versailles, no. 117, p. 87; interrogation of Mar. 18, nos. 5-7, p. 333; Mar. 26, nos. 88-89; and of Mar. 28 (the question), p. 404.

51. BPR, LP 548, "Indiculus," no. 9.

52. *PO*, 3rd continuation d'information, deposition of François Bonnemant, Jan. 10, p. 77.

53. *PO*, 4th interrogation at Versailles, no. 76, p. 80; interrogation of Jan. 29, nos. 279-81, p. 143; of Feb. 18, no. 539, pp. 165-66; of Mar. 26, nos. 105-110, p. 375; of Mar. 28 (the question),

p. 401; recollement of Bonnemant, Feb. 23, p. 263; confrontation between Bonnemant and Damiens, Mar. 6, pp. 289-90.

54. AN, X^{2B} 1362, dr IIE, depositions of Jean-Baptiste Ternois and Louis La Croix, April 22.

55. D'Argenson, *Journal et mémoires* 8:454, 9:149-50, 156, 164, 183. On duc de Chaulnes, see F.-X. de Feller, *Biographie universelle ou Dictionnaire historique des hommes qui se sont fait un nom par leur génie, leurs talents, leurs vertus, leurs erreurs, ou leurs crimes*, 8 vols. (Paris, 1847-1850), 2:581-82.

56. On the existence of such a person at Versailles at the time, see Luynes, *Mémoires* 15:469, 482; BPR, LP 549, unnumbered fol., "lettre du 22 janvier"; *PO*, "Précis historique," p. xix. For Saint-Florentin's letter, see François Ravaisson, *Archives de la Bastille*, 18 vols. (Paris, 1866-1904), 16:447-48, Saint-Florentin to Berryer, Feb. 3, 1757.

57. Luynes, Le Paige, and Le Breton all referred to him as someone "connu." For an example of how mortal this stigma could be, see Perrine-Joseph-Renée Macé's pathetic letter to the attorney general (BN, JF 2069, fol. 306) in which she requests a pension in consideration of what "elle avoit souffert et souffroit encore de cette accusation, tant par les horreurs des prisons qui lui sont encore présent que parce qu'elle est obligée aujourd'huy de déguiser son nom étant réduitte par sa triste situation et son peu de fortune à se mettre en condition. . . ." She goes on to state that her family has rejected her and an employer has fired her solely by reason of her association with Damiens and his trial.

58. See Marc-René, marquis de Montalembert, in Feller, *Biographie universelle* 6:67-68. Damiens was present at the siege of Philipsburg in his capacity as the captain Dubas' lackey (see *PO*, "Recueil des informations," p. 1).

59. Ravaisson, *Archives de la Bastille* 16:447-48, Saint-Florentin to Berryer, Feb. 3; and *PO*, "Précis historique," p. xix.

60. *PO*, 3rd continuation d'information, deposition of François Bonnemant, Jan. 10, p. 77; his recollement, Feb. 23, p. 263; and confrontation with Damiens, Mar. 6, pp. 289-90.

61. *PO*, information par addition, depositions of Jean-Baptiste Chirol and Ennemond-Clément Lapiejade, Mar. 8 and 12, pp. 190-91; and confrontations between these two and Damiens, Mar. 8 and 12, pp. 297, 300. Chirol's testimony is the one referred to in text.

62. This was also the opinion of the prince de Cröy, who for his part advanced a different hypothesis concerning the *quidam*. Ac-

cording to Cröy, Damiens indeed responded, "Eh bien, j'attends," to the question, "Eh biens?" posed by a person whom Damiens had encountered shortly before and to whom he had announced his intention of offering his services to a certain master. This person, whoever he was, willingly admitted the exchange with Damiens and corroborated the guard's recollection of its terms, but the guard confused him with someone else who had passed by at about the same time and hence continued to give a faulty physical description. Thus "ce garde de la porte, mal interrogé, persista à mal rendre son signalement, ce qui causa cette erreur et ce louche qu'il étoit bien aisé d'éclaircir, comme je l'avois dit d'avance." (See Cröy, *Journal inédit* 1:403.)

63. *PO*, pp. 394-95, 397.

64. For example, see BN, JF 2072, fol. 271, undated letter from the *procureur fiscal* at Jouarre to attorney general concerning a vagabond; or BN, JF 2077, fols. 162, 167, report by Pandenay, royal advocate at Saumur, to the lieutenant of police Berryer concerning a certain François de L'Etang, who bore a resemblance to *quidam*; or Barbier, *Journal* 7:52, who reports another such arrest on the grounds of supposed resemblance.

65. Louis-Gabriel Lainé's deposition (*PO*, Jan. 2, pp. 179-80) concerning the abbé de La Chapelle's revelations, which tended to implicate the Habsburgs, was actually dropped from the procedure at the request of the secretary for foreign affairs (see BN, JF 2070, fols. 181-82, Rouillé to attorney general, Feb. 6). Another pair of depositions, which tended to implicate England (*PO*, information par addition, Guirot Imbert and Joseph Duperieux, Jan. 22, pp. 173-77), led nowhere.

66. *PO*, interrogation of Antoine-Joseph Damiens, Feb. 16, nos. 11-14, p. 232; BN, JF 2068, fols. 95-96, interrogation of A.-J. Damiens by Vanden Driesche at Saint-Omer, Jan. 13. See also BN, JF 2069, fols. 73-74, Cröy to comte d'Argenson, Jan. 19.

67. BN, JF 2068, fols. 104-105, interrogation of Antoine-Joseph Damiens by Vanden Driesche, Jan. 11; fol. 92, by Pierre Chenon, Jan. 13; fol. 120, interrogation of Marie-Catherine Damiens by Vanden Driesche, Jan. 11. See also fol. 78, procès-verbal by Pierre Chenon, Jan. 11-13, a list of A.-J. Damiens' possessions; and BN, JF 2069, fols. 280-81, a list of his books.

68. *PO*, 4th interrogation at Versailles, nos. 79-81, p. 80; interrogation of Antoine-Joseph Damiens, Feb. 16, nos. 9-11, p. 232.

See also Cröy to comte d'Argenson, Jan. 19, in BN, JF 2069, fols. 73-74; and this volume, pp. 28-30.

69. *PO*, 6th interrogation at Versailles, nos. 169-70, pp. 104-105.

70. For the "best priests" reference, see *PO*, 2nd interrogation at Versailles, no. 39, p. 58; for the Jesuits' "way of thinking," interrogation of Jan. 25, no. 266, pp. 141-42; for the definition of Molinism, interrogation of Jan. 29, nos. 305-311, pp. 144-45.

71. On this, see Kreiser, *Miracles, Convulsions, and Ecclesiastical Politics*.

72. On Jesuit rumor, see Ravaisson, *Archives de la Bastille* 16:430, a Jesuit to the abbé ———, Jan. 8; on La Timonière, see AB 11964, fols. 63-64, his original declaration; and fols. 100, 126-27, his arrest in 1757; on Noailles and attorney general, BN, JF 2072, fols. 96-100.

73. AB 10202, dossier dated 1756, May 1, police observer's report on who was in evidence at Saint-Médard.

74. *PO*, 2nd interrogation at Versailles, no. 48, p. 59; and this volume, p. 15-17.

75. *PO*, interrogation of Jan. 25, nos. 198-262, pp. 136-37; nos. 264-65, p. 141; and nos. 267-68, p. 142. On Le Corgne de Launay, see *Nouvelles écclésiastiques ou mémoires pour servir à l'histoire de la bulle Unigenitus* (hereafter *NE*) (1758), pp. 15, 18, 118; (1759), p. 114; (1760), p. 65. Another of the doctors who declaimed against the parlement at the table that Damiens served was a certain Souvestre of the college of Navarre (see *NE* [Aug. 7, 1759], p. 129).

76. *PO*, interrogation of Jan. 25, no. 266, pp. 141-42; for prison utterance, BN, JF 2070, fol. 158, Feb. 26.

77. *PO*, interrogation of Jan. 29, nos. 289-95, p. 144.

78. Some examples of these suspicions and speculations are Robert de Saint-Vincent, "Mémoires," p. 186; Barbier, *Journal* 6:441; [Grosley], *Lettre d'un patriote*, pp. 7-8; and BN, Mss Fr 7573, p. 5, some speculations by Durey de Mesnières to this effect.

79. The Damiens affair itself, of course, focused attention on the Jesuits and theoretical and practical regicide and gave rise to streams of "histories" on this subject, which swelled into an ocean flood by the time of the order's suppression a few years later (see Rétat et al., *L'Attentat de Damiens*, pp. 267-94; and Van Kley, *The Jansenists*, pp. 33-36, 62-71, 94-96). In 1757, however, the following histories of the wars of the League and the assassinations and attempted assassinations of Henry III and Henry IV, which emphasized the role of

the Jesuits, were readily available and in fact consulted: Jacques-Augustin de Thou's *Histoire universelle . . . depuis 1543 jusqu'en 1607*, trans. from Latin by P. F. Guyot-Desfontaine, N. Leduc, et al. (ed. in 16 vols. in 1734, and 11 vols. in 1740); François de Mézeray's *Abrégé chronologique de l'histoire de France* (ed. in 6 vols. in 1701, 7 vols. in 1706, 3 vols. in 1717, 10 vols. in 1740, and 14 vols. in 1755); Etienne Pasquier's *Recueil des pièces historiques et curieuses*, including his *Catéchisme des Jésuites* (ed. in 2 vols. in 1717); the abbés Fabre's and Goujet's continuation of Claude Fleury's *Histoire ecclésiastique*, esp. vols. 29-31 (ed. in 36 vols. in 1690-1783); Louis Ellies Dupin's *Histoire de l'église et des auteurs ecclésiastiques du XVIe siècle* (ed. in 5 vols. in 1701-1703); Pierre Quesnel's (according to Barbier) *Histoire des religieux de la compagnie de Jésus* (ed. in 4 vols. in 1740, 2 vols. in 1741, and 4 vols. in 1751); Nicolas Petitpied's *Juste Idée que l'on doit se former des Jésuites et leur vrai caractère, avec un recueil de pièces concernant leur bannissement du royaume pour avoir enseigné et fait mettre en pratique qu'on peut tuer les rois* (1755; reprint ed., 1761); César-Ergasse Du Boulay's *Historia Universitatis Parisiensis* (ed. in 6 vols. in 1665-1673); and last but not least, the "great" Antoine Arnauld's *La Morale pratique des Jésuites* (ed. in 8 vols. in 1669-1695; reprint ed., 1716). To these histories or quasi-histories we may append judicial harangues such as the original Antoine Arnauld's *Plaidoyers . . . contre les Jésuites . . . avec la relation de ce qui s'est passé au rétablissement des Jésuites en 1604* (1716 and 1735); and polemics such as the anonymous *Anti-Cotton, livre où est prouvé que les Jésuites sont coupables et auteurs du parricide éxécrable commis en la personne de Henri IV d'heureuse mémoire* (1610; new ed. in 1733, 1736, 1738, 1744, and 1745).

80. For remark in Orléans, see BPR, LP 549, unnumbered fol.; for Arras, BN, JF 2075, fol. 88, denunciation of *commis aux aydes* at Abbéville to attorney general, Jan. 15.

81. *PO*, interrogation of Jan. 18, no. 145, p. 132; of Jan. 29, no. 319, p. 146; of Mar. 17, no. 20, p. 330; of Mar. 26, no. 126, p. 381; of Mar. 28 (the question), p. 402.

82. *PO*, interrogation of Jan. 29, no. 319, p. 146; of Mar. 17, no. 20, p. 330; Mar. 26, no. 163, p. 381.

83. *PO*, interrogations of Feb. 18, no. 491, p. 161; of Mar. 17, no. 7, p. 328; of Mar. 26, no. 142, p. 378. A certain Philippe-Marie Tal was brought from Fies to Paris to account for this remark, although he does not seem to have been its author (see *PO*, infor-

mation par addition, deposition of Philippe-Marie Tal, chaplain-priest to m. de Fies, Mar. 13, p. 195).

84. *Mandement de son éminence monseigneur le cardinal de La Rochefoucauld, archévêque de Bourges, pour faire une messe solemnelle et un Te Deum en actions de grâce de la protection singulière que dieu a accordée à ce royaume, en conservant la personne sacrée du roi*, in BN, JF 2068, fol. 339.

85. [Grosley], *Lettre d'un patriote*, pp. 39-45; BPR, LP 548, unnumbered "Indiculus," no. 6; and "quelques faits," nos. 1-3, 5-7.

86. [Grosley], *Lettre d'un patriote*, pp. 41-42; BPR, LP 549, no. 43 bis, Feb. 25; unnumbered notes entitled "Faits qui peuvent être importants à approfondir," no. 3; and "quelques faits," no. 4.

87. Barbier, *Journal* 6:480-81, 485-86, 508-509, 529, 534.

88. For Damiens' letter to the king and accompanying billet, see *PO*, 3rd interrogation at Versailles, pp. 69-70; for Henri Belot's deposition, see 3rd continuation d'information, Jan. 10, pp. 77-78; for Damiens' explanation, see 3rd interrogation at Versailles, nos. 57-59, p. 66, and end of interrogation, p. 68; 4th interrogation, nos. 71-73, p. 79; interrogation of Jan. 29, nos. 371-76, p. 150; of Feb. 18, nos, 510-15, pp. 163-64; of Mar. 26, nos. 128-31, 136-40, pp. 377-78; and confrontation with Belot, Mar. 6, pp. 288-89.

89. [Grosley], *Lettre d'un patriote*, p. 69.

90. Ibid., p. 59; [Grosley] *Déclaration de guerre*, p. 26; BPR, LP 548, unnumbered fol.

91. *PO*, interrogation of Mar. 26, nos. 112, 116, 160, pp. 376, 380.

92. *PO*, interrogation of Mar. 28 (the question), pp. 403-404; confrontations with Gautier and the marquis de Ferrières, Mar. 28, pp. 406-407; interrogation of Gautier, Mar. 30, pp. 426-27; and testimonies in favor of Gautier, pp. 429-37. The duc de Luynes (*Mémoires* 15:491-92, and 16:2-4) confirms that Ferrières was a "ci-devant conseiller au parlement."

93. On the incident involving king, see d'Argenson, *Journal et mémoires* 8:136-37. On Gautier's 1740 embastillement, see *PO*, deposition of Jacques Corbay, Apr. 6, p. 437; interrogation of Apr. 9, pp. 438-39; and of Apr. 23, p. 446. On the incriminating deposition of Claude Barrière de La Plaine, see BN, JF 2072, fols. 38-39, May 16 and Aug. 2; and AN X^{2B} 1362, dr IIG, May 16. On Jansenist ambiance, see Luynes, *Mémoires* 16:16. It is true that Pierre Gondron, to whom Claude de La Plaine ascribed the incriminating remarks

about Gautier, denied ever having uttered them (BN, JF 2072, fol. 38, Aug. 2); nonetheless, the following statement by Gautier in his very last interrogation seems close to an admission of guilt: "il se peut faire qu'il ait dit comme bien d'autres que certains écclésiastiques étoient cause des troubles qu'au surplus aucune personne de ses amis n'a cessé de le voir pour ce sujet" (AN, X^{2B} 1362, dr IIE, Aug. 4). Moreover, Luynes (*Mémoires* 15:492) asserted that Ferrières finally admitted to knowing Damiens "parce que ce scélérat lui portoit quelquefois des arrêtés du parlement. Damiens a dit que m. de Ferrières parloit mal de l'archévêque."

94. BPR, LP 548, no. 43 bis, Mar. 11.

95. D'Argenson, *Journal et mémoires* 8:454, 9:149-50; and letter from the comte de Maurepas to Feydeau de Marville, May 15, 1747, in A. de Boislisle, ed., *Lettres de m. de Marville, lieutenant général de police, au ministre Maurepas*, 3 vols. (Paris, 1896-1905), 3:214-15. The editor describes Montalembert at that time as captain of Conti's guards.

96. *PO*, interrogations of Apr. 9, no. 5, p. 438; and no. 9, pp. 438-39; see also Fr. Weil, "L'Abbé Prévost et le 'gazetin' de 1740," *Studi Francesi* (1962), 474-86; and E. Showalter, "L'Abbé Prévost et le 'gazetin' de 1740: nouveaux documents," *Studi Francesi* (1970), 257-60.

97. *PO*, 4th continuation d'information, depositions of Alexandre Ingoult and Jean Gabriel, Jan. 12, pp. 82-83; interrogations of Jean Aubrais, Noël Selim, Quentin Ferard, pp. 98, 106-112, but esp. of Noël Roi, Jan. 17, pp. 113-14; deposition of other *convives*, pp. 339-42, but esp. André-Georges Drou, March 14, pp. 339-40. For Le Paige's reaction, see BPR, LP 549, unnumbered fol. entitled "Lettre du 12 février 1757." As if putting himself in Le Gouvé's place, Le Paige's rendition of what Le Gouvé said is, "qu'il est à craindre que tous nos troubles ne nous ramenent les scènes de la ligue."

98. BN, JF 2070, fols. 283-84, anonymous note to attorney general. "Le malheureux Damiens dit flammand n'a été connu que sous ce dernier nom pendant l'espace de 18 mois environ qu'il a demeuré (mais à deux reprises) ches mr Baye [*sic*] de Lys conseiller au parlement rue des massons il y a environ cinq six ou sept ans. La nommée marie la faye cuisinière alors ches le sudit conseiller qui scait sa demeure puisque le lendemain de l'assassinat il l'envoya chercher je crois aux environs du cloistre St. Benoit ches un nommé mr fils ou quelque nom approchant pour scavoir de la cuisinière si

elle luy avoit connu sous le nom de damiens." Fol. 95 enables us to identify the author of the anonymous note as the curé of Saint-Sulpice.

99. BPR, LP 549, unnumbered papers consisting of procurations by Clément de Feillet and scenarios devised by himself and his brother Clément de Barville; and BN, JF 2072, fols. 79-89, and 78, La Guillaumie to attorney general, Joly de Fleury, Mar. 21. La Guillaumie wanted all evidence of his association with the affair suppressed "jusqu'aux moindres traces," including this letter, which he wanted the attorney general to burn.

100. BPR, LP 549, unnumbered fol., entitled "Mémoire sur la peine de tallion," and in general, the 11th, 13th, and 14th letters to Le Paige's fictitious "madame." See also Luynes, *Mémoires* 15:472-74, 486-88.

101. BPR, LP 548, no. 43 bis; and Pierron's reflections on Clément de Feillet's plan in BN, JF 2072, fol. 81. See also Cröy, *Journal inédit* 1:339.

102. See esp. BPR, LP 548, no. 43 bis, Feb. 19.

103. BN, JF 2071, fols. 201, 204, attorney general to ministry, Mar. 26 and 29; and fol. 365, "Projet de conclusion" by Pierron. The sentence against Damiens' family was also modeled on that against Ravaillac's.

104. BPR, LP 549, unnumbered papers, 14th letter to "madame"; and "Remarques sur l'arrêt contre Damiens et sur le séance de 29 mars lendemain de l'arrêt."

105. Luynes, *Mémoires* 15:493-94; *PO*, "Précis historique," pp. xl-xli; "Relation de l'éxécution de Damiens, qui a été faite le lundi 28 mars 1757," and "Détail de ce qui s'est passé le lundi 28 mars 1757, jour de l'éxécution de Robert-François Damiens," at end of *Supplément au procès*, pp. 1-10; "Rapport de l'exempt Bouton," in Ravaisson, *Archives de la Bastille* 16:472f., and reprinted in A. L. Zavaes, *Damiens le régicide* (Paris, 1937), pp. 201-214; "Exécution de Robert-François Damiens le lundi 28 mars 1757 en place de Grève," AN, AD III, 8; and "Detail de l'éxécution de Damiens faite en place de Grève le 28 mars 1757," MS in author's possession.

106. On Gueret's appointment, see BPR, LP 548, unnumbered fol., Mar. 11; BN, JF 2071, fols. 31, 34, letters from Gueret to attorney general, Mar. 7 and 8; and Luynes, *Mémoires* 15:446. On Gueret's history, see *NE*, table, esp. p. 198, Sept. 30, 1730; and Gueret, *Lettre d'un curé de Paris à m l'archévêque de Paris*, in BPR, LP 535, no. 17. See also this volume, p. 110.

107. BN, JF 2071, fol. 24, Sorbonne's memoir to attorney gen-

eral, Mar. 23; fol. 28, attorney general to Bel of Sorbonne, undated; and fol. 26, Sorbonne's response, naming Marcilly, Mar. 28. In appointing the latter over Bel, the Sorbonne bypassed a request by Gueret to be accompanied by Bel if he had to be accompanied by anyone else at all. See BN, JF 2071, fol. 53, Gueret to attorney general, Mar. 27. On Marcilly's ecclesiastical past, see *NE* (July 10, 1759), p. 113.

108. "Détail abrégé et très véritable de plusieurs faits qui ont précédé ou suivi l'éxécution de Robert-François Damiens, assassin du Roy," in BN, JF 2072, fols. 305-307. This manuscript was sent to attorney general by one Dumont, royal advocate at Macon, who complained that students at the Jesuit college were circulating it in the town (BN, JF 2071, fol. 308, Dumont to attorney general, Apr. 25). In response (fol. 309, May 3), the attorney general opined that it merited only "mépris."

109. *PO*, interrogation of Gautier on Mar. 30, p. 426; and on Apr. 2, no. 14, p. 439. See also Luynes, *Mémoires* 16:3, 35.

Notes to Chapter 3

1. This numerical breakdown is based upon Jules Flammermont's *Remontrances du parlement de Paris au XVIIIe siècle*, 3 vols. (Paris, 1888-1898; reprint ed., Geneva, 1978). Anything short of a formal remonstrance I counted as a representation, whether the harangue was by the first president alone, the gens du roi, or by a more numerous delegation of the parlement. I counted remonstrances on behalf of provincial parlements as a separate category, even though they could be grouped variously under the other three categories, depending on the issue that originally provoked the royal displeasure. From yet another point of view, they could all be grouped under the jurisdictional-constitutional category, because what the parlement of Paris objected to in each of these instances was the king's unconstitutional rough handling of a sister—or perhaps daughter—court.

2. Ibid., 1:453

3. J. Tascherau, Paul Marchal, et al., *Catalogue de l'histoire de France*, 15 vols. (Paris, 1855-1895), esp. vols. 2 and 5.

4. The parlements in question were principally Besançon (1760), Rouen (1763), Toulouse (1764), Pau (1765), and Rennes (1765-1779).

5. These occasions arose in 1759, 1761, 1763, and in 1768. The famous lit de justice held in December 1770 that preceded Maupeou's

dissolution of the parlements concerned the parlement of Paris' constitutional pretensions and practices.

6. *Edit du roi, portant suppression de deux chambres des enquêtes, et de plusieurs offices dans le parlement de Paris. Donné à Versailles au mois de décembre 1756* (Paris, 1757).

7. Manuscript evidence of these negotiations is to be found in BN, JF 336, file 36141. When they began in May 1756, these negotiations were secretive and restricted to the attorney general, Guillaume-François Joly de Fleury; the first president, René-Charles Maupeou; and the comte d'Argenson. But they progressively widened to include, first the solicitor general and a few more presidents, then all the presidents, and finally the entire parlement, which was invited to make suggestions concerning the government's edict.

8. *Déclaration du roi, pour la discipline du parlement. Donné à Versailles le 10 décembre 1756* (Paris, 1757). For analysis of the parlement of Paris' parti janséniste and the political clout it could wield, see my *The Jansenists and the Expulsion of the Jesuits from France, 1757-1765* (New Haven, 1975), pp. 37-61.

9. *Déclaration du roi, concernante les affaires de religion. Donné à Versailles le 10 décembre 1756* (Paris, 1757).

10. Neither Jean Egret, who concludes that the declaration of Dec. 10, 1756, was "loyally executed" (*Louis XV et l'opposition parlementaire, 1715-1774* [Paris, 1970], p. 86), nor Philippe Godard, who maintains that the king gave the clergy "entire satisfaction" in principle, while admitting that parlementary practice might have deviated from this principle from time to time (*La Querelle des refus de sacrements, 1730-1735* [Paris, 1937], pp. 130, 257-59), have appreciated the parlementary victory that the surface registration of this declaration in September 1757 imperfectly concealed (see this volume, pp. 102-104, 149-58).

11. Augustin Gazier, ed., *Fragment inédit des mémoires du chancelier d'Aguesseau* (Paris, 1920), pp. 7-11.

12. Ibid., pp. 29-35; Robert Kreiser, *Miracles, Convulsions, and Ecclesiastical Politics in Early Eighteenth-Century Paris* (Princeton, 1978), pp. 17-38.

13. [Louis-Adrien Le Paige], *Observations sur les Actes de l'Assemblée du clergé de 1765* (n.p., n.d.), pp. 166-71. See also *NE* (Nov. 20, 1765), p. 189.

14. Pierre-Guérin, cardinal de Tencin, *Instruction pastorale, et ordonnance de monseigneur l'archévêque prince d'Embrun, portant défense de lire et de garder divers écrits publiés sous le nom de m. l'évêque de Montpellier*

(Grenoble, 1730), pp. 26-27; and cited by *NE* (1731), p. 49. For Christophe de Beaumont, *Mandement et instruction pastorale de monseigneur l'archévêque de Paris, touchant l'autorité de l'église* . . . (Paris, 1756), p. 53.

15. *Déclaration par lequel le roi explique de nouveau ses intentions sur l'éxécution des bulles des papes données contre le jansénisme, et sur celle de la constitution Unigenitus*, in Léon Mention, ed., *Documents relatifs aux rapports du clergé avec la royauté*, 2 vols. (Paris, 1893-1903), 2:62-69.

16. Godard, *La Querelle des refus de sacrements*, pp. 1-65; precedents assembled by Chancellor Lamoignon in AN, AP 177mi 74, nos. 1-10.

17. On one occasion the cardinal de Fleury wrote to La Fare, "vous regardés le dernier concile Romain comme authentique, quoiqu'il n'ait point été reçu en France ni autorisé. Vous traittés la constitution comme règle de foy qui n'a été regardé que comme jugement dogmatique de l'église universelle par presque tous les évêques, et par le concile d'Embrun que comme *circa fidem* appartenant à la foy." (AN, 257 AP 14, dr 2, no. 149, Fleury to La Fare, undated.) For Fleury's reaction to a particular instance of refusal of sacraments, see the letter he ordered the comte de Maurepas to write to La Fare, dated Feb. 25, 1741, in AN, 257 AP 19, dr 4, no. 124.

18. See in general, Georges Hardy, *Le Cardinal de Fleury et le mouvement janséniste* (Paris, 1925); and Emile Appolis, *Entre Jansénistes et zélanti: Le 'Tiers Parti' catholique au XVIIIe siècle* (Paris, 1960), pp. 80-89.

19. Egret, *Louis XV et l'opposition parlementaire*, pp. 50-52.

20. Ibid. It is the duc de Choiseul who suggests in his *Mémoires*, ed. F. Calmettes (Paris, 1904), pp. 110-11, that Christophe de Beaumont might have originally received the secret encouragement of Louis XV himself, who was unable at that point to grasp all the consequences of such an enterprise. As for billets de confession, see the list of precedents assembled by episcopal spokesmen in 1752 to justify their use in BN, JF 1502, fol. 15, but which in spite of their intentions failed to justify the archbishop of Paris' use of them.

21. Flammermont, *Remontrances* 1:457-82; and Legier Desgranges, *Madame de Moysan et l'extravagante affaire de l'Hôpital général, 1749-1758* (Paris, 1954). The lawyer Edmond Barbier suspected that Jansenism was at the bottom of this affair (*Chronique de la régence et du règne de Louis XV, 1718-1763*, 8 vols. [Paris, 1857-1866], 5:67, 94, 128), as did the marquis d'Argenson (*Journal et mémoires du*

marquis d'Argenson, ed. E.-J.-B. Rathery, 9 vols. [Paris, 1859-1867], 6:440-41, 454, and 7:31).

22. Roland d'Erceville, "Journal," in AN, AB XIX 3336/2, fol. 1; and Barbier, *Journal* 4:373-74.

23. Rolland d'Erceville, "Journal," AN, AB XIX 3336/2, fols. 6-8, 19-22.

24. Ibid., fols. 23-26.

25. BN, JF 1487, fols. 21-78, but esp. nos. 40, 43, 54-59, 61-63, 75-78. These manuscripts consist for the most part of extracts from the parlement's registers.

26. BN, JF 1487, fols. 71-107. For the actual conclusions of the gens du roi, see fol. 104, Mar. 21, 1752; or AN, AP 177mi 74, no. 52. For the text of the arrêt of Apr. 13, 1752, see Flammermont, *Remontrances* 1:498.

27. BN, JF 1568, fols. 371-72; 1569, fol. 1.

28. Barbier, *Journal* 5:226.

29. Tascherau, Marchal, et al., *Catalogue de l'histoire de France*, esp. vols. 2 and 5.

30. See the debates between the councillors Drouin de Vandeuil and Philippe Thomé on precisely this subject in Rolland d'Erceville's "Journal," AN, AB XIX 3336/2, fols. 33-34.

31. Text in Mention, *Documents* 1:114-50.

32. Godard, *La Querelle des refus de sacrements*, p. 146.

33. This argument, omnipresent in fragmentary form in the Jansenist-parlementary literature of the period, is expressed in most systematic and concentrated form in the following sources: the gens du roi's confidential response to the clergy's objections to the parlement's arrêt of April 18, 1752, in AN, AP 177mi 75, nos. 16-17; [Claude Mey and Gabriel-Nicolas Maultrot], *Apologie de tous les jugements rendue par les tribunaux séculiers en France contre le schisme . . .*, 2 vols. (France, 1752); [Gabriel-Nicolas Maultrot], *Mémoire sur le refus des sacrements à la mort, qu'on fait à ceux qui n'acceptent pas la constitution, et une addition concernant les billets de confession* (n.p., 1750); and the parlement of Paris' remonstrances of Mar. 4, 1751, and Apr. 9, 1753, in Flammermont, *Remontrances* 1:414-43, 506-609. See also Godard, *La Querelle des refus de sacrements*, pp. 139-54, 170-92.

34. The appel comme d'abus was a legal device that since the late fifteenth century had allowed either the attorney general or an aggrieved particular to appeal the judgments of ecclesiastical courts to the parlements on numerous possible grounds, among them procedural irregularities, violations of canon or French law or more spe-

cifically the Gallican liberties, and infringements on secular jurisdiction. Article 37 of the edict of 1695 stipulated that the parlements were not supposed to judge the *fonds*, or substance, of such appealed cases but simply to determine whether the ecclesiastical judgment contained an *abus* or not, and if so, to reassign the case to a superior ecclesiastical jurisdiction for a definitive and substantial judgment. But the parlements paid no more attention to this provision than it had to similar ones in the past. (See Godard, *Le Querelle des refus de sacrements*, pp. 146-48.) Aside from the indirect means referred to above, the parlements contrived another way to make the appel comme d'abus more immediately and directly relevant to the case under discussion, which was to consider the act itself of refusal of sacraments to be the equivalent of an ecclesiastical judgment. The parlements could then "appeal" this "judgment" and declare it "abusive" on grounds both that the "judgment" had not been preceded by a canonically regular sentence of excommunication (factual notoriety was not recognized by French law, only legal notoriety) and that opposition to *Unigenitus* was not punishable by either legal or de facto excommunication because this bull was not a rule of faith—not even, hard-core opponents would add, a law of church and state. For the most part, however, the parlements did not take this tack but rather employed the surer one of criminal procedure.

35. Godard, *La Querelle des refus de sacrements*, pp. 217-39. For a forceful and exceptionally lucid exposition of this part of the parlementary argument by a contemporary, see Louis-Adrien Le Paige's memoir for the prince de Conti on the subject in BPR, LP 537, no. 90.

36. The cas privilégié, in Old Regime law, was a crime committed by an ecclesiastic over which the royal judge, rather than the ecclesiastical judge, had the "privilege" of exclusive jurisdiction as much because of the crime's seriousness and threat to public order as because it merited an "afflictive" or "defamatory" punishment, which the ecclesiastical judge was unqualified to pronounce. Obvious examples are homicide, highway robbery, counterfeiting, etc., although a definitive list was perhaps purposefully never made of them. In contrast, the délit commun was a purely "ecclesiastical" crime such as drunkenness, which was unpunishable if committed by a lay person, and over which the ecclesiastical judge naturally possessed exclusive jurisdiction. A rather complicated system governed "mixed" cases whereby the ecclesiastical and royal courts judged conjointly, the ecclesiastical judge for the délit commun and the royal judge for

the cas privilégié. See article 30 of the edict of 1695; Daniel Jousse, *Commentaire sur l'ordonnance criminelle de 1670*, 2 vols. (Paris, 1769), pp. 510-22; the elder Joly de Fleury's remarkably clear explanation of the relevant jurisprudence in BN, JF 1484, fols. 213-15; and *Dictionnaire universel dogmatique, canonique, historique, géographique, et chronologique des sciences écclésiastiques*, 6 vols. (Paris, 1760-1765), 2:333.

37. *Arrest du Conseil d'état du roi. Du 21 aoust 1752*, in AN, AP 177mi 74, no. 35.

38. *Arrest du Conseil d'état du roi, qui casse et annulle, comme attentatoire à la juridiction de l'église, une procédure faite au bailliage de Tours, en matière spirituelle et de sacrements. Du 23 aoust 1752*, in AN, AP 177mi 74, no. 36. For Lamoignon's reaction, see his "Réflexions sur le projet de remontrances arrêté au parlement le 24 janvier, 1753," in carton 75, no. 68.

39. BN, JF 1493, fols. 156-57, attorney general to Rouillé, Sept. 8, 1753.

40. BPR, LP 547, fol. 3, "Première mémoire ou lettre de moi à mr. le prince de conti, 9 dec. 1756."

41. Rolland d'Erceville, "Journal," AN, AB XIX 3336/2, fol. 8; and Flammermont, *Remontrances* 1:497, the king's response of April 18.

42. Flammermont, *Remontrances* 1:504-505.

43. *Arrest du Conseil d'état du roi. Du 21 novembre 1752*, in AN, AP 177mi 75, no. 29. The clergy regarded the wording of this arrêt as tantamount to acknowledging the "parlement's maxim that every public refusal of sacraments is a privileged case." See note by Lamoignon concerning the *agents généraux*'s reaction to the arrêt of Nov. 21, 1752, also in no. 29.

44. The correspondence between Chancellor Lamoignon and the dauphin, which contains abundant evidence of their shared dévôt sympathies, is to be found in AN, AP 162mi (archives du marquis de Rosanbo). Due to an interminable lawsuit, these documents are unfortunately not now accessible.

45. "Réponse du Roy au parlement le 17 avril 1752," in AN, AP 177mi 74, no. 25; and "Réponse du Roy le lundy 29 aoust 1757," in BN, JF 336, file 3614[1], fol. 211.

46. "Remontrances du 15 avril 1752," in Flammermont, *Remontrances* 1:495.

47. Ibid., p. 497.

48. In effect, this was the whole message of the parlement of

Paris' famous remonstrances of Apr. 9, 1753, also in ibid., pp. 506-609.

49. Rouillé, at least, described the project as a secret. See his letter to the retired attorney general, dated July 24, 1752, at Compiègne, in BN, JF 1493, fol. 92.

50. At least four different proposals were given consideration by the special commission appointed by Louis XV. The two given most attention were the elder Joly de Fleury's proposal, consisting of eleven articles (in BN, JF 1493, fols. 59-71), together with its author's observations and account of episcopal objections, and another (among Lamoignon's papers in AN, AP 177mi 75, fol. 33 bis) described by the elder Joly de Fleury as a "nouveau projet, donné par le Roy à m le cardinal de Rochefoucault, novembre 1752," in BN, JF 1494, fol. 111, where it is also found. It was most probably drafted by Louis-Antoine Rouillé, secretary of state for foreign affairs. The prince de Conti, Louis XV's secret advisor and negotiator in these matters, contributed another (BN, JF 1494, fols. 51-66), and yet a fourth, of uncertain authorship (AN, AP 177mi 74, no. 64, and BN, JF 1484, fols. 202f.) is especially interesting because, alone among the proposals, it attempts to embody two recommendations that the king was forever urging upon his parlements: namely, to send delicate cases to him personally for judgment and to refrain from imposing "afflictive" or "defamatory" sentences upon offending ecclesiastics.

51. Rouillé, especially, insisted upon "la necessité de rétablir l'ordre des jurisdictions," Rouillé to the elder Joly de Fleury, Aug. 9, 1752, in BN, JF 1493, fol. 125. See also fol. 191. This would mean that the royal courts could take cognizance of such cases only by means of the appel comme d'abus and the cas privilégié, the latter being defined as horrendously scandalous behavior on the part of the priest, such as refusal of sacraments accompanied by gratuitous insults. For Joly de Fleury's summary of the general goals of the draft declarations, see fols. 131-32, 135-38.

52. BN, JF 1493, fols. 2-3, Rouillé to the elder Joly de Fleury Jul. 19, 1752.

53. BPR, LP 517, no. 59: "avis d'un de ceux qui ont opiné devant le Roi lors de l'arrêt du 21 novembre 1752"; plus this note by Le Paige: "je le crois de l'écriture de Rouillé ministre et secrétaire d'Etat." It is, as can be ascertained by a comparison between the handwriting of this "avis" and that of any of Rouillé's many communications to Joly de Fleury.

54. The interpretation of the privileged case as a gratuitous insult

accompanying a refusal was advanced by the cardinal de La Rochefoucauld, according to a letter from Grandeville to the chancellor, Jan. 27, 1753, in AN, AP 177mi 75, no. 56. A reference by the elder Joly de Fleury to a conversation he had had with La Rochefoucauld (BN, JF 1493, fols. 135-38, under rubrique of article 9) confirms that this was the cardinal's view, and suggests that it was his own as well. See also Joly de Fleury's letter to Rouillé, Aug. 28, 1752, in fols. 144-45.

55. Discussion by special commission of article 7 of one of the proposed declarations in AN, AP 177mi 75, no. 1 bis. It could be argued, however, that the declarations' distinction between a provoked refusal and a passive refusal implicitly constituted such a definition.

56. BN, JF 1484, fols. 202f., esp. articles 6, 7, 9, and 12. The elder Joly de Fleury's critical observations concerning these articles are in fols. 213-15.

57. AN, AP 177mi 74, no. 71, Lamoignon's "observations sur un projet que le Roy m'a confié."

58. AN, AP 177mi 74, no. 54, "Mémoire sur l'arrêt du parlement du 18 avril 1752," as well as carton 75, no. 68, "Réflexions sur le projet de remontrances arresté au parlement le 24 janvier 1753."

59. BN, JF 1494, fols. 215-16, Rouillé to the elder Joly de Fleury, Apr. 22, 1753; and fol. 1494, fol. 243, same to same, Oct. 14, 1752.

60. *Arrest du Conseil d'état du roi. Du 29 avril 1752*, the preamble; and "Réponse du Roy aux députés du parlement au sujet de l'arrêté du 5 may, 1752," in AN, AP 177mi 74, no. 31. "Je connois," the king answered in the latter, "l'importance des objets qui me sont annoncés, c'est pour cette raison que je me propose de former incessament une commission composée de prélats et de magistrats de mon royaume pour discuter une matière aussy intéressante pour le bien de la Religion que pour le tranquillité de l'Estat et prendre sur leurs avis les mesures que je jugeray les plus convenable pour faire entièrement cesser tout sujet de trouble et de division." This response is also in Flammermont, *Remontrances* 1:503.

61. On the committee's composition, see BPR, LP 517, no. 17, Le Paige's note on the title page of his *Lettres pacifiques*; on its agenda, BN, JF 1495, fol. 2, Lamoignon to the elder Joly de Fleury, May 30, 1752; and fol. 3, Joly de Fleury to Lamoignon, May 31, 1752.

62. All of this emerges with exceptional clarity from Lamoignon's account of the commissioner's individual reactions to the twelve

articles of one of the proposed royal declarations in AN, AP 177mi 75, no. 1 bis. Grandeville privately admitted his chagrin at being more in accord with the clergy than with the other lay councillors on the commission (see no. 63, Grandeville to chancellor, Mar. 15, 1753).

63. BN, JF 1493, fols. 156-60, letters from the elder Joly de Fleury to Rouillé, Sept. 8 and 10, 1752.

64. The bishops of Valence and Toulouse are the examples cited. See BN, JF 1493, nos. 203, 222, and 224, letters from Rouillé to the elder Joly de Fleury dated Sept. 14, 22 and 28, 1752. The reference to the archbishop's zeal is in the first of these.

65. For a description of La Rochefoucauld, see BN, JF 1493, fols. 153-54, Rouillé to the elder Joly de Fleury, Sept. 7, 1752; for Soubise, see fol. 93, Joly de Fleury to Rouillé, Jul. 30, 1752; and for the archbishop of Paris, see AN, AP 177mi 75, no. 53, Grandeville to Chancellor Lamoignon, Dec. 13, 1752. Rouillé's ruminations on the situation are in BN, JF 1493, fol. 262, Rouillé to the elder Joly de Fleury, Oct. 28, 1752; and fol. 224, same to same, Sept. 28, 1752.

66. BN, JF 1493, fols. 139-40, 147-48, letters from Ogier to the elder Joly de Fleury, dated Aug. 29 and 31, 1752.

67. BN, JF 1494, fols. 215-16, Rouillé to the elder Joly de Fleury, Apr. 22, 1753.

68. On Trudaine, see BN, JF 1495, fol. 10, Trudaine to the elder Joly de Fleury, Oct. 14, 1752; on Grandeville, see AN, AP 177mi 75, no. 49, Grandeville to Chancellor Lamoignon, Nov. 11, 1752; on d'Auriac, see BPR, LP 517, no. 17, note by Le Paige.

69. BN, JF 1492, fol. 68, the elder Joly de Fleury to Rouillé, Feb. 9, 1753; BN, JF 1493, fol. 93, same to same, Jul. 30, 1752.

70. AN, 177mi 74, no. 44, Castanier d'Auriac to Lamoignon, Mar. 15, 1753; and 75, no. 63, Grandeville to Lamoignon, Mar. 15, 1753.

71. BN, JF 1493, fols. 232, 243, 256, letters from Rouillé to the elder Joly de Fleury, dated Oct. 3, 14, and 25, 1752.

72. BN, JF 1494, fols. 215-16, Rouillé to the elder Joly de Fleury, Apr. 22, 1753.

73. BN, JF 1493, fols. 131-32, the elder Joly de Fleury to Rouillé, Aug. 18, 1752; AN, AP 177mi 75, no. 29, note by Lamoignon.

74. The comment concerning the authors of the remonstrances are Grandeville's in AN, AP 177mi 75, no. 61, Grandeville to Lamoignon, Mar. 14, 1753.

75. For a detailed account of these events, see Flammermont, *Remontrances* 1:512-20.

76. Egret, *Louis XV et l'opposition parlementaire*, pp. 59-60.

77. BN, JF 2103, fols. 85-86, 89, letters from solicitor general and attorney general to Joly de Fleury *père*, May 22, 1753.

78. BN, JF 2103, fols. 87, 94-95, letters from solicitor general to Joly de Fleury *père*, May 29 and 23, 1753, respectively.

79. BN, JF 2103, fols. 72-73, 156-57, letters from solicitor general to Joly de Fleury *père*, May 18 and Jul. 16, 1753, respectively.

80. BN, JF 2103, fol. 100, Rouillé to the elder Joly de Fleury, May 24, 1753; and fols. 111, the latter to Rouillé, same date.

81. BN, JF 2103, fols. 133-34, attorney general to Joly de Fleury *père*, June 21, 1753.

82. For evidence of Conti's efforts, see BN, JF 2103, fols. 138-39, 140-43, 147, 149-50, 153, letters from attorney general to Joly de Fleury *père*.

83. BN, JF 2103 fols. 131-32, 140-41, letters from attorney general to Joly de Fleury *père*, June 20 and 24, 1753, respectively.

84. BN, JF 2103, fols. 140-43, letters from attorney general to Joly de Fleury *père*, June 24 and 23, 1753. The reference to "catechizing" is from fols. 133-34, same to same, June 21, 1753.

85. Characterization of d'Héricourt as gentle is by solicitor general in letter to his father in BN, JF 2103, fols. 160-61, Jul. 18, 1753.

86. BN, JF 2103, fols. 158-59, attorney general to Joly de Fleury *père*, Jul. 18, 1753; and fols. 160-61, solicitor general to same, same date. For a first-hand acount of Bourges' point of view on the negotiations, see Robert de Saint-Vincent's and Durey de Mesnières' "Journal anecdotique sur la vie du parlement à Bourges"; in AN, KK 821, especially the section 14-31 written by Robert de Saint-Vincent. Belouze was not held in high repute by the colony at Bourges, not only for the reason under consideration, but also because he favored theatrical performances, balls, and other un-Jansenist forms of recreation.

87. For a sense of the differences in point of view regarding *Unigenitus* between the parti janséniste entrenched at Bourges and the more moderate gens du roi at Pontoise, see the correspondence between the elder Joly de Fleury and the councillor Louis-Alexandre Angran, in BN, JF 1483, esp. fols. 215-18, letters from Angran to Joly de Fleury, Dec. 1753.

88. BN, JF 2103, fol. 168, attorney general to Joly de Fleury *père*, Jul. 20, 1753.

89. Egret, *Louis XV et l'opposition parlementaire*, pp. 62-63.

90. *PO*, interrogation of Jan. 18, no. 139, p. 131.

91. Charles-Philippe d'Albert, duc de Luynes, *Mémoires du duc de Luynes, sur la cour de Louis XV, 1735-1758*, ed. L. Dussieux and E. Soulié, 17 vols. (Paris, 1860-1865), 13:444.

92. BN, JF 1494, fols. 227-31, Apr. 26, 1753. That at least the enquêtes would have rejected it is evident from Angran's negative reaction to it in fols. 240-41, Angran to the elder Joly de Fleury, undated.

93. BN, JF 2103, fols. 196-97. That it was sent by Machault is evident from fol. 195, Machault to attorney general, June 7, 1753.

94. On Conti as promoter of the law of silence, see *Mémoires et lettres de François-Joachim de Pierre, cardinal de Bernis, 1715-1758*, ed. Frédéric Masson, 2 vols. (Paris, 1911), 1:324; d'Argenson, *Journal et mémoires* 8:316; and BPR, LP 530, fol. 144, "de Compiègne, 14 juillet, 1754." Conti's role is also everywhere stressed in letters from Rolland de Challerange to Saint-Hilaire in Bourges in BPR, LP 532, unnumbered.

95. Rolland de Challerange calls attention to Pothouin's role in a letter to Saint-Hilaire in BPR, LP 532, June 13 and Jul. 9, 1754, unnumbered fol., as does Luynes in *Mémoires* 13:444. For Le Paige's initial reactions to the Declaration of Silence, see his "précis des réflexions sur le projet de déclaration présentée au parlement le 4 septembre, 1754," in BPR, LP 535, no. 4; for his more mature and optimistic reflections, see no. 6, a note dated Sept. 7, as well as no. 13, "Réflexions sommaires sur l'enregistrement de la déclaration du 2 septembre, 1754."

96. Text in BPR, LP 535, no. 5, "Versailles le 2 septembre 1754"; or in Flammermont, *Remontrances* 1:610-11.

97. Flammermont, *Remontrances* 1:612; BPR, LP 535, no. 5.

98. Luynes, *Mémoires* 13:445; d'Argenson, *Journal et mémoires* 8:344. See also Barbier's corroborative commentary in *Journal* 6:54-56.

99. Flammermont, *Remontrances* 1:613-14.

100. For Lallemant case, see BN, JF 1487, fols. 183-91; 1563, fols. 100-120; d'Argenson, *Journal et mémoires*, 8:375-76, 379-380, where the "grande joie parmi le peuple de Paris" is stressed; and Barbier, *Journal* 6:75-85, where Lallemant is described as a "fille lingère dans la place Maubert," a "soeur ou fille d'un chaudronnier, au bout de la rue Galande." For Henri Griveau's straightforward although impolitic translation of the wording of one of the parlement's arrêts, see BN, JF 1568, fol. 312, Pierron to attorney general.

The parlement's definitive arrêt in the Lallemant case is dated Feb. 3, 1755.

101. For Cerveau's cooperation in the Lallemant case, see BN, JF 1563, fols. 100, 104, 114, 120; and in the Breton case, see MS 1567, fols. 124, 133-34. For the Deshayes and Demoiselle Coffin case, see MS 1567, fol. 125; and MS 1568, fol. 240; and for his dubious domestic situation, see, MS 1570, fols. 152-53, "Précis des plaintes qui ont été portées contre S. Deshayes prêtre depuis 1755 à 1759."

102. BN, JF 1563, fols. 104, 114, 120; and MS 1567, fol. 150. See also d'Argenson's comments about the parlement's jurisprudence in this matter, in *Journal et mémoires* 8:426, 432.

103. BN, JF 1567, fol. 153.

104. Coquelin's "original sin' was to have administered the sacrament of extreme unction to the sometime convulsionary Milady Edward, Duchess of Perth, in response to the parlement of Paris' arrêt to this effect of Jan. 14, 1755. See BN, JF 1563, fol. 120; and MS 1568, fol. 247; as well as Barbier, *Journal* 6:110; and d'Argenson, *Journal et mémoires* 8:414.

105. BN, JF 1568, fols. 221, 248-49, 330-34; d'Argenson, *Journal et mémoires* 8:426-28; Barbier, *Journal* 6:110-11, 290.

106. Barbier, *Journal* 6:111; d'Argenson, *Journal et mémoires* 8:243, 428.

107. "Remontrances au roi, concernant les refus de sacrements," in *Collection des procès-verbaux des assemblées générales du clergé de France, depuis l'année 1560 jusqu'à présent, redigé par ordre de matières* (henceforth *Procès-verbaux des assemblées générales du clergé de France*), 9 vols. (Paris, 1778), vol. 8, pt. 1, no. 5, pp. 183-84.

108. BN, JF 1569, fols. 60f.

109. Barbier, *Journal* 6:143-46; Flammermont, *Remontrances* 2:4.

110. Flammermont, *Remontrances* 2:5-6. A much more conciliatory royal response to the parlement's arrêt of Mar. 18, 1755, which was not adopted, exists in the handwriting of Joly de Fleury *père* in BN, JF 2103, fols. 233-34. The same is true of the royal council's arrêt quashing that of the parlement, for which a more conciliatory but abortive version can be found in fols. 229-30. See also Barbier, *Journal* 6:146-48, 149-52; and d'Argenson, *Journal et mémoires* 8:441, 455, 458.

111. Flammermont, *Remontrances* 2:10-11.

112. For an example previous to the clergy's remonstrances of Oct. 1755 and the archbishop's *Mandement et instruction pastorale* of

Sept. 1756, see the bishop of Boulogne's letter of Oct. 1, 1754, to the attorney general of the parlement of Paris, in BPR, LP 535, no. 31.

113. See the abbé de Targny's "Recueil de pièces sur le jansénisme" in BN, Mss Fr 3335, fols. 176-78; but also d'Argenson, *Journal et mémoires* 8:441, 444, 447-48, 455, 458; Barbier, *Journal* 6:134-40; and Godard, *La Querelle des refus de sacrements*, p. 38.

114. Barbier, *Journal* 6:183-84.

115. *Procès-verbaux des assemblées générales du clergé de France*, vol. 8, pt. 1, pp. 455-60.

116. For formal presentation of remonstrances and king's response, see ibid., pp. 550-53; for specific objects of remonstrances, see "Remontrances au roy concernant les refus de sacrements," in ibid., no. 5, pp. 187-88; as well as Barbier, *Journal* 6:212-15.

117. Ibid., "Remontrances au roy concernant les refus de sacrements," no. 5 pp. 180-83.

118. Ibid., p. 554.

119. BN, JF 2103, fols. 274-77, 382-410.

120. BPR, LP 537, no. 120, "J'ai l'honneur d'envoyer à v.a.s. le projet qu'elle m'a demandé," Jan. 1, 1756; and no. 119, Murard's "Mémoire sur la nécessité indispensable de maintenir la déclaration du 2 septembre 1754."

121. BPR, LP 537, no. 90, memoir by Le Paige.

122. BPR, LP 537, no. 88, "Autorités et citations concernant le droit qu'ont les princes et les magistrats de faire des injonctions aux écclésiastiques de se conformer aux règles de l'église et de remplir les fonctions de leur ministère"; and BN, JF 1483, fol. 62, note by retired attorney general: "écrire pour le prince de Conti 3 cahiers."

123. Flammermont, *Remontrances* 2:12-22; and BPR, LP 539, nos. 5-45. See also Egret, *Louis XV et l'opposition parlementaire*, pp. 72-76.

124. Flammermont, *Remontrances* 2:22-102; Barbier, *Journal* 6:222-24, 242-45, 250-62, 264-76.

125. In general, see BN, JF 1477, fols. 175-76, 184-87; and MS 2103, fols. 285-335; in particular, see Barbier, *Journal* 6:192.

126. BN, Mss Fr 3335, fol. 208.

127. BN, JF 2103, fol. 335, Conti to attorney general, undated.

128. A blow by blow account of parts of the crucial session as this division opened up exists in BN, JF 1477, fols. 179-80.

129. *Procès-verbaux des assemblées générales du clergé de France*, vol. 8, pt. 1, pp. 555-58. See also BPR, LP 537, no. 37; Maurice Boutry,

ed., *Choiseul à Rome, 1754-1757: Lettres et mémoires inédites* (Paris, 1895), pp. 56-57; and Barbier, *Journal* 6:212-15, 219-20.

130. *Procès-verbaux des assemblées générales du clergé de France*, vol. 8, pt. 1, pp. 554-59.

131. Emile Appolis, *Entre Jansénistes et zélanti: Le 'Tiers Parti' catholique au XVIIIe siècle*, pp. 155-76.

132. On Choiseul's negotiations in general, see Boutry, *Choiseul à Rome*, pp. 4-218; for the text of *Ex Omnibus*, see pp. 320-27, or *Procès-verbaux des assemblées générales du clergé de France*, vol. 8, pt. 1, no. 5, pp. 274-78.

133. [Le Paige], *Observations sur les Actes de l'assemblée du clergé de 1765*, pp. 182-209.

134. Cardinal de Bernis, *Mémoires et lettres* 1:326; BPR, LP 546, no. 215, a note by Le Paige; and no. 219, "anecdote importante," where Le Paige cites Durey de Mesnières as his source. The latter was on social terms with Choiseul. The controversial terminology in *Ex Omnibus* is contained in the opening line: "Tanta est profecto in Ecclesia Dei autoritas Apostolicae Constitutionis quae incipit *Unigenitus*," etc. Toward the end of the same paragraph, *Unigenitus* is also called a "regula."

135. These suspicions by contemporaries are in all probability confirmed by the contents of AN, K 682 and 698, which were unfortunately inaccessible to me in 1976-1977 because they were in the process of being microfilmed.

136. Pierre de Nolhac, *Madame de Pompadour et la politique* (Paris, 1928), pp. 74-110; Adrien Thierry, *La Marquise de Pompadour* (Paris and Geneva, 1959), pp. 159-68. The Pompadour's "conversion" did not, of course, escape the notice of contemporary memoirists. See Barbier, *Journal* 6:245-50, 262-63; and d'Argenson, *Journal et mémoires* 8:414, where he notes that "la marquise de Pompadour répand souvent des pleurs sur les malheurs de l'Etat. Elle affecte aujourd'hui d'être alarmé pour la religion à l'occasion de l'exile des évêques. . . ."

137. Nolhac, *Madame de Pompadour et la politique*, p. 91. D'Argenson, again, notes (*Journal et mémoires* 8:430) that "présentement elle [Pompadour] est pour le clergé, sous prétexte de craindre pour la vie du Roi; elle se port à des ménagements qui empêchent la fin de l'affaire du clergé et des magistrats."

138. Emile Campardon, *Madame de Pompadour et le cour de Louis XV au milieu du XVIIIe siècle* (Paris, 1867), p. 67; Gaston Capon and Robert Yve-Plessis, *Paris galant au dix-huitième siècle: Vie privée du*

prince de Conty, Louis-François de Bourbon (1717-1776) (Paris, 1907), pp. 99-110.

139. On the king's "secret," see in general Didier Ozanam and Michel Antoine, *Correspondance secrète du comte de Broglie avec Louis XV, 1756-1774*, 2 vols. (Paris, 1956), 1:xi-cxiv; Edgar Boutaric, *Correspondance secrète de Louis XV sur la politique étrangère avec le comte de Broglie, Tercier . . . et autres documents relatifs au ministère secret . . .*, 2 vols. (Paris, 1866), 1:1-194; and the duc de Broglie, *Le Secret du roi: Correspondance secrète de Louis XV avec ses agents diplomatiques, 1752-1774*, 2 vols. (Paris, 1878).

140. Ozanam and Antoine, *Correspondance secrète du comte de Broglie avec Louis XV* 1:xxxv; Boutaric, *Correspondance secrète de Louis XV sur la politique étrangère* 1:73.

141. Cardinal de Bernis, *Mémoires et lettres* 1:230; Richard Waddington, *Louis XV et le renversement des alliances: Préliminaires de la Guerre de Sept Ans, 1754-1756* (Paris, 1896), pp. 297-98.

142. Broglie, *Le secret du roi* 1:124-25, 138-42, 165-70.

143. Cardinal de Bernis, *Mémoires et lettres* 1:226-27. For attitudes of d'Argenson and the dauphin, see p. 296; Barbier, *Journal* 6:473; and Boutaric, *Correspondance secrète de Louis XV sur la politique étrangère* 1:73-75.

144. For Joly de Fleury's death, see Barbier, *Journal* 6:279; and BPR, LP 539, no. 83, "Discours prononcé le vendredy 26 mars par m Séguier, avocat général, au sujet de la mort de m Joly de Fleury, ancien procureur général." Rohan Butler's *Choiseul: Father and Son* (Oxford, 1980), which I was able to consult only as this manuscript was going to press, contains a somewhat finer appreciation of the maréchal de Noailles' role in the earlier phases of the controversy. See in general pp. 1007-16, 1033-38, and 1059-67.

145. BPR, LP 539, no. 85. The association between Conti and Noailles went back to the duchesse de Châteauroux, who favored both. See Ozanam and Antoine, *Correspondance secrète du comte de Broglie avec Louis XV*, 1:xvi.

146. See this volume, pp. 138-40; also BN, JF 1483, fol. 62; MS 1562, fol. 48, attorney general to Conti, Jan. 6, 1756; and MS 2103, fols. 382-410, memoirs by Joly de Fleury *père*.

147. BPR, LP 541, no. 68, Le Paige to Conti, Mar. 31, 1756. For memoirs concerning the Declaration of Silence, see this volume, pp. 138-39, 313 nn.120-22.

148. George Armstrong Kelly, "The Machine of the Duc D'Orléans," *Journal of Modern History* 51 (December 1979):667-84.

149. Charles-Jean-François Hénault, *Mémoires du président Hénault*, ed. François Rousseau (Geneva, 1971), p. 269.

150. BPR, LP 539, no. 65, Conti to Le Paige, "lundy au soir." No. 164 helps date the letter as of Aug. 2, 1756. "On veut toujours refuser les remontrances," Conti's warning to Le Paige begins, and so on.

151. BPR, LP 556, no. 63.

152. [Louis-Adrien Le Paige], *Lettres historiques sur les fonctions essentielles du parlement, sur les droits des pairs, et sur les loix fondamentales du royaume*, 2 vols. (Amsterdam, 1753-1754). On this work, see Elie Carcassonne, *Montesquieu et le problème de la constitution française au XVIIIe siècle* (Paris, n.d.), pp. 271-81; Egret, *Louis XV et l'opposition parlementaire*, pp. 75-76; and Jean Imbert, *Cours d'histoire des idées politiques jusqu'à la fin du XVIIIe siècle, redigé d'après les notes et avec autorisation* (Paris, 1966-1967), pp. 295-99.

153. Edmond Hughes, "Un episode de l'histoire du protestantisme au XVIIIe siècle," *Société de l'histoire du protestantisme français, Bulletin historique et littéraire* 26 (1877), 289-303, 337-50, esp. p. 297. See also John Woodbridge, "The French Protestants' 'Secret': The Prince de Conti's Conspiracy Against Louis XV in 1756-1757," paper presented at the eighth annual conference of the Western Society for French History, Oct. 23-25, 1980, in Eugene, Oregon. On the basis of some new documents, Woodbridge argues that this whole "episode" was considerably more serious—and more compromising for Rabaut and the Languedoc Protestants—than Hughes' article and its title suggest.

154. Boutaric, *Correspondance secrète de Louis XV sur la politique étrangère* 1:212-14, letters from Louis XV to the comte de Broglie, dated Nov. 9, 27, and Dec. 24, 1756.

155. Christophe de Beaumont, *Mandement et instruction pastorale*. See also Barbier, *Journal* 6:369, 370-71, 382-406.

156. See this volume, pp. 289-90 nn.18-21.

157. On the bishop of Orléans' original exile, see Barbier, *Journal* 6:92; and d'Argenson, *Journal et mémoires* 8:391-92.

158. Text of Arrêt is in BPR, LP 537, no. 44. For origins of Cougniou affair, see d'Argenson, *Journal et mémoires* 8:354, 357, 366-67; and Barbier, *Journal* 6:194-95.

159. BN, JF 1562, fols. 51-53, Le Clerc de Doüy to attorney general, Jan. 26, 1756. See also fols. 53-54.

160. Montmorency de Laval, *Ordonnance de monseigneur l'évêque d'Orléans, portant interdit de l'église de Saint-Pierre-Lentin, et défense de célébrer*

le service ordonné par l'arrêt du parlement, le 29 août 1755, in BN, JF 1561, fols. 314-15.

161. *Procès-verbal de ce qui s'est passé au parlement de Paris, du 12 novembre au 11 décembre 1756 dans l'affaire du refus de sacrements* (n.p., n.d.), pp. 7-11. On Poncet de La Rivière's exile, see d'Argenson, *Journal et mémoires* 8:401-402.

162. *Second mandement de monseigneur l'archévêque de Paris. . . . Du 7 novembre 1756* (n.p., n.d.), in BN, Mss FR 22093 (29); for Beaumont's refusal of sacraments to nun in faubourg Saint-Jacques, see BN, JF 1562, fol. 220, attorney general to six ministers, Dec. 3, 1756.

163. *Procès-verbal de ce qui s'est passé au parlement de Paris, du 12 novembre au 11 décembre 1756 dans l'affaire du refus de sacrements*, pp. 1, 6, 11; Flammermont, *Remontrances* 2:156; and Barbier, *Journal* 6:396-98. On the Châtelet's condemnation of Beaumont's *Mandement*, see AN, AP 177mi 108, no. 97, Moreau to Chancellor Lamoignon, Nov. 4, 1756. For the parlement's arrêt regarding the curé of Saint-Pierre-Lentin, see BN, JF 1562, fol. 185, attorney general to ministers, Nov. 13, 1756.

164. *Citation canonique en forme de sommation et de monitoire faite par monseigneur l'éveque d'Orléans à maître François Ducamel curé de la paroisse de Saint-Pierre-Lentin en la ville d'Orléans. Du 17 novembre 1756*, in BN, JF 1562, fols. 202-203. See also fol. 211, Ducamel to attorney general, Nov. 29, 1756; Flammermont, *Remontrances* 2:153-55; and *Procès-verbal de ce qui s'est passé au parlement de Paris, du 12 novembre au 11 décembre 1756 dans l'affaire du refus de sacrements*, pp. 3-5.

165. On the lit de justice of Aug. 21, 1756, see Flammermont, *Remontrances* 2:112-30; on the capture of fort Saint-Philippe, see Ernest Lavisse, *Histoire de France illustrée depuis ses origines jusqu'à la Révolution*, 9 vols. (Paris, 1911), vol. 8, pt. 2, p. 273.

166. BN, JF 1562, fol. 211, attorney general to Conti, Dec. 1, 1756; BPR, LP 547, nos. 3-5, Le Paige to Conti, Dec. 9, 1756.

167. Cardinal de Bernis, *Mémoires et lettres* 1:328-30. See also d'Argenson, *Journal et mémoires* 9:370-71; and Barbier, *Journal* 6:403.

168. Barbier so describes the Parisian mood in *Journal* 6:408.

169. See the rump Grand' chambre's representation of Jan. 19, 1757, on this subject, and the king's response to these in *NE* (Feb. 22, 1757), p. 38, as well as presidents Molé and Le Pelletier's representations of Aug. 21, 1757, in *NE* (Oct. 2, 1757), p. 161. See also Henri de Revol's draft remonstrances in BPR, LP 532, unnumbered. That this was indeed the chief bone of contention, as

far as the king's declaration on religious affairs was concerned, is also indicated by Chancellor Lamoignon's attention to this distinction, in a memoir to the king, in AN, AP 177mi 74, no. 46, dated "aoust 1757." This memoir is wrongly classified with material having to do with the year 1752. The chancellor's execrable handwriting is undoubtedly to blame.

170. This was particularly true of the edict's suppression of seventy-five offices and the five *commissions des requêtes du palais*. The Grand' chambre objected, in truth, to the elimination of the last two chambers of enquêtes and the office of president in all these chambers, but its objections were stated less strenuously than those of the others. (BN, JF 336, file 3614[1], fols. 56-70.)

171. The fascinating story of the composition of these remonstrances is told by Rolland d'Erceville, "Histoire des remontrances du 9 avril 1753," in BN, Mss Fr, new acq. 8496 (518). A summary of this history is found in Van Kley, *The Jansenists*, pp. 52-53, 55-57.

172. Cardinal de Bernis, *Mémoires et lettres* 1:328-29.

173. D'Argenson, *Journal et mémoires* 9:364, 366.

174. The list is in Barbier, *Journal* 6:443; or BPR, LP 547, fol. 66. On Lefebvre de Saint-Hilaire and *Ex Omnibus*, see d'Argenson, *Journal et mémoires* 9:358.

175. Barbier, *Journal* 6:459-60. Le Paige reports (BPR, LP 547, fol. 67) that the original list contained thirty names, which was however considered excessive and containing everyone who was "enlightened" in the parlement. The king himself then wrote the names of the sixteen who were exiled.

176. Nolhac, *La Politique de madame de Pompadour*, pp. 179-82. For contemporaries' accounts, see cardinal de Bernis, *Mémoires et lettres* 1:366-68; *Mémoires de M. le baron de Besanval*, ed. A.-J. de Ségur, 3 vols. (Paris, 1805), 1:303-14; Emmanuel prince de Cröy, *Journal inédit du duc de Cröy, 1718-1784*, ed. vicomte de Grouchy and Paul Cottin, 4 vols. (Paris, 1906-1907), 1:376-77; *Mémoires de madame Du Hausset, femme de chambre de madame de Pompadour*, ed. Quentin Crauford (Paris, 1824), pp. 138-46; *Mémoires authentiques du maréchal de Richelieu, publiés d'après le manuscrit original pour la Société de l'histoire de France*, ed. A. de Boislisle (Paris, 1918), pp. 139-48; and Charles de Mathei, marquis de Valfons, *Souvenirs du marquis de Valfons, vicomte de Sébourg, 1710-1786*, ed. Georges Mauvion (Paris, 1906), pp. 239-54.

177. For Machault, Hénault joins Bernis in insisting upon this

reason in *Mémoires*, pp. 243-44; for d'Argenson, only Barbier suggests the disagreement about the Austrian alliance as decisive in *Journal* 6:473.

178. BN, JF 2070, fol. 158, Feb. 17.

179. BPR, LP 547, no. 91, Le Paige's account of negotiations to end the parlementary crisis.

180. Cardinal de Bernis, *Mémoires et lettres* 1:334-47; Flammermont, *Remontrances* 2:164-72; BPR, LP 547, no. 149, Le Paige's account of end of the crisis. See also Barbier, *Journal* 6:565-77.

181. The king's responses of Aug. 29 and Sept. 1, 1757, and in BN, JF 336, file 3614[1], fols.211-12, 227; along with *Arrest de la cour de parlement. Du 5 septembre 1757*; and the parlement's arresté and response of the king concerning the sixteen exiled magistrates on the same date, fols. 238-40. The king's response of Sept. 1, 1757, is also in Flammermont, *Remontrances* 2:167-69.

182. Quoted from *Sentence du Chastelet de Paris, qui bannit à perpetuité hors du royaume, le nommé Germain Picquenard, desservant la cure de Montmargny, pour avoir refusé publiquement les sacrements à une de ses paroissiennes. Du samedi 12 septembre 1761* (Paris, 1761), p. 2.

183. *NE* (Oct. 22, 1757), p. 174.

184. BPR, LP 547, no. 168.

185. This is likewise the meaning that Barbier attached to the wording of the parlement's registration, in *Journal* 6:576-77, 581.

186. This is the number of such cases that left traces in the Joly de Fleury collection. A thorough inventory of the registers or minutes of the parlement of Paris and the Châtelet would undoubtedly turn up more.

187. For evidence of consultations with the cardinal de Bernis, see BN, JF 1569, fol. 115, solicitor general to attorney general, Sept. 27, 1758; for the activities of Clément de Feillet, see fols. 131, 352, 411, and 412-13, Molé to attorney general, May 14, Nov. 18, and 20, 1758.

188. Seven of the fifteen cases in question were handled by the Châtelet. The royal council had summarily annulled two previous criminal procedures initiated by the Châtelet in such cases, one on Nov. 12, 1752, and the other on Mar. 6, 1754, in the parishes of St.-Jean-en-Grêve and St.-Nicolas-des-Champs, respectively. On both occasions Louis XV had forbidden the Châtelet's four "services" to assemble; after 1757 he allowed them to do so.

189. See, for example, BN, JF 1566, fols. 11-12, "Etat des

procédures qui doivent faire l'objet du compte à rendre au parlement le 6 fevrier 1767."

190. "Mémoire présenté au roi par l'assemblée [de 1758], au sujet de la déclaration du 10 décembre 1756," in *Procès-verbaux des assemblées générales du clergé de France*, vol. 8, pt. 1, no. 2, pp. 237-39.

191. "Remontrances de l'assemblée générale du clergé [de 1760] au roi," in *Procès-verbaux des assemblées générales du clergé de France*, vol. 8, pt. 1, no. 6, p. 240.

192. For example, "Reponse du roi" to clergy's memoir of 1758 on the subject of the declaration of Dec. 10, 1756 in *Procès-verbaux des assemblées générales du clergé de France*, vol. 8, pt. 1, no. 2, pp. 239-40. The king's response to the general assembly of 1760's remonstrances repeats the same themes (see no. 6, p. 297).

193. "Remontrances de l'assemblée générale du clergé [de 1765] au roi," in *Procès-verbaux des assemblées générales du clergé de France*, vol. 8, pt. 2, no. 8, p. 454.

194. *NE* (June 26, 1757), p. 108. See also the cardinal de Bernis, *Mémoires et lettres* 2:51-59. Beaumont's obstinacy in this matter was the principal reason for his exile to Périgord.

195. Cardinal de Bernis, *Mémoires et lettres* 2:56.

196. The following remark by the cardinal de Bernis shows that the change in royal ecclesiastical policy was indeed the reason for the episcopal changes in question: "m. de Digne [de Jarante de la Bruyere] à l'évêché d'Orléans, et m. de Troyes [Poncet de La Rivière] a donné sa demission; je travaille à obtenir la même chose de l'évêque d'Auxerre [Caritat de Condorcet] pour avoir la paix dans notre intérieur" (see *Mémoires et lettres* 2:181, Bernis to the duc de Choiseul, Jan. 30, 1758). Two other episcopal changes are undoubtedly part of the same pattern. Melvin de Montazet replaced the cardinal de Tencin at Lyons in 1758, and Jean Antoine de Beaumont de Juines replaced Louis Guy de Geurapin de Vauréal at Rennes in 1759. The government did not succeed in obtaining the resignations of either Beaumont in Paris, Condorcet in Auxerre, or Antoine de Brancas in Aix. On the religious communities of Saint-Charles and Saint-Loup, see *NE* (Jan. 23, 1758), pp. 19-20; and BPR, LP 547, no. 206, note by Le Paige.

197. On the change in sacramental procedure, see BN, JF 1562, fols. 259-301; on the celebration of service for Cougniou, see *Extrait des registres du parlement. Du 30 décembre 1757*, in fols. 264-65. See also *NE* (Jan. 23, 1758), pp. 19-20.

198. *Déclaration du roi, qui révoque l'arrêt du Conseil du 20 novembre*

1751 et les lettres-patentes du 28 janvier 1752; ordonne en conséquence qu'on se règle à l'avenir, pour tout ce qui concerne l'administration de l'Hôpital général de Paris, et autres y unis, comme avant l'année 1749. Donné à Versailles le 15 mars 1758, in BPR, LP 547, no. 276.

199. *Arrest de la cour de parlement, qui condamne un libelle intitulé, La Réalité du projet de Bourg-Fontaine, demontrée par l'éxécution . . .* , in BN, Mss Fr 22093 (170), p. 3.

200. AB 10202, Christophe de Beaumont to lieutenant of police Berryer, Apr. 26 and Sept. 30, 1753. For such a police report, see dossier on year 1756, report of May 1. However voyeuristic an interest in these documents might incidentally be, close attention to them is of some help in identifying the parlement's parti janséniste. Among the regulars, for example, were madame Roland de Challerange and the lawyers Gillet, Texier, and Gerbier *fils*.

201. AB 10202, Beaumont to Berryer, Mar. 17, 1757.

202. BN, JF 1569, fols. 110-11, request by *marguilliers* of Saint-Médard; fol. 112, lieutenant of police Jean-Baptiste Bertin to attorney general, Nov. 29, 1758; fols. 117-20, memoir by solicitor general.

203. BN, JF 1569, fols. 110-11, and 119, solicitor general to attorney general, Sept. 27, 1758.

204. BN, JF 1569, fol. 124, the president d'Ormesson to attorney general, Oct. 5, 1758.

205. BN, JF 1569, fol. 178, solicitor general to attorney general, Oct. 4, 1759; and fol. 185, Bertin to attorney general, Oct. 2, 1759.

206. BN, JF 1569, fols. 306-314, a summary of the affair by the attorney general. On the disappearance of the furniture, see fol. 345, the first substitute Pierron to the attorney general, May 3, 1758.

207. BN, JF 1569, fol. 389, summary by the attorney general.

208. *Arrest de la cour de parlement. Extrait des registres du parlement. Du 17 janvier 1759* (Paris, 1759). The priests were condemned in two separate judgments, one for Bonnet and another for L'Ecluse, Thérèse, Dubertrand, and Cousin.

209. BN, JF 1570, fols. 7-9, Moreau to attorney general, Nov. 8, 1759.

210. *Arrêt de la cour de parlement, servant de règlement pour les pauvres de la paroisse de Saint-Nicolas-des-Champs*, in BN, JF 1570, fols. 86-91.

211. BN, JF 1569, fols. 346-47, the police inspector Poussot to attorney general, May 8, 1758.

212. BN, JF 1570, fols. 68-69, d'Argonne to attorney general, May 13, 1764: fols. 83-84, an account of expenses compiled by *marguilliers* for the year 1765, which includes the books; fols. 92-93, *desservant* Brière to attorney general, June 24, 1765; fol. 97, Pierron to attorney general, Oct. 6, 1765; and fol. 98, note by substitute Boullenois, Oct. 19, 1765.

213. BN, JF 1570, fol. 109, request by *marguilliers*; fol. 112, note by Pierron; fols. 126-27, Jean-Etienne Parent to attorney general, May 31, 1769.

214. BN, JF 1570, fols. 261-62, a police report on the parish of Saint-Séverin for attorney general, Mar. 11, 1769.

215. BN, JF 1570, fol. 327.

216. "Remontrance au roy concernant les refus de sacraments," in *Procès-verbaux des assemblées générales du clergé de France*, vol. 8, pt. 1, no. 5, p. 182.

217. Lefranc de Pompignan, *Défense des Actes du clergé de France concernnant la religion, publiée en l'asemblée de 1765, par m l'évêque du Puy* (Louvain, 1769), p. 348.

218. On the intersecting curves representing the deepening and interiorization of the faith (Christianization) on the one hand, and the decline in conformity to the norms of Christendom (dechristianization) on the other, see Jean Delumeau, *Catholicism Between Luther and Voltaire*, trans. Jeremy Moiser (London and Philadelphia, 1977), pp. 203-231.

219. H.-X. Arquillière, *L'Augustinisme politique: Essai sur la formation des théories politiques du moyen âge* (Paris, 1955), pp. 154-69.

220. I am not unaware that terms such as "secularization" and "dechristianization" are ambiguous and controversial; this is the reason why I have briefly indicated what I understand by them. On secularization, see for example David Martin, *The Religious and the Secular: Studies in Secularization* (New York, 1969), esp. pp. 48-57. On dechristianization, see René Rémond, "La Déchristianisation: État de la question," *Concilium* 7 (1965):131-36; Bernard Plongeron, *Conscience religieuse en révolution: Regards sur l'historiographie de la Révolution française* (Paris, 1969), pp. 101-177; and Michel Vovelle, *Piété baroque et déchristianisation en Provence au dix-huitième siècle: Les Attitudes devant la mort d'après les clauses des testaments* (Paris, 1973), esp. pp. 593-613. No more than others, obviously, have I resolved the problem of whether and to what extent such exterior and quantifiable indices as attendance at mass, requests for requiem masses, or the frequentation of the sacraments indicate anything about the state of

interior faith. Damiens himself seems to have retained some sort of faith after the abandonment of external practices.

Whatever the decline of such practices be called, it seems to have taken place in two distinct stages in the course of eighteenth-century France: a small and mainly temporary one around 1730 followed by a larger and much more sustained one after 1750. In the Provençal dioceses he examined, Michel Vovelle credited the "precocious" or shorter one (where it occurred) to the influence of Jansenist prelates (*Piété baroque et déchristianisation en Provence*, pp. 599-600); as did Timothy Tackett in *Priest and Parish in Eighteenth-Century France: A Social and Political Study of the Curés in a Diocese of Dauphiné* (Princeton, 1977), pp. 43-54, 67. Yet could not the Jansenist controversy, which reached its apogee in the years after 1750, also be related to the larger and more sustained decline in cultic indices registered during the same period? I emphasize the Jansenist *controversy*, to which of course there were at least two parties, rather Jansenism and its abstemious sacramental sensibility alone. In doing so, I am perhaps only repeating a suggestion made by Pierre Chaunu in "Jansénisme et frontière de catholicité (XVIIe et XVIIIe siècles)," *Revue historique* 227 (1962):121-23, who in turn only modified in passing on some observations by Gabriel Le Bras in *Etudes de sociologie religieuse*, 2 vols. (Paris, 1955-1956), 1:325-432.

Notes to Chapter 4

1. Jean-Etienne de Caulet, *Discours prononcé dans l'église cathédrale le dimanche 30 janvier 1757 avant de célébrer une messe solemnelle pour remercier dieu de la conservation de la personne sacrée du roi*, pp. 9-12, in BN, JF 2068, fol. 344. For a very similar episcopal reaction, see *Mandement de monseigneur l'évêque de Miriophis, pour faire chanter le Te Deum en actions de grâces de la guérison du roi*, in BPR, LP 548, no. 41.

2. [Jean-Pierre Grosley], *Lettre d'un patriote, où l'on rapporte les faits qui prouvent que l'auteur de l'attentat commis sur la vie du roi a des complices, et la manière dont on instruit son procès* (n.p., "ce 11 mars"), p. 58.

3. Quoted in Emile Regnault, *Christophe de Beaumont, archévêque de Paris*, 2 vols. (Paris, 1882), 1:378-79.

4. *NE* (May 22, 1757), p. 85.

5. [Jean-Pierre Grosley], *Lettre d'un solitaire sur le mandement de m. l'archévêque de Paris du 1 mars 1757* (n.p., "ce 28 mars"), pp. 6-10.

6. François de Fitz-James, *Mandement de monseigneur l'évêque de*

Soissons . . . en préservant le roi, in *Oeuvres posthumes de monseigneur le duc de Fitz-James evesque de Soissons*, 2 vols. (Avignon, 1769), 1:18-20.

7. [Grosley], *Lettre d'un patriote*, pp. 58-59.

8. Ibid., pp. 2-3.

9. Jacques-Bénigne Bossuet, *Politique tirée des propres paroles de l'Ecriture sainte*, ed. Jacques Le Brun (Geneva, 1967), pp. 65, 179.

10. Ibid., pp. 84, 93-94, 201.

11. Bossuet, *Sermon pour le dimanche des rameaux prêché devant le roi sur les devoirs des rois*, in *Oeuvres de Bossuet, évêque de Meaux*, ed. abbés Hemey d'Auberine and Caron, 42 vols. (Versailles, 1815-1819), 13:356.

12. Bossuet, *Politique tirée des propres paroles de l'Ecriture sainte*, pp. 28, 291-93, 298-99. See also *Cinquième avertissement aux protestans sur les lettres du ministre Jurieu contre l'Histoire des variations*, in *Oeuvres* 21:460-61.

13. Henri-François d'Aguesseau, *Fragments sur l'origine et l'usage des remontrances*, in *Oeuvres complètes du chancelier d'Aguesseau*, ed. M. Pardessus, 16 vols. (Paris, 1819), 10:19, 24-26.

14. Ibid., p. 23. See also ibid., p. 30, and *Essai d'une institution au droit public*, in *Oeuvres complètes* 15:260-61.

15. For Bossuet on this subject, see *Sermon prêché à l'ouverture de l'assemblée générale du clergé de France, le 9 novembre 1681, à la messe solennelle du saint esprit, dans l'église des Grands-Augustins; sur l'unité de l'église*, in *Oeuvres* 15:507, 534-35.

16. D'Aguesseau, *Mémoires sur les ouvrages d'Almain et de Richer*, and *Autre mémoire sur le même sujet*, in *Oeuvres complètes* 8:527-41.

17. Bossuet, *Sermon sur l'unité de l'église*, in *Oeuvres*, 15:501; d'Aguesseau, *Mémoires sur le bref par lequel le pape a condamné l'écrit intitulé: Cas de conscience*, in *Oeuvres complètes* 8:375.

18. D'Aguesseau, *Réquisitoire pour l'enregistrement de la bulle contre le livre des Maximes des saints, le 14 août 1699*, in *Oeuvres complètes* 1:265.

19. Bossuet, *Politique tirée des propres paroles de l'Ecriture sainte*, pp. 65, 258-60; and *Sermon pour le dimanche des rameaux prêché devant le roi sur la justice*, in *Oeuvres* 13:386.

20. Bossuet, *Politique tirée des propres paroles de l'Ecriture sainte*, pp. 112, 292; *Sermon sur l'unité de l'église*, in *Oeuvres* 15:517.

21. D'Aguesseau, *Réquisitoire pour l'enregistrement de la bulle contre le livre des Maximes des saints*, in *Oeuvres complètes* 1:260; and *Mémoires*

historiques sur les affaires de l'église de France depuis 1697 jusqu'en 1710, in *Oeuvres complètes* 8:217-18.

22. D'Aguesseau, *Fragment d'une cinquième instruction qui n'a pas été achevée, sur l'étude du droit écclésiastique*, in *Oeuvres complètes* 15:130-31.

23. Ibid., p. 130; and d'Aguesseau, *Fragments divers sur l'église et les deux puissances*, in *Oeuvres complètes* 15:159-60.

24. On defense of recalcitrant bishops, see Georges Frêche and Jean Gudreau, *Un Chancelier Gallican: Daguesseau, et un cardinal diplomate: François-Joachim de Pierre de Bernis* (Paris, 1969), pp. 33-34; and abbé Dorsanne, *Journal contenant tout ce qui s'est passé à Rome et en France dans l'affaire de la constitution Unigenitus*, 6 vols. (Rome, 1753), 1:204-18.

25. AN, AP 177mi 74, dr 9, no. 12, "Copie de la lettre que m. le chancelier a écrite par ordre du roi au parlement de Bordeaux le 24 décembre 1731."

26. D'Aguesseau, *Mémoire pour le roi sur le projet de déclaration des douze évêques en 1710, pour expliquer l'acceptation de la bulle Vineam domini . . . dans l'Assemblée du clergé de 1705*, in *Oeuvres complètes* 8:403.

27. D'Aguesseau, *Mémoire sur la Théologie de Poitiers*, in *Oeuvres complètes* 8:516-19.

28. D'Aguesseau, *Mémoires sur la censure du Mandement et de trois lettres de m. l'évêque de Saint-Pons, prononcée par le pape, par un bref du 18 janvier 1710*, in *Oeuvres complètes* 8:439; and *Mémoire au sujet du bref au roi contre l'acceptation de 1705*, in *Oeuvres complètes* 8:413.

29. On the appeal of 1717 specifically, see Edmond Préclin, *Les Jansénistes du XVIIIe siècle et la Constitution civile du clergé: Le développement du richérisme, sa propagation dans le bas clergé, 1713-1791* (Paris, 1929), pp. 71-77. On Jansenist conciliarism more generally, see David Hudson, "The Nouvelles Ecclésiastiques, Jansenism, and Conciliarism, 1717-1735," a paper soon to be published by the *Catholic Historical Review*.

30. On this phenomenon in general, see Préclin, *Les Jansénistes du XIIIe siècle et la Constitution civile du clergé*.

31. D'Aguesseau, *Mémoires sur les disputes de théologie, au sujet de l'infaillibilité du pape dans le droit et dans le fait*, in *Oeuvres complètes* 8:504. More royalist than the king, more ultramontanist than the pope, and more zealously anti-Jansenist than even the cardinal-minister de Fleury, an episcopal firebrand such as Etienne de La Fare of Laon was in the 1730s already the very prototype of Christophe de

Beaumont. See his correspondence with the cardinal de Fleury in AN, 257, AP 14-20.

32. The censured propositions 72-78, 88-99 of *Unigenitus* concern or imply this ecclesiology. On *Judicium Francorum*, see Franklin Ford, *Robe and Sword: The Regrouping of the French Aristocracy after Louis XIV* (Cambridge, Mass., 1902), pp. 92-95; and Elie Carcassonne, *Montesquieu et le problème de la constitution française* (Paris, 1926), pp. 33-39.

33. This, at least, is the impression conveyed by d'Aguesseau's testimony in *Mémoires historiques sur les affaires de l'église de France depuis 1697 jusqu'en 1710*, in *Oeuvres complètes* 8:217-18.

34. Jean Orcibal, *Jean Duvergier de Hauranne, abbé de Saint-Cyran et son temps* (Louvain and Paris, 1947), pp. 352-54; and Alexander Sedgwick, *Jansenism in Seventeenth-Century France: Voices from the Wilderness* (Charlottesville, Va.), pp. 156-66.

35. Aimé-Georges Martimort, *Le Gallicanisme de Bossuet* (Paris, 1953), pp. 346-63; Sedgwick, *Jansenism in Seventeenth-Century France*, pp. 174-77.

36. Mr. Carroll Joynes and Professor Keith Baker of the University of Chicago have called my attention to the direct and major dependence of this brand of Gallicanism upon such late medieval conciliarists as Pierre d'Ailly, Jean Gerson, Jacques Almain, and John Mair. On these figures, see Martimort, *Le Gallicanisme de Bossuet*, pp. 17-20; Victor Martin, *Les Origines du gallicanisme*, 2 vols. (Paris, 1939), 2:31-54, 131-47; Quentin Skinner, *The Foundations of Modern Political Thought*, 2 vols. (Cambridge, 1978), 2:34-50; and Brian Tierney, *Foundations of the Conciliar Theory: The Contribution of the Medieval Canonists from Gratian to the Great Schism* (Cambridge, Mass., 1955).

37. Préclin, *Les Jansénistes du XVIIIe siècle et la Constitution civile du clergé*, pp. 1-12, 41-51, 60-65, 151-62.

38. [Louis-Adrien Le Paige], *Lettres adressées à mm. les commissaires nommés par le roi pour délibérer sur l'affaire présente du parlement au sujet du refus de sacrements ou Lettres pacifiques au sujet des contestations présentes* (n.p., 1753); and [Claude Mey and Gabriel-Nicolas Maultrot], *Apologie de tous les jugements rendus par les tribunaux séculiers en France contre le schisme, dans lequel on établit: 1 l'injustice et l'irrégularité des refus de sacrements, de sépulture et des autres peines qu'on prononce contre ceux qui ne sont pas soumis à la constitution Unigenitus; 2 la compétence des juges laïcs pour s'opposer à tous ces actes de schisme*, 2 vols. (France, 1752).

39. This is hardly surprising, seeing as how Mey was one of the

remonstrances' authors. See Rolland d'Erceville, "Histoire des remontrances du 9 avril 1753," in BN, Mss Fr, new acq. 8496 (518), p. 155; and Robert de Saint-Vincent, "Mémoires," pp. 145-50.

40. [Le Paige], *Lettres pacifiques*, pp. 22,38, 43, 81, 85.

41. Ibid., 19, 30. Elsewhere he calls them "malentendus" (p. 44), "vaines questions de fait" (p. 47), and "brouilleries" (p. 82).

42. Ibid., pp. 6-7, 46, 79, 80.

43. Ibid., p. 81; or "qui consiste enfin, quand on se trouve d'accord sur la foi, à scavoir sacrifier tout le reste au bien de la paix, et à laisser au tems, ainsi qu'aux procédés pacifiques, le soin de ramener au vrai les esprits qui se trompent" (p. 3).

44. This becomes apparent in ibid., pp. 27-28. On the subject of this solicited bull, see my *The Jansenists and the Expulsion of the Jesuits from France* (New Haven, 1975), pp. 71-77.

45. On Le Paige's use of these terms, see *Lettres pacifiques*, pp. 10, 22, 27.

46. Ibid., p. 22.

47. Ibid., p. 47.

48. Ibid., p. 79.

49. Ibid., pp. 7-8.

50. *Lettre à l'auteur des Lettres pacifiques* (n.p., 1753), p. 39; and BPR, LP 517, no. 15, unsigned letter dated Oct. 30, 1752.

51. [Le Paige], *Lettres pacifiques*, pp. 6-7n, 24n.

52. Ibid., p. 83.

53. [Mey and Maultrot], *Apologie* 1:41, 86.

54. Ibid., p. 481.

55. Ibid., p. 40. In the same passage the authors go further: "ce n'est que lorsqu'elles [oppositions] ont été levées, qu'ils ont acquis leurs notoriété, et durant tout le tems de ces obscurcissments, les doutes qu'on pouvait avoir sur leurs décisions, n'ont point passé pour révolte, pour indocilité, pour un crime digne de l'anathème."

56. Ibid.

57. Ibid., pp. 487-89, 513.

58. Ibid., pp. 482, 484-85.

59. The term "député" is the authors' own. See ibid., p. 507.

60. Ibid., pp. 516-17.

61. For a few examples of appeals to the "happy centuries" of the early church, see ibid., pp. 507, 508-510, 513, 610.

62. On this subject, see Préclin, *Les Jansénistes du XVIIIe siècle et la Constitution civile du clergé.*

63. [Mey and Maultrot], *Apologie* 1:626.

64. This is more specifically the subject of *Apologie*'s second volume.

65. *Lettre de m. l'évêque de XXX à monseigneur l'archévêque de Rheims, sur les Actes de l'Assemblée de 1765, envoyés à tous les évêques du royaume* (n.p., n.d.), p. 6; or *Réflexions sur les efforts du clergé pour empêcher l'éxécution de la loi du silence au sujet de la Bulle Unigenitus* (n.p., n.d.), p. 38; or [Mey and Maultrot], *Apologie* 2:109-10.

66. [Mey and Maultrot], *Apologie* 1:625-26; 2:119. *Remontrances du parlement au roi du 9 avril 1753* (n.p., 1753), pp. 2, 18, 23, 32-33, 52, 54-55, 58, 82, 83, 160, 163.

67. *Remontrances du parlement au roi du 9 avril 1753*, pp. 55-56, 123.

68. *Parallèle de la conduite du clergé avec celle du parlement à l'égard des Jésuites* (n.p., 1762), p. 73; and *NE* (Jan. 4, 1770), p. 3.

69. *Réflexions sur le despotisme des évêques, et les interdits arbitraires* (n.p., n.d.), pp. 3, 9-10. Or the following passage from *Les anathèmes, ou Lettre à monseigneur l'évêque de XXX sur la publication qu'il a faite dans son diocèse des nouveaux Actes du clergé* (n.p., 1766), p. 17, is typical: "Cependant, monseigneur, ne seroit-il pas avantageux de mettre sous les yeux des ignorants ce qu'ils doivent croire? Car l'ignorance dans laquelle ils sont n'est pas tellement invincible, qu'elle excuse de tout péché eux et ceux qui sont préposée à leur instruction." The well-known Jansenist emphasis on lay access to the scriptures also comes to mind in this connection.

70. For example, *Lettre d'une demoiselle de considération, dévôte des Jésuites, à un de ses amis, copiée sur l'original 22 avril 1754* (n.p., n.d.); or *Lettre écrite de Paris à un ami de province, sur l'éducation des jeunes gens dans les collèges des Jésuites, par un homme de qualité* (n.p., n.d.); or *Les pourquoi, ou Questions sur une grande affaire pour ceux qui n'ont que trois minutes à y donner* (n.p., 1762); or *Lettre à m. XXX chevalier de l'ordre de Malte, touchant un écrit "Sur la destruction des Jésuites en France*" (France, 1765). Other titles are referred to elsewhere in this study.

71. Préclin, *Les Jansénistes du XVIIIe siècle et la Constitution civile du clergé*, pp. 248-53.

72. Augustin Gazier, *Histoire générale du mouvement janséniste*, 2 vols. (Paris, 1923), 1:17-18; and Van Kley, *The Jansenists*, pp. 34-36, 152-62.

73. Préclin, *Les Jansénistes du XVIIIe siècle et la Constitution civile du clergé*, pp. 463-504.

74. Quoted in Philippe Godard, *La Querelle des refus de sacrements*

(Paris, 1937), p. 277. See also Carcassonne, *Montesquieu et le problème de la constitution française*, pp. 381-82.

75. BPR, LP 541, no. 6, Revol to Le Paige, Oct. 24, 1757, dated by reference to no. 7.

76. *Journal et mémoires du marquis d'Argenson*, ed. E.-J.-B. Rathery, 9 vols. (Paris, 1859-1867), 8:281-82.

77. For refusal of sacraments analysis, see ibid; for references to England, ibid., 6:320, 464; and 7:51.

78. Ibid., 8:153.

79. [Louis-Adrien Le Paige], *Lettres historiques sur les fonctions essentielles du parlement, sur le droit des pairs, et sur les loix fondamentales du royaume*, 2 vols. (Amsterdam, 1753-1754), 1:12, 96-97, 159-60, 171-72, 312.

80. Ibid., pp. 32, 153.

81. Ibid., pp. 96-97.

82. Ibid., pp. 32-33.

83. Ibid., p. 12.

84. Ibid., pp. 32-33, 98, 236-37.

85. Ibid., p. 150.

86. Almost simultaneously, another Jansenist constitutional theoretician, the abbé Pierre Barral, similarly made popular consent essential to the monarchy. Quoting Bossuet, of all people, he concludes that kings "ne peuvent donc pas contre le voeu de leurs Sujets établir de nouvelles loix, ou renverser les anciennes. Il faut que ses Sujets y consentent" (see Barral, *Manuel des souverains* [n.p., 1754], pp. 26-27).

87. [Le Paige], *Lettres historiques* 1:11-12. See also Carcassonne, *Montesquieu et le problème de la constitution française*, pp. 21-22, 89-91.

88. [Le Paige], *Lettres historiques* 1:18-19, 90-92.

89. Ibid., pp. 12, 89, 92.

90. Ibid., pp. 152-53.

91. BPR. LP 547, fols. 93-94, Mesnières' comment in Murard's draft: "Cette expression ne sera du goût de plusieurs parlementaires. Ils prétendent que c'est la nation qui a formé la loy de l'enregistrement, et qu'elle est aussy ancienne que la monarchie, qu'elle fait partie du contract etc."

92. [Le Paige], *Lettres historiques* 1:11-12. See also pp. 18-19, 85-86, 88-89, 92.

93. Ibid., 2:16.

94. Flammermont, *Remontrances* 2:26-27, 32.

95. Ibid., pp. 31, 34-35. The footnoted appeal to Bossuet's *Politique tirée des propres paroles de l'Ecriture sainte* is on p. 34.

96. Ibid., p. 138.

97. BPR, LP 541, no. 6, Revol to Le Paige, Oct. 6, 1757.

98. [Le Paige], *Lettres historiques* 1:142n.

99. BPR, salle de travail, carton des catalogues, "Copie d'un manuscrit écrite par mlle Rachel Gillet d'une notice faite par m. Rondeau, prêtre de l'Oratoire, sur Adrien Le Paige."

100. BPR, LP 571, no. 26, Le Paige to Murard, May 20, 1772.

101. Jules Flammermont, *Le Chancelier Maupeou et les parlements* (Paris, 1885), pp. 308, 315, 318, 540, 544-45.

102. For how clearly this fact emerged during the Maupeou "revolution" of the 1770s, see D. Carroll Joynes' Ph.D. diss., "Jansenists and Ideologues: Opposition Theory in the Parlement of Paris, 1750-1775" (University of Chicago, 1981), esp. the last chapter.

103. For example, Jean Imbert, *Cours d'histoire des idées politiques jusqu'à la fin du dix-huitième siècle* (Paris, 1966-1967), pp. 295-99; J.M.J. Rogister, "The Crisis of 1753-1754 in France and the Debate on the Nature of the Monarchy and of the Fundamental Laws," in *Studies Presented to the International Commission of the History of Representative and Parliamentary Institutions* (Göttingen, 1977), pp. 105-119; and "Louis-Adrien Le Paige and the Attack on *De L'Esprit* and the *Encyclopédie* in 1759," *English Historical Review* 92 (Jul. 1977):522-39.

104. [Abbé Bertrand Capmartin de Chaupy], *Observations sur le refus que fait le Châtelet de reconnaitre la Chambre royale* (France, 1754); *Réflexions d'un avocat sur les remontrances du parlement, du 27 novembre, 1755, au sujet du Grand conseil. A M. le président de XXX* (Londres, 1756); [Pierre-François Lafiteau], *Entretiens d'Anselme et d'Isidore sur les affaires du temps* (France, 1756); and François de Paul Lagarde, *Traité historique de la souveraintè du roi et des droits en dépendant*, 2 vols. (Paris, 1754).

105. [Lafiteau], *Entretiens d'Anselme et d'Isidore sur les affaires du temps*, pp. 203-204.

106. Ibid., pp. 12-13.

107. Ibid., p. 190.

108. Ibid., pp. 110-113.

109. Ibid., pp. 13, 107-109.

110. [Capmartin de Chaupy], *Réflexions d'un avocat sur les remontrances de parlement*, pt. 1, pp. 14, 48-49.

111. Ibid., pp. 52-53.

112. Ibid., pp. 78-79.

113. Ibid., pp. 57-60, 65-78.

114. Ibid., pp. 80-83. The quotation comes from the remonstrances of Nov. 27, 1755 (see Jules Flammermont, ed., *Remontrances du parlement de Paris au XVIIIe siècle*, 3 vols. [Paris, 1888-1898; reprint ed., Geneva, 1978], 2:35).

115. [Capmartin de Chaupy], *Réflexions d'un avocat sur les remontrances du parlement*, pt. 1, pp. 53-55.

116. [Lafiteau], *Entretiens d'Anselme et d'Isidore sur les affaires du temps*, pp. 13-14, 195-96.

117. Ibid., pp. 191-95; [Capmartin de Chaupy], *Réflexions d'un avocat sur les remontrances du parlement*, pt. 1, pp. 144-45.

118. Van Kley, *The Jansenists*, pp. 163-207.

119. [Louis-Adrien Le Paige and Christophe Coudrette], *Histoire générale de la naissance et des progrès de la compagnie de Jésus en France, et analyse de ses constitutions et privilèges*, 4 vols. (Paris, 1761), 3:225, 294; 4:28-29, 48, 58, 73. See also Van Kley, *The Jansenists*, pp. 34-36, 93-97, 111, 152-58.

120. Van Kley, *The Jansenists*, pp. 152-58. The quotation is from the anonymous *Réplique aux apologies des Jésuites* (n.p., 1761-1762), pt. 3, p. 54.

121. [Claude Frey or Pierre-Claude de Neuville], *Observations sur l'institut de la société des Jésuites* (Avignon, 1761), p. 45.

122. *Réponse à quelques objections publiées contre l'institut des Jésuites*, in BN, JF 1612, fol. 186.

123. [André-Christophe Balbani], *Appel à la raison des écrits et libelles publiés par la passion contre les Jésuites de France* (Brussels, 1762), pp. 88.

124. Gustave-François-Xavier de Lacroix de Ravignan, *Clément XIII et Clément XIV*, 2 vols. (Paris, 1854), 2:205, Henri de Fumel to king, Sept. 23, 1761.

125. *Réplique aux apologies des Jésuites*, pt. 3, p. 52.

126. Van Kley, *The Jansenists*, pp. 156-57.

127. *Réplique aux apologies des Jésuites*, pt. 3, p. 52.

128. *Questions proposées à l'auteur de l'Appel à la raison* (n.p., n.d.), pp. 17-19.

129. *Réflexions sur le despotisme des évêques*, pp. 46-47.

130. *Compte rendu des constitutions des Jésuites, par m. Jean-Pierre-François Ripert de Monclar, procureur général du roi au parlement de Provence* (n.p., 1763), pp. 83-84, 90.

131. *Comptes rendus du parlement séant à Toulouse, toutes les chambres*

assemblées, par deux d'entre mm les commissaires, au sujet des constitutions et de la doctrine des soi-disans Jésuites (n.p., 1762), pp. 106, 134; and *Compte rendu par un de mm les commissaires nommés par le parlement de Besançon pour l'examen de l'affaire des Jésuites, sur l'institut et les constitutions desdites Jésuites, au parlement* (n.p., 1762), pp. 261, 275.

132. *Comptes rendus du parlement séant à Toulouse*, p. 134.

133. Flammermont, *Remontrances* 2:180, 186, 201. Carroll Joynes of the University of Chicago has called my attention to numbers of passages in the remonstrances of Apr. 9, 1753, which, if they do not employ the term "absolu" in a clearly pejorative sense, do not use it in an especially favorable one either. (See *Remontrances du parlement au roi* [n.p., 1753], pp. 138-39, 151, 160.) Typical of these borderline cases is the following sentence from p. 146: "Les récompenses dans une main, et le *pouvoir absolu* [my italics] dans l'autre, voila, SIRE, avec quelles armes on attaque la liberté et la conscience de vos Sujets, pour les soumettre à la Bulle *Unigenitus*." Although it could be construed as protesting against absolute authority as such, the explicit identification of "absolute" with "arbitrary" or "despotic" is not yet effected.

134. Flammermont, *Remontrances* 2:435.

135. Ibid., pp. 503, 518, 549. These quotations come from the remonstrances dated Sept. 6, 1765, and Feb. 13, 1766.

136. Ibid., pp. 566-86. See esp. pp. 573, 576.

137. [Louis-Adrien Le Paige], *Réflexions de l'auteur des "Lettres pacifiques" sur les lois que les souverains sont en droit de faire pour rétablir la paix dans leurs états, quand ils sont troublés par les disputes de religion* (n.p., n.d.); *Autorité royale justifiée sur les fausses accusations de l'Assemblée générale du clergé en 1765* (n.p., n.d.); *De l'autorité du clergé, et du pouvoir du magistrat politique sur l'exercise des fonctions du ministère ecclésiastique. Par m. XXX, avocat au parlement*, 2 vols. (Amsterdam, 1766).

138. "Exposition sur les droits de la Puissance spirituelle," the second part of *Actes de l'Assemblée générale du clergé de France sur la religion, extraite du Procés-verbal de ladite assemblée, tenue à Paris, par permission du roi, au couvent des Grands-Augustins en mil sept cent soixante-cinq* (henceforth *Actes*) (Paris, 1765), pp. 11-46. Our zealous abbé J.B.J. Le Corgne de Launay is indeed the real author of the assembly's *Actes* if we can trust the anonymous author of the following polemical pamphlet: *Supplément aux diverses remarques faites sur les Actes de l'Assemblée du clergé de 1765, ou Dissertation sur trois textes de l'Ecriture, qui*

s'y trouvent ou falsifiés ou mal cités, ou mal appliqués, adressée à m. le Corgne-de-Launay, rédacteur des Actes (n.p., 1766), in BPR, LP 586.

139. *Actes*, pp. 15-27.

140. Ibid., pp. 31-39.

141. The parlement's parti janséniste typically engineered the court's condemnation of the *Actes*. Guillaume Lambert, councillor in the second chamber of enquêtes, saw to the actual condemnation by the assembled chambers on Sept. 4, while his good friend Le Paige laid the groundwork for what later became the remonstrances of Aug. 30-31, 1766, in response to a request for his advice on Sept. 12. He found the *Actes* to consist of "principles that no one has ever contested" plus "very inconsequent consequences that have been drawn from them." See BPR, LP 562, no. 29, note by Le Paige "pour la cour après la lecture rapide des actes qu'on m'avoit fait passer ad hoc"; and no. 19, memoir by Lambert. See also *NE* (Nov. 6, 1765), pp. 183-84; (June 30, 1766), p. 21; (Dec. 9, 1767), p. 197; and Flammermont, *Remontrances* 2:596.

142. Of these titles, only *Plaintes légitimes, ou Réclamation contre les Actes de l'Assemblée du clergé de France* (n.p., n.d.) is not cited elsewhere in this chapter. Louis-Adrien Le Paige's authorship of *Observations sur les Actes de l'Assemblée du clergé de 1765* (n.p., n.d.) can be ascertained by a note in Le Paige's handwriting in his personal copy of this work, in BPR, LP 785, no. 12, p. 127. This note contains (1) a paragraph written by Le Paige in 1765 but not published with his *Observations*, warning that if the French bishops persisted in their "maximes révoltantes ils s'exposent aux plus grand périls," including a reaction such as the Protestant Reformation, which "embrasserent avec empressement une nouvelle hérésie, pour se délivrer du fardeau de ces évêques, en abolissant l'Episcopat"; and (2) Le Paige's reflections on the omitted passage as an octogenarian in 1790: "L'auteur ne voulut pas laisser imprimer ce morceau, pour ne pas être un prophète de malheur. Mais il l'a conservé: et l'on voit aujourd'hui comment 25 ans après, en évitant cependant les 2 crimes [l'hérésie et l'abolition de l'Episcopat] tout le reste s'est réalisé quant à la personne des Evêques." Le Paige accepted the Civil Constitution of the Clergy.

143. *Actes*, p. 15. The French translation of the text reads: "Deux puissances sont établies pour gouverner les hommes: l'autorité sacrée des Pontifes et celle des Rois; l'une et l'autre viennent de Dieu, de qui émane tout pouvoir bien ordonné sur la terre." Nearly all the pamphlets published on the occasion objected to this punctuation,

as did the parlement of Paris as well as its attorney general, Guillaume-François Joly de Fleury. See Flammermont, *Remontrances* 2:621; and Joly de Fleury's manuscript, "Réflexions sur les Actes de 1765," in BN, JF 1479, fol. 85.

144. Jean-François-André Le Blanc de Castillon, *Réquisitoire du 30 octobre 1765*, in BPR, LP 562, no. 238, pp. 22-23.

145. *NE* (Mar. 27, 1766), p. 54.

146. [Gabriel-Nicolas Maultrot], *Les Droits de la puissance temporelle, défendue contre la seconde partie des Actes de l'Assemblée du clergé de 1765 concernant la religion* (Amsterdam, 1777), pp. 7-8. This belated contribution to the controversy was provoked by the reprinting of the *Actes*, along with the *Procès-verbaux* of the general assemblies, by Guillaume Desprez during the 1770s. For stylistic and organizational reasons, this pamphlet is treated as if it had appeared along with the others around 1765. If, as Barbier assures us, the author is the Jansenist canon lawyer Maultrot, it represents no advance over what he with the abbé Mey and Le Paige were saying in the 1750s and 1760s. So if the pamphlet was not actually written in 1765, it clearly should have been. A few paragraphs from this work are reproduced in René Taveneaux, *Jansénisme et politique* (Paris, 1965), pp. 190-95.

147. Le Blanc de Castillon, *Réquisitoire*, pp. 29-31, 97-98.

148. *NE* (Mar. 27, 1766), pp. 54-55. The parlement of Paris, in its remonstrances of Aug. 30-31, 1766, made the same comparison between 1682 and 1765 (see Flammermont, *Remontrances* 2:599-600).

149. Pierre de Marca's *De Concordia Sacerdotii et Imperii, seu de libertatibus Ecclesiae gallicanae* was first published in Paris in 1663; a third Paris edition appeared in 1703. Zeghert Bernhard Van Espen's *Opera canonica in quatuor partes distributa* first appeared in two volumes on Louvain in 1700; another Louvain edition followed in 1721. A Paris edition in seven volumes of Noël Alexandre's *Historia ecclesiastica Veteris Novique Testamenti, ab orbe condito ad annum post Christum natum millesium sexcentesimum* appeared in 1699; the thirty-six volumes of Claude Fleury's *Histoire écclésiastique* were published in Paris from 1691 to 1738. The maxim that the church was in the state, not the state within the church, was most specifically taken from Saint Optatus, the fourth-century bishop of Mileve (see Carolus Ziwsa, ed., *S. Optati Milevitati libri VII* [Prague, 1893], p. 74, 1.3: "non respublica in ecclesia, sed ecclesia in respublica"). For some examples of appeals to this principle in the controversy over the *Actes* see Le Paige, *Observations*, pp. 38 and 102, where Optatus of Mileve is

specifically mentioned. See also Le Blanc de Castillon, *Réquisitoire*, p. 87.

150. The best examples of these principles at work are Mey's and Maultrot's *Apologie* and Le Paige's *Lettres pacifiques*.

151. Sedgwick, *Jansenism in Seventeenth-Century France*, pp. 107-138; and Louis Cognet, *Le Jansénisme*, "Que sais-je?" no. 960 (Paris, 1964), pp. 62-75.

152. [Maultrot], *Les Droits de la puissance temporelle*, pp. 26-27.

153. [Mey and Maultrot], *Apologie* 1:348; and *Lettre d'un philosophe militaire à monsieur l'archévêque de Rheims, en qualité de président de l'Assemblée générale du clergé de France en 1765; sur les affaires du temps, et sur les Actes du clergé* (n.p., n.d.), in BPR, LP 586, p. 8.

154. In the author's words, "la formule dans laquelle elle est proposée" or "la forme sous laquelle il est conçue" ([Mey and Maultrot], *Apologie* 1:176).

155. [Le Paige], *Observations*, p. 40.

156. *Requête d'un grand nombre de fidèles adressée à monseigneur l'archévêque de Rheims, président de l'Assemblée générale du clergé* (n.p., 1765), p. 64.

157. [Maultrot], *Les Droits de la puissance temporelle*, p. 27.

158. [Le Paige], *Observations*, pp. 71, 79-80.

159. Ibid., p. 91.

160. [Maultrot], *Les Droits de la puissance temporelle*, p. 82.

161. Le Blanc de Castillon, *Réquisitoire*, pp. 57-58.

162. [Etienne Mignot], *Traité des droits de l'état et du prince sur les biens possedés par le clergé* (n.p., 1755); and *Voix du prêtre* in *Recueil des voix, pour et contre les immunités du clergé* (London, 1750), pp. 46-49. The latter justifies regular taxation of ecclesiastical property on the grounds of public good or "good order": "Non, Sire, la Religion ne scauroit autoriser des abus que la raison condamne, l'observance des loix de l'Etat doit préparer les voyes à celles de l'Evangile. La Religion est nécéssairement liée à l'ordre public, le bon ordre de la société est la première base des Actes de Religion." The quotation from the *Actes* is from pp. 29-30.

163. [F. J. de Chastenet, marquis de Puységur], *Discussion intéressante, sur la prétention du clergé d'être le premier ordre d'un état* (La Haye, 1767); [François Richer], *De L'Autorité du clergé, et du pouvoir du magistrat politique sur l'exercise des fonctions du ministère écclésiastique*, 1:149-94, and *Lettre d'un philosophe militaire*, pp. 177-78.

164. [Cerfvol], *Du Droit du souverain sur les biens fonds du clergé et*

des moines, et de l'usage qu'il peut faire de ces biens pour le bonheur des citoyens (Naples, 1770), pp. 121-46, but esp. p. 138.

165. Jean-Etienne de Caulet, *Dissertation à l'occasion des Actes de l'Assemblée générale du clergé de France de 1765 sur la religion* (n.p., 1767).

166. Bossuet, *Sermon sur l'unité de l'église*, in *Oeuvres* 15:540-41, 548-49.

167. Since parochialism and laicism were not preoccupations of the assembly of 1682, its Gallican declaration did not take the bother to reject them unless the preamble had these deviations in mind by its reference to those "desunt qui earum [Gallican liberties] obtentu primatum b. Petri ejusque successorum Romanorum pontificum a Christo institutum, iisque debitam ab omnibus christianis obedientiam, Sedisque Apolisticae, in majestatem imminuere no vereantur." This interpretation is all the more probable in that those to whom these deviations are attributed are explicitly distinguished from "Haeretici." For Bossuet's very emphatic episcopalism (and rejection of Richerism), see Martimort, *Le Gallicanisme de Bossuet*, pp. 181-82, 398-400, 402, 415-16, 541, but esp. 552-55, 644-45.

168. Lefranc de Pompignan, *Défense des Actes du clergé de France concernant la religion, publiée en l'assemblée de 1765, par m. l'évêque du Puy* (Louvain, 1769).

169. Ibid., p. 306; and "Remontrances au roi, concernant les refus de sacrements," in *Procès-verbaux des Assemblées générales du clergé de France*, 9 vols. (Paris, 1778), vol. 8, pt. 1, no. 5, p. 174.

170. Lefranc de Pompignan, *Défense des Actes du clergé de France*, p. 394.

171. Ibid., pp. 304, 306.

172. Ibid., pp. 384, 389, 310.

173. Ibid., p. 245.

174. Ibid., p. 169. Also J.B.J. Le Corgne de Launay, *Défense des droits des évêques dans l'église contre le livre intitulé les Pouvoirs légitimes*, 2 vols. (Paris, 1763).

175. Lefranc de Pompignan, *Défense des Actes du clergé de France*, pp. 170, 202. See also pp. 198-202, 328-29, 331.

176. Ibid., pp. 202, 233.

177. Ibid., pp. 203, 205.

178. François de Fitz-James, *Ordonnance et instruction pastorale de monseigneur l'évêque de Soissons, au sujet des assertions extraites par le parlement des livres, thèses, cahiers composés, publiés, et dictés par les Jésuites*, in *Oeuvres posthumes* 1:289-90.

179. Lefranc de Pompignan, *Défense des Actes du clergé de France*, p. 472.

180. *Mémoire au sujet de l'instruction pastorale*, in Fitz-James, *Oeuvres posthumes* 2:197-200, 212-13, 224-25. The royal commissioners were Roche-Aimon, Montazet, Dillon and Jarente, archbishops of Narbonne, Lyons and Toulouse, and bishop of Orléans, respectively (see 1:lxix-lxx). The general assembly's inclination to convene a provincial council to examine the bishop of Anger's 1703 pastoral instruction, which had similarly expressed a high view of the declaration of 1682, perhaps also indicates something of the majority of bishops' thinking on this subject (see *Procès-verbal de l'Assemblée générale du clergé tenue à Paris, au couvent des Grands-Augustins, en l'année 1765, et continuée en l'année 1766* [Paris, 1773]. Sept. 27, 1765, pp. 440-41; and Jacques de Grasse, *Ordonnance et instruction pastorale de monseigneur l'évêque d'Angers, portant condamnation de la doctrine contenue dans les Extraits des assertions* [n.p., n.d.], pp. 14, 16-17).

181. Henri-Jacques de Montesquiou, *Instruction Pastorale de monseigneur l'évêque de Sarlat au clergé séculier et régulier et à tous les fidèles de son diocèse. 28 novembre 1764* (n.p., n.d.), pp. 11, 16.

182. Montmorin de Saint-Herem, *Lettre pastorale de mgr. l'évêque de Langres au clergé de son diocèse. 1 août 1763* (n.p., n.d.), p. 9.

183. *Actes*, p. 43. If it is true that the church is in the empire, Christophe de Beaumont hastened to add, quoting Ambrose, then the emperor is also in the church, "pour nous faire entendre que les loix de l'Eglise, en matière spirituelle, obligent l'Empereur, et qu'il ne peut jamais s'élever au dessus de ces Loix" (see Christophe de Beaumont, *Mandement et instruction pastorale de monseigneur l'archévêque de Paris, touchant l'autorité de l'église*. [Paris, 1756], p. 20).

184. BPR, LP 535, no. 31, bishop of Boulogne to attorney general, Oct. 1, 1754.

185. [Lafiteau], *Entretiens d'Anselme et d'Isidore sur les affaires du temps*, pp. 109-110.

186. Ibid., pp. 177-78.

187. Lefranc de Pompignan, *Défense des Actes du clergé de France*, pp. 128-30. Despite the fact that nearly all the proponents of anti-constitutional absolutism cited in this chapter are Catholic bishops or priests, it is not my intention to associate too closely the development of ideological or "integral" absolutism and the episcopacy as an order, particularly in view of the eleventh-hour rapprochement between the parlements and the clergy and the growing capacity of the latter to sound like Montesquieu in proportion as the threat to

its immunities came from the monarchy itself. On this, see Michel Peronnet, "Les Assemblées du clergé de France sous le règne de Louis XVI, 1775-1788," *Annales historiques de la Révolution française* 34 (1962):8-35; and Jean Egret, "La dernière Assemblée du clergé de France," *Revue historique* 219 (1958):1-15. It is reassuring to note, however, that even in 1788 Lefranc de Pompignan, then bishop of Vienne, was demanding absolute obedience to the crown—even at the cost of eight million livres in *don gratuit*

188. Lefranc de Pompignan, *Défense des Actes du clergé de France*, pp. 128-30.

189. Ibid., p. 223.

190. D'Argenson, *Journal et mémoires* 8:148.

191. [Lafiteau], *Entretiens d'Anselme et d'Isidore sur les affaires du temps*, pp. 219-20.

192. Ibid., pp. 190, 195.

193. Ibid., pp. 110-11, 195-97.

194. *Procès-verbaux des assemblées générales du clergé de France*, vol. 8, pt. 2, no. 111, p. 369.

195. *Réflexions impartiales d'un François papiste et roialiste sur le réquisitoire du maître Omer Joly de Fleury et l'arrêt du parlement de Paris du 1 juin 1764 qui supprime les brefs de N.S.P. le Pape Clément XIII au roi de Pologne, duc de Lorraine et de Bar et à m. l'archévêque de Paris* (à Alais, chez Narcisse Buisson imprimeur à l'enseigne du probabalisme, ce 12 juin 1764); and *Lettre d'un cosmopolite sur le réquisitoire de m. Joly de Fleury, et sur l'arrêt du parlement de Paris du 2 janvier 1764 qui condamne au feu l'instruction pastorale de m. l'archévêque de Paris du 28 octobre 1763* (Paris, 1765). See also *NE* (Aug. 28, 1765), p. 142, on the subject of this *Lettre*.

196. *Cri d'un françois catholique après la lecture du réquisitoire de m. Le Blanc de Castillon sur les Actes du clergé* (Soleure, 1766), p. 12. The Jesuit is Joseph-Antoine-J. Cerutti, *Apologie de l'institut des Jésuites*, 2 vols. (n.p., 1763), 1:10.

197. On Helvétius, see David Wormer Smith, *Helvétius: A Study in Persecution* (Oxford, 1965); and Alan Charles Kors, *D'Holbach's Coterie: An Enlightenment in Paris* (Princeton, 1976), pp. 31-35, 56-59, 315-19, 323-24.

198. Claude-Adrien Helvétius, *De L'Esprit*, 4 "discours" paginated separately (La Haye, 1759), 3:132.

199. Christophe de Beaumont, *Mandement de monseigneur l'archévêque de Paris portant condamnation d'un livre qui a pour titre De L'Esprit* (Paris, 1758), in BN, Mss Fr, 22093 (181), pp. 20-21.

200. Rogister, "Louis-Adrien Le Paige and the Attack on *De L'Esprit* and the *Encyclopédie* in 1759," *English Historical Review* 92 (July 1977):526-29.

201. *NE* (Jan. 16, 1759), pp. 14-15. The issues of Nov. 12 and 18, 1758, pp. 181-88, had reviewed *De L'Esprit* from an ethical and philosophical perspective.

202. Ibid., Feb. 13, 1759, pp. 29-30.

203. The attorney general Joly de Fleury denounced *De L'Esprit* (and the *Encyclopédie*) before the parlement of Paris on Jan. 23, 1759; the parlement condemned both on Feb. 3 (see Smith, *Helvétius: A Study in Persecution*, pp. 62-63).

204. *NE* (Jan. 16, 1759), p. 15. See also issue of Feb. 13, 1759.

205. Christophe de Beaumont, *Mandement . . . portant condamnation d'un livre qui a pour titre De L'Esprit*, p. 20.

206. Regnault, *Christophe de Beaumont archévêque de Paris* 1:378-79.

207. *NE* (Jan. 16, 1759), p. 15; Van Kley, *The Jansenists*, pp. 137-52.

208. This, in effect, is what J.M.J. Rogister does in "Louis-Adrien Le Paige and the Attack on *De L'Esprit* and the *Encyclopédie* in 1759," pp. 530-34, 538-39, which aspires to refute Elie Carcassonne, Jean Egret, David Hudson, me, and untold others on the subject of Le Paige's political thought.

209. The lines of division over aristocracy and privilege as such, when these became important toward the end of the century, tended to cut across and therefore confuse the issues outlined in this study. It is this which in no small measure accounts for the gradual rapprochement between the episcopacy and the parlement after 1774. For an example in a neighboring Catholic country of how controversy between "ultramontanists" and "Jansenists" lay at the origins of modern conservatism and liberalism, see Richard Herr, *The Eighteenth-Century Revolution in Spain* (Princeton, 1958). To a greater extent than in France, the Enlightenment was not very divisive; it was shared by both parties to the Jansenist-ultramontanist controversy.

210. Helvétius, *De L'Esprit* 3:130-31, 137. For an excellent example of how the refusal of sacraments controversy could radicalize the political thought of the philosophes, see Keith Michael Baker, "A Script for a French Revolution: The Political Consciousness of the abbé Mably," *Eighteenth-Century Studies* 14 (Spring 1981):235-63.

211. For example, BPR, LP 547, no. 91: "Actuellement, la cour

[Versailles] est aux abois par le besoin d'argent, par la perte de son crédit, par le dénument de tout espérance de détacher les membres qui ont doné [*sic*] leur démission. C'est elle qui fait les avances. C'est donc le moment de tenir bon."

Notes to Chapter 5

1. In the famous letter he dictated to the guard Belot, Damiens himself identified the side of the parlement and the "good" or appellant priests as that of the "people." See *PO*, 2nd interrogation at Versailles, no. 39, p. 58; 3rd interrogation at Versailles, pp. 69-70.

2. BN, JF 2070, fol. 276, Berryer to attorney general, Feb. 8. For the case of this rumor in general, see fols. 275-79.

3. BN, JF 2076, fol. 108, attorney general to Saint-Florentin, Aug. 23. For Jacques Mirlavaud's case, see fols. 94-168.

4. BN, JF 2070, fols. 275-79.

5. See pp. 91-92.

6. BN, JF 2076, fol. 55, Saint-Florentin to attorney general, Jan. 22; fols. 50-51, memoir on subject; fol. 48, attorney general's note on commissioners' resolution on the subject.

7. AN, Y 15813 (Commissioner Miché de Rochebrune), "Déclaration de Jean Persy et de Louis-Christophe Larquois de Courboissy, au sujet des discours séditieux imputés au nommé Le Blanc. Du 1 mars 1757."

8. AN, Y 15813, "Déclaration d'André Aubryé dit Aubry, de Philippe Henry Bery, d'Antoine Percheron, de l' abbé Yun et de la femme Fossier au sujet des discours séditieux imputés au nommé Chaumet, des 18, 19, 20, et 23 mars 1757."

9. See this volume, pp. 89-91; and *PO*, "Précis historique," p. xxxii.

10. See this volume, pp. 251-53; and *PO*, pp. 410-11.

11. AB 11965, fols. 166, 181. For the text of Lefevre's "rhapsody," see fols. 152-63.

12. BN, JF 2076, fols. 94-95, Mirlavaud to attorney general, June 10; and fol. 104, same to same, Aug. 14, 1757. For the whole case, see fols. 94-290.

13. *Supplément au procès* (Paris, 1757), pp. 53-54.

14. AB 11968, fols. 149-50, 107-168, reports by *mouche*; fols. 172-78, 216-22, interrogation by Rochebrune. For original denunciation by Maréchal, see fols. 147, 117-22.

15. BN, JF 7072, fols. 157-58, Moreau to attorney general, Oct. 4, 1758, but in general, fols. 153-62; and AN, Y 15816, interrogation of Jean-François Le Vacher by Rochebrune, Aug. 17, 1758. The crucial question and answer read: "Interrogé s'il ne souvient que dans la même conversation ledit Sr. Heraud [*sic*] en parlant de la révocation de deux chambres des enquestes du parlement de Paris, dit, je crains bien que le ministre qui a donné au Roy un tel conseil ne soit puni tost ou tard et la suitte le prouvera ou bien il faut que le Roy se dédire de bien des choses?

A dit qu'il se souvient seulement que ledit Sr. Heraud [*sic*] dit que le Roy pouroit se dédire de bien des choses."

The earlier portion of the interrogation makes it clear that the above remarks took place in the context of an argument about the inevitable bull *Unigenitus*.

16. See this volume, pp. 69, 72-73. For the Kattman affair, see BN, JF 2070, fols. 137-51; and for the Chauveau case, BN, JF 2073, fols. 126-25. Chauveau's original letter is in AB 11979, fol. 79.

17. Respectively, AN, Y 11475 (Commissioner Doublon), Jan. 1757; and BN, JF 2070, fol. 123, "Billet contre les Jésuites trouvé dans le Palais et qui m'a été remis." The latter reads: "Tant que nous aurons des Jésuites en France le parlement et le peuple seront malheureux puisque le roy ne veut pas s'en défaire il faut les brulé [*sic*] dans leur maison."

18. For the advice to the parlement, see BN, JF 2074, fol. 30, which reads: "Les parlement [*sic*] fléchissent, vous deves chef des peuples faire nos remontrances les peuples vous obéiron [*sic*], vous n'êtes (?) en place." For other aspects of this anonymous communication, see in general fols. 21-34.

19. For the placard in the Châtelet courtyard, see BN, JF 2073, fol. 161, note by attorney general, Oct. 24, 1758; for lit de justice billet, see BPR, LP 549, unnumbered fol. The following are some others reported by Le Paige: "France ne te réjouis pas; une autre fois on ne le manquera pas" (Jan. 12, Luxembourg Gardens); "Le tiran qui a échappé au bras vengeur, n'échappera pas pour longtemps" (Hôtel de Ville); "Frappez frappez, françois / et redoublez vos coups / le Roy n'est pas mort / le plus grand mal de tous" (a billet distributed among notaries).

20. BPR, LP 551, no. 62.

21. *Arrest de la cour de parlement, qui condamne Jean Moriceau de La Motte, huissier aux requêtes de l'hôtel, à faire amende honorable et à être*

pendu, pour avoir tenu des propos séditieux contre le roi, le parlement, et des personnes en place. Du 6 septembre 1758, in BPR, LP 551, no. 62. See also AN, AP 177mi 108, nos. 34, 39, Moreau to Chancellor Lamoignon, Aug. 30 and Sept. 7, 1758.

22. BN, JF 2073, fols. 205-206, subdelegate to intendant of La Rochelle, Mar. 16; fols. 215-16, the local criminal lieutenant's investigation (*information*); and in general, fols. 205-223.

23. BN, JF 2075, fol. 89, original denunciation to attorney general by Bacler, *commis aux aydes* at Abbéville, Jan. 15; and fol. 88, an investigatory memoir dated Feb. 13, which clarifies the matter. See also *PO*, "Précis historique," p. xxix.

24. BN, JF 2076, fol. 192, Domingon, *procureur du roi* at Issoire, to attorney general, Jan. 14.

25. BN, JF 2072, fols. 294-95, Peyfrond de Bacot to attorney general, Lyons, Jan. 15.

26. BN, JF 2072, fol. 279, unsigned to attorney general, La Chatre, Jan. 15. The attorney general's correspondent refers to himself as "*votre substitut*" and "*du prévost de la chatre.*"

27. BN, JF 2076, fol. 192.

28. AN, Y 13653 (Commissioner Chastelus), deposition by Jacques Roy, Jan. 8.

29. AN, Y 13653, depositions by Louis Fougues or Fouques and Charles Despré.

30. AB 11979, fol. 122, d'Hémery to Berryer, Jan. 14; and fol. 399, note by Berryer.

31. BN, JF 2076, fols. 23-24, anonymous to attorney general, Cirray en Poitou, Mar. 10, 1764.

32. BN, JF 2076, fols. 262-63, Poulain to attorney general, Provins, Oct. 22, 1764.

33. BN, JF 2075, fols. 179-80, *information* executed by Roger Parent, civil and criminal lieutenant at bailliage of Chaource, Dec. 9, 1766.

34. BN, JF 780, fol. 262; and *Arrest de la cour de parlement, qui condamne Jacques Ringuet, prêtre du diocèse de Cambray, à faire amende honorable . . . et à être pendu en place de Grève, pour avoir tenu des propos séditieux et fanatiques contre le roi, le parlement et l'état*, in fol. 293.

35. Pierre Gaxotte, *Le Siècle de Louis XV* (Paris, 1933), pp. 158-61.

36. See this volume, pp. 143-44; and Jacques-A.-M. Crétineau-Joly, *Histoire religieuse, politique, et littéraire de la compagnie de Jésus*,

6 vols. (Paris, 1844-1846), 5:181ff; Thierry, *La Marquise de Pompadour*, pp. 159-68.

37. BN, JF 2077, fols. 72-73, De Montaulain, *premier juge* of the duchy of Pigney, to attorney general, Jan. 12; fols. 74-81, correspondence between attorney general and Saint-Florentin on the subject.

38. BN, JF 2072, fols. 122-23, depositions by François Gorgu, Feb. 7 and 25.

39. BN, JF 2076, fol. 35, Née de Charmois to attorney general, Apr. 10. See fols. 30-36 for case as a whole.

40. AB 11967, fols. 126-31, 157-64, "Déclarations des nommés Arnoult, Castel, Garré et Duchesne, au sujet des discours affreux tenus par le nommé Liebert, le 7 octobre 1757"; fol. 171, curé of Saint-Landry to lieutenant of police Berryer, Nov. 22.

41. BN, JF 2077, fols. 121-22, "Copie de la dénounciation faite au procureur du roi du bailliage royal et siège présidial de Rheims le 19 décembre 1765"; fols. 123-24, Marlot, *procureur du roi* to attorney general, Dec. 21, 1765; fol. 125, Bertin to attorney general, Dec. 24, 1765.

42. AN, AP 177mi 118, no. 2, Jan. 2.

43. BN, JF 2076, fols. 64-65, Le Veillard to attorney general, Dreux, Apr. 19, 1759; fol. 68, same to same, Apr. 26, 1759.

44. BN, JF 2076, fols. 59-63, depositions of Alexandre-François Collette de Chomberu, master surgeon, and Claude-Jean-Jacques Haran, apothecary, Apr. 17, 1759.

45. BN, JF 2076, fols. 68-69, Le Veillard to attorney general, Dreux, Apr. 26, 1759. See also fol. 70, Saint-Florentin to attorney general.

46. BN, JF 1566, fol. 67, declaration by Edme Thoyoy to the police commissioner Charles-Daniel de La Fosse, May 7, 1752.

47. BN, JF 1566, fol. 27, Aug. 7, 1754.

48. BN, JF 1569, fols. 47-48, deposition of Jean Vicaire, shoemaker, to attorney general, 1752.

49. BN, JF 1566, fols. 28-29.

50. *Sentence rendue en la chambre criminelle du Châtelet de Paris qui condamne Elizabeth Chauvin, fille ouvrière en linge, au blâme, pour avoir insulté un prêtre quetant dans l'église. Du 23 mars 1759*, in BPR, LP 551, no. 97. See also *NE* (Jul. 31, 1759), p. 127.

51. BN, JF 1569, fols. 359-60, the inspector of police Poussot to attorney general, June 6, 1758; fol. 419, Moreau to same, Mar.

28, 1759. See also AN, AP 177mi 108, no. 60, Moreau to Chancellor Lamoignon, Mar. 23, 1759.

52. AN, Y 15816, "Procès-verbal contenant des déclarations de voisins et l'interrogatoire de Claude Le Roy en démence, en éxécution des ordres de m. le lieutenant de police. Du 7 décembre 1758."

53. AN, Y 15814, "Procès-verbal et interrogatoire de Pierre Arnault insensé conduit au grand chastelet et ensuite à Bicestre. En vertu de l'ordre de m. le lieutenant de police. Du 18 octobre 1757."

54. AB 11964, fol. 100, Rolliere to parlement's commissioners, Jan. 24. For biographical information on La Timonière, see fols. 139-40; for his original declaration, fols. 63-84, Feb. 14, 1750. The waxen figure of the king reminds one of the waxen images of Henry III that pro-League Parisian priests kept on altars and caused to be pierced forty times during masses of forty hours in 1588 (see Orest Ranum, "The French Ritual of Tyrannicide in the Late Sixteenth Century," *The Sixteenth Century Journal* 11 [Spring 1980]:68).

55. AN, Y 15813, "Interrogatoire de François Arguetil à Bicêtre, en éxécution des ordres de S.M. Du 24 janvier 1757."

56. BN, JF 2072, fols. 166-67, Artus aveugle's billet sent to attorney general; fols. 168-70, his declaration to Commissioner Chastelus, Feb. 21. For biographical information, see ibid., fol. 185; and on question of his sanity, fols. 185-86, Hommet, oeconome at Bicêtre, to attorney general, June 4, 1761.

57. BN, JF 2072, fols. 328-41, depositions of Nicolas Roy and Pierre Sallin at prévôté of Mitry, July 6 and 9.

58. BN, JF 2072, fols. 317-20, 325, depositions of Jacques Vergot and François and Nicolas Gourier to Le Pape, lieutenant of the constabulary at Melun, May 7, 9, and 28. In a letter (fol. 330) to *procureur du roi* Moreau at the Châtelet, dated June 4, 1759, Le Pape called Lepine a "fou." He was eventually consigned to Bicêtre after a trial at the Châtelet.

59. AB 11979, fols. 140-45, memoir by Duval on Pansin; and fols. 146-51, interrogation of Denis Pansin by Rochebrune, Jan. 27.

60. BN, JF 2075, fols. 141-42, interrogation of Oct. 14, 1758; fols. 137-38, information of Aug. 3, 1758; and fol. 133, Cuvelier to attorney general, July 6, 1758.

61. François Ravaisson, *Archives de la Bastille*, 18 vols. (Paris, 1866-1904), 17:161, 167, 170, 176-77, 180-81. A similar case is that of a certain Schneider, a soldier in the Swiss guards, who began to receive nocturnal revelations to the effect that he should assassinate the king. On Nov. 28, 1759, he was taken to the Bastille, where

he attempted to commit suicide and from whence he was soon transferred to Bicêtre. He was still there in 1762. See pp. 257-62.

62. For the Durand case, see BN, JF 2072, fols. 147-48, 151, Durand to attorney general, Jan. 23; for Du Truche de la Chaux, see BN, JF 368, fol. 46, arrêt sentencing him to the gallows; fols. 69-70, interrogation of Jan. 23, 1762; and fol. 51f., his declaration confessing all to the lieutenant of police Sartine, Jan. 14, 1762. He is included in the period 1757-1758 because his career as informant of imaginary plots began at that time. Then, he investigated probably nonexistent peasants engaged in delivering important packages from Jesuits in Bourges to those in Paris. He claimed to have discovered this sinister correspondence with the help of a certain Dubreuil in Orléans, whom he tried unsuccessfully to relocate. In 1759 he received a hundred pistolles for these efforts. (See fols. 69-70.)

It is difficult to know whether to include in the present category the case of Morlot, an unemployed cook, who on Dec. 19, 1759, claimed to have heard men in an alley off the rue de la Tannerie planning an attempt on the lives of the king, the archbishop of Paris, and the curé of Saint-Paul. The king and the archbishop could have given the supposed plot a certain political consistency, but the addition of Gueret, the curé of Saint-Paul, renders the plot's objective politically ecumenical. Under interrogation he confessed that it was a "fable" he concocted "à cause de la misère où il se trouvait, et que son beau père l'avait menacé de le renvoyer, lui et sa femme." (See Ravaisson, *Archives de la Bastille* 17:257-62.)

63. For the Ricard case, see *PO*, interrogation of Feb. 22 at Mondidier, pp. 507-509; or this volume, pp. 42, 70, 73. For the Breton case, see AB 11953, fols. 66-67, his original declaration to Le Clerc Du Brillet, Mar. 13; fols. 73-74, Inspector d'Hémery to lieutenant of police, Mar. 24. See also BN, JF 2073, fol. 155, note by attorney general.

64. BN, JF 2072, fols. 233-34, deposition of Gabriel Bienvenu, June 5. Fols. 219-26 contain basically corroboratory depositions as part of *information* conducted by Pierre-François Dublineau, lieutenant of the constabulary and presidial judge of Châteaugontier. Bellier, however, denied these charges in his interrogation on May 21, fols. 227-31.

65. For the anonymous peasant, see BN, JF 2078, fol. 15, Lamoignon to attorney general, Mar. 9; for Dupont, see BN, JF 2073, fols. 248-52.

66. For the Clermont-Ferrand incident, see BN, JF 2072, fol.

190, La Michodière to Saint-Florentin, Jan. 13; for the Mayenne incident, see BN, JF 2076, fols. 245-47, information conducted by Pierre Boueffay, civil and criminal lieutenant of the ducal bar of Mayenne, May 23-24. Gonnet, of course, denied having said this in his interrogation of May 27, fols. 251-54.

67. BN, JF 2073, fols. 248-53.

68. BN, JF 2072, fol. 281, Meilland to Rouillé, Mar. 14.

69. BN, JF 2073, fols. 182-84, 190, interrogations administered by Reaucourt, assessor in the Rheims constabulary, and Jacques Savé, lieutenant of the constabulary, in Apr. 22-23. See also fols. 185-86, deposition by Marie-Jeanne Mozet on Apr. 23 as part of Reaucourt's *information*. Some question arises concerning Le Cocq's sanity because he was wounded in the head as a soldier during the War of the Austrian Succession, and when interrogated on May 7 by Rochebrune at the Bastille (fols. 195-99), Le Cocq definitely conveyed this impression by responding to questions about the king in terms of supernatural personnages. I am nonetheless personally inclined to regard this performance as exactly that, because in Rheims Le Cocq knew very well what he meant by the king, namely Louis XV. So pointed was his mauvais discours that the authorities seemed all too eager to dismiss him as a "fou."

70. AB 11979, fols. 383-84, declarations by Gadibois and interrogation administered by Honoré-François Lambert, lieutenant of the constabulary at Orléans. See also Berryer's correspondence on this subject in fols. 457-80.

71. BN, JF 2073, fols. 227-28, Gallimard to attorney general, Oct. 13, 1759. The domestic servant Paumier was accused of having uttered a similar remark while drinking in a Paris cabaret on June 10, 1758, to the effect that "Damiens ought to be a great saint in Paradise, and the Holy Scripture says that the King will be assassinated." His accuser, Desvigner, it is true, later toned this down to "if Damiens suffered his torments patiently, he is a saint," and was subsequently unable to recognize Paumier in confrontation. (See Ravaisson, *Archives de la Bastille* 17:139-41.)

72. BN, JF 2073, fols. 259-61, interrogation of Mirault at Tours, but for the affair in general, see fols. 256-310; and BN, JF 2077, fols. 218-75. A few echoes of the affair are to be found in *PO, Supplément au procès*, pp. 51-53.

73. AN, Y 15815, "Déclaration de Joseph Rodier cy-devant cavalier au régiment Dauphin compagnie de la Tour. Du 27 mars 1758." See also Ravaisson, *Archives de la Bastille* 17:136.

74. AN, 154 AP II, file 18, no. 50 bis, Borjon to Lamoignon, Dijon, Jan. 12. In the same vein is a conspiracy denounced in June 1759 by a certain B. Manem, which had as its goal the ruin of the monarchy by means of civil war, the destruction of the royal family, and the transformation of France into a republic with Marseilles as the capital. Damiens' attempt represented the partial misfiring of the plot, which was masterminded by one Laserre. (See Ravaisson, *Archives de la Bastille* 17:89-90.)

75. AB 11968, fols. 167-68, report of the police observer Dupuis, Mar. 13, 1758.

76. AN, Y 15813, deposition of Louis-Christophe de Courboissy, Mar. 1.

77. Ibid., déclaration of André Aubryé, Mar. 18.

78. See this volume, p. 147.

79. *PO*, 4th continuation d'information, testimony of Alexandre Ingoult, prior of the royal abbey of Saint-Prix in Saint-Quentin, and Jean Gabriel and his wife, Jan. 12, pp. 82-84.

80. *PO*, interrogation of Jean Aubrais or Saint-Jean, Jan. 15, pp. 97-98. See also his interrogation before the Grand' chambre and princes and peers, Apr. 4, pp. 411-12.

81. *PO*, interrogations of Noële Selim, wife of Jean Chevalier, and Quentin Ferard known as Condé, Jan. 16, pp. 106-112. See also their interrogations before the Grand' chambre, Apr. 4, pp. 412-13.

82. *PO*, interrogation of Noël Roi known as Roi, Jan. 17, pp. 113-14; as well as before the Grand' chambre, Apr. 4, pp. 413-14.

83. *PO*, depositions by Jacques Tribolet d'Auvilars, Jean-André Gairal, Jacques Le Noir and Georges Drou, Feb. 18, pp. 339-41.

84. Ibid., pp. 107, 110-11, 113.

85. Jeffrey Kaplow, *The Names of Kings: The Parisian Laboring Poor in the Eighteenth Century* (New York, 1972), pp. 46-47, 107.

86. I can lay claim to thoroughness only in the case of the papers of the gens du roi (the Joly de Fleury collection), who pay no systematic attention to mauvais discours and the like until 1757 and thereafter. In their case, it was clearly the Damiens affair that awakened their vigilance in the first instance. But soundings in the Bastille Archives and the papers of the Paris commissioners of the police also point to the conclusion that the phenomenon either failed to interest the authorities or hardly existed for them to notice before the early 1750s. Interestingly, the imagined plots and conspiracies that occupied the police in the years immediately prior to about 1755 had

mainly to do with madame de Pompadour or with such ministers as d'Argenson and Machault, and they therefore involved the king only indirectly.

87. AN, X^{2B} 1367, first interrogation of Severd dit Parisien, June 9, 1750; and addition d'information, June 12 testimony of Marguerite Benoist, June 13, 1750.

88. René-Louis de Voyer, marquis d'Argenson, *Journal et mémoires du marquis d'Argenson*, ed. E.-J.-B. Rathery, 9 vols. (Paris, 1859-1867), 8:35, 121.

89. Ernst H. Kantorowicz, *The King's Two Bodies: A Study in Medieval Political Theology* (Princeton, 1957).

90. Marc Bloch, *The Royal Touch: Sacred Monarchy and Scrofula in England and France*, trans. J. E. Anderson (London and Montreal, 1973), esp. pp. 224-25.

91. On the quasi-episcopal and sacramental character of European monarchies, see in general Fritz Kern, *Kingship and Law in the Middle Ages*, trans. S. B. Chrimes (Oxford, 1968), esp. pp. 51-61.

92. BN, JF 2075, fol. 134, attorney general to Saint-Florentin, undated.

93. BN, JF 2074, fol. 197, note by attorney general apropos of Ferlin / Courtin affair, Feb. 1759. For the Châtelet's sentence in this case, see fol. 196, Moreau to attorney general, Feb. 15, 1759.

94. BN, JF 2077, fols. 99-100, attorney general to first president, Oct. 15, 1765.

95. BN, JF 2076, fols. 31-32, Barentin to Rouillé, Apr. 2.

96. BN, JF 2074, fol. 202, attorney general to Berryer, May 26.

97. BN, JF 2073, fols. 160-61, interrogation of Legris by Pierre Grandin, *procureur du roi* and subdelegate of the intendant, Mar. 5.

98. BN, JF 2076, fols. 256-57, attorney general to *procureur fiscal* of Mayenne, June 7.

99. BN, JF 2073, fols. 94-95, deposition of Anne Boissard, wife of Deshayes, Feb. 25; fols. 103-104, interrogation of Lagrené by Jean-Léon Boyetet, criminal lieutenant of the bailliage of Orléans.

100. BN, JF 2073, fols. 52-75, correspondence between the attorney general Joly de Fleury, Le Clerc de Doüy, and Saint-Florentin; fols. 83-88, memoir on the subject by Joly de Fleury for Saint-Florentin; fols. 118-22, entreaties from wife. The quotation from Saint-Florentin is from fol. 63, Saint-Florentin to attorney general, Sept. 20; and that from attorney general is from fol. 72, attorney general to Saint-Florentin, Sept. 1, 1759.

101. [Jean-Pierre Grosley], *Lettre d'un patriote, où l'on rapporte les*

faits qui prouvent que l'auteur de l'attentat commis sur la vie du roi a des complices, et la manière dont on instruit son procès (n.p., "ce 11 mars"), pp. 53, 68-69.

102. BPR, LP 548, no. 43 bis, session of Feb. 25.

103. BN, JF 2076, fol. 98, Saint-Florentin to attorney general, June 23.

104. BN, JF 2078, fol. 15, Lamoignon to attorney general, Mar. 9.

105. See this volume, pp. 72-73.

106. BN, JF 2072, fols. 126-41. The quotations from the attorney general and the marquis de Paulmy are from fol. 140, Paulmy to attorney general, June 19; and fol. 141, attorney general to Paulmy, July 3.

107. *Supplément au procès*, pp. 37-39, 46-47, 51-55.

108. Jean Bosquet was originally detained because he "se meloit de débiter les nouvelles contre les personnes en place" and "disoit que c'étoit les anglois qui étoient les auteurs de l'attentat de Damiens" (see AB 11979, fol. 622, Bertin to Saint-Florentin, Jan. 29, 1762).

109. On Bosquet, see ibid.; on Gadibois, see AB, 11979, fol. 476, Berryer to Saint-Florentin, undated; on Lefevre, see AB 11965, fol. 166, *placet* to Saint-Florentin.

110. BN, JF 2073, fol. 169, Moreau to attorney general, Mar. 16.

111. BN, JF 2075, fol. 53, Saint-Florentin to attorney general, Feb. 17, 1771; and fol. 52, attorney general's response, Feb. 25, 1771.

112. AB 11951, fol. 122, original denunciation (letter of Pagot, intendant of Limoges, June 1757); fols. 133-34, undated interrogation.

113. AB 11951, fols. 93, 138, and 159, note dated June 1762.

114. AB 11956, fols. 49-55, interrogation of Firman de Rome by Rochebrune, Feb. 2; Ravaisson, *Archives de la Bastille* 16:445, d'Hémery to Berryer, Jan. 27.

115. AB 11956, fols. 43-48, interrogation of Jérôme by Rochebrune, Feb. 1; and fol. 17, the poem itself. Line no. 17 contains the expression "monstre de l'enfer."

116. AB 11956, fol. 108, Duval to Saint-Florentin, undated; fol. 111, note by Abadie; fol. 131, Duval to Saint-Florentin, undated; fol. 134, de Rome to Lieutenant of Police Berryer, undated.

117. AB 11956, fol. 83, *placet* from Jérôme and Meusnier to Lieutenant of Police Berryer.

118. BN, JF 2077, fol. 303, Anne's original deposition of June 25, 1758, to Jourdain; fol. 308, the curé Dubois to Lamoignon, June 20; fol. 303, interrogation of Patin by Jourdain, June 20; fol. 304, interrogation of Françoise Perdu, cotton spinner, June 26; fol. 305, of Marie Oudin, widow of Perdu, June 26; fols. 305-306, of the wife of Houssian, June 27; fols. 306-307, of Jean-Baptiste Houssian, June 27; and fols. 307-308, of Jacques Goulard, June 30.

119. BN, JF 2077, fol. 310, bailliage's *revendication*; fol. 312, Saint-Florentin to attorney general, June 29, 1758; fol. 318, attorney general to Saint-Florentin, July 1, 1758; and fol. 317, Saint-Florentin to attorney general, July 1, 1758.

120. BN, JF 2077, fols. 327-28, *information* administered by Nicolas Sourdat, criminal lieutenant of bailliage and sénéchaussée of Troyes, July 5-7, and Aug. 7-8, 1758.

Notes to the Conclusion

1. *Arrest de la cour, contre la famille de Robert-François Damiens. Extrait des registres du parlement, du* 29 *mars* 1757, in *PO*, pp. 417-18.

2. BN, JF 2071, fol. 328, Pierron to attorney general, undated.

3. BN, JF 2071, fol. 204, attorney general to ministry, Mar. 29, 1757.

4. BN, JF 2071, fol. 120. Concerning Elizabeth Molerienne's birthplace and family, see BN, JF 2069, fol. 221, interrogation of Elizabeth Molerienne by Berryer at Bastille, Jan. 10.

5. BN, JF 2071, fols. 121, 123, 125, 127-30, correspondence between Saint-Florentin and attorney general.

6. BN, JF 2071, fol. 112.

7. BN, JF 2069, fols. 306-309, *placet* to attorney general. See also p. 294, note 57.

8. BN, JF 2072, fol. 8, Marcotte, *maître des eaux et forests*, to attorney general, Mar. 7, 1761. Only the envelope is there, with a note by the attorney general concerning its contents.

9. *NE* (Aug. 14, 1757), pp. 134-35.

10. Ibid., p. 135; AB 11958, fol. 87, Paulmy to Berryer, Oct. 29, 1757.

11. BPR, LP 547, no. 305, copy of a letter from Le Paige to the first president Molé, July 31, 1758.

12. BPR, LP 549, unnumbered MS, "15e lettre. Elle contient le récit de la question et de l'éxécution de mort, le lundi 28 mars

1757." On the comparative advantages of the Parisian vs. the Avignonese "questions," see MS 548, no. 43 bis, Feb. 25.

13. *PO, Supplément au procès* (Paris, 1757), pp. 19, 21, 24.

14. BN, JF 2071, fol. 365, "Projet de conclusion."

15. Edmond Préclin and Victor L. Tapié, *Le XVIIIe Siècle*, 2 vols. (Paris, 1952), vol. 1, *La France et le monde de 1715 à 1789*, pp. 256-57, 416-17.

16. François Ravaisson, *Archives de la Bastille*, 18 vols. (Paris, 1866-1904), 17:254-81, 328-451.

17. *Procès-verbaux des assemblées générales du clergé de France*, 9 vols. (Paris, 1778), vol. 8, pt. 2, no. 5, pp. 566-67: "Tandis qu'ils (the Protestants) ont craint d'être réprimés, ou que leurs démarches ont été observées, ils sont demeurés dans le silence; et leurs Assemblées étant rares et peu nombreuses, n'ont causé presque aucune inquiétude. Mais quand ils ont apperçu que les troubles de l'Europe fixaient l'attention de Votre Majesté, qu'elle était obligée d'employer ses forces pour protéger ses alliés et défendre ses frontières, ils se sont montrés avec audace. . . ." The remonstrances of 1760 concur: "Ce grand ouvrage (the revocation of the Edict of Nantes) s'avancait vers sa perfection, lorsque de malheureux événements ont interrompu l'observation des Loix que vos prédécesseurs, et vous-même, Sire, avez portée au sujet des Religionnaires. Depuis ce moment, presque toutes les barrières opposées au Calvinisme, ont été successivement rompues." (See vol. 8, pt. 1, no. 6, p. 294.) The fact that the clergy's formal complaints concerning Protestants began at this time (1760) and were renewed regularly thereafter is perhaps corroborative evidence for the decisiveness of the year 1757 or thereabouts. Burdette C. Poland in *Protestantism and the French Revolution* (Princeton, 1957), pp. 67-69, also designates the environs of 1757 as the watershed period in the evolution toward de facto toleration.

18. "Ce jansénisme, ayant perdu son grand mérite, son intérêt véritable, par l'extinction des jésuites en France, s'est transformé dans le parti du patriotisme. Il faut rendre justice a celui-ci [Jansenism], il a toujours eu beaucoup d'attraits pour l'indépendence; il a combattu le despotisme papal avec un courage invincible; le despotisme politique n'est pas une hydre moins terrible à redouter, et il faut diriger aujourd'hui vers cet ennemi toutes les forces désormais inutiles dans l'autre genre de combat." Quoted in Jules Flammermont, *Le Chancelier Maupeou et les parlements* (Paris, 1883), pp. 510-11.

19. Johan Huizenga, *The Waning of the Middle Ages*, Anchor Books edition (Garden City, New York, 1954), p. 335.

Bibliographical Note

I HAVE NOT concluded this study with an exhaustive bibliography of the materials it has used, both because each chapter's first citation of every work repeats the full bibliographical information, and because, for the Damiens affair in particular, Pierre Rétat's recently published *L'Attentat de Damiens: Discours sur l'événement* (Lyons, n.d.) has included a bibliography more complete than any that I myself would have assembled. Where my own book's bibliography chiefly differs from his is in its somewhat more intensive exploitation of the archival sources and in its chronologically more extensive attention to the polemical pamphlet literature of the period. The most important of the archival sources I have used are the Bibliothèque de Port-Royal's entire Le Paige Collection, nearly all the manuscripts relating to ecclesiastical and religious controversies in the Bibliothèque Nationale's Joly de Fleury Collection (MSS. 2068-2077 concern the Damiens affair in particular), the papers of the Paris commissioners of police for the years 1757-1758 in the Archives Nationales' Châtelet (Y) series, the relevant portions of the Lamoignon de Malesherbes papers in the possession of the Tocqueville family (AN, AP 154 or 177mi), as well as the original dossiers of political prisoners in the Archives de la Bastille for the years 1757-1758. The AN's AB XIX series (particularly no. 3192) also yielded some very useful information, while the parlement of Paris' original trial record (AN, X^{2B} 1362) proved more valuable than I thought it would be. The best guide to the period's polemical pamphlet literature is J. Taschereau's and Paul Marchal's *Catalogue de l'histoire de France*, 15 vols. (Paris, 1855-1895), supplemented by books reviewed in the *Nouvelles écclésiastiques* and whatever Louis-Adrien Le Paige himself assembled on a given subject in his personal library that is still intact in the Bibliothèque de Port-Royal. Le Paige's often helpful speculations concerning the authorship of anonymous works can be corroborated or corrected by comparison to Antoine-Alexandre Barbier's *Dictionnaire des ouvrages anonymes*, 5 vols. (Paris, 1872), and Police Inspector d'Hemery's manuscript "Journal" in the BN's Anisson-Duperron Collection. A. de Backer's and C. Sommervogel's *Bibliothèque des écrivains de la Compagnie de Jésus*, 3 vols. (Paris, 1869-1876), is frequently useful in determining the authorship of *dévot*-inspired books and pamphlets.

Events in this country since 1963 have provoked a vast literature on the subject of political assassination that is admittedly quite unrepresented among the secondary works cited by this book. Two such works stand out by their quality: James Kirkham's, Sheldon Lewis' and William Crotty's, eds., *Assassination and Political Violence: A Report to the National Commission on the Causes and Prevention of Violence* (Washington, D.C., 1969), and Murray Havens', Carl Leiden's, and Karl Schmitt's *The Politics of Assassination* (Englewood Cliffs, N.J., 1970). Yet as a whole I found this literature frustratingly unhelpful, at least for my specific purposes. On the one hand, studies of the temporal and spatial distribution of political assassination have not permitted us to go significantly beyond the truism that such assassinations tend to occur in times and places characterized by intense political and social conflict. And although psychoanalytical studies of lone political assassins, on the other hand, have come up with a suggestive list of shared biographical variables—typically motherless or fatherless, friendless and introspective, vocationally unstable and unsuccessful, and increasingly disorganized generally—the diagnosis of "paranoid schizophrenia" toward which these studies gravitate functions more as a label than as a true diagnosis and fails to display much more explanatory power than "melancholy" did in the eighteenth century. Moreover, this literature is for the most part devoid of any serious historical dimension; it is seemingly unaware, for example, that in the West at least the solitary political assassin is a phenomenon of rather recent origin, dating only from the sixteenth-century wars of religion. This absence of a historical dimension does not hold, of course, for some of the many recent studies of particular political assassinations. Charles Rosenberg's *Trial of the Assassin Guiteau*

(Chicago, 1968) throws a brilliant light on the state of psychology toward the close of the nineteenth century, and in using François Ravaillac's assassination of Henry IV as a vehicle for touring the entire international, political, and ideological terrain of early seventeenth-century France, Roland Mousnier's *L'Assassinat d'Henri IV* (Paris, 1964) constituted a model and inspiration for the present study.

It is in such attention to the wider popular, political, and ideological contexts of an assassination that perhaps chiefly distinguishes my own study from a second genre of secondary works very inadequately acknowledged in the citations, namely that bearing on Damiens particularly. The best of these works, A. L. Zavaes', *Damiens le régicide* (Paris, 1933) and André Bouton's *Damiens le régicide. Les Secrets de son procès d'après des pièces originales du procédure récemment découvertes dans la Sarthe* (Le Mans, 1955), are rather narrow in scope and nod only occasionally in the direction of these contexts. (The "secrets" of the second of these studies consist of some evidentially unwarranted speculations about the political significance of Damiens' service with madame de Verneil Saint-Rheuse, the mistress of the marquise de Pompadour's brother.) By comparison, the brief chapter that Jules Michelet consecrated to Damiens in his *Histoire de France*, 19 vols. (Paris, n.d.), accords a relatively larger place to the popular milieu and even ecclesiastical-religious context and remains in both content and style an inspired piece of prose. Most other works specifically on the subject of Damiens represent attempts at psychoanalysis. In Maurice Allain's and J. Rogues de Fursac's "L'Attentat de Damiens. Etude de psychologie historique," in *Revue politique et litéraire, Revue bleue* 47 (2nd semester, 1909): 241-47, 281-85, 308-12, the reader will find an emphasis similar to mine on the psychological aftermath of Damiens' theft of 240 louis from his last master and the fatal intersection in Damiens' psyche between his personal dilemma and the realm's political crisis. Yet this study, as well as Emmanuel Régis' "Les Régicides," in the *Revue philomatique de Bordeaux et du Sud-Est* (1900), pp. 529-49; André Besson's *Damiens. Etudes de psychopathologie historique* (Paris, 1930); and D. Cabanès' "Le Coup de canif de Damiens," in *Légendes et curiosités de l'histoire* (Paris, 1921), pp. 1-114; are couched in the jargon of an archaic psychology already so impenetrable as themselves to necessitate a hermaneutical effort of no small proportions.

Finishing this brief survey of studies insufficiently acknowledged in the citations are the inevitable ones published too recently to have influenced either my documentation or my conclusions. Relying on J.M.J. Rogister's Oxford dissertation, entitled "Conflict and Harmony in Eighteenth-Century France: Reappraisal of the nature of relations between the Crown and the Parliaments under Louis XV," which I was unable to consult, Rohan Butler's *Choiseul: Father and Son* (Oxford, 1980), pp. 1007-16, 1033-38, and 1059-67, contains a finer appreciation of the roles of the maréchal de Noailles and the controller general Machault in the early stages of the refusal of sacraments controversy than the reader will find here. And Daniel Roche's *Le Peuple de Paris* (Paris, 1981), esp. pp. 27-30, and 66-94, calls attention to the gradually deteriorating material situation of the mass of eighteenth-century Parisian domestics who, like Damiens, performed neither the most skilled domestic tasks nor worked for the highest noble families. In also insisting upon the extent of their provincial origins (about 90 percent) and the frequency with which they changed masters, Roche's collective portrait of Parisian domestics reinforces the banality of Damiens' particular case. Finally, an earlier reading of François Furet's brilliant *Penser la Révolution française* (Paris, 1979) would probably have slightly reoriented my discussion of mid-century Jansenist ecclesiastical and constitutional thought. In particular, I would have more strenuously called attention to the contribution of Jansenist ecclesiology, with its vesting of sovereignty in the whole church and its strong distrust of even conciliar representation, to what Furet describes as the peculiarly irrefrangible or nonrepresentational character of the French revolutionary conception of political sovereignty.

Index

INDEX

Library of Congress Cataloging in Publication Data

Van Kley, Dale K., 1941-

The Damiens affair and the unraveling of the ancien régime, 1750-1770

Bibliography: p.

Includes index.

1. *Louis XV, King of France,* 1710-1774—*Assassination attempt,* 1757.
2. *Damiens, Robert François,* 1715-1757.
3. *France—History—Louis XV,* 1715-1774.
4. *France—Church history—18th century.*
5. *Jansenists—France—History—18th century.*
6. *Jesuits—France—History—18th century. I. Title.*

*DC*133.3.*V*34 1983 944'.034'0924 83-42583

ISBN 0-691-05402-9